In Post-Communist Worlds

Also by the author

Policing from the Schoolhouse:
Police-School Liaison
and Resource Officer Programs

In Post-Communist Worlds

Living and Teaching in Estonia, Lithuania, Ukraine, and Uzbekistan

MARTIN SCHEFFER

iUniverse, Inc.
New York   Bloomington

In Post-Communist Worlds
Living and Teaching in Estonia, Lithuania, Ukraine and Uzbekistan

iUniverse books may be ordered through booksellers or by contacting:

iUniverse
1663 Liberty Drive
Bloomington, IN 47403
www.iuniverse.com
1-800-Authors (1-800-288-4677)

ISBN: 978-0-595-48519-2 (pbk)
ISBN: 978-0-595-60610-8 (ebk)

Printed in the United States of America

iUniverse rev. date: 8/17/2009

For you, Judy,

Astute observer and eager participant

All my love

Contents

We are posted the third year in the large regional city of Kharkiv located on the eastern border with Russia. I describe how this part of Ukraine retains the distinctive look and feel of Communism, and discuss the serious political divisions between one part of Ukraine where people feel Russian, and the other half of the country where the people do not feel Russian whatsoever. Several stories tell of our humorous adaptation to life in an upper class, but quite badly run down, czarist-era summer home. I have absolutely wonderful students and take the time to describe several of them. This chapter also includes some scary stories of winter energy shortages involving long twice-daily power blackouts. There are chapter segments inspired by our visits to Odessa, to Chisinau, Moldova, and by our visit to the Chernobyl Museum in Kyiv. Travel descriptions also include a train trip to the Crimea with a village home stay, and a visit to historic Yalta. Oh, and one more very Russian part of life: included in this chapter is what I learned about the proper way to drink vodka and eat caviar.

We begin our final year in the ancient capital city of Tashkent stranded all night at the airport. This incident prompts me to muse over the limitations brought about by more than four hundred pounds of luggage and taxi drivers who are unsure about addresses due to post-Soviet language and place name changes. Again, I feature the personalities and activities of some of my great students. In a segment titled "Yaks and Yurts," I describe flying in old Soviet planes and etiquette in Kyrgyzstan yurts. More stories include: hospitality in a Soviet-style sanatorium, and adjusting to scrutiny and restriction in a totalitarian society. Highlights are provided of our trips to beautiful Lake Issyk-Kul in Kyrgyzstan, and to the intriguing, historic Silk Route cities of Samarkand and Bukhara. The chapter concludes with a brief essay on feudalism in the cotton culture of Uzbekistan.

This chapter is built around the organizing theme of Soviet-style public transportation. It features an essay relating my practically incredulous commute experiences in the old and unimaginably crowded Vilnius trollybuses. In contrast, I describe traveling in the beautiful and efficient metro underground subway systems in their Kharkiv and Tashkent versions. The reader will be taken along on scary minivan rides and learn how I dealt with the uproar created when, upon entering a bus, I fell, face down, into a big basket of wild mushrooms. There are several stories about protocol in public conveyances, including how to get in and out, when to sit and where to stand, when to pay, and what happened to me when I got caught not paying. This chapter covers a potpourri of such observations on the little rules of post-Soviet life gained from the opportunities that local travel provides to study people, sometimes up uncomfortably close.

"Over there" was a term frequently used in the CEP to refer to the great expanse of the former Soviet Russian Empire. Over there, I take the reader into my universities, talk about relations with faculty and administrators, and recount the best stories to come from all the little joys of being a visiting lecturer. This chapter tells how I was initially numbed, both physically and mentally, by what passed for classrooms, teaching, and testing routines. I become embroiled in a high-stakes power play for control of a newly formed sociology department. In a different posting, my contract is jeopardized by an ideological conflict with my chairwomen. In Kharkiv, I stumble into a fantastic approach to teaching. It is an example of every teacher's dream.

Urban Soviets live in apartments (flats). I describe the two most common types of flats in detail, using our experience as examples. We also spend a year in a czarist-era dacha (summer home). There are stories, among many others, about our neighbors, our landlords, and our cleaning ladies. Other stories include our encounters with eccentric and temperamental telephones, washing machines, toilets, and kitchen appliances. I explain why, in Tashkent, I had to hold clandestine student meetings in our flat. I also add some heartwarming accounts about introducing my students to the joys of Halloween and Christmas parties. Finally, the chapter provides some innovative solutions to our constant battle with cockroaches and mosquitoes.

People throughout most of the former Soviet Russian Empire normally travel intercity as well as long distance by train. This chapter begins with a description of Soviet-style trains. This includes our experience with the basics of overnight train rides, including the informal rules of riding and sleeping in compartments with strangers. Some of the steps we had to take to maintain personal security are explained along with lighter subjects such as how and when to order tea or use the bathroom. I describe the routines and constant frustration of border checks and bribes. Along the way are stories of extortion, sex, crime, and even stinky feet.

The reader will learn in this chapter how we shopped for food and just about everything else in time-worn traditional ways. The shopping scenes I describe take place in outside markets, bazaars, off of the sidewalks, in the subways, from the kiosks, and in the flea markets. Interesting details of each shopping venue are revealed. The reader will feel what it is like to be overwhelmed by the size of Central Asian markets, learn about the pleasures of befriending the merchants, and how to bargain for things. Our shopping experiences are illustrated through a number of unique and humorous examples.

Located in Central Asia, the Aral Sea was the world's fourth largest inland body of water; and now it has almost disappeared. The Soviets had dammed the rivers that fed the sea in order to divert water for use in growing ever larger amounts of cotton. In this chapter I give an account of the tremendous environmental and human impact of this practice and the consequent loss of the sea. I describe a phantasmagoric dry lake bed scene observed during my early morning visit to the area. I share insights about the local reaction to the disaster based on conversations I had with people who live in the nearby city of Nukus. The chapter ends with two heartwarming stories of triumph over adversity.

The CEP was an early post–cold war example of America's deep-rooted and worldwide interest in assisting efforts to stimulate democracy building and economic liberalization. The chapter begins with an explanation of the vital connection between economic liberalization, democracy, and civic society. I explain how this connection is summed up in the concept of open society, a concept popularized by the writing of George Soros. In the main portion of the chapter, I illustrate the civic education work of the CEP through my speech note summaries and the description of a major university teacher-education project I participated in while posted in Uzbekistan.

The CEP identified its program as "Strengthening Democracy through Education." A major part of this program involved instruction in how to conduct undergraduate-level research projects on topics of relevance to building civic society. Best papers were presented at CEP–sponsored regional and international student conventions. This chapter describes my own and my students' involvement in this activity. Topics include research preparation, difficulties students had working in a second language, typical paper titles, and predelivery anxiety. There are stories about my efforts to overcome bad educational practices such as bribery, cheating, and plagiarism. Another part of the chapter recounts how my CEP office mate and I, under Judy's direction, organized and directed a major regional conference. In a similar vein, the chapter ends with a description of Judy's and my involvement in the lead up to and operation of the first Model United Nations Security Council simulation ever presented in Central Asia.

This concluding segment begins with a few reminiscences from the four years of our life with the Civic Education Project. Next, I review the accomplishments of some of my students in a section titled "A New Generation of Leaders." The Epilogue finishes with an essay called "The State of the Transition to Democracy and Liberal Economy in Post-Communist Worlds: Sketching a Mixed Record of Obvious Success, Debatable Reform, and Downright Resistance."

CEP Certificate—Course Announcement—Shashlik Party Sign-Up Sheet—Nukus Workshop Schedule—Suggestions for Writing Proposals—Call for Papers

List of Photographs

All photographs are by the author and his wife unless otherwise noted.

Maps

Map of the Baltic States with permission of Graphic Maps.
Other maps courtesy of the University of Texas Libraries.

Preface

Above all else, the stories in this book recount the details of a grand adventure. Faced with the need to identify the book's essential nature, my first thought was to label it a narrative of my professional activities as a university educator working abroad, but other overlapping categories also came to mind. From another perspective, a large portion of the book was a travelogue, a genre made quite compelling by many of the places visited, including the stunning, the exotic, the hazardous, and the horrible. In yet a third category, the book could be considered a memoir of the four-year companionship of two people having the time of their lives a long way from home, participating in one of the most significant change events of human history Ah, that was it! We were having the time of our lives. Essentially, I decided, the book is an adventure story.

My wife Judy and I were both educators, in our mid-fifties, with over thirty years in the educational system. Judy was burned out. For me, work was becoming too sedate, too routine. I was getting bored. Judy was a grade school teacher, and I was a university professor. Our hobbies were gardening, camping, in fact any outdoor activity that gave us an excuse to appreciate the scenic beauty of Idaho. But our passion lay elsewhere. We had long ago become hooked on foreign travel adventure. I had traveled and worked in Europe while a university student, and couldn't stop telling Judy about my experiences until, fifteen years into our marriage, she agreed to accompany me on a trip abroad. We left our twin ten-year-old daughters with grandparents and spent two months traveling, on a shoe-string budget, through Italy, France, Switzerland, Yugoslavia, and Greece. It took just a few days into the trip to convert Judy into a dedicated tourist.

Several more trips—to Southern Europe, North Africa, and Turkey—followed as quickly as we could save up enough money. Fortunately, we had the time. A hand-painted sign that hung next to Judy's school desk clearly indicated the three most important reasons why we were both teachers: June, July, and August! By now our house was filled with souvenirs and picture scrapbooks.

There were additional opportunities for overseas travel when my university established a Studies Abroad program and I was selected to teach for a semester in the Basque region of Spain, and for two summers in Central Mexico. These postings served to whet Judy's and my appetite to expand our travel horizons even further. I could think of nothing better than to qualify as a truly peripatetic professor: "Have lecture notes, will travel to foreign countries!" would become my mantra. Yet, Spain and Mexico were only interludes from my regular university position: all too brief, quite difficult to obtain, and very demanding in preparation for courses that most likely would be offered only once. Teaching abroad during the school year also required moving heaven and earth to spring Judy from her grade school classroom. Being rather parochial in outlook, the school district's central administration was exceedingly reluctant to grant any teacher an educational leave of absence, no matter how uplifting. Our taste for foreign travel and the difficulty of making long-term travel arrangements while still in our jobs were two reasons we were both ready to do something quite different. We both quit our jobs, and I joined a small "Peace Corps for teachers" type of organization. Within just a few months, we were ready to spend four very adventurous years in the former Soviet Russian Empire.

We spent our first year, 1995, in Lithuania, and our second year in Estonia. We then spent a year back home, long enough to convince us that we were not through with our big adventure. We decided to return to Central/Eastern Europe for a year in Ukraine. Then, after another year at home, boredom and an unfulfilled appetite for an even more exotic experience brought us back to work, this time to Central Asia for a year in Uzbekistan.

Following our final return to Idaho, it was certain that our storytelling overwhelmed our children, our friends, and everybody else who would listen to us. Most of them strongly urged me to write a book about our experience. I was also receiving words of encouragement for such an endeavor from my former students, special friends, and department colleagues who had been such an important part of our lives during our time abroad. Some lightheartedly joked that they only wanted their name in a book. A few actually ended up getting their picture in as well!

More convincingly, several students, friends, and colleagues also pointed out that the interesting and unusual nature of what Judy and I had experienced should definitely be recorded in print. Living in so many places in the former Soviet Russian Empire, so early after the fall of Communism, had provided us a rare close-up view of life during a very significant but relatively brief window of time. We had been witness to the immediate aftermath of the peaceful disappearance of the most dreaded totalitarian regime of modern time.

Our friends back home often asked: what had life been like under Communism? What were the challenges facing people now as they sought to rebuild their lives and participate in their newly free, and, in some cases, newly formed societies? What was it like to teach university students and their former Soviet teachers, and what is so important about learning sociology? It was at this point that I thought: why not respond in print with our stories and our insights into these and other similar questions?

We had arrived right in the middle of the first post-Communist decade. It was a period of intense disjunction for millions of former Soviet citizens. In the United States, academicians were unemotionally describing the trials and tribulations of these people as a "transition." In contrast, from our new vantage point, we were struck by the extensive amount of personal disillusion, insecurity, and impoverishment. Almost everywhere we looked there was stark evidence of physical collapse. Politically, it seemed that society was near the point of anarchy. Key social indicators, cautiously stated in development reports issued by the United Nations, revealed a social fabric that was under extreme stress. The statistics clearly documented rapidly declining living standards, hyperinflation, and a rising rate of organized crime, growing alcoholism, increased abortion rates, and diminishing life expectancy.

Judy and I confronted the human face of these statistics every day. However, we also became aware of another side of life. In the midst of the suffering and disorganization, we could see clear evidence of perseverance and many small steps being taken toward a brighter future. We observed numerous public instances of individual sharing and helpfulness toward others. We were most impressed with the cheerful, forward-looking spirit that was evident in many of the university students.

As I contemplated the writing of this book, it seemed almost unimaginable that Judy and I had actually experienced the kinds of stories I was preparing to put into print. Right up until practically the day the Soviet Union was secretly dissolved in December 1991, like just about everybody else, we had thought that the Iron Curtain would remain and that Communism and the cold war would continue. We were part of the cohort of Americans who grew up learning how to duck under our school desks during practice air raid drills. In high school we read about bomb shelters and discussed what the effects would be of a twenty-megaton nuclear blast on an American city. Television news contained graphic pictures of mushroom clouds and multiple warhead intercontinental ballistic missiles on parade through Moscow's Red Square. In college we saw the movie *Dr. Strangelove* and lived through the gripping tension of the Cuban missile crisis. Who could then guess that three decades later, the Soviet Russian Empire, the "evil empire" as President Reagan had often referred to it, would be history and we would have a chance to travel freely and live in this always intriguing, previously remote and forbidden land.

I decided to take up the challenge of translating our experience into the pages of a book. Fortunately, I had a lot of firsthand material to draw upon. Judy and I had written several hundred e-mail letters to friends and family. Our daughter Karen had saved these letters. In addition to the letters, I had brought back more than two file drawers of documents: announcements, course evaluations, speech outlines, employment contracts, brochures, meeting agendas, activity reports, newspaper clippings, even the large calendars on which we had written each day's upcoming agenda. It was enough to fill any professor's easily cluttered office. All the needed material was in place. Now all that remained was to organize such an overwhelming scatter of material and begin writing.

The reader is about to enter into the world of the former Soviet Russian Empire less than four years after its collapse. The post-Communist world we entered was the end product of over seventy years of totalitarianism, accumulated policy mistakes, environmental disasters, and simple contempt for the average citizen. This vast empire had been comprised of Russia, the Eurasian republics, and the countries of Central and Eastern Europe. The total was an incredibly huge area locals presently refer to as "former Soviet space." After the fall of Communism this enormous region contained the geographically and economically much-diminished country of Russia, along with twenty-three other "newly independent states."

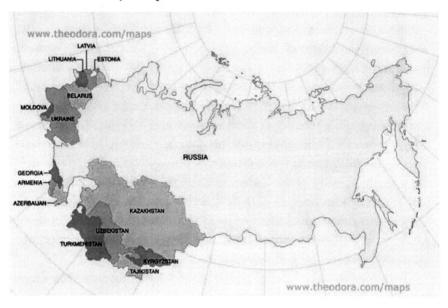

The Soviet Union refers to Russia, Eastern Europe, and the Eurasian republics. The descriptor "Soviet Russian Empire" as used in this book includes the Soviet Union along with the Central European states (not shown), such as Hungary, Albania, or Romania. Some scholars also include Mongolia.

The total of twenty-four newly independent states include those, such as Estonia, whose history involved a long period of Russian subjugation, followed by a brief period of freedom that was lost in the forced reoccupation by the Soviets. Also included as part of the Central European, "Iron Curtain" countries are Poland and Czechoslovakia (the latter now two countries: the Czech Republic and Slovakia). In these countries, the Soviets had come to power through treachery and sham elections following the end of World War II. These countries are often referred to as the Soviet "client states."

In another region of the vast Soviet Russian Empire, the category of once-independent nations also includes such Eurasian republics, as Azerbaijan, Georgia, and Armenia. Finally, there is a forth region of the former Soviet Russian Empire containing five truly new independent states. This region is Central Asia: once a part of the conquest of Alexander the Great, later the center of the empire of Genghis Khan, ultimately to become a part of Russia in the nineteenth century in a "great game" with the British to see who could colonize the area first. These former Soviet republics, now newly independent states such as Turkmenistan and Uzbekistan, are starting their transition from scratch with no previous national identity and no history of ever being a country.

With the fall of the Russian Soviet Empire, each of the twenty-four newly independent states immediately began a period of "transition." This was a Western term normally used by academicians and government officials to encompass all of the changes that each country would make as it began to move away from the institutions associated with Communism and totalitarianism. How long would the separate transitions take? Would they be peaceful? Would they be successful? There were no simple criteria on which to make such judgments. What kinds and variety of changes would be represented? Only time would tell, but when the dust was determined to have settled, Western economic and political theorists hoped to see stable liberal economies and democratic political systems in place and running peacefully.

Without exception, the leadership of the newly independent states made it clear that they did not wish to follow the Soviet model and that, in words at least, they planned to borrow heavily from Western political, economic, and human rights practices as they began to reform their countries. Buoyed by such statements, and anxious to prevent a return of authoritarian governments and managed economies, the United States and several other rich countries were willing to provide technical and material as well as monetary assistance in support of many, if not most, of the transition programs. However, on matters of lending and giving, the question soon was raised and continued to be debated: how might Western groups and institutions best assist these transitioning states? Many organizations and a lot of money were involved in answering this question. A large variety of programs were initiated.

Of direct pertinence for Judy and me, it was in this overall context of helping the transition of twenty-four countries out of Communism that one very small nonprofit organization began to pursue its specialization of higher education assistance and reform. This was the Civic Education Project (CEP). It would become my organization and employer. The CEP was also Judy's and my source of travel and adventure, the reason for all those e-mails, and more than just my work, it was practically our life for four years. It was time enough to accumulate many good stories.

This book was conceived and written with a diverse audience in mind. At the broadest level, the general reader will enjoy the people-watching stories and the informal, lighthearted, and humorous descriptions of the experiences and insights we accumulated while living and teaching in three very different regions of the former Soviet Russian Empire.

At another level, people who like reading accounts of foreign travel will find this book enough of a guide to at least spark enthusiasm for places they may not otherwise have thought to visit. More specifically, readers with a professional interest in post-Soviet history will appreciate the less technical change of pace represented in this book. This is because many of the stories I tell are written from the point of view of the way the people we met understood and made sense of their world. College teachers will have occasion, while reading this book, to experience vicarious pleasure and empathy in the efforts of a professor trying diligently to teach his students under often confoundedly challenging circumstances.

And finally, our two children, Karen Moss and Kimberly Johanek, will also want to read this book. Beyond doing this to humor me, they will undoubtedly want to better understand what madness drove their parents to enjoy living and working in such austere and difficult surroundings, far away in strange-sounding places, while leaving them to manage all our affairs at home.

In thinking of such a diverse readership, I am particularly conscious of the image that recent immigrants from the former Soviet Russian Empire might gain from reading this book. They will surely recognize the world I describe, but will it correspond to the world they lived in? In some cases the answer may be at least a qualified yes. However, in other ways what I have written, particularly my analysis portions, may appear somewhat of a caricature. The view will seem in some ways to be slanted, insensitive, quite "out of the know." I can remember as a student being surprised by the argument made by my university anthropology professors who said that books written by social scientists about people of different cultures, even those based on the most exhaustive field work, will most certainly appear strange if not just a little laughable to those who are being described.

An important parenthetical note needs to be added here. Going far beyond strange and laughable, what I have written can also be seen by some individuals in a deadly serious light. As I was nearing completion of the book, I sent a draft of my chapter on Uzbekistan to one of my former students. What I received back was a letter from a third party, living out of country, accusing me of writing a "Borat and Martin" story that was totally unappreciative of the culture and traditions of the Uzbek people. This could be just another example of seeing the situation I described differently, but I took it as being a way of saying that offering a critical view of the country's totalitarian political structure is not acceptable in the context of introducing the names and/or actions of particular individuals. The writer pleaded with me not to indicate the name of my student in the context of certain stories, and by implication, any other of my Uzbekistan students, or friends either. To do so, the writer pointed out, would almost certainly risk damage to their reputation, their family's reputation, their career, and possibly even worse.

The letter forced me to more fully recognize just how thoroughly people can be intimidated in a totalitarian society, and that I needed to take precautions to insure the needed degree of anonymity. I am thankful that this issue was brought to my attention in time to make the necessary revisions within the approximately two and a half chapters that contained such potentially dangerous material.

At times the reader will also note that the narrative detours into a little different or unusual slant on things. This is because I have used my training as a sociologist to guide what I see and think is important; even to give a little lecture here and there. Perhaps most significantly, the observations and experiences that fill these chapters are those of two people who did not speak Russian; having only a traveler's acquaintance with the national languages of the four countries where we were posted. In one sense, this was a major handicap, but viewed another way, it allowed for a special understanding that began from naivete and relied heavily upon an increased effort at listening and watching. Much of what we learned came from constantly pestering my English-speaking students, friends, and colleagues with our questions.

Granting all its seeming hardships and limitations, for two people looking for unique experience and adventure, the Civic Education Project had placed us in some of the best of all possible worlds. In addition to all the wonderful cultural experiences, we lived so far north in Estonia that we could eat a restaurant dinner outside early in the summer at midnight while the sun was still brightly shinning. In Lithuania, we lived through the longest, coldest, and most snow-filled winter on their records, and certainly in our lives! In Ukraine, we were located so far east, out on the Russian steppe in the middle of just about nowhere, that most people had never seen an American before, and speaking English in public was sure to turn many heads. In Uzbekistan, in addition to experiencing the jolt of severe totalitarianism, we adapted quite well to life in 100 degree or higher temperatures and fierce windstorms at the sandy edge of one of the world's largest deserts.

So now I want to take the reader along through the ups and downs of these years. I will bring you into our consciousness as I think back over the many different, delightful, humorous, sometimes crazy, experiences. I will also describe times when our feelings were of sadness, frustration, and incredulity, almost always stemming from our confrontation with the brutal legacy of Communism.

The key to a full appreciation of what you will read in this book lies in both our sense of adventure and the context in which our experiences occurred. Throughout our four years and all that transpired to fill them, we were always intensely conscious of who we were, and of where we were. We were Americans/Westerners in the former "Soviet space" to see and feel and live and work in the immediate aftermath of Communism, to inhabit other people's worlds quite different from our own. This is what makes intentional travel and living abroad such a rewarding adventure. Judy and I hope you enjoy reading this.

A Note on Word and Spelling Usage

There are several words that denote a portion of the vast "Soviet space" I have mentioned. The most common is the Soviet Union, or USSR, meaning the Union of Soviet Socialist Republics. This union consisted of Russia and fifteen republics. But this was not all of the "space" that the Soviets controlled. Added to the total were also the several "Iron Curtain" countries of Central Europe. There was also Mongolia. I have chosen the words "Soviet Russian Empire" to encompass all these political entities.

In the chapter on Ukraine, I have chosen Ukrainian rather than Russian spellings of the major place names. Kiev thus becomes Kyiv and Kharkov becomes Kharkiv, Odessa now is Odesa and so on, spellings less well-known but certainly more appropriate.

In Appreciation

Most importantly, I wish to thank my students. They were delightful personalities and were certainly some of the very best I have ever known. Many of my students became almost like family to Judy and me, attentive to every aspect of our welfare, our main source of English-speaking contact day in and out, our tour guides, and most joyously, our eyes and ears into a deeper understanding and appreciation of post-Soviet life. It was, as the following pages will easily reveal, a case of "no students, no book." Thank you students ever so much.

The Civic Education staff deserves big thanks as well. It was comforting to be able to rely on their knowledge and efficiency as a secure lifeline while so far away from home. Judy and I both wish to give particular thanks to our country directors, and especially to our first director, Jana Tetoris. The country directors were our first-line administrators. To be good at our job, we depended on them to be good at their job. They were, and Jana set the bar high. She knew how to get the most out of her charges, and she also knew how to have fun!

This book could not have been written without undergoing the critical eye of two of my longtime friends and former colleagues. Canfield Smith, retired professor of Russian and Soviet history graciously reviewed an early draft of the manuscript, offering both valuable technical advice as well important editorial comments. Charles G. Davis, emeriti professor of English, provided both an editorial critique as well as many helpful suggestions in the preparation of my final draft. Thank you both.

Finally, when it came to "crunch-time," our daughter Kimberly came to the rescue, constructing and converting files, formatting, uploading, and with countless other computer details, saving her father many headaches while proving the tech-suaveness of the younger generation.

So here's to post-Communist worlds, to my CEP students, my supervisors, colleagues, and especially to my wife. I may have given the lectures, but Judy was always helpfully, lovingly, right in the middle of that part of my work and everything else that really mattered.

LET THE STORIES BEGIN!

1
The Civic Education Project

Deciding to Teach in the Former Soviet Russian Empire

Judy and I had often talked to each other about our growing desire to quit our jobs as educators and do something really different. What began as a fantasy turned ever more serious as time went on. We considered many hypothetical scenarios, including what we might do and where we would do it. Almost all of the scenarios involved living in a foreign country. We didn't think about living or working in what was until recently the vast empire of Soviet Russia. Certainly there were many exciting possibilities ranging from Poland and Georgia to Kyrgyzstan and Mongolia. Even Russia was starting anew as a separate, smaller country. Yet something as unique and exciting as spending time behind the former Iron Curtain did not initially appear to us as a possibility; perhaps it was a holdover of the cold war mentality of seeing the Communist world as off-limits.

While we were considering the matter of what and where, the geopolitical world was undergoing a huge change. The Soviet Union had dissolved by secret vote, Communism was gone, and a very exciting and historic transformation was underway. The former Soviet Russian Empire had devolved into two dozen independent countries, some regaining their freedom, others newly independent; all seeking their own new future. These events would end up answering our questions about where to locate.

Toward the beginning of 1994, Judy started it all, moved beyond the hypothetical, and announced that she was going to quit her job. It didn't come as a big surprise. It was a good time to leave. She would receive a quitting bonus of half her salary. Not about to stay home and bake cookies while I went to work, Judy suggested that I also retire early and then we could both travel. Having long sailed as a hobby, I thought about piloting a thirty-five or forty-footer around the world. But, I protested, all this seemed pretty abrupt. I had only just turned fifty-six years old! Besides, we probably could not afford to retire. At about this point, Judy stated the challenge. She said, facetiously, I thought, I hoped, "Then I will travel. I can write you from every port."

What was the possibility of both of us leaving our positions so early? I started to think about what I would do if I were to find myself with "nothing to do." We started checking out these questions. We met with Layne Hepworth, our insurance agent and financial planner. Even in 1994 his computer easily "crunched the numbers," producing an elaborate multicolored spread sheet and graph that said, in effect, quit now, disappear for at least two years while remaining self-sufficient. We could then safely return to live in retirement at our current economic level using cash reserves, an annuity, and taking the early federal and state pension options. It did not take long for us to mull over this advice. We were ready. Now we just needed somewhere interesting to go for at least two years and, of course, to manage to stay out of our bank account and away from our credit cards.

Our decision parameters were simple. Judy wanted to continue our frequent travel to foreign countries and be free to do what she wished. I also thoroughly enjoyed foreign travel, but wanted to continue teaching and would need some sort of academic appointment. Only a few possibilities seemed to fit our requirements. I checked the employment section of several copies of the weekly *Chronicle of Higher Education,* a national higher education newspaper. There were some academic positions open in several foreign countries, especially Southeast Asia and the Middle East. These normally required a minimum two-year stay. In this category was a particularly interesting job location in the high Atlas Mountains of central Morocco. We had traveled in Morocco and really liked the people and the culture. There was also a unique graduate-level teaching position in China, operated in conjunction with a prestigious American university.

A second, quite different approach to our goal was to work through the University of Maryland Extension Division. They provided university classes for American armed forces throughout the world.

Professors were usually given one-or two-year appointments. An attractive variation of this category of employment was to spend a year with a program called "University Afloat," teaching classes on board a fairly sizable ship while sailing around the world and stopping at many of the most famous ports of call. It was hard to imagine seriously teaching a class to students while we sat, gently rocking, soaking up sun and warm ocean breezes in our deck chairs. Would anybody learn anything? Would anybody care?

The possibilities also included a Fulbright teacher exchange. The Fulbright program had been a main source of teaching-abroad opportunities for two decades or more. I had tried for one of these appointments many years earlier, but by selecting Paris, with Rome as my alternative, the competition easily outstripped my qualifications. I would have had more luck with less popular venues. However, I decided not to try the Fulbright program this time. The main drawbacks of the program were that the application had to be made almost a year in advance, most appointments were for only one year, and I would have needed to remain actively employed at my university for at least two additional years following my return.

Minus the Fulbright program, the application phase began. What a chore this can be. Each employer usually required filling out a multitude of forms that seemed to request information on every academic twist and turn I had made since graduation from high school. I typically needed to send letters of recommendation, graduate school transcripts, and sample course syllabi. One application also required two essays, one discussing my reasons for wanting to teach, and the other indicating how I might change my teaching style and course content to fit the training and experience of my new students. I thought, how would I write this last essay? I decided to write about the flexibility I had developed teaching in a wide variety of settings. These included an air force base where the classroom was located less than one hundred yards from a busy jet runway, and a state penitentiary constructed in the late 1800s complete with a "hole," gallows, a firing squad area, and a classroom filled with inmates serving life sentences for rape and murder.

While waiting for a response from some of the earlier applications, I ran across a new, very small employment ad, also in the *Chronicle*.

A nonprofit organization called the Civic Education Project (CEP) was looking for people with academic experience and a background in the social sciences, willing to commit for a year of teaching and outreach activities in Russia or one of the other newly independent countries of the former Soviet Russian Empire. "Challenging living conditions" were promised and pay would be "subsistence level." For the first time Judy and I started thinking about living behind what used to be the Iron Curtain. This was just the type of opportunity we had hoped to find. It was mid-December 1994. I submitted the usual paperwork as quickly as possible. In March, I flew to Seattle for a finalist interview conducted by Ron Kim, a CEP program officer. Ron was in his twenties, an example of the predominance of young people who made up the CEP staff. Just a year earlier, Ron had been a CEP visiting lecturer in Latvia.

Less than three weeks following my interview, on April 3, we received word that I was hired and had been assigned to a country adjacent to Latvia! Ron must have had a hand in the placement process as well. Judy joyfully handed in her resignation. I took a leave of absence from my university—just in case. Within a few days, the CEP contract arrived in the mail for me to sign. It came along with a "Notice to Applicants" that specified the conditions of my employment. Under "Living Conditions," it reiterated, this time in considerable detail, the warning I had seen in the position announcement in the *Chronicle* to the effect that the living and working situation could be "difficult and frustrating." We should expect that food could be in short supply and almost certainly of very limited variety. We should also anticipate coping with badly overcrowded public transportation, slow and very unreliable government services, and "Stalinist style" apartments. The apartments were described as dreary, poorly maintained, and subject to sporadic hot water or hardly any water or electricity at all during certain hours of the day, or for several days at a time.

The disclaimers continued. When there was drinking water, it almost certainly would be unhealthful unless first boiled and filtered. Under the heading "Working Conditions," the warning was equally frank. Most universities lacked even basic resources, and many professors would either be too busy trying to make a living working several jobs or too demoralized or cynical to pay visiting professors much heed.

For signing on to the CEP, I would be paid a living stipend of $5,500, which I could take while on the job or have deposited in our bank at home. Round-trip flight costs, housing, and medical insurance would be paid for. I would earn local university salary. Our sense of adventure stimulated by these descriptions, I signed and returned the contract immediately, undeterred by the warnings; actually both of us were quite excited to live and work under such challenging conditions.

The Civic Education Project

The CEP was a young organization, only four years old when I joined in 1995. In fact, members of its staff were still in the process of writing and codifying a slim little *Policies and Procedures* manual. The CEP offered a maximum of freedom for individual judgment and initiative to its 125 faculty members. There were nine field supervisors called country directors, each responsible for the program in their area of the former Soviet Russian Empire. Each country director usually had one or two part-time assistants. There were two small central administration offices: one located on the Yale University campus in New Haven, Connecticut, and the other in Budapest, Hungary. The Budapest office included two regional directors with responsibility for the programs and activities managed by the country directors.

One of the regional directors was Nandini Ramanujam. Educated in India, Nandini held a doctorate in economics and had begun her service in the CEP two years previously as a visiting lecturer in Lithuania. A very talented lady, Nandini had learned to speak Lithuanian fluently in less than six months. She modestly attributed this fete to the major influence of Hindu Sanskrit on the Lithuanian language. Lithuanian is one of the oldest and the least unchanged of Indo-European languages. Judy and I frequently enjoyed the pleasure of Nandini's company, usually over dinner while she made her official rounds through the Baltic and Eurasian regions.

The president was Donna Culpepper, newly arrived at CEP following a twenty-four-year career as a Foreign Service officer with USAID. Donna presided over our small operation with a budget of less than two million dollars. Six years later when I left the CEP for the last time, Donna had capably guided this organization to a level of operation spanning two continents, essentially the entirety of "Soviet space."

Visiting lecturers, or "fellows," as we were also called, were recruited from many countries, and were posted to one of about sixty universities throughout much of the former empire. Having begun in 1991 in the Czech Republic, the CEP, by the time I joined four years later, was operating as far north as tiny, moderately well-off Estonia just south of Finland, all the way through Central/Eastern Europe to totally impoverished Albania located directly east across the Adriatic Sea from Italy. In between these north/south extremes there were Russia, Bulgaria, Romania, Slovakia, Ukraine, Moldova, Hungary, Poland, Belarus, Lithuania, and Latvia.

Over the years that we were part of the organization, the CEP continued to broaden its geographical coverage, adding Macedonia in the west and extending its operation eastward in and beyond the Caucasus to include much of Central Asia. By 2001, when Judy and I left the CEP, the organization was celebrating a decade of service. The total number of fellows had grown to about two hundred academics. The CEP was by then operating with partner universities in almost every one of the twenty-four countries that were formally part of the empire—all the way, on a east-west plane from Moldova to Mongolia. It was an immense territory.

Some of these countries presented especially difficult working conditions and imposing geographical environments for CEP country directors and teaching fellows. For instance, from the stories we heard, it must have taken an especially dedicated and hardy soul to have been posted in Ulaan Baatar, the capital of Mongolia. It was a place where the wind blew fiercely much of the time and the winter temperature might easily drop to as much as - 50 degrees for more than a week at a time. Under these circumstances, central heating for the apartments and for the university was sorely taxed. Noticeably large numbers of orphan children survived this cold by living in the relative warmth of the city's sewers.

Yasmin Lodi was our brave CEP person posted to the State University of Mongolia. Located out in what seemed the middle of nowhere, we only got to know Yasmin and enjoy her always cheerful and upbeat personality at conferences and retreats she attended that were nearer to our own location. Born and raised in India, Yasmin was an immense help in our planning an itinerary for a month-long winter trip that Judy and I made to India. With her graduate degree from Purdue University, Yasmin had developed her CEP talent for quickly turning adversity into opportunity in Romania before transferring her third year to Mongolia. While living in Central Asia, we thought about visiting Yasmin in Mongolia. It did not look too far away on a map, and a good educational reason for official CEP travel was usually easily available. On the other hand, transportation to and from that part of the world was so limited and unpredictable that we put the matter out of mind. The plane flight from our location in Tashkent to Ulaan Baatar where Yasmin worked required a long and arduous two-day trip routed, like a dog's leg, more than a thousand miles out of our way through Moscow.

A story like this makes it clear just how impossible it would have been for the CEP to operate over such a far-flung and constantly expanding territory before the Internet and the reasonably priced laptop computer arrived on the scene. Probably 95 percent or more of all communication between CEP country directors and lecturers, and among lecturers, was by e-mail. Local phones were very unreliable and fax machines were practically unheard of.

I can vividly recall how absolutely amazing it was in 1995, to sit down at our laptop PC, open up the rather primitive DOS-based e-mail program, and instantly communicate with a staff member in New Haven, a colleague in an adjacent country, or our children living in Boise and Washington, DC! The New Haven office even sent weekly two or three-page world news updates to all visiting lecturers via e-mail. I can remember a friend sending us the verdict in the OJ Simpson Trial within a few minutes of its announcement. The e-mail system didn't always run smoothly, however. Individual PC software was sometimes incompatible. There were horror stories of our main server at Yale University running amok and sending hundreds of copies of the same message to most, if not all, CEP members. This happened several times. One CEPer told the story, with annoyance obvious in his gestures, of using two fingers to rapidly open and delete the flood of more than a thousand incoming messages only to quickly be inundated to the point of giving up!

The CEP operated, in the form that I knew it at least, for thirteen years until 2004. What a whirlwind period of time, and we had been there for a good portion of it! No grand mission had been accomplished. Instead, our successes were more in keeping with the idea of "a thousand points of light," small steps in a big landscape that I feel confident added up to a significant overall contribution.

The CEP had begun as the result of the coming together of the right historical moment, a chance encounter between a few academics, and the enthusiastic and crucial financial support of a well-known philanthropist. Stephen Grand, a doctoral student at Yale University, had gone to Czechoslovakia in the summer of 1990 to do research for his dissertation. While there he met several professors who explained to him how they were experiencing a great deal of difficulty developing the competency necessary to teach newly popular Western subjects like political science, sociology, or economics. Their universities were broke, their library resources pertaining to these subjects were almost nonexistent, and books and curricular material were equally scarce. How were these academics, who only a few months earlier had been professors of Marxism-Leninism, going to make the change? The need for assistance was clear. It was also obvious that these professors represented only small sample of the much larger number of academics, throughout the former empire, who were facing the same problem. "So that is their problem," you might say. However, in this instance, the importance of the matter could be seen to extend far beyond the limited arena of academics needing to learn something new.

At stake in helping the professors develop and implement Western-based social science curriculum was—if one believes as I do that knowledge drives change—an immense opportunity, using a relatively minuscule investment, to make a significant contribution to the furtherance of human freedom. Professors who could effectively teach and direct research in Western subjects, such as government and economic liberalism, would be a major influence on their students who would then be in a position, along with their professors, to apply what they learned in helping their countries transform out of Communism. Suffice it to say here that providing such academic assistance became the work that the CEP set out to do.

To this obviously limited state of Western academic knowledge it should be added that most of the Soviet teaching methodology was built around easily corruptible oral examinations, and a mind-numbing instructional lecture style referred to by students as "reading the classes." The CEP set out to model and to suggest the benefits of a form of teaching that rewarded critical thinking and student involvement in the learning process; both important qualities leading to effective citizenship in a democracy. I visited many lecture rooms where the ex-Soviet professors would typically stand behind overly large lecterns and read entire lectures from their notes. Admittedly, the elements of this style of lecture were certainly not invented by the Soviets, and, in fact, have a long history. I have seen the telltale physical remains of this approach to learning: rows of benches and little lecture balconies placed high up the side of the front wall in the museum sections of fourteenth century European universities. In America, this kind of teaching happened more than occasionally even forty years ago when I was a student, and such abuse surely has not completely disappeared. Jokes about this and the professor's yellowed notes are still easily recognized by most American college students. Imagine, though, a system in which an overwhelming majority of entire classes relied exclusively on this practice.

The first CEP visiting lecturers quickly learned that they would not only be teaching a subject matter that was entirely new to their students, they would also be modeling a quite revolutionary style of teaching as well. No long lectures by "a sage on the stage." CEP lecturers often would sit on the edge of the desk when informally addressing the class. Students were invited to offer and defend their own views. All this was quite a novel and exciting experience for the students. So was being asked to take responsibility for a class presentation and see it through, to show independent thinking, or to contribute as a member of a small group project, and be graded on your effort by the group members. Students felt empowered by these and similar teaching techniques.

The CEP used the words "active learning" to describe essentially what is a broad approach to teaching that stresses student participation in their learning. Small group discussion, panels, paper presentations, simulation games, and critical-thinking strategies are some examples of this form of pedagogy.

Fortunately for the CEP, for university social science professors, and most importantly for everybody who has taken our classes and workshops, the funding for the CEP remained secure and reliable. Donors were enthusiastic in their support of the CEP's mission and its Peace Corps–style approach for pursuing it.

Most prominent among these donors was the well-known philanthropist George Soros. Mr. Soros had grown up in Hungary under both the Nazi and Soviet regimes. After immigrating to America and becoming one of the richest men in the world, Soros established the Open Society Foundation with the aim of supporting democracy-building projects behind the Iron Curtain. By the time the Soviet Russian Empire was dissolved, Soros had already begun developing foundation branch offices in a majority of the capitals and large regional cities of the newly independent countries that had formed out of the empire. The CEP got most of its funding through a special Open Society Foundation program set up to support a broad array of higher education initiatives. Several governments, including our own, also added their contributions to the CEP, along with a number of other private foundations and corporations scattered around the world. The CEP was an international entity in every sense of the word.

Very briefly, the CEP's plan follows the mission statement contained in most of its brochures, information sheets, and other printed hand-out material. The CEP was "an international voluntary organization rooted in the belief that democratic society requires critically minded and informed individuals ... with attitudes and values respecting pluralism and habits of thoughtful, tolerant debate on public issues." Their statement continues: "The aim of the CEP is to help restore, in the countries of the former Soviet block, the capacity of individuals to make independent, informed decisions about the economic, social, political, and legal issues facing their societies" (CEP Brochure, 1995). To accomplish these objectives, the CEP focused mainly within the classroom, but it also gave a large amount of attention through outreach activities to helping the region's social science teachers and their universities develop into centers of research and teaching excellence in the social and policy sciences.

The CEP recruited a cadre of visiting lecturers from a pool of academics and graduate students who were able to take a year away from their work, and were sufficiently idealistic, adventurous, adaptable, and able to withstand a major dose of cultural shock, especially as this translated into living and working conditions that at times were unimaginably trying. Next, the CEP plan provided basic professional coordination over long distances sufficient to insure the successful academic and outreach performance of each lecturer. A key element of this part of the plan was the funding of many forms of academic and student enrichment.

Still another part of the CEP's plan was to help develop a local cadre of young professors who would be instrumental in rebuilding social science higher education in their own countries. This ultimately came to be called the Local Faculty Fellows program. The program assisted these young people in going abroad for a year or two of additional graduate training in a Western university. Once back home, these new fellows were given a generous (by local standards) two-year stipend and integrated into all CEP programs and activities. The program was a recruitment and retention success as it began to fill a much-needed gap in the diminished faculty numbers at most universities

Finally, definitely not to be overlooked was one especially important part of the plan; have lots of fun! The CEP country directors and staff worked hard to insure that there were plenty of occasions for gaiety and camaraderie, or should I say, comradeship? Frequent visits to the teaching sites by the country directors and regional supervisors were opportunities to eat out as a group "on the house" at some of the better local restaurants. Additionally, each country director organized two retreats a year. These were usually three-day stays at interesting out-of-town places, even sometimes out-of-country locations, and again, by local standards, with good accommodations and tasty food. There were also plentiful libations, a custom in this part of the world. Sightseeing, horseback riding, tobogganing, rafting, and swimming were some of the activities that could be included in a retreat. It might sound like we spent too much of our budget "kicking up our heels," as it were, but one important idea behind these events was to help compensate for the often remote, sometimes lonely, and almost always materially challenging daily life of the lecturers.

This was the organization, the plan, and the basis of a life that Judy and I were part of for four of the six years between 1995 and 2001. It was a truly wonderful experience, an opportunity to live in ways much different than anything either of us could possibly have imagined ahead of time. Being together, we didn't experience the loneliness that the CEP literature had warned about. As for the material privations and other challenges, we loved them all and considered them absolutely essential to the life we found so appealing. Over the years we were abroad, Judy and I learned a great deal about how to improve the effectiveness of our academic impact on the students as well as the variety and quality of our professional outreach activities. Each year we did more, and we did it better! Even though she had no official obligations, Judy's efforts counted equally in our success. It was a team effort in most every way.

Getting Ready to Leave Boise

Our adventure began with preparations to leave our home in Boise. Getting ready and packing up amounted to quite an interesting effort. The preparation involved far more than a casual observer might have concluded if they had only seen our car full of baggage parked at our bon voyage party the night before we left. Reading the following account of our preparations may unintentionally dissuade someone who might want to follow in our path. I hope not, as the rewards far exceeded the effort.

We received confirmation of our first posting with the CEP early in April 1995. We would need to be ready to leave for Lithuania in just over four months. Half way through our preparations, in July, I left for a delightful, if a little hectic, trip to Yale University in New Haven, Connecticut, for a weekend orientation. It was a long flight to Chicago with a transfer to New Haven. I was lucky to arrive in time to catch the last of a pizza picnic dinner. During the next two days, I listened to the usual welcomes and general remarks in Sudler Hall, a beautiful Gothic structure, as is most of the architecture of Yale University. I sat in George H. W. Bush's seat in this hall, experiencing the symptoms of afternoon drowsiness. I wondered how often George might have fallen asleep in that comfortable chair.

All new CEP visiting lecturers learned firsthand from returning lecturers some of the privations we could expect as well as the joys we would find in the totally new world we were about to enter. We were all treated to a humorous but nevertheless sobering slide show of a visiting lecturer's difficulties with his uncooperative university administration and very basic living conditions in Tirana, the capital of Albania. The school would be open one day and closed the next. Misunderstanding over the purpose of the lectureship could not seem to be resolved, and trying to keep things working in the apartment was a constant struggle.

The orientation included breakout meetings organized by discipline and also by country. In these meetings, I met my country director and the individual lecturers with whom I would work very closely over the coming year. We did some team-building exercises. The new and returning lecturers were twelve interesting and friendly young people, most just out of graduate school, about half of them new hires like myself. One was from China, one from Columbia, another from India, and the rest were Americans. Our country director was a Brit.

Four years later, Judy accompanied me to Yale for one additional orientation prior to our stay in Ukraine. This time, thinking the trip would be easier, we flew to New York City and took the Connecticut Limo to New Haven. We ended up in the largest Friday evening rush hour either of us has ever witnessed. Following the conference, we rented a car and spent three days driving along Connecticut's beautiful coastline from New Haven to the Rhode Island boarder. To a Westerner used to wide open Pacific beaches, it was depressing to see how much of the Atlantic coastline has been allowed to fall under private control. Finding one of the few places to access the beach was quite difficult.

Back home from my first orientation, we immediately began our preparation to leave. We had made a beginning checklist of things that needed to be done. As our plan was to stay with the CEP for a minimum of two years, we began our preparations by selling both of our family cars and buying "Tilly," an old "beater" 1974 Dodge sedan. This would also give us something to drive before leaving for our posting, and also during the month that we would be home the following summer. Tilly didn't cost much to purchase and ran well following an automatic transmission rebuild, but she certainly looked the worse for wear with her advanced age and peeling blue paint.

Next, we started to ready our seventy-plus-year-old house for caretaking by one of my students, her husband, and their two young children. This assignment included responsibility for Ben, our German shepherd dog. I made up a "House-Sitter's Manual" of several typed pages, which described a long list of things including how to operate the spa, where to get service for broken appliances, necessary maintenance chores for the house, how to care for the dog, and many other important considerations. In hindsight, I doubt they read any of it. Then we began to move all of our household goods into our detached oversized double garage, carefully covering everything with blankets and tarps. Also parked in the garage was a fully restored old MGTD roadster and a second project MGA sports car tucked on its side against the far wall surrounded by numerous boxes filled with its inner parts. Even at this we were still able to leave room in the garage for the house sitter to access the workbench and tools that would be necessary for the constant maintenance required by an old home.

By June, the house was ready for its caretaker tenants and we were ready to spend the last two months at our mountain cabin. We hitched Tilly up to our utility trailer made from an old pickup back end, and loaded it up with camping stuff and everything we planned to take with us overseas. Ben rode in the back seat. Like most big dogs, he enjoyed riding most of the time with his head out the window. We handed the keys over to the tenants and pulled out of the driveway. What a sight we must have been. Truly this was a scene from *The Grapes of Wrath*.

Our house was located in the historic North End District of Boise in a neighborhood filled with stately mansions and upper middle class bungalows. Although our young house-sitter family took reasonably good care of our place, their lifestyle contained features that definitely did not fit into the quiet charm of the area. We had not done our homework, and after only a brief initial meeting with my student's husband, we turned the house over to their safekeeping.

Unbeknownst to us, the young man was a motorcycle mechanic and racer who quickly converted his small part of the garage into a repair and fiberglassing shop for himself and his friends. Fiberglass items dripping with fresh resin were laid up on our tarp-covered furniture. There were late night tune-ups followed by noisy test trial runs up and down the quiet tree-lined streets. Junk motorcycle parts cluttered the driveway and Tilly, sitting under her ragged tarp in the driveway, accumulated a number of large bumps of fiberglass resin from being used as a drying rack.

My student turned out to have her own peculiar hobby as well.

She raised rabbits, which along with their hutches and droppings, grew to fill most of our small backyard. Being in a rather close-knit neighborhood we began to get e-mails from residents reporting the goings on. Much of the evidence of these activities remained when we briefly returned the following summer. Our house sitters were almost moved out, but certainly more than enough evidence remained to give adequate credibility to the neighbor's tales of visual, auditory, and even olfactory hardship. No doubt a few of the neighbors seriously wondered about us. They were glad to see us come back and probably hoped that our absence was a one-time moment of irresponsibility.

Our daughter stayed in our house during our second year abroad. Being a poor graduate student, she lived mostly in the bedroom/sitting room and kitchen, closing off the heat to the rest of the house to save money. It was a wonder that the water pipes did not freeze. Foolishly, we tried using a house sitter a third year only to return to a considerable amount of damage due to a couple of very small children and tales from neighbors of what seemed an endless number of relatives who moved into the house for extended periods of time. At least the outside looked nice this time as the husband worked for a lawn care company. Following their stay, and our continuing interest in remaining with the CEP, we decided to eliminate the need for house sitters. We sold our place and moved to a townhouse in a gated community. During our last year in the CEP we were able to just turn the door key and leave.

Bringing the story back to our preparations to leave Boise on our first posting, it was now toward the end of the summer. We were back from the cabin, on our way to the airport, ready to start our big adventure. We stopped by our house just long enough to drop off the dog and park Tilly off to the side of the driveway. It was a very strange sensation to see another family living in our house, to see their furniture and decorations in place of ours. At this moment I suppose we might have considered whether this adventure we were about to undertake was worth all the effort and sacrifice. The answer would be *yes* a thousand times, but neither of us was sure of this then. We didn't even think about it in all the excitement of finally leaving! We were actually ready to bring our carefully packed bags to the airport.

The trip to the airport gave me time to reflect on the tedious experience of packing our many bags. Shortly after joining the CEP, we had begun to think about all the things that we would need to pack. After a preliminary consideration of the volume of goods and belongings that would be involved, we hit upon the idea of using secondhand military duffel bags. The first of a total of seven that we would end up taking on round-trip flights overseas was actually my own U.S. Army duffel bag, issued exactly forty years earlier and still clearly containing my military identification number on its side. This fairly unordinary travel gear turned out to be an ideal selection. Through careful packing, each bag could hold up to the then typical seventy-pound weight limit for an overseas flight.

The bags were easily available at the local army surplus store, were very inexpensive, and would easily fold away in a small stack when not in use. They could be locked at the top, and their look of impoverishment, the likelihood of containing military issue contents, or both, probably reduced the bags attractiveness to thieves. They could, and were, hefted, squeezed, bounced, dragged, and sat on with impunity. Nothing ever got damaged. Once, while sitting in our plane still in the boarding process at the terminal in New York City, I remember looking out the window to see one of our duffel bags fall hard to the tarmac as the baggage train made a wide turn at high speed. Some of the later model military duffels are rubber lined, an important consideration we learned after a few of our bags got a complete soaking while being transferred between planes in a classic Atlanta summer thunderstorm. "Camouflage green" dye faded into some of our clothing. Fortunately we were able to wash it out later.

Not only did our duffel bags have all these redeeming features, with careful attention to packing they also offered a safe and secure way to bring all of our foreign shopping treasures back home. In preparation for our several return flights, we would leave some of our worn-out clothing and give away no longer needed books and personal effects. By doing this, Judy and I were able to make room in our duffel bags for a surprising array of locally purchased items of folk craft, clothing, china, glassware, and souvenirs. In all of our plane trips home, never once did anything get bent, torn, or broken! I considered this to be quite an amazing feat, considering that our last trip home included a complete forty-six-piece set of classic cotton motif Uzbekistan ceramic tableware, each piece wrapped in clothing and scattered throughout the bags. On an earlier trip, our duffel bags even included a large array of Belarusian cut crystal pieces, beginning with several gift sets of small vodka shot glasses! No need here to elaborate on the central place of vodka in the daily life of people in most of the former Soviet Russian Empire.

Enough about packing souvenirs for the trips back. What gets packed in all seven of these duffel bags for the trips over? Only the essentials get packed, of course. Yet, when the destination will be half the way or even more around the world to places with minimally functioning economies, when we will be living in a places we have barely heard of, then the things that are packed become more than just essential or utilitarian. Most everything we would pack became a microcosm of our life, a precious bit of personal security. So what do we need or, worse, just really have to have? Consider the matter of books. Packed among all the other stuff were ten to fifteen heavy academic books, a couple university catalogs, and sample student recruitment materials, a half dozen notebooks full of lectures, and enough paperback novels to last Judy several months. Also included were a couple of cookbooks, a heavy tome describing the basic plot of most of the more well-known operas, and two address books.

Books! They made up almost a quarter of the total space and more than that in weight! However, each item was considered crucial to the operation. For example, there was my university catalog and promotional literature, such as a "view book," a recruitment brochure containing a minimum of print and a number of large glossy pictures of students enjoying education and leisure pursuits at the university. We packed these rather fancy printed items we take for granted in American higher education yet, such items had never been seen before by academics and administrators in the countries where I would be posted. Students marveled at the big Boise State University recruiting poster that I kept pinned to the wall behind my desk. "Wow! Look at that big picture of your football stadium with the blue turf" they would say. No, no, I would retort, "look instead at those smaller pictures of classrooms with smiling students interacting with their professors!"

The CEP Yale office supplied every lecturer with several lists of "things to bring or do before leaving." First, there was a rather short but comprehensive list of over-the-counter medications and other drugstore products. Some of these items were also on a special list of things that would be difficult or impossible to find, especially for the CEPers posted to some of the more remote locations. These included eye drops, dental floss, and lip balm. Another list mentioned among other items, a sink plug, chili sauce, a corkscrew (hmm...), a shower curtain, and a water filter with sufficient replacement cartridges. By the time we had finished packing from these lists, our bags contained a small medicine chest worth of stuff, including, just in case, sterile disposable syringes—hospital supplies being quite unreliable—and, of course, enough of our prescription medications to last for 11 months.

In the miscellaneous category, we brought a very important little shortwave radio and a medium-size stereo radio and tape player. To power our radio, laptop computer, and compact printer, we packed a voltage converter to switch the local 220 current to 110 volts. We would still need to purchase special adapters in order to plug our American-style flat-pronged electrical plugs into the special Russian-style three-round-pronged plugholes. Later, we would need to purchase other adapters in order to use appliances made in Western Europe since their three prongs are slightly larger than the three prongs used throughout the former Soviet Russian Empire.

Other lists produced more items for the duffel bags. We packed a cheap coffeepot and vacuum-packed coffee, a few rolls of toilet paper, and a small photo album of family pictures. These pictures, along with a large paper-bound photo book of Idaho, would provide a simple and effective opportunity to make small talk with new friends and acquaintances. They could also be used to effectively bridge the language barrier in answering a lot of typical questions about who we were, where we were from, and what our family was like.

Finally, we threw in a plastic sack full of several hundred little colored plastic lapel pins. Some we obtained from the Idaho Department of Commerce and were shaped like the State of Idaho; the others were from the Idaho Potato Commission. You can guess what they looked like. I gave these pins away to all of my students and to anybody else we thought might appreciate our little effort at good will. Students wore them proudly. The potato sellers at the "farmer style" markets we frequented all got a little plastic spud engraved with the word "Idaho." They turned out to be a big hit.

By our second year, our bags included the all-important roach traps. These critters were a ubiquitous feature of life everywhere we lived. The preferable trap contained "food" that could be taken back to their nest where they and the others could die out of our sight. However, we first tried the roach "motel" variety of trap, placing them every night on the kitchen counter of our Estonian apartment. But it became more than we could stand to get up in the morning, make coffee, and watch several dozen of the roaches slowly dying while doing "push ups" on the sticky surfaces of their cardboard motel boxes. Mothers would often have their babies during the night and sometimes there would be hundreds of little ones all wiggling around in the mire.

All of these items and many more were carefully laid out along with all our folded and rolled clothing in the "staging room," a location in our house or cabin that went through several incarnations, depending upon where we were living prior to leaving. The room would be taken over by a mass of stuff that could be visualized all at once, enough to fill more than seven duffel bags, a little over four hundred pounds all in all, almost a quarter of a ton! Some of our lecturer friends packed less, a few much less, but, remember that Judy and I, along with our cat, intended to "create a home" as one of my country directors aptly described it. Actually, a few lecturers brought even more.

The story told by some of my Lithuanian students was that an older lady who had previously occupied my position at the University of Vilnius went so far as to bring her Mercedes convertible from Germany where she had been teaching American military personnel. This bit of eccentricity would have stuck out like a sore thumb anywhere in Lithuania as few people drove cars and absolutely nobody owned a convertible.

Another packing example involved Elizabeth Ryder, a young woman who was trying her hand at teaching for the first time. Having arrived fresh from her first couple of years in a law practice in Chicago, "Lizzy" brought what appeared to be her complete professional wardrobe packed in a large number of big bright red plastic trunks. There would be little need for all these business suits and accessories. However, she was definitely the best dressed of all of us whose general working attire was much more casual. I commonly wore black jeans along with sweaters, or a favorite sport jacket. I brought a wool suit as there were a few times when, as the senior CEP lecturer, a suit was appropriate for special occasions. I found that a good wool suit could be turned inside out, rolled and packed tightly in a duffel bag, left in this manner for a week or two, removed, hung up and yet come out of all this with no need for pressing.

When everything had been collected in the staging room, it was time to pack. Each bag was numbered and its contents written down in a notebook in case the bag became lost in transit. A master list was also kept at the same time. The checklist included the essential category of "passport/visa." We had our passports from earlier travels. Gaining the necessary visas was what we needed. They were expensive, in some instances particularly so for Americans who were charged more just because we were known to have the money. Of course, the CEP paid for these. To provide an example , our two visas just to enter Kyrgyzstan and Uzbekistan cost $510 dollars and required that we submit our passports, special order forms, passport photos, visa application forms, and letters of invitation. The last item was rather unique. Many of the former Soviet block countries wanted to know who was going to take responsibility for our visit. In my opinion, this requirement was a vestigial survival of an empire whose ideology required that paranoia become part of everyday life. Usually there was a time-consuming bureaucracy involved in obtaining visas, and after all the paperwork, faxes, telexes, and waiting, we were never sure we would get what we wanted.

Packing completed and the visa requests in the mail, Judy and I were able to turn to a last few tasks that needed our attention. We needed to execute a power of attorney, and both of us had to get a medical and dental checkup. Now all that was left was to throw in a bottle of Tabasco sauce, review our life insurance, and update our will. Finally! We were ready to leave!

2
Lithuania: First Impressions
of Post-Communist Life

A Flurry of New Experiences

This chapter is the first of four introducing our initial and most interesting observations and experiences in four country postings. I begin this chapter in Riga, Latvia, where we first landed behind what had been, until three years earlier, the Iron Curtain, the westernmost border of the former Soviet Russian Empire. This chapter records our first year in Lithuania where we were posted to Vilnius, its capital city. I describe a predominance of first impressions that embody a considerable degree of naiveté about the unique world we had just entered. We had much to learn about Soviet and Russian history, geography, and the politics of transition. Some of our learning came from books, but a large part of it was built up from noticing the little things, the routine items and events that were new to us. These caught our attention first and continued to be the source of the small delights of each day. With only a few exceptions, especially toward the last chapters, the stories in this book always begin with the observation of little things.

Riga, Latvia: Our First Few Days behind the Iron Curtain

After leaving Boise, Idaho, our adventure began with a few days touring Washington, DC, and a visit with our daughter Kimberly who was a U.S. Army officer stationed at Walter Reed Hospital. Then we were off to Dulles Airport, full of anticipation and jitters for a red-eye flight bound for Frankfurt, Germany. Following a long layover, we made a final two-hour flight northeast behind the former Iron Curtain to Riga, Latvia, our initial destination. The site of our regional office, Riga, would be our location for several days of in-country orientation.

I distinctly remember the bumpy landing on the very uneven sections of concrete runway and the miniscule, crudely constructed, and dilapidated nature of the airport: yet Riga was a capital city of almost a million people! This first impression, along with several others I would make in the first few days, would turn out to be emblematic of some of the most distinctive features of post-Communist Central/ Eastern Europe if not the whole of the former Soviet Russian Empire. Right from the start, the condition of the runway and the airport made clear that most people did not fly, but rather, as we were soon to find out, used long-distance trains. It also suggested that a lot of the Soviet-built environment was constructed hastily, without attention to detail, and was in bad need of repair or replacement. The banal and shoddy nature of Soviet building construction was an inescapable fact of everyday life and a striking contrast to the elegant architecture of the surviving older buildings.

The Baltic states. Also shown is Kalinigrad Oblast and the Courland Spit connecting the Oblast, by sea, to Lithuania

Once known as "the Paris of the Baltic region," Riga's city center is built around a large attractive park. Several of the surrounding buildings show off a wild variety of art nouveau friezes, colonnades, reliefs, and decorative sculptures. Some sculptures depict human and animal figures, while others include fruits and flowers. Red and crème colored articulated trams clatter and bend their way along their rail tracks around one side of the park and on to various destinations throughout the city. These trams look like they might have been manufactured in the 1930s or 1940s with their decidedly quaint old-fashioned appearance.

Riga's old quarter, lying between the park and the Daugava River that bisects the city, is a visual delight of old German-style buildings. At the main plaza entrance to "Old Riga" was a new McDonald's restaurant. While it was hardly in keeping with the architecture of the area, it was nevertheless a very popular place. Just around the corner was our student dormitory/hostel, a definitely "bare bones" place to stay if there ever was one.

Although we could not recognize it at the time, in the space of just a few blocks, were three more central features that would be a frequent part of our life over the next six years. These features were, first and foremost, strikingly beautiful old town centers. Second, was a plethora of austere and delapated buildings, including hotels, which could only intermittently, if at all, furnish heat or hot water. Finally, there were, joy of joys, McDonald's restaurants, some of the very few places where we could always count on a clean bathroom.

Not quite ready to venture out too far on our own, Judy and I began the first day of our stay in Riga with coffee at McDonald's. The place was full of people eating hamburgers. It was obvious they were happy and did not care about the lack of a breakfast menu. It was a little early for us to try a beer, typically a menu item at McDonald's resturants outside of the United States. We sat outside the restaurant at the edge of the adjoining plaza enjoying the warm morning sun. That morning, a man who was sitting at the table next to us actually was having a few "McBeers" for breakfast. I could tell that he was about to initiate a conversation. Asking of our whereabouts, he began to speak in poor but understandable English about how he had a relative in the United States and how much he liked Americans. This occasion also turned out, as it were, to foretell two more frequent features of this part of the world: a high degree of alcohol use, and abuse, and a very friendly attitude toward America and Americans. It seemed to me that everybody had a family member, or knew somebody who was now an American.

The CEP orientation meetings were an in-country gathering and initial cultural acclimatization for our Baltic states group, a total of fifteen faculty and two staff members. Our supervisor was Jana Teteris, a competent, personable, fun-loving young person in her mid-thirties, a citizen of Britain whose parents had fled their native Latvia just ahead of the Communist takeover in 1939. Jana had been raised bilingual.

The CEP had presented an opportunity for her to make an extended first visit to her parent's homeland. Now in her second year as a CEP country director, Jana was one of many second-generation children of the Latvian diaspora who were returning to work, maybe to start a business, and sometimes to claim confiscated family property.

There were twelve visiting lecturers in our Baltic group, who, except for me, were all single young men and women: an economist from Columbia, a law school graduate from the UK, and the rest from the United States. Three were coming back for their second year. There were also four young faculty fellows from the region. Artis was from Latvia, and Jonas, Darius, and Ramunas were from Lithuania. One of our group, Vello Pettai, was an Estonian-American whose parents, like Jana's, had fled their homeland ahead of the Soviets. Vello had grown up in New York, and, also like Jana, had grown up bilingual. He was a PhD candidate in comparative politics at New York's Columbia University when he decided to spend a year as a CEP visiting lecturer at Tartu University, Estonia's major institution of higher education. He was able to teach his classes there in Estonian. While the students quickly came to appreciate his up-to-date knowledge and active learning approach to teaching, they found his quaintly old-fashioned grammar a humorous but frequently difficult linguistic anachronism reflecting the fifty-year language hiatus of his parents' generation.

Our orientation meetings were held at the University of Latvia, a large Gothic-looking, centuries-old building that faces the main city park. Our regional office was in two small adjoining, freshly remodeled, first-floor rooms. The remodeling, along with the new computers and other furnishings in our office, presented a sharp contrast to the drab look of the rest of the building's ancient, worn-out looking interior. During these first few days, we learned about CEP's expense reimbursement system as each of us would be fronting all our housing and educational expenses for upwards of a month at a time. We met several German academics who were employed in a program somewhat like ours, although only in the three Baltic States. Some of these individuals would become some of our best friends and colleagues while in Lithuania and the next year in Estonia.

Sightseeing Riga and Its Environs

On a couple of afternoons, the entire Baltic contingent went sightseeing. We visited the Baltic Sea coast at a nearby town that was part of the beach strip city of Jurmala. All of us brought our swimsuits, but even in late August, the water was quite chilly. Another day, we took a bus ride to explore what would be the first of a large number of strikingly beautiful castles that Judy and I would visit everywhere in the Baltic region, almost always sharing the very picturesque features of stone walls with long interior balcony-style loggia, round-roofed turrets, and square-roofed towers capped in red tile.

These fortifications typically began their first incarnation in the eleventh or twelfth century. They were destroyed, rebuilt, and remodeled several times over the ensuing years before ending up in their present form sometime between the fifteenth and seventeenth centuries. Now, in various states of ruin and repair, they can be found in the countryside or as a complement to the old town centers of nearby cities, easily awaking one's imagination of what it might have been like during the rule of the Teutonic knights. Standing in their midst, it was easy to conjure up scenes of chivalry, shining armor, jousting competitions, and much more.

While walking through Riga's Old Town one afternoon, several of us decided to visit the Museum of the Occupation of Latvia. We had found the museum quite by chance. It was a fortunate discovery. The recently finished, windowless museum focused on what life was like under the long occupation of the Soviet Union. The visit became a valuable primer on Soviet history for Judy and me. It would help to inform our experience, over the next several years, with the effects of the Soviet way of thinking and doing things. In hindsight, it was fitting that we would wander into this museum so early in our stay.

The museum touched on a wide number of subjects spanning a fifty-one-year period of Soviet totalitarian occupation, 1940 to 1991. Almost all the exhibits seemed to leave two main impressions with Judy and me. The first concerned the large technical and material gap that clearly existed between the material quality of life of the Soviet citizens and of Americans, and yet this was the region with the highest standard of living anyplace in the Soviet Russian Empire. It was like looking back at least three decades in our own time.

The other impression was deeply disturbing, resulting from the tenacious and maniacal manner in which the Soviet authorities had gone about their radical reform of society. Force and terror appeared in the exhibits as the common denominators in practically all areas of life. I had previously read of the forcible way in which collective farms had been established throughout the empire, including Stalin's planned starvation of millions of Ukrainian farmers who would not cede personal control of their land to the state. The same reaction to collectivism and the same official response, we would later learn happened in Central Asia as well.

Since Judy and I were both educators, it was equally incredible and very sobering to see the exhibits showing how the Soviets completely and forcibly changed the Latvian national K–12 school curriculum. The use of completely different lesson plans and textbooks was immediately required. History was thoroughly changed simply by edict! It was the new occupational government's "well meaning" intention that Latvian youth should lose much of their previous connection to their culture and instead grow up to be Communists. This educational process began by prohibiting the learning or the use of the Latvian language.

The goal of "Russification" and creating the new "Soviet person" was evident in many of the exhibits. Again and again, the museum collection brought forth a clear message: Communism was not just good, it was morally right, and it was glorious! Posters and old pictures showed holidays celebrated by massive parades, buildings decorated with red bunting, and thousands of flags flying from almost every location.

We would see the evidence of these large and colorful parades everywhere we went in the former Soviet Russian Empire. The Communist Party introduced new holidays to celebrate such events as the Bolshevik Revolution or victory in the Great Patriotic War (aka World War II). A very frequent theme of celebration was the exultation of the worker.

The pictures in the museum also made it clear that the name and the presence of Lenin in painting or statue had hardly ever been out of people's sight. In the Baltic States, almost all official traces of Lenin, as well as other Communist symbolism, had been removed from public spaces shortly following independence, long before our arrival.

However, from a tourist's perspective, we were delighted to see that his presence remained a popular item with street venders and in flea markets where one could easily find busts, lapel pins, letter openers, and an endless variety of medals, pictures, and paintings. There was an overwhelming abundance of Lenin memorabilia. It really drove home just how extensive the cult of Lenin had been. I remember thinking that it will take years and thousands of future tourists in order to get rid of all this stuff. More impressively, Judy and I would later see plenty of Lenin, larger than life, still on his pedestals in the parks and other street settings in other parts of the empire

The Bolsheviks had initiated the Communist revolution. They, and the members of the Communist Party that followed, were fanatics, fully indoctrinated, and absolutely certain of the morality of turning the history and way of life of millions of people upside down in order to create the ideal Soviet society. In the 1960s, I had read the popular book *The True Believer* by Eric Hoffer. The Museum of Occupation made horrifyingly real what Hoffer had said about the dangers of the crusading mind-set of extremists, no matter what their beliefs might be.

As the CEP orientation began to wind down, the new crop of lecturers started to leave for their respective places of university employment. With a few exceptions, every teaching site could be reached within at least a day's travel by train or bus, or, in our case, by minivan. The van was quite ragged inside and out and just large enough with barely enough power to carry Judy and me, all our duffle bags, and a large box of academic materials and supplies. Also stuffed into the little van were the locally provided box of criminology hardcover textbooks and a second box containing a large number of bound photocopied articles I would use in all four of my classes during the upcoming academic year. We left Riga at midmorning with the van engine coughing and sputtering, alternately sharing the single remaining backseat or the duffle bags to sit on. Luckily, the strong smell of gas fumes eventually went away. Our drive would take about five hours. We crossed the border into Lithuania and turned on to the country's only semblance of a freeway for the trip to Vilnius, Lithuania's capital city. As the day wore on, I finally began to think that the minivan would actually get us to our destination.

We drove straight through, eating a box lunch while on the road.

We needed only to stop once at a designated roadside rest stop (the sign indicated "Services" in Lithuanian). It was a muddy turnoff from which a short trail led into the woods and two very smelly holes in the ground. Even after years of our life visiting primitive Idaho campgrounds, we had never witnessed anything so atrocious. No McDonald's at a convenient freeway offramp anywhere on this trip. In fact, no McDonald's anywhere in Lithuania! Probably a good thing, as it was high time we cut our umbilical cord with America. A whole new world awaited us.

Lietuva: The Land of Rain

Our route passed through several small Lithuanian towns and near even smaller rural villages. There were large unbroken expanses of farm fields and equally large areas of forest containing pines mixed in with an abundance of birch trees. Referred to by its people as "Lietuva," the land of rain, Lithuania is a country about the size of South Carolina. It was predominately green and tree-covered with rolling hills. It reminded me of Oregon's Willamette Valley where I had grown up and Judy and I had met as university students. Lithuania is still a heavily agricultural country with small farm holdings. The largest of the three Baltic countries, Lithuania had a population of about four million people composed mainly of native Lithuanians, but with fairly sizable first and second generation minorities of Russians, Belarussians, Ukrainians, and Poles.

While small enough in size not to threaten the new nationalist sense of identity, this ethnic mixture continued to highlight the fact that Lithuania is located in the geographic center of Europe. In fact the exact center, as calculated by the French, is less than twenty miles north of the Lithuanian capital. It is marked by a large flat-topped rock about five feet in diameter. All this is dutifully recognized by geographical societies and even the *Guinness Book of World Records*.

Soviet-period postcard picture of Lithuania's fourteenth-century castle at Trakai epitomizes the awe-inspiring medieval beauty of the Baltic region

The stamp of Communism and military occupation by the Soviets were only the last indignity of occupation of this centrally located little country by what seemed like every neighboring nation. Sitting just north above Poland, Lithuania is the southernmost of three small contiguous countries, often referred to collectively as the Baltic states. Stacked one above the other, sharing a Baltic Sea coastline as their western border, the most southern country is Lithuania, then to its north is Latvia, and to its north is Estonia.

Our initial trip through Lithuania's countryside and small urban areas revealed many distinctive qualities. There were large multistory apartment blocks smack dab in the middle of tiny rural farm communities. Except for the larger cities, these apartments, the results of Soviet agricultural collectivization, were fortunately outnumbered by attractive little one-story wooden houses usually painted in shades of blue or mustard and decorated around their windows and along their roof peaks with distinctive wooden carvings, which are a Lithuanian folk specialty. A few houses even had thatched roofs. Usually the houses sat on lots large enough to contain a fruit and vegetable garden, maybe a few chickens, or even a cow, and usually a washline partly full of clothes. The overall appearance was rural and peasant, suggesting some degree of self-sufficiency.

Our entry into Vilnius took us first through a suburban area filled with the same drab prematurely aging high-rise apartments we had seen earlier in the day on the outskirts of Riga. Most of the buildings had been originally built in the 1960s and 1970s. They had been sided completely or partially with ceramic tile. Most of the tile color was now badly faded and many tiles had long since come unglued and fallen to the ground. Communism had certainly put its banal stamp on this feature of city life. However, beyond this ugly parameter Vilnius began to reveal its striking beauty.

The main part of the city contained much of the same wonderful nineteenth-century architecture we had observed in Riga. In our first walk through town, Judy and I would discover that, also like Riga, Vilnius had its "Old Town" section. Although more extensive, it seemed just as Medieval, but with a more baroque rather than German look. The city's Old Town reflected a strong historical alliance with Catholic Poland. During this period, Vilnius became the capital of a fifteenth-century empire that stretched east, far into Russia, and south to the Black Sea. Today, the view across the Old Town part of Vilnius presents a forest of Catholic spires and a few Protestant steeples, most topped with delicate wrought-iron crosses. Russian influence is also evident in Orthodox Church cupolas that poke up here and there with their brightly painted and gleaming gold or silver gilding. Most of these places of worship had been recently renovated. After Lithuanian independence from Communist control in 1991, these places of worship were some of the first structures to receive private money to make long-needed repairs.

Judy and I would experience the pleasure of walking through the old part of the city the very next day. After that, we found what seemed like an endless number of excuses to keep coming back. What made this area especially nice for the person on foot was that vehicle traffic was severely restricted by the predominance of narrow winding streets with sidewalks—often no more than a foot or two wide.

As an American, especially one living in the West, it was hard for me to believe that some of these ornate, colorful buildings containing places of worship, shops, restaurants, and bars, even a major university, could be as old as six hundred years. In Idaho, at least outside of a few cities, any structure very much older than one hundred years has likely fallen to the ground or, with luck, may at least continue to function artistically as part of a ghost town. As the little van neared our apartment in the downtown area, it was obvious that Vilnius would most certainly be a delightful place in which to live, work, and explore.

The van pulled through the archway into the partially paved drive in the inner courtyard of our large U-shaped apartment building. We were met by Vito, our landlord, who had thoughtfully planned to serve tea and cookies upon our arrival. The entrance to our apartment stairwell made a powerful first impression. There were two large beat-up looking, creaky-sounding wooden doors, one in front of the other, leading to an unpainted concrete staircase. With the help of our van driver, we managed to get all our stuff up the four flights of stairs and into the tiny little apartment. Vito got the tea ready, serving it from a fancy teapot into our little glass cups. I sat on a soft chair and took a first long look around the front room. It was small and packed with furniture. The room looked like a museum. Big vases sat on an aging wooden parquet floor. Large pictures filled the walls, and a wide variety of ornaments and porcelain knickknacks seemed to be everywhere.

Also present for tea was Susan Cooper, a perky, young Californian who had recently finished two years in Lithuania as a member of the Peace Corps. Susan was now working part-time as the Lithuanian coordinator for the CEP. She had found our apartment, negotiated the rental contract at the inescapably inflated price charged Americans, and would, the following day, show us around the city and my university workplace. Following tea, Susan took us to a tiny nearby grocery store where we bought a few things for dinner. The first trip to a grocery store in a foreign country is always an exciting new experience: new foods, different packaging with odd labels, a little bit like the ethnic food portion writ large of an American supermarket. It would turn out to be our primary grocery store during our entire stay in Vilnius.

Later, that first evening, back at our apartment, alone just the two of us, very tired but still pumped up with adrenalin, Judy and I began to unpack our bags and search the limited amount of storage space for suitable places to put things away. Day one was about to conclude in our new life as residents, not just tourists, behind the famous Iron Curtain.

We were just one of many foreigners who were coming to Vilnius, many attracted by the rapid growth of consulting opportunities in one form or another. For example, early in our stay, Judy and I met a German man while grocery shopping in a store on the other side of town. He gave us a ride back to our apartment in his little Alfa Romeo sedan. We were glad for the company and for the ride as our bags were heavy. His business card indicated that he was in financial "enterprise restructuring."

Another consulting example involved one of our second-year CEP lecturers who met a California girl in Vilnius. She was working as a full-time advisor to one of the larger banks in the city. Not over thirty years old, she was well paid, well enough to afford the rent on a very nice apartment with a gorgeous view. I was not surprised to learn that the apartment had originally been occupied by a senior KGB operative. Another man we met in a restaurant looked quite a bit the professor with his gray hair, matching beard, and tweedy sport jacket. He was from Ireland and was consulting with government officials on environmental and national park issues. Judy and I were to see a wide variety of consultants during our four years in the former Soviet Russian Empire. Consulting in the new "transitioning" states was definitely a gold mine of professional opportunity.

There were other newly created professional opportunities as well. Early in the fall, Judy and I received an e-mail from a close friend in Boise informing us that one of his friends, Steven Anderson, would be arriving in Vilnius. Steve was on leave of absence from his position as editor of Boise's monthly *Business Review* newspaper. Under terms of a modest grant, Steve was coming to Vilnius to spend several months observing and writing about the changing economic climate. A friendship quickly developed with Steve and continued following our return home. While in Vilnius, Steve and his Lithuanian interpreter, Katerina Salgina, grew romantically attracted to each other. Within a year of Steve's return to Boise, Katerina was able to win a Green Card through an immigration lottery and join Steve in Boise.

Time for Two Local Excursions before Winter Settled In

We had arrived in the Baltic region in time to enjoy the last weeks of summer and to witness the absolutely gorgeous soul-enriching colors of fall. The profusion of color reminded me of the pictures of our own Northeastern states in October. Every shade of fall was represented in Vilnius. I found myself commenting over and over to Judy as we took our almost daily walk exploring the city, "It just doesn't get any better than this."

Fall was still in full color when we decided we could wait no longer to travel the short distance from Vilnius to Trakai National Park to visit the Gothic island castle of Grand Duke Vytautas. By the early 1400s, the region's German Teutonic occupiers had been completely overthrown, the last vestiges conquered. Through the coming together of several Lithuanian tribes under Vytautas's leadership, Vytautas's castle had become the seat of newly won Lithuanian power. What makes the castle setting absolutely stunning is its location on a very small little island in the middle of a sizable lake. The castle had been fully but not overly restored. Not having to contend with a rush of tourists, it was delightful to walk anywhere on the castle grounds totally undisturbed. We walked around the island on a small dirt path that wound along near the water's edge through a mix of weeds, pasture grass, trees, and brush. It was hard to believe that a treasure such as this castle could still remain in such natural surroundings. Anywhere in Western Europe it might easily have been over-restored, dedicated to tourism, and made into Disneyland.

The castle needed no traditional mote. Instead it was reached then as now by a long wooden pedestrian causeway. A regatta of small sailboats was in progress the day we arrived. The view could not have been more picturesque as we left the commuter train station and began about a half mile walk toward the castle down a gently sloping hill through the little town of Trakai with its brightly painted old wooden houses. We stopped for a beer and a Lithuanian delicacy; small toasted slices of very dark heavy bread saturated in an oily garlic mixture. Just below the town was the path to the causeway and the castle.

A week or so later, Judy and I made a second short trip out of town. We took a local train and got off at the village of Paneriai. We wanted to see what remained of the dreadful event that had taken place here: one of many gruesome reminders of Lithuania's more recent past. From a nearby abandoned train station next to a large train switching yard, we walked down a small road about half a mile into the woods to a place where Germans, and some Lithuanian collaborators, had systematically eliminated about one hundred thousand Jews, most of them from the Vilnius Ghetto.

The woods were quiet, peaceful, and very beautiful during our fall visit, but the evidence of atrocity was obvious and quite unsettling. Several clearings revealed large sunken pits about twenty feet deep and two hundred feet across. These pits were reminders of where the Jewish people—men, women, and children—were first shot and then burned on pyres. Their remains were then crushed and buried in hope that no easily noticed evidence would remain. There were Nazi killing fields like this scattered throughout the three Baltic countries. Only a few years after the Nazi occupation, the Soviets would add to their number. It was difficult for Judy and me to live in this part of the world without encountering, intentionally or by accident, the extensive amount of ethnic and political atrocities that had occurred, either by Nazis or Communists.

In the midst of our fall outings, it would have been hard to believe that soon the joyous weather would change, plunging us into the longest, coldest deep freeze Judy and I had ever experienced. It was especially hard for Lithuanians as well as the winter would turn out to be the longest and coldest on record. The daily trip to visit our little market and to explore more of the city and its environs grew difficult and at times treacherous as weeks of constant snow began to pile up on the frozen streets and sidewalks. In one of my e-mails to our daughters in early February, I noted that the high temperature was expected to be about 5 degrees Fahrenheit. I wrote that Judy had already been to the grocery store that morning—all several layers of her, including long johns and two pairs of mittens.

Back at our flat, we ate more chicken soup along with wonderful heavy dark rye bread. We got out a little supplemental electric portable heater to place near our feet as we began to spend more of our spare time confined to our apartment by the weather. We made use of this opportunity to read through the small library of paperback books we had brought with us for just such occasions. As the winter stretched on, Judy decided to try a facial suntan lamp that our landlord had left for our use. It looked a little like a flood lamp in a box. She spent what seemed like only short periods of time facing into the lamp while wearing little black eye covers. Needing more sunshine than we were getting, the sun lamp seemed to help recharge Judy's batteries, but it also gave her a nasty sunburn accompanied by enough pain to dissuade here from trying the lamp again.

Shopping

We were not about to let the coming of winter slow us down that much. There were just too many new things to see and do, too many strikingly different features of Vilnius waiting for us to experience in this "center" of Europe, this post-Communist world we had only recently entered.

Our big down jackets were able to keep us warm enough even though they were not very attractive for evenings out. This was particularly noticeable now that we had discovered the opera and ballet theatre that was only a few blocks away. We had begun to attend performances on a frequent basis. It was a new experience for both of us, especially for me. I had never been to a ballet and only one opera, back during my freshman year at university. The building was quite new and very modern in architectural style. It was just one more of the many winter locations to which a large number of women would wear their full-length fur coats. Mostly in light shades of crème and brown, it seemed like these coats were made from just about every kind of fur-bearing animal. Some of the coats were just plain gorgeous even though it was clear that most of the coats had been in service for many years. Later, when we lived in Ukraine, the women would wear beautiful fur hats as well.

Judy and I decided that shopping for a fur coat might make a good excuse to brave the outside elements for a walk to the few stores where we had seen such coats for sale. I do not recall the prices exactly. However, they were definitely very reasonable by American standards, even though still a lot of money if measured against our CEP budget. More disconcerting than the cost were the questions about where Judy might wear such a coat back home in Boise, and more importantly, what would our friends think? We were aware of the still lingering attitude toward killing animals for their fur. Judy decided against a fur coat—well, almost.

We didn't recognize the reasons immediately, but as we began to shop for tourist things and locate places to purchase necessities, we found the going a bit difficult. It struck us that there was little in the way of a commercial look to the city. It was hard to determine where to get things and what might lie behind store facades. Missing was the vibrant, colorful jumble of advertising and electrified store signs that characterize our cities. Of course, these commercial features had been left out by design. Under Communism why advertise when the state owned all the stores and there was no competition? The initial impression was that the "business sectors" of the city had a distinctively drab appearance. Judy scolded me for liking the situation to one of a lady without her makeup. I remember previously thinking, while living at home in Boise, about how nice it would be if our city streets were not so cluttered with billboards and a jumble of neon advertising signs. Now, with streetlights just about the only source to brighten the way through Vilnius in the evenings, I missed all the glitzy distraction of electrified signs.

Stores were never identified by someone's name or by a cute boutique title. Instead, little painted pictures on the lower portion of store windows, maybe eight to ten inches high, were the most common form of identifying what might be sold within. Painted in browns and greens, these pictures were typically simple outlines of fruits and vegetables, a loaf of bread, cuts of meat, or a roast bird on a platter. Other stores had pictures of books or common items of furniture or electrical things.

Some of these stores no longer sold anything or without announcement had completely changed their line of merchandise. I had not realized how much we take the informative clutter of commercialism for granted. It took quite awhile to overcome this sense that something important was missing as we walked about the city. The limited amount of commercialism could also be seen in the absence of "yellow pages" in a telephone book. In fact, there were no telephone books at all. We were told that during Soviet times, in an effort to prevent the possibility of organized resistance, ordinary people were not permitted to own a telephone book, copying equipment, or even an accurate map of the city. Fortunately, good maps were just becoming available, but they were difficult to find.

So how did we shop or find anything? Certainly, by comparison to what we were used to in the United States, there was not a whole lot of anything to buy. There really hadn't ever been much in the way of consumer goods under Communism, and now there was even quite a bit less. The theory was that centrally planned collective activity rather than a chaotic private market with all its glitz was the way to produce wealth. The situation in Lithuania had grown even worse as the local economy had suffered, like the rest of the Soviet Russian Empire, through more than two decades of especially hard times. Most knowledgeable observers in the West had been unaware of how bad the Soviet economy had been. The reigning assumption was that the Soviet standard of living was about three quarters of what we enjoyed in the West. In fact it was closer to a third, but we did not find this out until the Iron Curtain fell and it was possible to get an unfettered look on the other side. Now, what was left of the prior Soviet economy following seventy years of collectivism was in shambles.

The first years after Communism had witnessed further economic decline in most, if not all, of the newly transitioning countries. The year Judy and I arrived, Lithuania actually saw the first up-tick in the economy, following declines of 30 to 40 percent for each of its first four years of independence. So finding what one needed became somewhat like a scavenger hunt for everybody. One way we learned to find things was to walk into and make a quick perusal of every store that looked like it might contain something interesting. This took us in and out of a large number of doors, enlivened our walks and quickly helped us build a pretty thorough mental map of where to find at least the limited kinds of merchandise.

In some cases, things could be found by their smell. We located a small meat market in the basement of one building this way. Once inside the building, there is a smell. It is hard to describe, just kind of meaty, but not offensive. We purchased pork here quite often from a short robust man with dark hair that was always poking out in curls from his Chicago Bulls baseball cap. He clearly remembered us on each subsequent visit from our initial inquiry as to the nature of the meat we had pointed to. The cut was unfamiliar. "Oink oink?" I had cheerfully inquired.

Word of mouth was another way to locating what we might need. Students were especially helpful in this regard. No matter how helpful though, such tips and references could quickly get out of date as little stores would rapidly come and go. For example, a little grocery store opened up about five blocks from our apartment on a route we walked quite often. To our surprise, our basement butcher had set up his new shop there! The long narrow store fronted a busy sidewalk. It had a small, but exciting selection of imported canned goods (yes, items like this were exciting). We shopped there several times, but within a month, it was gone and so was our butcher.

While out on our walks, one of the best sources of shopping information was a little guidebook that had recently started up called *Vilnius in Your Pocket*. It was printed in English, lighthearted in approach, and hip to all the latest scenes. New editions were printed every two months in an effort to keep up with a city that was beginning to change ever more rapidly. There were introductory tidbits on history and language and major sections on hotels, dining, shopping, transportation, and sightseeing. One more recent edition brought back to me by a friend had as its front page title; *"Beer, Probably the Best Guide in the World."* Problem solved. The success of this guide quickly spawned similar guides for other cities in Lithuania and Latvia, and later, in other adjacent countries as well.

Oh, yes, Judy did end up getting a fur coat. After a couple of months of looking out our apartment window at a building entrance kitty-corner across the street, I realized we had not checked it out. It turned out to be a secondhand store filled with clothing from Germany. As a "rich" American, I felt a bit embarrassed after entering the store. Before I had time to contemplate the matter, Judy found a black calf-length coat that looked like new and fit her perfectly. It had a collar that turned up above her ears. The coat was very good looking, noticeably heavy, and easily capable of keeping anybody warm in the coldest Lithuanian weather. I enquired of one of the clerks as to the origin of its fur. *"Muton"* (Mutton), she said. Her answer didn't initially register. Remembering the butcher, I sounded out, "baa-a-a?" Both clerks broke out in laughter. OK, I had it right. We purchased the coat for very little money. In remembrance of the event, we called the coat "Ba-ba." Judy wore it for the next two years before giving Ba-ba away to the Estonian fiancée of one of our CEP lecturers. Being constructed of sheep hide, in purchasing this coat we didn't figure we were breaking any taboos concerning the misuse of exotic or endangered animals.

We continued to shop in our "perhaps we will find something new" manner, always in a bit of wide-eyed wonder, with patience, and much firsthand investigation. With this approach, and with help from our friends and my students, we found most everything we needed during our stay in Lithuania except shoelaces for Judy.

As might be expected, while out on our numerous walks, we seemed to find just about everything we encountered worth describing. Take weddings for example. After such a long period of Communist rule and enforced atheism, religious weddings did not appear to have regained popularity. Instead, the majority of young couples appeared to prefer to get married in the Palace of Weddings. Almost windowless, the building was an ultra-modern two-story construction of large vertically placed concrete slabs, several of which projected well above the building's roof line. This municipal building was located just a few blocks up the hill above our apartment. On several occasions, Judy and I would walk by, noticing that the building had taken on the appearance of a real wedding mill. A line of several dozen people and a few brides to be in their white wedding gowns would slowly be moving through the street-level side door, while an equally large number of happily wedded couples, their attendants and family members would be exiting the upper floor moving down the wide front staircase to be greeted by other well-wishers. We never waited to see how long the process took, but I suspect the whole ceremony lasted less than half an hour "door to door."

Sustenance

So how could I have gone this far in the chapter without saying something about food? First of all, we are not connoisseurs, and, if we were, it might have been an expensive if not difficult passion to pursue. We were told that most people were not eating out very much, and if there were some high-end restaurants, and I am sure there were, at least they were not in obvious sight to the passerby. It wouldn't have been much help in locating such restaurants to consult our excellent tourist guide on this matter, not with a cover describing the contents inside as a "survival kit."

Actually, we ate out almost half of the time. The remainder of the time I was saved by the fact that Judy is an excellent cook, and having remembered to pack a few cookbooks with simple recipes, we enjoyed many scrumptious meals at home. Working in a very cramped kitchen, which also included our only table, Judy quickly learned the quirks of operating a temperamental gas stove and how to move food in and out of a miniature-size refrigerator with a broken freezer compartment door. Judy cooked many delicious meals in this little kitchen. We would eat at our little white painted kitchen table under a very large oil painting that hung at a sharp angle from the wall, enough of an angle so that from our seats we could clearly see its depiction of a large bowl containing various fruits.

The rest of our meals we ate out. We tried the Taro Restaurant conveniently located at the ground-floor corner of our apartment building. We also visited a couple of other equally Soviet-period places just a few blocks away on Gedimino, the main street through the city. The food in these restaurants was usually very plain and was served in small helpings. Later, we realized that "plain and small" was pretty standard everywhere. In the Soviet-style restaurants, we typically would sit in a large, high-ceiling room that was gaudily decorated using gobs of colored plastic and aluminum, especially on the ceilings. There would be a big serving buffet in the middle of the room from which the food and table silver were organized before bringing it to our table.

It was hard to understand the menus as they normally did not contain an English translation, and when they did, the menu items rarely corresponded to the translations. A humorous example of this occurred while we were living in Kharkiv, Ukraine. Accompanied by our country director and his assistant, we began to check the menu at a high-end restaurant only to break out laughing. The featured meal was "boiled language." The waiter was perplexed until our country director filled him in. "Tongue" and "language" are the same word in Russian.

Fortunately, there were many interesting places to eat in addition to the Soviet-style restaurants. We tried some authentic Lithuanian food in the Old Town. We liked *blynai*, a pancake made with grated potato. We ate a great number of traditional vegetable salads, usually served with a mayonnaise dressing. There were a wide variety of these salads that were all very popular. There were no lettuce salads, nor could one find lettuce in a grocery store. The salads were, like so much of Lithuanian fare, proportionately quite small. I considered that this might be one reason why younger Lithuanians, the women especially, were so noticeably slender.

We also tried *cepelinas,* which definitely does not arrive at the table as a small portion. Even though a national favorite, we tried it only once. Later, referring to our *Lonely Planet* guide book, we realized why this Zeppelin-shaped dumpling would take more patience than we had in order to learn to enjoy—or digest. It was a potato dumpling alright, but our guide book seemed to define it more entertainingly than delectably as "a parcel of glutinous substance alleged to be potato dough, with a wad of cheese, meat, or mushrooms in the center." I remember that it seemed to go right to the bottom of our stomachs and stay there for a very long time.

One other popular food item remained for us only a curiosity. It was called *spirgai,* salted pig fat. We saw people eating chunks of it plain or as a thick spread on bread. Squeamish about even a little bacon fat, we passed up this delicacy, although it was offered to us on several occasions. Our CEP colleague, Tom Velek, told us how early one evening, he ran across the entry hall of his apartment building in Minsk, Belarus, upon hearing the screams of a family next door. He found a very overweight grandmother lying face down on the floor choking on some food she had been eating at the dinner table. Tom managed to get the lady up on her feet successfully applying the Heimlich maneuver. The next day he was rewarded for saving her life with a knock on his door. Opening the door Tom was joyously greeted by the grandmother. She gave him a big hug and proudly presented him with a very large slab of spirgai.

In rather ethnocentric fashion, our three favorite restaurants ended up being places frequented by ex-pats, embassy personnel, and many of the consultants I mentioned earlier in the chapter. One restaurant was the Prie-Parlamento, which as its name suggests was located just a block from the Lithuanian Parliament building. Its menu was in English and contained a variety of Lithuanian and British/Irish dishes. We both liked the Sheppard Pie. We ate here frequently, savoring the food and braving the cigarette smoke, which at the time was a common denominator in all Lithuanian restaurants. Wednesday night was "English Speaker's Night."

Judy and I met a few individuals whom we really liked and a highly ranked member of the American Embassy whom we really disliked. All he talked about was how he hated his posting in Vilnius!

The owners of the Prie-Parlamento had a second pub-style place to eat just a block from the Old Town location of the University of Vilnius. One can easily guess its name: the Prie-Universiteto. Judy and I really liked this place because its interior furnishing reminded us of an English pub-style place where we often went for a coke date while students at the University of Oregon. In fact, the English-style pub was, along with pizza establishments, undoubtedly the two most frequent home grown and probably locally owned foreign-type food restaurants to spring up throughout most of Central/Eastern Europe since Soviet times.

Our favorite pizza place was called Rita's. It was located in the basement of a building just a short walk across a large park just a block from our apartment. Until recently, the park had featured a big statue of Lenin. The story was that people used to put bread in his outstretched hand and dog poop in the hand he held behind his back. On the other side of the park was the pizzeria owned by Rita Sleptuve. An American Lithuanian who had grown up in Chicago, she came to Vilnius soon after independence to form several businesses and get involved in politics. Rita's pizza place duplicated the U.S. theme of a hip and racy Chicago dive, and her menu was as close as possible to American fare. It served great food and an opportunity to connect with our American lifestyle. In addition to pizza, the menu also included barbequed ribs and baked potatoes. This was always our order, along with two potatoes each as they were quite small. It was impossible anywhere to find the type of large "Idaho" potatoes we were used to.

Pedestrian Life

It is obvious by now that walking was the main way we and most other Vilnius residents got around. The city center and adjacent Old Town were principally designed at a time when most people walked almost exclusively, and they still do in large numbers. However, for several reasons, the life of the pedestrian had become rather dangerous. Judy and I needed to be very careful when walking just about anywhere in the city. Like just about every city we lived in or visited in the former Soviet Union, the sidewalks in Vilnius presented serious dangers to life and limb. This is not to say that they weren't full of people most of the time. They were often very crowded. Only America might be described as "the land of the empty sidewalk." No, the security problem wasn't a matter of too many people. In part it was the fact that the sidewalks were suffering from poor construction and years of neglect. The other part of the problem stemmed from how a good number of these people behaved as pedestrians.

I will first explain the poor construction and neglect of the sidewalks. They contained a number of lidless manholes and many with lids askew. This danger was something we carefully looked out for, preferably in time to take evasive action. While visiting us, one of our friends from Boise actually stepped on a manhole lid that was ajar and quickly dropped one leg to below his knee before he was able to extract himself. It might have been that the manhole covers were removed by thieves interested in the scrap value of cast iron. The city's main newspaper often mentioned that many of the newly wealthy people had made their money "in metal." As for manhole covers, I had heard that this practice went on in other parts of the world as well, but from my early experiences in Lithuania and Latvia, the difference was that nobody seemed to attend to their replacement.

There were also pieces of angle iron poking up several inches here and there. These dangerous stubs appeared to have been part of signposts at some earlier time. It seemed odd that they had not been more carefully removed or cut off flush. And finally, waiting to stub your toe, were the individual concrete squares used to pave the sidewalks. Other than varying somewhat in size from a foot to more than two feet square, these chunks of concrete made up the standard sidewalk surface in every city. Many of these squares had either prematurely disintegrated down to their exposed metal reinforcements, ended up tilted at a sunken angle, or were missing all together. This was another reason to look down frequently to take care where we were walking.

If all this was not enough to watch out for, there was—no kidding—an unimaginably large number of banana peels that lay about on the sidewalks. Lithuania was in the midst of a banana craze. Suffice it to say that the sidewalks got slippery long before winter set in.

More ominously than banana peels were other pedestrians who could really make the sidewalk a dangerous place. We had to be careful to make a wide birth around some of these dedicated pedestrians coming the other way. Making matters worse, there seemed to be little sense of order or walking on the right. Older women in particular (the Russian word is *babushka*) were determined to walk briskly straight ahead, even on the most crowded of sidewalks. It seemed like most of these women were short and wide. I got used to dodging these bulldozing ladies, but Judy was constantly getting forcefully turned part way around as they made body contact, whacking her shoulders on one side or the other.

If negotiating the sidewalks in good weather required a heightened level of alertness, during the long winter, the sidewalks presented new challenges, and in the spring, they literally were places of death for more than a few hapless individuals. As the sidewalks became permanently covered with ice and the sand available to sprinkle on at least a few of them ran out, people reverted to "the Baltic shuffle," walking "like a cow" as one of my students put it. Arm in arm, Judy and I would walk, with legs apart, taking little sliding steps forward while trying to keep both feet on the ground. The city tried at first to clear the ice from the sidewalks, but it was a losing effort. Before the small budget ran out, a large number of these same shoulder whacking old women would appear around the city early every morning with heavy steel breaker bars and begin to pound the sidewalk ice into large chunks that they would pile along the side of the streets. The sound of their methodical pounding could be heard each morning in our apartment, sometimes helping to wake us up for the day. In some cases, men would show up later in the day in trucks that looked like a rusty, rather exact copies of old American Studebakers, and cart the ice away. Later in the winter, the public coffer depleted, the ice was left to pile up along the side of the streets frequently reaching heights of four or five feet or more.

During the early spring in Vilnius, big blocks of ice that had been building on the rooftops over a four-month freeze were finally beginning to loosen up. Icicles up to three feet long that had formed on the eaves of the city's mostly two and three story buildings were poised like downward-facing missiles ready to break away and crash to the sidewalk or down on the unsuspecting pedestrian. As the concept of personal liability was only just beginning to appear in the new laws, most of these obstructions, while illegal, went unattended by municipal officials as well as new private owners. Later, when the icicles were falling in profusion and quite a few people had become seriously injured, and even two women were killed in instances that we knew of, did a few merchants began to rope off their part of the sidewalk and send someone up on the roof to whack away at these protruding menaces. By now, most people had taken to walking in the streets anyway.

It was a long, cold winter. As the very first signs of spring began to arrive—a small bird at our windowsill, touches of green at the ends of bush and tree tips—Judy and I would lengthen our walks to explore new sections of the city. We also began to spend more time wandering the narrow cobblestone streets of the Old Town. We would often enter the little shops or linger in front of some of the hundreds of sidewalk merchants displaying amber artwork in every conceivable form. Lithuania's Baltic seacoast contains one of the world's largest deposits of this translucent fossilized resin, which ranges in color from light yellow to dark brown. In a few of the special jewelry items it was possible to see the complete remains of tiny flies and crawling insects that had been caught up in the tree pitch from which the amber was formed millions of years ago.

We would walk past a church that the Soviets had literally turned into a storage barn for construction and road repair equipment. One church, St. Kazimeras, built in 1604, was actually made into a museum of atheism! Some of these buildings were very run down. One section of the old town was almost completely abandoned, its one and two story stucco facades and rotting wooden doors and window trims looking very forlorn. It was sad and required that one look a bit selectively among the many visual delights of the area. While a lot of fixing up was underway, it still seemed like the country had just awakened after about a three-decade Gulliver-like sleep among the Lilliputians: a sleep during which time stood still and no money was spent to fix anything! In some cases, the areas of the city that had been rebuilt during Soviet times were filled with unattractive gray stucco buildings. And, as previously mentioned, there were also those hastily constructed high-rise apartment monstrosities out on the low hills in the distance, ringing the edge of the city.

I began to realize that a poor economy was not the only reason, and likely not the main reason, for the deteriorating state of so many buildings. Lacking private ownership or the opportunity for financial return on investment, there was really not much incentive for anybody but government to do anything. Some of the deterioration had stopped by the time we arrived. Things were beginning to change. For example, people were purchasing and fixing up the inside of their apartment units, often obtaining free title to the unit with coupons provided through a popular housing privatization program. The newspapers were reporting a debate over what percentage, if any, of outside foreign investment should be allowed in the ownership and reconstruction of the city, especially the buildings in the Old Town.

Life after Communism

Our walks filled us with many new impressions. One, example, which occurred quite frequently, was the rather dramatic architectural juxtaposition of historic beauty and the design and construction priorities contained in the Soviet vision of socialist modernity. In a strange sort of way we felt as if we were living in the shadow of the Soviet Russian Empire, which definitely hadn't made industrial First World status, while actually experiencing the poverty typically associated with a Third World country. This was an impression that carried through all the places we lived or visited in the former empire. It was very disconcerting. I had expected a higher standard of living, obviously having ignored all the warnings that the CEP had provided about the mess the Soviets had left behind. Certainly the early years of independence were taking a toll on many people. There was a look of quiet resignation in the faces of many, especially the older people. Public drunkenness was common. Old women and men begged at the entrance to buildings. In the dead of the winter, beggars would sit for hours separated from the icy sidewalk only by a thin piece or two of cardboard. I honestly did not understand how they stayed alive.

I kept thinking of the dislocations and impoverishment that had befallen Lithuanians enumerable times before. That large stone marking Lithuania as the center of Europe kept coming to mind. While being in the "center" is now considered a great business advantage, historically it seemed to have been a liability. Always accompanied with great dislocation and destruction, the Germans, Poles, Swedes, Russians, and others had been in, and out, of this little country. The Germans had managed one of the longest occupations, remaining the dominant power in the Baltic area for about three hundred years until losing control to the Swedes in the middle of the sixteenth century. About two hundred years later, Peter the Great seized the Baltic coast from the Swedes, and the Russians held sway until the First World War when the Germans again took over the region for the duration of the war. The interwar years brought a brief period of independence for the Baltic countries, a time of respite that was lost to forced Soviet occupation in 1939. The Germans invaded the region for the third time in 1941 and briefly occupied all three countries until being defeated by invading Soviet forces in 1945. This was also the Russians third return to the region.

Thus, it seems obvious that the penalty for being in the center of Europe was frequent war and occupation. And now, the old people were undergoing the wrenching dislocation of fundamental change once again. If any consolation, at least this time it was economic rather than military. As usual, being the oldest and economically unproductive, these people were in constant danger of being squeezed out of their small share of the much-diminished economic pie. Pensions were being reduced, not paid on time, and sometimes delayed for months at a time. Old people had to rely on their children for most of their support. It was far from a satisfactory arrangement as the children were often out of work and might be close to destitution themselves. Only those elderly who had children or relatives in the farming areas usually were able to get enough food to eat.

Inadequate pensions and the anger and frustration with the Russians were evident in our landlord's remarks one evening while having dinner in our apartment. "Those dirty Russians," Vito, kept saying. Now in his late fifties, Vito had been born to Polish- Lithuanian parents. Like his father, he had worked as a journalist under close Soviet censure, hated it, and was now living in more or less forced retirement. His mother and father had been deported to Siberia by the Soviets shortly after the war and had both perished there. Vito lived with his son's family while renting his flat to us in order to help make ends meet financially. He gave the impression that he would go out of his way to be accommodating to Judy and me, but the language barrier made it hard to assess his sincerity. We were left to make small talk over dinner or during his visits. At least we thought there was a language barrier. Later, when arguing his case for trying to raise the rent, or justifying his unauthorized cohabitation with his girlfriend in our unit while we were away for Christmas holiday, we noticed that his English had improved considerably!

As for the young people, the world was quickly becoming theirs to possess. We found them in the coffee shops and the newly opened pubs and discos. And, of course, we talked about this topic in class. They seemed optimistic about their future. A favorite pastime involved debating what was Lithuanian in their culture, and enjoying the thought of once again having an independent national identity. Their hand-held calculators were quickly replacing the standard abacus, which continued to be seen everywhere in the markets and still was the main instrument of accounting. However, in a few newly opened banks and other fashionable stores, computers sat on stylish Scandinavian desks. It seemed new business signs were popping up every week along Gedimino, the city's main street. And yes, before our year was over, McDonald's made its appearance to much fanfare and appreciation. People would put on their best clothes and linger over a hamburger and a cardboard cup of coffee for an hour or more!

What seemed to be the most amazing was the incredibly young age of a small new group of successful entrepreneurs. Where we would expect our business owners, managers, and surely our CEOs to be at least approaching middle age, here Judy and I would see banks and sizable businesses managed by young men and women in their late twenties and early thirties. My students told me that many people in their forties and up were just too heavily steeped in the Soviet way of thinking to be able to make the adjustment to capitalism as quickly or as successfully.

Most businesspeople, although disproportionately older and female, had very small establishments and still used an abacus to figure totals. The big state-owned department store was defunct, its two locations in town now occupied by a hundred or more usually one-person stalls called *mugues*, each selling essentially the same wide and incongruous assortment of mostly imported merchandise. Mugues were located everywhere in the city, sometimes on the sidewalks, but more often tucked into hallways, in the foyers of small stores, and in basements. We felt the urge to stop and examine it all: housewares, toiletries, shoes (but no laces), candy, clothing, and much more, everything the intrepid entrepreneurial trader could stuff in a few Chinese-made giant woven plastic bags while on a shopping trip to Poland. "Polish crap," Jana

Teteris, our young country director would quickly volunteer. Judy and I continued to shop the mugues during our stay in Vilnius. We were always on the lookout for a pair of standard brown shoelaces. We never could find them. Too bad we were not looking for bananas!

Bananas

Bananas seemed to be everywhere we went in Vilnius. I had never seen so many bananas! In the few short years since independence, Lithuania had been, for all intents and purposes, introduced to the banana and had seemingly become the unofficial banana capital of Eastern Europe! Imagine living in the second half of the twentieth century, in a developed part of the world, and not having had bananas. People just loved this newfound delight. Cases of bananas from Central America were stacked high in the little grocery stores and next to sidewalk kiosks that displayed them in bunches strung in long lines on wires between lampposts, street signs, tree trunks, or anything that the merchant could use to anchor the wire. People frequently ate them while walking the sidewalks, depositing the skins in the little street-side trash receptacles until they were overflowing with the wilting remains. We were told that, prior to our arrival, television announcements had been aired to instruct people on how to peel and eat a banana. It was the reverse of our approach of beginning the peeling from the stem end. Street-side banana eating continued, only slightly abated as the weather began to turn colder and heavy rains made people scurry along the sidewalks. We were amazed to see that sidewalk banana eating turned out to be a year-round activity no matter what the weather.

We lived only two blocks from Gedimino, the cobblestone main street in the nineteenth-century center of Vilnius. From our third-floor window, we looked across a large park anchored on the south end by what was originally a large czarist-period Russian mansion. Under the Soviets, it became the Palace of Labor. Now it was used, in part, for Protestant church services, which Judy tried out with one of her local friends. It never ceased to impress me that one of the most beautiful places in one of the most scrumptious locations in town was given over for use in honor of the laboring man. In Boise, our union hall was a small plain-looking building in a non-descript part of the city. On the other hand, in contrast to Vilnius, high up on his private hill overlooking

Boise sits the home of one of the world's wealthiest businessmen. It would be pretty hard to imagine the labor hall up there! Communism had certainly turned our way of thinking upside down.

All winter long we watched out our kitchen windows as the children sledded down the gentle slope of the nearby park, creating a beautiful Currier and Ives scene for our enjoyment. The boys and girls were using old-fashioned sleds that seemed to me to be quite dangerous. Their metal construction could easily injure one of the other children if they were to run into them. I enthusiastically described the American use of inner tubes in place of sleds to Evelina, an eleven-year-old girl who lived upstairs in our apartment building. She would frequently enjoy afternoons practicing her English with Judy and me over peanut butter and crackers at our little kitchen table. I broached the subject. I drew diagrams. She didn't think much of my idea. Even young people get used to doing things a certain way!

Spring Retreat at the Beach

Drippy icicles were still hanging from the eves and patches of snow remained in the shadows of the buildings and trees when Judy and I got a long-awaited chance to leave the cold winter routine of Vilnius. We were taking a train, and later a chartered bus, out of town to participate in a four-day spring gathering of the Baltic region CEPers at a little coastal holiday settlement called Nida. Here, picturesque thatched wooden houses sat intermixed with modern Nordic-style cabins amidst a long strip of narrow ground separating the Lithuanian mainland from the Baltic Sea.

Approximately a half hour ferry ride had put our bus on the Courtland Spit and within another half hour we were in Nida. There was plenty of fresh air, a gorgeous series of large sand dunes marched down the coast, and the Baltic Sea beach was a beautiful light tan color. But, we would not need our beach gear as snow-covered ground had followed us all day on the drive from Vilnius and was up to six inches thick in places in Nida. Instead, we put on our heavy boots and hiked up and down the snowy sand dunes.

Several of us walked south along the beach until, after about a mile, we were warned by signs to go no further. We were near the border with Russia! It was our first glimpse of Russia, albeit a part of

Russia some of us, including Judy and I, had no idea existed. There was absolutely nothing to see but a few evergreens, more sand dunes, and the sea. It was exciting nevertheless, and we captured the view with photos of us pointing out the direction to Russia. What we were pointing to was Kaliningrad a very small struggling Baltic Russian seaport enclave, or state *oblast,* sitting, all by itself, between Lithuania and Poland. We had two CEP visiting lecturers stationed in the main city, also called Kaliningrad. It was definitely a hardship posting. Too bad for everybody involved. The area had long been the center of the region called Prussia. Now the city of Kaliningrad contained the dismal and severely disfigured remains of what was, prior to the Soviets, the famous Prussian city of Konigsberg.

The "Hill of Crosses" near Siauliai, Lithuania. A sacred place covered with thousands of wooden crosses ranging from small and plain to the most elaborately carved. The Soviets bulldozed the area three times, but each time, the Lithuanians persisted in building the crosses back.

On the way back from Nida, our bus took a short detour to the small town of Siauliai. Nearby was the Hill of Crosses, a high piece of open land of maybe eight or ten acres on which sat an absolutely topsy-turvy forest of mostly wooden crosses. Packed in tightly on both sides of a winding trail that ascends to the top of the hill were simple little crosses six to eight inches tall. Sticking out, here and there, among this flowering of little wooden sticks were icons and memorials, and most prominently, dozens of large, very elaborately carved crosses ten or more feet tall

The tradition of planting crosses here is actually quite old, extending back several centuries as a place of religious and nationalistic importance. Going there has taken on slightly different meanings to people at different times in history. While fundamentally a sacred place, it has functioned to reinforce ethnic and more recently national identity. During the 1800s, it grew large with crosses in remembrance of people who the Russians had sent to die in Siberia. Most recently, the Soviets tried to stamp out these symbols of Christianity with their bulldozers. They leveled the area three times only to see it quickly rebuild. Two years before we arrived in Lithuania, Pope John Paul II had visited the Hill of Crosses, thus insuring that this small sacred piece of ground would gain international recognition.

Shortly after our arrival back in Vilnius, we noticed a crowd of people gathering one evening in the big park directly across from our flat. It was a festival celebrating the end of winter. There was a larger than life effigy of the Old Witch of Winter, which would later in the evening be set afire accompanied by singing and a general atmosphere of gaiety. Judy and I wandered through the crowd, keeping reasonably warm near the several bonfires, hoping this old pagan ritual might make a difference. Sure enough, it wasn't long before Vilnius experienced a rapid warming period of spring weather—actually it became quite hot and uncomfortably humid. Summer clothing was again in style. What a relief it was from the long, hard winter.

A Ghastly Place

Down at the north end of the park was the former Soviet KGB (Committee for State Security) building, four stories tall and two full blocks of it! It was formerly a pretrial detention prison, and even fit the sinister needs of the German Gestapo during their wartime occupation. On the sidewalk in front of this building facing Gedimino Street were a memorial stone and the constant presence of small Christian crosses, framed pictures, various memorabilia, and fresh cut flowers sitting in upwards of a hundred vases of all sizes. Those lucky enough to escape the Soviet slaughter continued to remember family and friends who had lost their lives in this building.

Looking from the basement hallway into a padded cell where the screams accompanying brutal beatings could go undetected. Soviet KGB building in Vilnius, Lithuania.

Due to their paranoia over anyone thought to oppose Communism or its leadership, the Soviets forcibly processed about a third of the mostly best-educated portion of the population of Lithuania through this detention prison and a few others like it. Many were killed on site, and the rest were sent to Siberia. The same fate befell the people of the other Baltic states as well as large numbers of people throughout the Soviet Empire. Judy and I visited the basement of the Vilnius KGB detention prison building, now a museum officially called the Genocide and Resistance Center. It preferred to accept visitors on an advance appointment-only basis.

It had not been necessary to reconstruct the past in this museum. Everything was just as the Soviets had hastily left it five years before. Upstairs, officer's uniforms hung near the entrance, the chairs were positioned in front of the desks as they always were, the typewriters sitting ready for a new sheet of paper, as if they had just been used.

Our guide, a physically broken, but mentally strong man, met us at the door. Now in his late sixties, he had been tortured in the gloomy unheated basement. Speaking Lithuanian translated for us by Darius Zeruolis, our local CEP lecturer and friend, our guide invited us to put our hand on his chest and feel the misshapen bony protrusions that covered his ribcage. He had been beaten very badly in a room that he showed us. It was lined with mattress-type padding on the walls to help keep the sound of anguished cries from reaching the street. He showed us the tiny room containing a waist-high metal tub that would be filled with water. Our guide had spent several winter days and nights standing in the frigid water of this tank. Afterwards, he had been transferred to one of the twenty-three unheated basement cells. As we looked into the cell, he described how he had lived in this cell for over two months, a confinement so packed with other prisoners that only one or two individuals at a time had space to lie down on the concrete to rest. He showed us the courtyard where many of the internees were eventually shot.

There was also a room full of large bags of shredded paper, the last minute, and incomplete effort of the KGB to destroy evidence that would implicate them in these atrocities. The shredding was only a fraction of the evidence. It didn't help too much to hide what had taken place. In 1995, Lithuania was in the early stages of locating and bringing to trial many of these KGB operatives and officials. The newspapers carried a continuing number of news items and editorial opinion as to what should be the appropriate disposition of each case.

A Challenging Place to Teach

Later chapters will specifically describe my experiences as a visiting lecturer in all four countries, my classrooms, my students, and my colleagues. However, in a chapter on first impressions it seems fitting to provide a description of my initial experience at the University of Vilnius branch campus where I was assigned to work.

Out of a variety of universities that had existed behind the Iron Curtain, it is easy to contrast two types. There were beautiful old universities that had somehow managed to survive all the wars, and then there were the universities constructed by the Soviets, especially those built after World War II. While the architects usually provided these university buildings with a flamboyant, modernistic appearance, their unbelievably poor construction was destined to give them a very short life span.

My university was constructed about 1980 and consisted of several large rambling red brick buildings trimmed out in aluminum. Everything was quite dramatically falling apart. One needed to step carefully when approaching the building as most of the concrete squares making up the walks and steps were badly disintegrated. Students told me that sometimes the bricks would fall out of the walls for lack of sufficient mortar, or because it was poorly mixed. Workmen would mix the mortar on the light side, they said, and then take the rest away for their own private use or to sell on the black market. The university was the first, but not the only place where I saw broken windows repaired by placing two carefully cut pieces of used glass together in the same frame! Some windows just remained broken.

The entrance to my building consisted of two parallel sets of five glass doors, the two rows separated about five feet from each other. I would first walk over a high aluminum sill through the leftmost door in the line of otherwise locked front doors. Then, turning right, I would follow the matching inner line of doors until reaching the last door on the right, which would open, again over a high sill, into the foyer. This was a typical layout for entry doors of public buildings throughout the Baltic region. I do not recall that any of these doors ever contained a mechanism to assist their closure. When the wind blew, Lithuania became "The land of the slamming doors." Of course, this took its toll on the glass panels. A few were almost always broken and others had been partly boarded up.

Just inside the university was a "control" station, a feature I found in some shape or form in all universities, and, in fact, in just about every large building, regardless of use. In this case, it was a small glass-fronted room staffed with a terribly bored security guard. He, or often she, would hand me a sign-in sheet on a clipboard along with my office and classroom keys.

After signing in and collecting my keys, I would select a stub or two of chalk held out to me in an open cigar box, then cross the foyer, pass a gigantic coat rack, also a common feature in the universities and most other publicly used buildings, and begin the ascent of five flights of stairs. I thought about the topic of theft. Didn't anybody lose his or her jackets from these unattended racks? After weeks of constantly stumbling and falling as I went up the stairs, I closely examined the risers to discover that they differed in height by as much as two inches—definitely enough to trip over, but who would have thought of such a possibility as this?

Arriving at the top of the stairs, I would encounter the odor of the bathroom. I would be remiss if I didn't say something about the nasty bathrooms, generally unchanged from Soviet times. It is a feature of life in which there had been little or no improvement, especially now that maintenance budgets were practically nonexistent. Fixtures were often inoperative, or shut down or should have been, while others were constantly flushing. Fortunately, a few windowpanes were missing or the bathroom might have been too foul to even consider using.

Why focus on such a negative subject as bathrooms? There are some things or events that form impressions, sometimes so unflattering, if not shocking, that they can't help but remain an important part of our memory. The bathrooms just happen to be a good example. The Soviets may have tossed off bathroom cleanliness as just an example of bourgeois phobia. Be that as it may. Certainly the students seemed to take it all in stride. They were accustomed to such things, but definitely not Judy and me.

Imagine what was involved in taking every precaution possible not to have to use these stinking places, at school, while out shopping, or practically anywhere else. Think about how important it was to have a McDonald's located in the city, or a home grown spin-off called McChicken, which also sported clean bathrooms (incidentally, this establishment was being threatened with a lawsuit by McDonald's if they did not take the "Mc" out of their name). No matter what else you may think about McDonald's, or McChicken, they were a dependable oasis of clean bathrooms. And here is my main point. For us, nasty bathrooms will be written about and remembered because they were part of what gave life for us in this part of the world such a great intensity. You know you were really living when you stepped into one of these foul places!

Once on the top floor, it was just a few steps to my small narrow office located just across the hall from my classroom. It had a window looking out on an unfinished and partially abandoned high-rise dormitory building. There was a barely workable telephone on my desk. I was used to small offices, but found the large mirror and full-sized free-standing safe, which remained locked, to be quite unique accoutrements. There was a steam heat radiator that never produced much heat, and a handy closet with clothes hangers and shelves. But there was no bookcase, which is usually considered in American universities to be a standard fixture of almost any professor's office. So I kept my books in the closet. It was the only private office I would have during my four years as a CEP lecturer. I usually arrived at my office a couple of hours early on each teaching day so that students could enjoy "office hours." This was a novel educational concept for most of them.

My classes were over at 6:30 in the evening. Downstairs, I would turn in my keys and chalk and sign out. Not too long after my arrival at the university, one grizzly-faced guard was always gesturing to me with the standard flick of the index finger under his chin to drink some vodka with him. Of course that would mean that I first would have to go buy the bottle! I would politely decline. This same invitation would be repeated at my university in Uzbekistan. So much for "security" in this building!

A Very Memorable Year

While grim in some respects, it was obvious that Lithuania was finally on the mend and that the near future would be a bright one. Some features of the physical legacy of Communism would, however, likely remain for some time. For example, one wonders if many of the hastily and poorly constructed high-rise apartment buildings will become ghettos for low-income people. Some people were staying and fixing up their flats, but others, who could afford to move, were leaving for the new but growing phenomena of suburban single-family developments. Certainly Lithuania contained much beauty to write about, geographically, culturally, and artistically. Along with the other two Baltic countries, Lithuania offered us a historical window on the past, an opportunity to witness something of the living conditions and a hint of a time long past in most of Western Europe. Then there was our opportunity to experience the Soviet standard of living, which was not only very differently oriented to a noncommercial economy, but except for a very few instances, never produced a standard of affluence that would seriously challenge a predominantly rural way of life, its indigenous cultures, their separate languages, or their vast store of antiquities. For us, thank heaven that was the case. Lithuania offered us our first look at all of this. There was much about Lithuania and the other two Baltic countries that favorably caught our eye, impressed us deeply, and made living there a very positive experience.

3

Our Year in Estonia

The Jewel of the Baltic Sea

Our first and most enduring impressions of Estonia were of its fantastic natural and architectural beauty. Its Baltic coast contains broad sandy beaches and forested tree lines. Even more awe-inspiring were the many fine examples of fourteenth and fifteenth-century medieval architecture. We were never able to soak in enough of these beautiful buildings. Estonia is a tourist's delight to rival any other better-known location in Central/Eastern Europe. However, as we had found in Lithuania, to appreciate all the beauty, we needed to look beyond the easily visible evidence of Soviet occupation: the same ugly apartments and the dull uniformity of most public buildings. As in Lithuania, such distractions were part of a quickly changing façade and were bound not to last too long in their present form or condition. The landscape was changing very quickly.

Estonia's past is similar to its Baltic neighbors in some ways and very different in others. Like Latvia and Lithuania, Estonia had known a long period of German rule. There was the same distinctive influence of the Teutonic Order, for example, producing the same-style seven-hundred-year-old fortifications with their distinctive ramparts, logia, and red terracotta tiled towers. However, the German presence had been stronger in Estonia. When combined with the cultural elements introduced by nearby Denmark and Sweden, both of whom had also occupied Estonia, the effect was notably, even distinctively, different from what we had observed in Lithuania. In place of the more ornate, baroque, Roman Catholic influence so dominant in Vilnius's Old Town architecture, the Old Town in Estonia's capital city of Tallinn was more ascetic and functional, less ornate, even a bit severe in its appearance, what one might imagine as the expression of the values of the Protestant merchants who were responsible for much of its defining features.

All three Baltic countries had also been heavily influenced by Russian occupation, which lasted roughly two hundred years from the early 1700s until the end of the First World War. During this period Tallinn, then called Revel, became Russia's major seaport. There was direct train service to the Russian capital at St. Petersburg. Peter the Great maintained a summer home in Tallinn. Russians built homes and buildings in the neoclassic style, many of which remain in use today. Outside of his rather uncharacteristically small quarters in Tallinn, the czar also spent time in much more lavish style, taking spa waters and curative mud baths in another summer residence located in the Estonian costal town of Haapsalu. Judy and I visited this attractive little town for a day, but were leery of indulging in a mud bath by the sight of the black tarry substance. It was just too hard to imagine being covered from head to toe in such stuff. Estonia was not quite in the center of Europe, but not unlike Lithuania, its land, its people, and its culture were also the product of being at a busy historical crossroad.

Of the three Baltic countries, Estonia was changing the most rapidly, bravely pushing ahead in its implementation of democracy and liberal economic practice, setting the pace for others. Unlike most other parts of the former Soviet Empire, Estonia was lucky in being able to receive unjammed Western radio and TV broadcasts. In most areas of the former empire, the Soviets had worked hard to make such broadcasts unintelligible. But the Estonian signal reception came from Finland, which was only fifty miles away. As the two languages were reasonably similar, Estonians were able to remain knowledgeable of the world outside Communism and relatively free from its propaganda and distortions. When the Soviet Union collapsed, Estonia was ready to move quickly to implement change.

In a pattern seen elsewhere, even if more haltingly in other transitioning countries, implementing the future was a challenge that attracted a large number of Estonia's young people. Armed with the knowledge of liberal economics and democracy, it didn't take long to put these Western concepts into practice. In 1992, less than a year after

Communism had fallen, Estonia elected Mart Laar a thirty-one-year-old country school teacher to be prime minister. His ministers were also quite young, including one who was only twenty-seven years of age.

The new political cadre was well versed in the economic writings of monetarist and conservative Milton Friedman and the libertarian Friedrich Hayek. Laar and his team of ministers started off by quickly establishing a national flat tax. They kept a balanced budget and implemented a policy of free trade. Just as the theory predicted, things really started to happen in the Estonian economy. In the realm of communication, Estonia took the lead among the newly independent countries in implementing computer savvy throughout its educational system. The investment quickly began paying big dividends both socially and economically as the country became known as "E-stonia."

As it would turn out, the CEP did not need to remain in Estonia for very long. In most respects our work had already been done before we arrived!

An Initial Visit to Estonia

Judy and I had visited Estonia twice during my first year posting in Vilnius. Our initial visit was in October 1995, only about a month after arriving in Lithuania. An island near Estonia's Baltic coast was to be the location for our fall CEP retreat. Judy and I began our trip with an overnight train ride, the first of many trains we would take over the next four years. We arrived, quite sleeplessly in Riga, Latvia, at 5:45 AM, and found our way to the CEP regional office at the University of Latvia where we were joined by the rest of the Baltic CEP lecturers and staff, including two lecturers from Belarus and two others from the Russian Kaliningrad region. The rest of the trip to Estonia would be by a rather well-worn bus.

It was difficult to get all the CEP people together like this because of the distance that separated us, the need to obtain visas permitting us to move between often more than one country, and other less predictable factors such as the willingness of finicky border guards to honor our papers. Vello, our Estonian-American lecturer was turned back at the Latvian border because of a printing inaccuracy in his visa. Carlos, our CEP lecturer from Columbia, was almost always held up for close scrutiny on the stereotypical presumption that he was carrying drugs. Both lecturers were a day late in arriving at our retreat location.

The bus drove us from Riga north along the coast into Estonia where we took a ferry ride to Saaremaa, Estonia's biggest island. On the way, our old Hungarian-made bus bounced and fumed and needed frequent repair of something connected to its rear axle. On at least five occasions, the bus driver stopped on the steeply angled shoulder of the road. The routine was always the same. He would get out, jack up the rear of the bus dangerously still full of passengers, and with no other support to hold the bus up save for the jack, he would slide completely under the rear axle. Soon we could hear him loudly banging for several minutes on something with his sledgehammer. In this manner, we made it to our destination slowly, but surely.

As in other parts of the heavily wooded Baltic countries this time of the year, the foliage was in full color, the numerous birch trees in bright yellow and the hardwood trees in their shades of brown and red. The color provided a superb background to the thatched roofs and windmills, and especially to the large, well-preserved eight-hundred-year-old castle located near the outskirts of the island's small coastal town of Kuressaare, which was our destination.

Our retreat consisted of three delightful days of work and play in a well-maintained hotel that was originally constructed by the Soviets to house Olympic athletes who were training for track and field events. Now Swedish owned, it came complete with a sauna, a novelty to Judy and me, even though the sauna is a defining feature, as we would soon learn and enjoy, throughout this region of the world. Some of the saunas we would later encounter were modern and electrically heated like the one in Kuressaare, others were more traditional, being heated from outside the building with a wood fire and usually complete with fresh birch branches used to beat one's back to stimulate circulation. There was normally a source of cold water nearby, a shower or small pool, or more traditionally a creek or stream as the correct use of the spa involved the application of both heat and cold to properly open and close the body's pores.

Each hotel room had a heated tile floor in the bathroom including the routing of the heating water through a series of bent chrome pipes on the wall. This novel idea, which helped to turn brrrs into ahhhs, served as a towel rack and room warmer. We never saw another heated floor, but the towel rack turned out to be a quite common bathroom appointment, although never in such good working condition as this one.

Also helping to stimulate circulation was a "pick the best beer" contest that we played in between visits to the hotel sauna. Didn't I mention that our supervisor was fun loving? Jana had e-mailed each of us ahead of the trip requesting that we bring a couple of bottles of our local beer to the retreat. Judy and I brought the two most popular Lithuanian beers: Utenos and Kalnapilis. All the beer was in bottles as refilling was a traditional practice. The label on each bottle was covered in black paper and the bottles set out on a large table in the basement near the sauna entrance. About twenty-five or thirty brands were represented in the tasting contest. An enthusiastic blind sampling produced an Estonian winner, "Saku," a product of the Saku Olletehas, a brewery located in a small village near Tallinn.

The next day we shared some of our beer with a contingent of Swedish sportsmen lunching on crackers and raw salmon, which they had brought with them in one of their large coolers. The men were on a duck-hunting trip to the islands. It was their third consecutive trip, an excursion made possible only by the fall of the Iron Curtain.

During the cold war, the Soviet military had set up a listening and radar post along with other "sensitive" military operations on the island. Consequently, civilian crossings back and forth to the mainland were severely restricted with permission to cross only occasionally given to the islanders and very few others. The result was to freeze the normal socioeconomic development of the island, leaving it almost like a museum of a time long since past from which the island inhabitants were only now beginning to recover.

Along with its castle and picturesque farms, the island of Saaremaa contains a sizable meteorite crater and the equally visible remains of a large pagan worship site dating back at least two thousand years BC. To our untrained eyes, this site looked like a ring, maybe two hundred yards in diameter, made up of large tumbled-down rocks. But, it all seemed to take shape and come to life, as we stood there, at sunset, in the gathering windy darkness, listening to a local graduate student of history describe the structure of the site and the rituals that took place here. Paganism had remained in the Baltic region and was practiced and fiercely defended long after the conversion of most of Europe to Christianity.

Love at First Sight

While still living in Lithuania, Judy and I had occasion to travel back to Estonia a second time, two months later, in early December. As the senior faculty member of our Baltic contingent, I had been asked if I would serve as an academic coordinator. In most instances this meant that I was responsible for visiting each Baltic lecture site to help new CEP lecturers with project development, and to conduct a classroom visit and survey of student and administration opinion of all visiting lecturers. This assignment added a small amount to my stipend, but more importantly, it provided Judy and me the opportunity to travel, on per diem, to several cities and universities in each of our first three country postings.

Lecturer evaluations were thus the main reason for our second visit to Estonia. Our destination was the picturesque university city of Tartu, located in the southeast portion of this tiny country. The University of Tartu is Estonia's most respected school with a long and excellent reputation, especially in science. Judy and I arrived in Tartu by overnight train. The day began clear and very cold. The trees were leafless, and patches of snow covered most of the ground. We spent the morning walking the main streets of city, enjoying the many fine examples of classical architecture and thinking that the river that flows through the city would make a particularly inviting summer walk. After my class visits and interviews, we boarded an evening bus for the 120-mile ride to Tallinn, Estonia's largest city of about six hundred thousand population. Tallinn is located at the northernmost point of Estonia on the Gulf of Finland just 50 miles away from Helsinki on the other side. Our country director had been interested in developing CEP lecture sites in Estonia beyond the one existing in Tartu. Our presence in Estonia provided Jana the opportunity to broach the subject of lecturer appointments with administrators at a small public university in Tallinn. As a part of her proposal, Jana had arranged for me to have an interview with the dean and the department head and to give a lecture to a class of sociology students.

Our earlier trip to Saaremaa had heightened Judy's and my expectations of the reported beauty of Tallinn's Old Town section. It had largely escaped the ravages of World War II. Now a UNESCO World Heritage Site, the Old Town has remained relatively unchanged over the past six hundred years. The bus from Tartu got in late in the evening. We took a taxi through the relatively darkened town to our hotel without realizing much of where we were or what we might be passing by.

The next morning, after breakfast, the sun was beginning to come up, and we got our first good look at the city from our hotel window. High on Toompea Hill looming just in front of us was the fourteenth-century turreted wall surrounding the upper portion of Tallinn's Old Town. It was an awesome sight, an unforgettable vision of life as it might have looked hundreds of years ago in the time of the Teutonic Order of Knights.

Judy and I couldn't wait to leave the hotel. My appointment at the university was not until 11:00 AM, so we decided to walk the long way up to Toompea Hill and down through the lower part of Old Town. The sun glistened off a covering of fresh snow as we made our way across a small park and began climbing the stone steps leading up to the fortress hill. At the top we passed through a portal and immediately fell in love with all the beautiful sights around and below us. In view were nineteen of the original sixty-six turrets topping a mostly unbroken rampart that partially surrounded a fairyland full of early German-style slate-roofed buildings, tall Protestant church spires, and narrow winding cobblestone streets. The lower north side of the Old Town connected to an old seaport and the shimmering blue waters of the Gulf of Finland. There was even a large decorated Christmas tree standing in the center of Raekoja Plats, the main town square. The Christmas tree and the little white Christmas lights in the surrounding old buildings made a great impression on us. It was well into the month of December; yet in Vilnius we had yet to see Christmas decorations in the stores or visible in any public place.

Christmas tree in Raekoja Plats, Tallinn

We spent the better part of two days walking the snowy streets in Tallinn, coming back again and again to wander around the Old Town. We were elated to discover a big Finnish department store and a Finnish-owned grocery store, both as nice and as well stocked as anything we were used to back in Idaho.

Judy (wearing "Ba ba") shops in Tallinn's Old Town for handmade sweaters.

It snowed off and on both days we were in Tallinn. We bought some brightly patterned Estonian-style, hand-made woolen sweaters and mittens, some for us to use immediately and some for gifts. These and many other woolen items were being sold from little stalls built under the loggia overhang of a long stretch of Old Town's rampart walls. We climbed up inside a tower named "Kiek-in-de-kok," an old German word for "peep into the kitchen." Inside the tower was a small bar where we drank *hoogvein,*, a hot mulled wine that was a wintertime favorite and, as the name suggests, we were able to peek out through the tiny slit windows into the kitchens and living quarters of the lower part of the town, now lit up for the evening and glistening with new snow. It was truly love at first sight.

The lecture and interview were successful. Jana negotiated two new CEP lecture positions that were formalized in a contract that same day. Estonia would be our next posting during the coming year. Judy and I could not believe our good luck.

The Beginning of a Second Year with the CEP

The next year we returned to Tallinn shortly after midsummer, bringing with us Jan and John McFadden, two good friends from Boise. Our plan was to drop off some of our bags at an apartment Jana had rented for us, and then begin a two-week tour through parts of Russia and the three Baltic countries, visiting the places that had been our favorites from our previous year. We enjoyed playing tour guide, and the McFaddens were excited about the trip and our backpack-style of traveling, which by now had become our normal modus operandi for all our travel.

The morning following our arrival in Tallinn, we all checked out our new apartment. The location was across the street from a hospital emergency entrance complete with frequent ambulance sirens. At least it wouldn't have taken long to get medical attention. Even at that, it was hard to think of anything really positive about the apartment. It required walking up four flights of stairs. We were used to this bit of gymnastics from our previous year in Vilnius, but this year we had hoped for an elevator. We needed a building with five or more floors to get an elevator, a requirement in Soviet times.

The apartment was large enough, but it lacked anywhere near sufficient furnishings. The only table was a small round outdoor style white plastic thing with four plastic chairs. There was no other furniture except for a mattress on the floor of the bedroom and a broken TV set in the hallway. Fortunately for us, Tallinn had just established a realty market. We contacted an agent by phone, who showed us several rentals. Our final choice was a little more expensive, but it had a nice kitchen and it was fully furnished. That evening our new landlords, a middle-age Russian couple, came to arrange the contract. The wife explained the contract in broken English, and the husband grunted and gestured his agreement. Earlier that afternoon, John helped me move some of our duffel bags from the hotel to the apartment. The rest of the bags and boxes we moved from their summer storage location in the chairperson's office at my new university. Only two days late, we packed our backpacks and the next morning we left on our trip.

Our travel route began with the three Baltic countries, staying at least two nights in Riga and Vilnius. We then went east through Minsk, Belarus, and on to Moscow for three nights. From Moscow, we retraced our steps to stay a night in Kaunas in central Lithuania. So far the trip had been entirely by train, but in Kaunas, we boarded a well-worn but seaworthy hydrofoil boat, named the *Raketa* for a half-day trip down the Nemunas River, out across a large lagoon to the Courtland Spit for a two-night stay in Nida, a very pretty fishing and resort village facing the Baltic Sea. From there we headed back to Tallinn. It was actually a fairly relaxing and very enjoyable two-week itinerary that definitely served to reinforce our opinion of the Baltic region as an absolute delight and a travel bargain. Of course, it helps to take public transportation, stay in economical bed-and-breakfast lodging, and carry a backpack. It also is much more fun to have some favorite friends along. We would have continued our travel, but the summer was drawing to a close, and we all had to think about going back to our work.

The new academic year orientation was again held in Riga. There, Judy and I met a young British man named Simon Bevan, who would be my CEP colleague in Tallinn for the year. A very talented individual, Simon was trained as a solicitor (lawyer), but had not yet begun his practice. He had been a visiting lecturer the previous year in Poland, but, like us, he had been anxious to move to a new teaching site and experience a different country. Simon was well versed in and shared our newfound love of opera and ballet. He had learned the plot and the various scenes of the opera stories in order to impress an earlier girlfriend. He also possessed a great sense of humor that complemented his mischievous outlook on life. Simon knew how to be polite and well mannered, quite a proper gentleman, Judy and I thought, and certainly very mature for someone in his mid twenties. Yet in less formal occasions, Simon's wit, his funny stories, and his antics had the ability to make me feel twenty-five years younger. What a kick he could be!

Staying out late and having a good time could catch up with some of the young people in our organization, and Simon was no exception. Like so many youthful men and women, Simon was prone to living a bit dangerously at times. During the year, a man made an unsuccessful attempt to rob Simon while he was walking back to his apartment early one morning. No gun or knife was involved, and, in fact, I seem to recall Simon mentioning a fairly lengthy conversation he had with the man concerning the appropriateness of the attempted robbery. In the end, Simon was able to boast about chasing the man into a bar where he was apprehended and held until the police arrived. On another occasion, Simon arrived at his apartment quite hungry early one morning after having spent the evening in some of Tallinn's many attractive nightclubs and bars. He put a frozen pizza in the oven and then proceeded to fall asleep on the sofa. He woke up later in the morning to find that the pizza had overcooked, caught fire, filled the small apartment with black smoke and burned his stove beyond repair. Being British, Simon referred to his stove as a "cooker." In this case, the term seemed very appropriate.

If Simon was trying his best to burn down his university apartment, it would only be fair to note that I was doing my best to burn down a portion of the university! I plugged in a coffeepot early one evening in our department office and did not realize the cord was also connected to a heating coil used to boil water for tea. Later I turned off the coffeepot at its switch, leaving the cord plugged into the wall, and headed downtown to meet Judy and Simon at the opera. Luckily, during the performance, I began to wonder if I had, in fact, turned off the coffeepot. At intermission, I quickly hailed a taxi for the short ride back to the university. The school was officially closed for the evening. Nobody had yet discovered the concept of evening or night classes, but I found that the front door was open. Entering the main door in almost total darkness, I had a difficult time convincing the security lady, sitting in her little booth, that she knew who I was and should let me go, without a flashlight, upstairs to the department office. It was a good thing she let me go, for while I found that the coffeepot had been turned off, the heating coil hidden in the drawer below the counter where the coffeepot was, was still heating along! It had smoldered pretty much all the way through the wood drawer bottom filling the office full of smoke. Fortunately, the drawer had not caught fire.

As new employees, Simon and I were paid about $225 a month each, in local money, to teach two classes a semester. As new residents of Estonia, we were also required to complete a series of medical tests before we could officially join the workforce and be allowed to collect our first paycheck. I had not been required to take these tests in Lithuania the previous year nor had Simon during his first year in Poland. The tests were a pleasant farce except for a scary chest X-ray which was taken while I stood in front of a large, ugly, pale-green-colored machine. It was certainly of Soviet manufacture and looked to be fifty years old, even though it probably wasn't. I remember it seemed to buzz for an interminably long time before finishing its radiation picture of my chest.

Other CEP lecturers in some of the other postings also had to undergo similar examinations. The best full description of these tests was written in an e-mail letter sent to me five years later by Carter Johnson. Carter had been my young Canadian CEP colleague during the year that Judy and I spent in Uzbekistan. Fortunately neither of us had been required to have an examination while working in that country. However, a year later, Carter's luck ran out in his new posting in Moldova. With his permission, I have included a large portion of his e-mail description of the experience:

I recently completed my marathon medical tests and soon should be granted my first official "landed immigrant" status. The process though was amazingly tedious. One tuberculosis test involved this massive Dr. Who–era machine that scares me to death. I completed this a month ago, but apparently the results didn't work out, so I needed to do it again. They said that they don't advise more than one of these a year (radiation), but that I needed to do it again anyway. Everyone in this hospital is old and decrepit except those working in this office who are all middle-aged. I figure the constant running of the machine must kill off these workers before pensionable age.

The best tests though were the neurologist, dermatologist, and infectionist. After waiting an hour, I finally saw the neurologist in room 53 who sat me down, and asked me one question (this all in Russian, of course): "Your head, do you feel any pain?" No, I answered, and she stamped my form and told me I was healthy, neurologically speaking. Next, after waiting another hour and a half outside room 34, I met with the dermatologist. He sat me down and asked, "How's your skin?" Fine, I said, looking down at my hands—the only exposed skin in my sight—and flipping them over as if I was examining myself. "Are you sure it's clean?" he asked. "Yes," I said, "I'm very confident of that." So he pulled out his stamp and gave me the clear....

Finally, I went in to see the infectionist in room 66. "You need to give a specimen," he told me right away, "and then return to me with the results." What kind? I asked. He went through various words that I didn't understand until finally he said a word in Russian with a similar English word—he said, "Fekal…." Off I went to room 51 to give my specimen. There the woman first took a blood sample, put it in an old pipette, and told me I had a choice: return in two days to get the results, or pay her US$0.30 and get the results immediately. I duly paid up and she, without looking back at the pipette, stamped my form—"negative," it read. Then for the feces. She told me I could crap in a bag, give it to her, and return in a couple of days, or…. Then I asked her if I could return to the infectionist right away, or if I still had to wait a couple of days, since he would obviously know that I had paid a bribe. "Everyone knows how this system works, you can return to him right away." So I returned to room 66, he looked at my stamped form, and gave me his stamp of approval; infectionally, I was healthy it seemed.

The best part is that I told my landlady this story today, and she told me that she knows someone who works at the centre where they analyse the fekal specimens, and she says that when they receive a specimen, they don't even bother to analyse it at all and just put it straight in the garbage! The exception, she said, is people who really are sick, but these people—if you can believe it—have to pay a US$1.25 bribe to have an actual analysis done.

Actually, Simon's medical examination and mine in Estonia, while very similar, did not include bribes and were probably the most professional of the lot, a situation I would attribute both to culture and the much higher socioeconomic level of the country. Carter's experience in Moldova was near or at the other end of the scale in terms of medical standards and facilities; if for no other reason this can be deduced from the small size of the bribes. On at least one point of similarity, Simon and I were each asked to take a mental examination. Passing the test also required the correct answer to just one question: "Do you like girls?" the doctor inquired.

A Busy Fall

As in our previous year, we traveled out of country, spending our fall retreat in the little Latvian resort community of Sigulda, known as the "Switzerland of Latvia." There was the expected amount of professional work, of course, but work was happily overshadowed by play. This began with a leisurely trip down the Gauja River in a giant rubber raft, which, now that I look at the picture, we almost certainly managed to load beyond recommended capacity. Fortunately, the river flowed gently, even as we passed through the gorge next to our hotel.

The Soviets had trained their Olympic bobsleigh teams nearby. The long winding roller-coaster-like construction of the bobsleigh track remained and could be used by tourists who rode sleds with small wagon wheels attached. It was a wild ride that Judy and I were content to just watch. There was no beer tasting this time, but following a dinner held several miles from town, our country director naively allowed an open bar one evening, and Simon chose to show all who dared how to properly drink Tequila. Never mind that imported Tequila was very expensive and in short supply at the bar. The bartender quickly realized that the challenge to drink this powerful stuff was being taken up by a good number of us and would result in a nice profit that night. I could hear a car outside race off as the bartender's assistant went the several miles back to town to find a couple of replacement bottles.

Baltic states CEPers on a spring retreat in Latvia. Simon is in front, wearing dark glasses.

A New Family Member

We were anxious to return to our apartment following the retreat. We had a new member of the household to worry about. A week or so before leaving, Judy and I had added a tiny little kitten to our household. We called him "Saku" after the Estonian beer and how we came about getting him. His name also seemed fitting in part because of the white socks on his front feet. We had talked about going to the big outdoor market on the outskirts of the city to get such a furry little companion, but before we could act on this plan, I had unexpectedly been offered a little kitten by a sidewalk kiosk vender.

Upon leaving the university one evening, Simon, who was to be our dinner guest, and I had stopped to purchase a couple of last minute food items and some Saku beer to take home. Standing in front of the open kiosk window, I was admiring a big Russian Blue cat sitting on the counter when the lady proprietor reached down below the counter and came up with a tiny, barely weaned kitten, motioning for me to take it as a gift. I put it in the pocket of my raincoat for the trip back to our apartment. Saku barely had become used to the apartment and us when away we went on retreat leaving him to manage on his own over the next four days. Our return was a joyous reunion for the three of us, with Saku happily speeding up and down the apartment hallway.

Later, in the spring, we had Saku castrated, a rather uncommon procedure for most Estonian cats. Having his front nails removed was even more uncommon, really almost a first of its kind operation. The pet clinic did not attempt to dissuade us of our wish to have this done, but claimed not to have the proper expertise. Fortunately, with their help, we were able to schedule the procedure the following week with a visiting veterinarian from Sweden. Saku came home with big bandages on his front feet wearing the typical "lamp shade" collar. Earlier, when I asked my students to recommend a veterinarian for the nail removing procedure, they thought me terribly cruel and protested my intentions loudly. We went ahead anyway. It was a lot cheaper than having it done back in Idaho, as our plan was to take him back home with us when we left Estonia.

Saku quickly got used to being left alone in the apartment. I had been reappointed for a second year as academic coordinator, so this provided a few additional occasions for us to travel. One such trip would combine faculty evaluations at universities in three Latvian cities with a trip to Kaunas, Lithuania, for a Thanksgiving get-together with all the Baltic CEPers.

A Travel Interlude in Latvia and Lithuania

The travel portion of our life in Estonia was beginning to take on a familiar routine. Judy and I would pack our backpacks, take the tram from our apartment to the Old Town, walk up the narrow cobblestone streets to our favorite restaurant for a good pork chop dinner, and then it was just a short walk out beyond the town's western rampart to the train station. Here we would board the Baltic Express train for the overnight trip to Riga, the hub city for the Baltic region.

"Stalinist Art" poster (ca.1958), the Riga Motor Museum

First, on our Thanksgiving trip, I had scheduled a morning evaluation in Riga for John Cooney, who was teaching comparative constitutional law at the University of Latvia. In the afternoon, Judy and I took a bus to the Riga Motor Museum, which was located quite a distance out in the suburbs. The museum turned out to be well worth the effort to get there. Being an old car enthusiast, I wanted to see this museum that had been the only one of its kind in the Soviet Union, probably anywhere in the Empire.

Why the authorities had allowed this museum I am not sure, as the Soviets actively discouraged the development of any kind of car fetish. Mass car ownership was considered too capitalist and individualistic. Very few people had a car at the time nor had many more been able to acquire one during the first years of independence as they remained hard to find and quite costly. German cars were just beginning to show up on the streets. Some of them were stolen. German cars were the source of much interest while at the same time their modern driveline and impressive build quality turned out to be quite depressing to many men. They had dreamed of owning a Volga (the high end of Soviet-built cars) only to realize through comparison with the German models, how shoddily built and old-fashioned they were. In spite of such defects, the Volga continued to convey status, and the factory seemed able to find a ready supply of new customers for its cosmetically altered, but still carbureted, fuel-gulping models.

The museum contained over one hundred mostly European cars from early years through the last of the prewar models. The feature display included cars belonging to the top Soviet elite. Included were very lifelike figures of Stalin, Khrushchev, and Brezhnev. Stalin sits in the back seat of his Packard look-alike ZIM automobile, and Khrushchev stands alongside his car with a big smile, welcoming the museum visitor to take a ride. One vehicle, a Rolls-Royce Silver Shadow, was quite badly damaged. It was displayed just as it remained after Brezhnev drove it into oncoming traffic colliding with a truck. A startled Brezhnev sits behind the wheel. I remember thinking how cynical and quite out of keeping for a Communist leader to own the world's most capitalist and elitist of automobiles, in fact, he owned several.

The next day, Judy and I accompanied Jana and her boyfriend in his car to Valmiera, a small city a little more than an hour drive north of Riga. I was looking forward to seeing Vidzemes University, a newly formed private school, and conducting an evaluation for Artus Pabriks. Artus was in the final stages of obtaining a PhD degree from an American university. Along with teaching for the CEP, he was also, for all intents and purposes, serving as university president, a position to which he would be formally appointed within a few months. I normally did not evaluate local CEP faculty, but my evaluation of Artus was considered important enough by the university board of directors for the CEP to make an exception in this case.

Artus could not have been more than thirty years of age, and now he was about to be president. Actually, this was not atypical for talented young people during the early stage of transition from Soviet times. We had encountered many examples during our previous year in Lithuania. I had met Artus on two earlier occasions during our retreats. He was outgoing and possessed a clearly recognizable sense of confidence without any touch of arrogance or egotism. I sat in on a very lively meeting of his political philosophy class, conducted in English for my benefit and involving about two dozen junior and senior students. Artus easily passed my evaluation with high marks.

On the third day, Judy and I again left Riga, this time on a morning commuter train for about a twenty-five-mile day trip to Jelgava, a once stylish and important little city that had been practically bombed away during the two world wars and was now a very dreary looking place. Judy called it "Yucklava." It was almost as dreary as we had found it the previous winter when all of the Baltic CEPers had met there for a student conference held at the Latvian University of Agriculture. I was to conduct my faculty evaluation at this university.

On our walk over from the train station, it suddenly looked like this particular visit to Julgava might possibly turn out quite cheery. At least this is what Judy thought when she spotted a small gambling casino just a couple of blocks from the university. The building was not much bigger than a typical American convenience store. There were three big late-model, foreign-made SUVs parked in front, the telltale sign of a local Mafia-type hangout. I had a few extra minutes, and so, with Judy's prompting and against all better judgment, we decided to take a quick look inside. Disco music was playing. The Mafia-esque types were there alright, dancing, quite provocatively, with their lady friends near the back of the room. A bank of slot machines stood along the opposite wall. Judy went over to inspect the machines. I was motioned over to the bar where the bartender changed my U.S. dollars for playing tokens. Judy quickly hit a sizable jackpot and opted to stay at the casino while I left for the university.

I had a short meeting with the university's lady rector and then went upstairs to Quimei Yang's office. Quimei was in her first year as a CEP economics lecturer and a little nervous over my visit. She needn't have been, considering what she had experienced and accomplished in just the past six years. In 1989, Quimei was a pro-democracy activist who was arrested, along with her brother, in the Tiananmen Square crackdown. Her brother went to jail, while Quimei was given a choice: either go to jail or leave the country. She opted for the United States. How ironic it seems. In just six years, Quimei had come to America, completed her graduate education, and was now in Latvia teaching the principles of personal freedom and liberal economy, exactly what she had fought for in China. It was an uplifting example of globalization.

Oh yes, what about Judy's good luck? Well, she played the slot machine for awhile, earning no more jackpots but unable to use up but a small portion of her credit. She then tried to cash out, but the bartender would not cooperate and insisted that she continue to play off her credit. Judy got nervous and left. We both got a lecture from Jana when she found out where we had been. I doubt it cured Judy's passion for pulling the handle on cheap slot machines, and Latvia seemed to have enough of them to continue testing her resolve.

The next day Judy and I again left Riga for a train trip to meet the rest of our Baltic lecturer contingent in Kaunas, Lithuania's second largest city and past capital of the country. CEP anthropologist Craig Heller and his Spanish wife Ingrid Martinez Rico were our hosts for a Thanksgiving get-together. The dinner festivities were complete with a turkey, a rare commodity in this part of the world. After dinner, we watched a replay of the Florida vs. Florida State football game on a VHS tape that had been sent to one of the lecturers, compliments of his parents–living in Florida, of course. Jana put all of us visiting CEPers up at an inexpensive and very Soviet-style hotel. There was the customary large glass-fronted lobby containing the expected oversized modernistic sculpture. It was also customary that the best rooms were on the two lower floors. Our rooms were on the top floor, which, at only four floors, meant there was no elevator. There was also no heat in our room or hot water in the bathroom, but Judy and I had by this time become used to these inconveniences. I had also learned to prefer no hot water over the risk of being electrocuted by malfunctioning individual instant-shower hot water heaters. The little boxes sat next to the hot water faucet. One "tingling hot" shower was enough for me! Being late in November, our room was definitely quite chilly, even close to freezing, it seemed, but our separate beds each had enough blankets to ensure a warm sleep. At least the hotel did not seem to contain critters that would eat our snack food in the middle of the night. Our stash had been depleted a couple of nights previously while staying in our Riga hotel.

While in Kaunas, we visited another anthropologist and his wife, Roger and Vally Nance. They had come to Kaunas so that Vally could spend a couple of months working as a church missionary and exploring her family's Lithuanian roots. Vally's parents had lived all their life in Kaunas. Theirs was another example of the ever more common effort to explore and reconnect family following the forced isolation that was so common during Soviet times. Judy and I had been informed of the Nance's visit by one of my university colleagues in Boise. During our visit with Roger and Vally, we learned the whereabouts of a mutual friend we had known over thirty years ago. What a small world it is.

Before returning to Estonia, Judy and I took a bus ride the short distance out toward the edge of Kaunas to visit the site of the Ninth Fort. From the bus stop, it was a pleasant half-mile walk up a gentle slope to the Ninth Fort. The fortification was mostly hidden from view because it was built into the side of a large hill. The fort had been constructed by the Russians to ward off an anticipated World War I German invasion. It quickly failed to do so. The Germans had come back again during the Second World War to use the fort as a location for the mass killing of nearly eighty thousand Jews. When the Soviets arrived, they put up a typically monumental-size reinforced concrete and steel sculpture dedicated to the Jewish resistance. They also built a small museum to recount the details of the Nazi genocide. It was quite interesting to see how the present Lithuanian caretakers had updated the museum to tell a more balanced story, including several exhibits of the Soviet KGB's use of the facility as a location for killing and for arranging deportations to Siberia.

Several underground rooms at the fort were open for inspection. One room contained an old kitchen, another laundry items, and several metal bed frames in a third room were sitting next to curved walls into which prisoners had scratched dates and poignant messages about life.

Miss Estonia

One of my female Estonian students, knowing of my interest in old cars, gave me the telephone number of a man she said had similar interests, who lived in Tallinn, and supposedly had a few old cars in his collection. I made an appointment to see him. His Old Town office was located inside one end of a meeting hall containing several rows of folding chairs. Somewhat to my surprise, I discovered that this was where festivities connected with a Miss Estonia pageant were held. My fellow old car buff greeted me in fluent English. Valeri Kirss, a late middle-aged man, was in charge of this annual event, which I discovered was a long-standing institution in Estonia. It had its beginning in 1923 as a way of finding new actresses for a newly forming film industry. I found the prominent display of the pageant scene to be a bit ironic. At home, I had learned to see such pageants as old-fashioned if not rather sexist in nature. I was amused to see that the Soviets, who had been outspoken champions of feminist causes, had still enthusiastically supported this form of female exploitation.

An examination of the many photos hanging in the hall made it clear that Valeri had stayed with the pageant and the film industry for the past several years. He showed me around his office and the meeting hall. The place was loaded with memorabilia, giant trophy cups, and hundreds of autographed pictures of past incarnations of Miss Estonia. One large recent photo was personally signed for Valeri by Eha Nirigue, one of the pageant winners. She looked just like Marilyn Monroe complete with the wide toothy smile. Eha was now billed, in a title below her picture, as a "Russian Supermodel." Also at the bottom of her picture were noted her measurements, complete to her shoe size: a nine and a half.

So what about the cars? This turned out to be only a fading sideline. Vaeri continued his membership in an old car club but no longer owned any old cars himself. He had owned several in the past, featuring them and himself in several movies. One picture in his office showed him as a Nazi officer sitting in a war-time German command car that had been part of his collection.

Doing Capitalism behind the Former Iron Curtain

As the long, dark Estonian winter settled in, Simon and I discovered the excitement of the fledgling Estonian stock exchange. In fact, a small *Bourse*, as the exchange was called, had also begun in the other two Baltic countries, in Russia, and in many of Communism's successor states. We knew a couple of visiting lecturers in economics who were in a German program similar to ours. They were making highly profitable investments in what was definitely a bull market. I could not resist the temptation and opened an account with a bank using my VISA card and jumped in, buying shares in Rakvere, a meatpacking company and in The Baltic Fund, the first mutual fund to be created in the region.

I thought about buying some shares in Saku brewery in honor of our cat. I decided not to make the purchase, thinking it to be a questionable play after finding out that a secret Soviet radioactive waste depository had been discovered rather near where the brewery drew its well water. The mutual fund owned shares in about thirty companies, roughly an equal number in Lithuania, Latvia, and Estonia, including my meat company. I quickly learned how to read the Estonian language stock reports in the local newspaper and watched my investment double very quickly.

When Judy and I left Estonia, I sold the meatpacking shares and bought more of the mutual fund. Back home in Idaho, with visions of a continued run-up in share prices, I was able to follow my stock on the Internet, and to watch its price plunge well below my original stake! It was 1998 and Russia had defaulted on its foreign loan obligations, allowing the ruble to lose more than half its value. Along with my wallet, the economy of many newly independent countries took a big hit. This was because Russia had remained their main trading partner in a continuation of a pattern developed during Soviet times. Oh well, what goes up may come down. Most recently, my mutual fund was closed and my position was transferred to a different Eastern European fund. My stake climbed back above my original investment. The future for the fund will depend, in large measure, on what has been a slowly improving overall European economy.

Just think of it. In a matter of a few years, the Berlin Wall collapsed, the cold war was over, some of the former Soviet republics have now joined NATO and the European Union, and I was "doing capitalism," riding what one famous economist, referring to competition, had once called "the perennial gale of creative destruction." I had been doing this boldly on what was just a few years ago Communism's former home turf!

Dark Days Disappear into White Nights

Our year in Estonia, especially the cold winter, went quickly, in part because we spent over a month back home in Boise, Idaho, during the Christmas season. We enjoyed family, but we missed the snowy beauty, the pubs, and the tasty restaurant meals of Old Town. We especially missed my students. Judy suggested that on our return to Estonia, we bring back a large stack of corn tortillas and some medium hot salsa and have a Mexican party for the students. Mexican food had yet to arrive in the Baltic region. The young people loved the party, but with only a few exceptions, they could not handle the medium hot salsa. We were reminded once again of how bland the diet in the Baltic countries was.

In the early spring, the days began to grow noticeably longer. This was an especially welcome change considering that we were living as far north in latitude as Anchorage, Alaska. The long winter nights had for too long crowded out much of the daytime sun. People began to get out and do things. Outside eating was again available at some of the restaurants. A law school where I had been teaching a criminology class scheduled a boat ride to Helsinki and back. Faculty members were going to have a floating seminar aboard. Judy and I were invited to come along and visit Helsinki.

The distance to Helsinki was only about fifty miles, but the round-trip takes twenty-four hours to complete. The gigantic ferry—I believe it was of Swedish construction—left Tallinn early in the afternoon, slowed only imperceptibly on its trip by what looked like about six inches of ice which covered the water. At the entrance to the Helsinki harbor, we were met by a series of low-lying islands followed shortly afterward by the port of Helsinki. Judy and I got off the boat to look around the city. We window-shopped until midafternoon when the sun disappeared and it began to get dark and very cold. We stopped in a pub for a hot mulled wine, commenting on how prices were so much higher in Scandinavia than what we had become used to. The Western European cost of living had yet to make its appearance in our part of the Baltic region. This cost differential encouraged at least one very interesting social pattern: the "booze run."

On the evening trip back to Estonia, the giant ferry anchored just outside the Tallinn harbor overnight before docking. Staying out in the water this long—twenty-four hours—exempted the Finnish passengers from paying stiff duties on the large amount of alcohol and prescription drugs they would be taking back home that day. Usually the purchases were so extensive that they had to be trucked on board on personal handcarts. The boat provided an economical way to stock up on booze and drugs. The numerous amenities on board the boat made it easy to while away the extra hours spent at anchor for the ferry contained several restaurants and bars, a casino, and a dance floor with a live band. There was also a typically loud disco for the young crowd. It was appropriately located several floors below our sleeping deck with its cozy little staterooms. We slept quietly and soundly.

A week or two after our boat ride, the senior faculty member in my department invited us for a Saturday visit at his home in the rural village of Saku. Mart was a geography professor in his mid-sixties with a full head of gray hair and a goatee. His first name was probably the most common in Estonia. I had quickly discovered this bit of knowledge only a few days after moving to Tallinn when I had tried to select "mart" as part of my e-mail address. The man at the Internet office had laughed loudly, "You and several thousand other men," he said.

We looked forward to the visit with Mart and the chance to tour our cat's namesake village and brewery. The commuter train ride lasted about twenty minutes from downtown Tallinn. We got off on the landing next to a small wooden station where Mart was waiting for us and headed for the brewery just a short walk away. Unfortunately, tours were not available on Saturday. Mart reminded us of the story about a Soviet-era toxic waste site, possibly radioactive, that had recently been discovered only a few miles away. Quite predictably, the Soviet authorities had kept its existence a secret. Mart assured Judy and me that the brewery water, and the water that the village inhabitants drank from their wells, had been deemed safe by Estonian as well as international authorities. A Swedish company had also checked the situation out thoroughly, Mart said, before deciding to purchase a controlling interest in the brewery. Even then, jokes about glowing in the dark after drinking a Saku beer remained popular. Following a few more minutes walking, we entered a large clearing in the sparse forestland containing a widely scattered neighborhood of small wooden and stucco single-family homes, some painted in the typical Baltic shades of mustard, green, and sea blue.

Judy and I were given a tour of the orchard and grounds surrounding Mart's house. Inside, we enjoyed homegrown and homemade rosehip tea and apple cakes with Mart and his wife. While sunny, it was still quite chilly outside, so Mart had the little house's heating system running. It is worth describing. The wood fired stove was about four feet wide and a little less than two feet deep. Its face was beautifully painted ceramic as was its upper section, an equally wide plenum that ran all the way to the ceiling. The complete stove arrangement made up part of the wall that separated the entry hallway from the front room thus allowing heat to circulate into the bedrooms on one side as well as the front of the house on the other side. We had seen this type of stove in old public buildings and homes that once belonged to the czarist-era Russian elite. It was a system that remained relatively unchanged from less elaborate examples we had also seen in museums depicting farm life five hundred years ago. Sometimes the stoves served a dual function of also heating the home's sauna.

One final, equally interesting feature of Mart's house was an inside pit toilet located in an otherwise reasonably modern-appearing bathroom. Mart noted that most of the other houses also had them and that it presented no hazard to his well, which was out in the backyard. Mart and his wife had chosen to live in a rural area, in part, because here the Soviet policy allowed them home ownership. I noted later to Judy how the little house and lack of modern conveniences made very clear the wide differences in material standard of living between us two professors who were nearly identical in age and work history. Even fifty miles away, in Finland, Mart's standard of living would have been similar to mine, maybe even higher. It was another example of the material difference that Communism had made.

Later in the spring, Judy, Simon, and I left on an overnight train to spend a four-day weekend in St. Petersburg, Russia. Even though it was late spring, it was still pretty chilly that far north. Fortunately, we had lots of sunshine throughout the trip. This helped to light the many golden church cupolas and set off the beautiful pastel-colored eighteenth-century architecture of the city, the "Venice of the north." The bridges, canals, and palaces made a delightful scene. The Hermitage, the Marinsky Opera and Ballet, and other exotic and fascinating places beckoned our visit.

St. Petersburg was founded in 1703 by Peter the Great. As Russia's new capital, even though it was inconveniently located in the far northwestern corner of the empire, it was able to offer two strategic advantages: its new fortifications helped to defend Russia from the Swedes, and, as a port city, it would be Russia's "window on the West," a symbol of the czar's aspirations to European great power status.

The city's fortunes declined after the Bolsheviks moved Russia's capital back to Moscow in 1918. There was further neglect following the damage of a World War II siege by the Germans. The city languished through most of the Communist period. However, more recently, tourists have begun to visit the city in increasing numbers; new businesses are arriving, including some that are relocating from Moscow. The city looks to be poised for a new period of greatness.

We stayed five nights on the top floor (remember what this means?) in a typical Soviet hotel. We supplemented the hotel's breakfast of boiled eggs and grainy porridge with lunch at McDonald's, where else? Dinners were mostly tuna salad sandwiches served at a Subway-style place that was in our price range. Although we splurged a couple of times, Russian restaurant food was generally very expensive.

We almost did not go on this trip due to the difficulty of getting an official invitation on short notice to visit Russia. With only a few exceptions, we knew that it was impossible to go anywhere in the former Soviet Union without first having a "letter of introduction." This was certainly the case in Russia. The letter could come from a private party, a hotel, or in our case we usually obtained our letters from a university who would testify in writing that we were an invited guest for some official purpose or other. In the present case, I had a faxed copy of an invitation I had arranged from a student hostel in St. Petersburg, which we took to the visa annex of Tallinn's Russian embassy.

The visa annex was a grimy run-down two-story building, obviously used to accomplish less than prestigious work and organized to maximize intimidation. Simon, Judy, and I climbed the wooden stairs to the second floor and entered a dimly lit room full of poor, dejected-looking Russian nationals trying to get a visa to leave Estonia. We waited for almost an hour, standing in the crowded room, with absolutely no sign of business activity or movement by anybody in the room, other than the fact that everyone knew we were there, including, it would seem, the officials on the other side of the big room's inner door. This door had opened part way a few times allowing hurried conversation with one or more of the waiting supplicants, but nothing appeared to come of it.

Finally, the door opened wide, and we were motioned into the inner room. Here, in a room containing a long counter and several women engaged in what appeared to be official business, we filled out paperwork and handed over the invitation and our passports. I don't think any of us even flinched when the clerk told us to return in the afternoon, at which time we would learn of their decision to grant us visas. We were beginning to get used to the likelihood of state business being conducted in such a totally customer-unfriendly way. We would need to make an almost duplicate visit to this dismal place later in the afternoon. Fortunately, we only had to wait about half an hour this time before the door opened and we were again motioned inside only to be told by the clerk that faxed invitations were not acceptable. Don't ask me why she didn't tell us this on our first visit.

At this point our options for getting to St. Petersburg boiled down to getting an original signed invitation through the only means left at this late date, which was the "train method" of fast mail, or go through one of the new travel agencies and, of course, pay a lot more. We decided to visit a small travel agency where the owner took care of all the paperwork including our visas and getting us somewhat "better" accommodations. It was a big relief not to have to stand in that visa line again!

The train (or bus) method of sending or receiving mail was one that we had used before and would employ many times in the future both in Estonia and in Ukraine. It involved going to the station just before the train was going to leave for the desired destination. There we would select a wagon steward (always a lady it seemed) in charge of one of the wagons, and hand over our letter or package. Back at our flat, we would e-mail the intended recipient who would then meet the train, give the wagon steward a tip and retrieve the letter or package at the other end. We used this system to send overnight envelopes and small parcels, sometimes containing our passports and even large sums of money. It seems, on hindsight, to be an extremely questionable practice, but the locals use it all the time, and besides, we usually paid much higher tips. It took more time to make the arrangements, but people in this part of the world didn't seem to be in such a rush. It worked well. Of course, it was totally without security, but it was many times less expensive than DHL, the only professional overnight mail service in the region at this time.

Getting to Know our Landlords

Our apartment flat owners in Tallinn were Natalia and Vova Fjodorovy, a Russian Estonian couple in their late thirties. Vova, a muscular, athletic appearing individual, worked as a guard at the state penitentiary. His descriptions of the miserable conditions of work were shocking but certainly not unexpected. I had read that the Estonian government was planning to make extensive reforms to existing Soviet practice and improvements to the Soviet-era physical plant. Quite attractive, with a notably outgoing personality, Natalia was an unemployed chemist. She had worked in a Soviet factory that, like so many others, had closed shortly after independence and privatization. Her place of work had been one of the many examples of Soviet factories whose inefficiencies and outdated product couldn't even begin to operate in a competitive market and consequently went out of business.

It was a second marriage for both Natalia and Vova, and they had a three-year-old son whom they referred to as "little Vova." This outgoing couple had inherited the apartment we were renting through the death of parents, had purchased the unit for very little money in an early policy of privatization, and now rented it to foreigners like us for a very good price. Over the year, we became good friends.

Natalia exhibited a marvelously buoyant and outgoing approach to life. Using her rudimentary understanding of English, she and her husband Vova would often invite Judy and me to their apartment, and once to their country house for meals whose main course was always fish and game provided compliments of Vova's skill as a sportsman. Their friendship was always good natured and genuine. Natalia and Vova were gracious hosts, taking obvious thought to insure that we felt at home in their company. Sometimes we felt almost too much at home, as when they would get out the photo albums after dinner.

The photo collection contained a predominance of pictures of Vova and little Vova in sporting attire exhibiting freshly caught fish or fowl. There were also a good number of pictures of the family taken in the buff. This seemed in keeping, however, with the numerous *Playboy* centerfold nudes that decorated some of the walls of their little flat. Judy and I wondered if they might be nudists, but we didn't ask, and they never said anything about it.

We will always remember the trip to their *dacha* (a Russian summer or country house). It was located about an hour's ride beyond Tallinn near where the Gulf of Finland meets the Baltic Sea. The dacha was an old two-story wooden frame house set in a grassy clearing surrounded by woods and bordered on one side by a good-sized stream—quite an idyllic location. The house had also once belonged to one of their parents. It had since been divided into two units, with the Fjodorovys using the upstairs and renting out the downstairs portion. Outside, in the center of the lawn, protruding above a circular rock garden was an approximately five-foot-tall carved wooden phallus. "Life," said Vova waiving his arm in its direction making sure we knew what it was.

We also examined their vegetable garden, waded in the stream, and walked to the nearby beach for a swim. The beach still contained a number of high wooden guard towers, one about every half mile up and down the sandy shoreline. Soviet soldiers once patrolled from these high locations making sure that no one tried to escape the country by swimming out to waiting Swedish or Finnish fishing or pleasure boats that would stand just offshore. A year earlier, Judy and I had been in Berlin during our Christmas holiday and had a chance to inspect what remained of the Berlin Wall, but I think these guard towers made the point even more convincingly about what it meant to live in a closed society.

In the afternoon, back at the dacha, we had an outdoor picnic in full view of Vova's woodcarving. Neither Judy nor I was particularly anxious to try Vova's freshly caught chilled eel. They were uncooked, small, dark-colored, and slimy looking. Vova showed us how to tip our heads back letting one slide down whole. This could be followed by a shot of vodka if necessary. Judy refused to try her eel. One was enough for me. Fortunately, there were plenty of other more edible foods to choose from, almost all homemade. Later, after waiting for the wood fire to heat the water, Judy and I took an authentic old-fashioned sauna. The sauna was located in what looked like a tool shed adjacent to where we had our picnic. We passed up on the suggestion that we follow the sauna with the usual splash in the nearby stream. Noting that we had put on our bathing suits, our hosts, who presumably would have gone naked, refrained from sharing the sauna with us out of concern for our modesty.

Natalia did not mention that they had experienced any problem transferring the titles to either their parents' apartment or the dacha. The dacha, especially, could have presented a problem of claiming ownership. It had been constructed prior to the Soviet occupation of Estonia, which had occurred toward the end of World War II. Older structures like this were being reclaimed by their original owners, not just in Estonia but throughout the former Iron Curtain countries. The difficulties most often involved situations where family members were coming back to their formally Soviet-occupied home country, usually following a generation or more of living abroad. A claim would subsequently be filed on property once held in private ownership by now-usually-deceased parents or grandparents.

We came across several examples of this effort to regain claim to previously owned property. In one example of this, we had stopped into a small private art gallery, fronting a busy downtown street in Tallinn, early one evening and met the proprietor who was a tall, middle-age American lady. She told us of the long, and unfinished, legal process she was undergoing in order to gain ownership of the small three-story building. It had once belonged to her father.

A very interesting second example involved a large and very beautiful old frame house located on the Baltic coast near Riga that was presently occupied by the Russian ambassador to Latvia. There had been a long, and so far unsuccessful, effort to reclaim the property. The litigation had already been quite lengthy even though what we were told was that the documentation supporting the claim was solid. It was obvious that the present Russian occupiers had, for all intents and purposes, gained the property free of charge and did not want to give up such an obviously gorgeous place located in such a prime location. The last bit of information that we received had it that the Russians were trying to trade the property for some other equally valuable property. They presumably owned this other property more securely or at least convincingly.

Back to Our First Love

During our year-long stay in Tallinn we returned to its historical Old Town section what seemed like more than a hundred times. We could walk from our apartment flat in twenty minutes or, when the weather was bad, take one of the old-fashioned trams up to the main double-turreted east portal of the Old Town. During warm weather, we drank beer outside (Saku, of course) in Raekoja Plats, the Old Town's cobblestone central square.

In the early summer, as we were about to leave Estonia for the last time, we sat outside one of Old Town's quaint little restaurants late into the evening, but still in bright sunlight. If we had stayed in Tallinn only a few weeks longer, we could have watched the sun actually stay up all night. Night or day, winter or summer, there had always been something interesting to see in the central square. I always enjoyed looking at the carved dragon heads that functioned as roof rainwater spouts or the elaborate antique wrought-iron business signs jutting out next to the doorways of various beige, light blue, green, or white painted little shops.

A couple of banks had branch offices fronting Raekoja Plats square. They had funny sounding names like Hansapank and Forespank. It reminded us of the "Pood" signs that were everywhere in this country. Early in our stay in Estonia, we had reasoned that if "pank" was bank, then "pood" must be food? Not quite, we had quickly learned. It was the word for "store," any kind of store apparently.

Over the snowy winter, we had spent many hours and countless evenings in the Old Town. A favorite destination in the winter was a little restaurant just off Raekoja Plats where we would drink hot mulled wine and eat pork chop dinners around a big fireplace. Another favorite, a few blocks from the main square, was a little place called Fat Margaret, a small pizzeria that could not have held more than two dozen people, tucked into a squatty turret entrance tower next to the Old Town's north portal.

We had begun our year in Tallinn sitting in our shirtsleeves at one of the shaded tables surrounding Raekoja Plats. Now we were finishing up our stay in Estonia, sitting at one of the same tables, enjoying a last Saku beer, glad to be going home, but wishing there was another day so that we might just head off one more time for the Old Town to walk the cobblestone streets and fill our spirits with the joy and beauty of this wonderful place—truly a jewel of the Baltic Sea.

4

Ukraine: the Look and Feel of Life in Soviet Russia

Learning to Enjoy Life in a Difficult Posting

We stayed home for the academic year 1997–98, thinking that Estonia would be the end of our adventure. Our original plan had been to remain overseas for only two years. Judy gave away "Ba-ba," her warm lambs-wool coat. We should have known the consequence of trying to stay home. Predictably, boredom set in, and we rejoined the CEP the following year and were posted to Ukraine.

We had requested a location in Central Asia, but local university politics there made it very difficult to arrange a position for me. After a series of postponements, the CEP suggested I consider a position still available in eastern Ukraine. It was acknowledged to be a more difficult and less attractive posting than Lithuania or Estonia. The Chernobyl nuclear plant explosion had given Ukraine an international black eye. Worse, Ukraine remained deeply stalled in a form of post-Communist doldrums: unable to make progress economically or socially, suffering a fractious government, and rather unable to decide who they were as a people and where they wanted to take their future.

The economy had still been in major decline when, just prior to our arrival, Russia devalued the ruble. Because of the major economic ties between the two countries, this set off serious inflation of Ukraine's currency, the hryvna. We would notice this immediately upon our arrival as each exchange of dollars brought an ever greater amount of less valuable hryvna. The impact of rapid inflation was to further drive people into destitution. As much as half of the economy operated off the tax rolls, an unusually large shadow economy by even post-Soviet standards. Unemployment and social payment arrears had become major problems. Half of all Ukrainians were living below their official poverty line, about thirty-five U.S. dollars a month for an individual. These statistics were even more pronounced in the eastern region of the country where we would be located.

Ukraine, the largest country in Europe.

The posting was also considered difficult because it would not be in a capital city such as we had enjoyed in both earlier assignments. In fact, we would be quite some distance from the capital, Kyiv, or any other place of any size. Even though we would be located in Kharkiv, Ukraine's second largest city, our *Lonely Planet* guide book gave it only one paragraph, referring to the city as "the world's most polluted." The paragraph went on to warn of cholera and suggested that travelers stay away! In contemplating the environmental conditions of our new posting, neither of us could put Chernobyl completely out of mind. After all, several thousand people may have died as a direct result of radiation exposure, and the health of as much as two-thirds of Ukrainians, especially children, may have been compromised by this incident. In the end, none of these dismal statistics dissuaded us from taking the posting. After all, the environmental wreckage left by the Soviets was everywhere. By now, we were two-year veterans of the post-

Communist landscape and its hazards. We had learned to take such matters in stride as far more important was the adventure awaiting us.

Once we had been located in our new assignment, we thought for a while that we might have to turn right around and come home. The rapid rise in inflation was threatening to close legal sources for exchanging our money, thus forcing us into a difficult black market in order to get local currency. Luckily, the problem of hyperinflation began to subside, and our posting no longer appeared in jeopardy.

For all these reasons, the posting in Kharkiv was not the most popular place where CEP operated, but we had taken it. It turned out to be a good decision, and a very fulfilling year. Within a month of arrival, Judy was writing home about the pleasant ambiance of the city and the extremely friendly and helpful people. Our adjustment was made easier by a long Indian summer. Sure, there were the usual hardships, maybe more so than we had expected, but we adjusted just fine, and of course, we had all our inoculations.

Confronting the Matter of Mobsters

We began our stay in Ukraine in late August with a few days of in-country orientation in the capital city of Kyiv. The workshops and presentations concerning our work and what to expect in Ukraine were held in our hotel just across the Dnipro River from downtown Kyiv. The view from our hotel window was one of a long line of geometrically placed high-rise apartments separated by an equally long narrow park. The design seemed like a duplicate of the dreary and crime-ridden Robert Taylor public housing project in Chicago. Similarly, it was also a place of mostly very poor people.

One of the first workshop presentations was a bit unnerving. It was made by an individual from the U.S. Embassy Security Office, and concerned the overall crime and safety situation in Ukraine. The presenter was trying to be helpful. Instead, he was very alarming, quite needlessly, I felt. The speaker handed each of us thirty-five single-spaced pages of crime incidents, a synopsis of articles about Ukrainian crime, and six special pages relating crime cases involving American Embassy staff. Given no basis on which we could interpret this plethora of information, the unintentional effect was to make it appear that Ukraine was a criminal place bar-none!

It was true that business dealings could involve violence. Mafia types, Ukrainians called them *mafiya* meaning "mob," were fairly common. They often were in the news for their violent manner of settling disputes. Businessmen sometimes felt it prudent to hire bodyguards for protection from these thugs. However, Judy and I never felt alarmed by such goings on and never worried about our personal safety. We had become used to seeing only the effects of mob activity as the incidents generally occurred out of our sight.

This was the case, for example, during our stay in Vilnius, Lithuania, when its major newspaper had attempted to raise awareness of the problem of local Mafia-style operations in a series of articles. In apparent retaliation, the front of their office building was blown away one night. Judy and I had seen mob-looking characters in all three Baltic countries, usually driving American SUVs, and dressed in athletic warm-up suits with crew-cut hair styles. We had occasionally seen them trying to shake down restaurant owners. We would see the work of these criminals again in Ukraine. One quite gruesome example was related to us a few months after our arrival by Gary Waldron, a CEP lecturer posted in Donetsk, a large city on the eastern side of the country.

We had arrived on a cold early morning in Donetsk following an overnight ride on a very cockroach-infested train. I had come to this unexciting coal mining city of over a million people to conduct course and instructor evaluations. Gary met us at the train station. Gary suggested we begin our day with a pancake breakfast at his apartment flat. As we approached the entrance to the apartment, Gary showed Judy and me a large, approximately two foot diameter, bloody spot on the concrete in front of the main door. The night before, he said he had heard screaming and crying coming from the hallway in front of the door to his third-floor apartment. Opening it, he found his neighbor being manhandled down the stairs by two men followed by his hysterical wife. As an ex–Los Angeles policeman, Gary moved quickly to stop the abduction—until the guns came out. The killing took place immediately upon reaching the front door of the apartment building. It was all about control of a local brewery.

I am only aware of one other CEP lecturer who ever got dangerously involved in the gangster orbit. In this instance, the consequences would have been his fault as he knowingly, and foolishly, spent a few months dating the estranged wife of one of these men. I had fully expected him to leave the country in a body bag!

In addition to the somber warnings about the Mafia, the orientation gave us a chance to meet our other lecturer colleagues, a much larger number than in the Baltic CEP contingent. There were forty-one lecturers and staff members, a few with spouses or "significant others," and one Danish couple with a brand-new baby. Fifteen of us were foreign visiting lecturers representing the United States, Mexico, the UK, France, Denmark, and Germany. There were twenty-three local faculty fellows.

Our country director was Oleksandr Shtokvych, "Sasha," as we called him. He was a young Ukrainian who was starting his first year as our country director after serving as an assistant the previous year. He turned out to be very good at the job. His assistant was Sharon Weinberger, an attractive, exceptionally talented outgoing young lady in her midtwenties with a finance major and Russian history minor from Yale University. These two people were responsible for CEP's largest contingent of lecturers who were scattered over Ukraine as well as the adjacent countries of Belarus and Moldova. We all stayed in touch through a few visits, many e-mail messages, and parcels sent by the "train method."

Our initial impressions of Ukraine were made through eyes more seasoned and experienced. By now, we had become not only familiar with the CEP routine, we also knew what to expect while living and traveling in post-Soviet Central/Eastern Europe. Of course, the culture of each country was wonderfully different and the geography equally so. Ukraine was no exception. We looked forward to each country's unique and varied antiquities and folk traditions as most important prizes to be savored. There was also a certain similarity about Sovietized Eastern Europe, and Kharkiv was very Soviet. The local population even referred to their city as Kharkov, using the Russian spelling and pronunciation.

Most noticeably, after two years behind the Iron Curtain, we had reached the point where we felt a comfortable familiarity amid the usual plethora of standardized and often run-down Communist-era surroundings. As we entered a city for the first time, in the back of our minds we could almost hear a little voice saying, "Here we go again." A friend of ours, Canfield Smith, a retired Russian historian, wrote us while we were in Kharkiv offering his conclusion concerning the Soviet look and how it became that way. He wrote, "So much of the Soviet-era structures and institutions are crumbling, and so much of the tsarist era stands. There must be a message here; not to return the tsarists, but not to put intellectuals and peasants in charge!"

Kharkiv was a large manufacturing city of over a million and a half residents known for its giant tractor factory (which during Soviet times had produced more tanks than anything else), ICBM missile manufacture, the Antonov aircraft plant, and Turboatom, the maker of large steam turbines. Kharkiv was also the location of many institutions of post-secondary education including where I was posted: Kharkiv State University, the largest and one of the most respected universities in Ukraine. For Judy and me, Kharkiv was an opportunity to think and feel like we were back only a few years in time living in Soviet Russia. Adding to the sense of Soviet times was the fact that Ukraine continued the Soviet practice of conducting large-scale military training in Kharkiv. One could easily imagine an authoritarian militaristic society from all the Soviet look-alike uniforms that were always in view, especially around the area of the city where we lived.

Ukraine

Preparing for our new posting, we were surprised to note that Ukraine was the largest country in Europe outside of Russia, slightly larger than France, but somewhat less populated at about 50 million. Its size and location in the south central part of Europe and its close proximity to several Middle Eastern neighbors had resulted in a much different mix of historic and cultural influences than what Judy and I had observed in the Baltic region. The most immediately noticeable of these differences was the use of the Cyrillic alphabet and the prominence of Byzantine influences in religion and architecture.

Having begun to prepare for what I expected to be a Central Asia posting, I had started reading about Genghis Khan. Now that I was going to be in Ukraine, it was fascinating to think that he had played a significant role in this region as well. One of my students filled me in on the details. Genghis Khan's army had come all the way across Asia, entering the region in the 1230s, conquering its people, and sacking the city of Kyiv. Over three hundred years old at the time of Kahn's arrival, Kyiv was the center of Kyivean Rus, the first Slavic state, an area much larger than the boundaries that would come to define present-day Ukraine.

Following the predictable amount of political intrigue and military engagements, and roughly seven hundred years after Genghis Khan, Ukraine willingly became a part of Russia in 1654. Ukraine had actually been Russia's spiritual birthplace. Russian tradition begins with a Slavic victory over Varangians (Vikings) who inhabited the region and who called themselves *Rus*, referring to the area as *Rossiya*, the land of the Rus. However, Varangian leadership was allowed to continue, and soon afterward, in 862 the House of Riurik was established with its center in Kyiv (thus the Kyivean Rus). Only twenty-six years later, the Russians, as the people of the area had begun to call themselves, adopted Eastern Orthodox Christianity and the Cyrillic alphabet. Having combined the key elements of identity, religion, and language, Kyiv, and the area which became Ukraine continued to remain a big part of the Russian Empire, quickly taking on the accolade as the spiritual birthplace, but also the defining attribute as Russia's grain or food belt.

Ukraine briefly tasted independence after World War I, moving its capital from Kyiv to Kharkiv, but within a year, and with only moderate opposition, Ukraine was back under Russian control, this time by the Bolsheviks. The Nazis occupied all of Ukraine during the Second World War, letting Romanian counterparts do most of the dirty work of producing untold numbers of deaths and extensive damage and destruction to architectural antiquities. Hitler had looked upon the Slavic people of the region as a second-class race. It was common knowledge among Ukrainians that Hitler had elaborate plans to turn the Ukrainians into a slave population following the war.

Two Ukraines

Judy and I arrived to find Ukraine in what many of its countrymen hoped would be the final stages of trying to patch up a dangerous and highly destabilizing case of political split personality. The country was politically—one could almost say ethnically—divided right down its middle. Its capital, Kyiv, is set geographically at the fulcrum point of a division that more or less follows the north-to-south flow of the large Dnipro River. The river passes near Chernobyl in Ukraine's north to Odessa and the Black Sea in the south.

On the east side of the river, Russian nationalists, many if not most still harboring strong Communist sympathies, fill approximately half of the land area including Kharkiv where we lived. These people continued to hold Soviet-era values and wanted to move Ukraine toward closer ties with Russia and their northern neighbor Belarus, even to the point, as some actually hoped, of creating an "All Slavic Union."

The west side of the Dnipro River contained a predominance of Ukrainian nationalists who looked to the newfound success of democratic and market liberalization measures in Poland and to Western Europe generally for their inspiration. In a manner similar to the role played by Kharkiv for the Soviet sympathizers, the Ukrainian nationalists looked to Lviv near the western edge of Ukraine as their spiritual flagship city.

Thus, in so many ways, Ukraine might as well have been two countries. The two factions remained essentially unchanged. Even though seven years into independence, in our eastern part of the country, Russian, rather than the closely related Ukrainian language, was still most commonly spoken. Even the money continued to be unofficially called by the Russian words "ruble" and "kopeck." On three occasions, Judy and I observed large Communist Party parades through Kharkiv's main downtown street. A large portion of the city's inhabitants still considered themselves geographically stranded Russians!

If the divisions I made between the two sides of the Dnipro River seem too sharp, students who had lived on both sides of the river do not think so. Maybe reason will prevail. A newly minted and widely circulated proverb in Ukraine is that "He who doesn't feel hurt about the Soviet Union's collapse has no heart, but he who dreams about its revival has no mind."

Evidence of Ukraine's split personality was also easily observed in the continuing display of its many Communist-era symbols, especially in the seemingly hundreds of Lenin statues located just about everywhere, especially in the eastern part of the country. Another example of split personality comes from a November 1999 editorial in the English-language newspaper, the *Kiev Post*. The editorial noted, with irony if not indignation, that seven years after Ukrainian independence and the highly publicized effort to implement a free market economy, the country was still officially celebrating the November seventh anniversary of the Bolshevik coup of 1917 and the beginning of Communism. The editorial took pains to point out that the Bolsheviks, under Stalin, had been responsible for the deliberate starvation of millions of Ukrainians, "a land awash in blood," as this event is often called. "Why was this date still a national holiday?" the editorial asked. The answer seemed clear enough to me in the statistics documenting the continuing strength of Soviet values. The Communist Party had received 39 percent of the votes in the national election that had just concluded at the time the editorial was written.

Some Freedom, But Not Much Democracy

During our stay in Ukraine, Leonid Kuchma was reelected for a second five-year term as the country's president with 56 percent of the vote. He campaigned on a platform of bringing Ukrainians together. He had the advantage that, while he was from a political clan located in the eastern part of the country, he was successfully able to appear in support of the western part's interest in moving Ukraine ahead toward democracy, liberal economy, and Western Europe geopolitically. However, Kuchma engineered a "rigged" election. International election observers were appalled at the amount of voting irregularities. For example, in one eastern town, a cardboard voting box was hopelessly broken after a voter tried to stuff a thick pack of ballots through the small opening at its top.

As I look back now, several years later, it seems obvious that Kuchma did not have his heart set on following through on his campaign promises. His second term in office continued a pattern of corruption, insider favoritism, repression of the media, interference with the independence of the judiciary, and widespread abuse of the state administration. Needless to say, the division of Ukraine continued unabated. The election was also a portent of what would come five years later when Kuchma's hand-picked successor would try the same tactics—and worse: the opposition candidate was alleged to have almost been killed by poisoning.

Classic example of Stalin-esque "wedding cake" architecture, Warsaw, Poland.

Exploring the City of Kharkiv

Kharkiv is located on flat steppe land only about thirty miles from the Russian border. The Kharkiv region had also been settled by Slavic tribes in the tenth century. The city of Kharkiv was officially established in the 1650s, quickly growing to become Ukraine's second largest city, a position it has held ever since.

The city prospered under the Soviets who made Kharkov, as they called the city, Ukraine's capital between 1919 and 1934. A cultural renaissance occurred during this period, producing many artistic and literary achievements, and the establishment of numerous educational institutes, notably in aeronautical engineering and medicine. It was during this time that the city made several new additions to its existing stock of Russian-Byzantine–style buildings, especially the massive and distinctive type with the Stalin-esque "wedding cake" top structure. One large and very severe looking building, the Derzhprom, the House of State and Industry, presented a very art-deco style combination of bridgelike rows of windows tied together at the ends with vertical columns containing more windows. Its front reminded me of a concrete incarnation of a tic-tac-toe game. Two busy streets each passed under separate five-story openings of this building.

The overall mix of buildings provided many visual highlights to Judy's and my frequent walking excursions. Unfortunately, Stalin brought the renaissance period to an end but not before the heady times had insured that Kharkiv would develop into a pleasant city of broad avenues, many parks, and thousands of beautiful chestnut and acacia trees. This was a very hospitable and interesting location for Judy and me to spend the year. As for a reported problem with water pollution, we just did not spend much time near the river that mucked it way through the city. The adage "out of sight, out of mind," applied in this case.

A Great Colleague and Unexpected American Neighbors make Our Stay Memorable

I had an absolutely wonderful American CEP colleague in Kharkiv. Newell Cook was closer to our age than just about every other visiting lecturer we had yet to meet. Trained at both Harvard and Yale, Newell was known for being an innovative treasurer and auditor for the city of Boston. More recently, he had been employed in Ukraine with USAID. He had lived the customary high life style for several years, sequestered in Kyiv and, more recently in Kharkiv before becoming disillusioned with the program and deciding to join the CEP instead. During his year with me in the CEP, Newell continued as an advisor to a few high government officials while doing an absolutely superb job teaching his CEP students.

Newell was a good friend. Dinner at his elegant eighth-story apartment was an opportunity to enjoy wonderful gourmet cooking. "Cook could really cook," we soon found ourselves saying. It was an enjoyable challenge helping him round up the ingredients for some of his recipes. A good dry red wine was always hard to find, so, when located, Newell always bought a case! After his multicourse dinners, we would talk, watch a movie, or go over current CEP activities. Newell showed us the blueprint plans for a fabulous retirement home he was getting ready to construct in the Virgin Islands. Tragically, that dream never would come to pass. Newell became quite ill with esophageal cancer toward the end of the school year and died shortly after returning home to his wife and daughter in America. He was fifty-six years old.

Judy and I were definitely much more isolated from the outside world than we had been in Vilnius or Tallinn. Aside from Newell and our students, there just didn't seem to be very many other people in Kharkiv who were native English speakers, or very adapt at using English. Unlike our previous two postings, there was no place in Kharkiv to purchase copies of the country's single English-language newspaper published in Kyiv. No place, that we could locate, sold the international edition of newspapers or magazines, and no American or British TV broadcasts were available to us unless, like Newell, we had purchased a very expensive satellite dish. We didn't even have a TV set until Newell graciously lent us one of his that conveniently had a built-in VHS player. We used it almost exclusively to play movies that were traded around within our CEP contingent or borrowed from Newell's large library of titles.

To accompany our movie watching, we made sure to buy popcorn while in Kyiv during one of our many visits. It was hard to believe that a place as large as Kharkiv had no popcorn for sale, but we couldn't find any and neither could our students. Our up-to-date news came via our small short-wave radio on which we could listen to BBC broadcasts. Their programs would fade in and out during the day, while usually maintaining a reasonably strong signal for the 10:00 PM BBC World News broadcast. The effort to impeach President Clinton was the longest running top news story. Finally, a few back copies of my favorite weekly news magazine, *The Economist*, would find their way to our dacha via visits from CEP colleagues or trips to Kyiv.

We were feeling somewhat isolated. It didn't take us long to locate the only English-language oasis in the city: the single-room British Council library located in the main building of my university. I obtained a library card, and we visited this place quite regularly to check out books and VCR movies. Each visit presented the same difficult choice of how to get up to the library's eighth-floor location. We could climb the arduous, but safe and sound, stairs or ride the single functioning, rather unsafe-appearing, elevator that serviced the entire university building.

We always chose to live on the edge and take the Russian-made elevator. Its compartment was long and skinny. It probably had a load limit posted somewhere inside, but nobody in the usually long waiting line paid any attention. When the door opened on the main floor, the queue would immediately disappear and people would pack into the elevator like you couldn't believe—until a bell would ring to signal "Whoa, that is enough." Ignoring the bell, more people would attempt to jam in. The elevator would just sit there until some of the hapless would-be riders stepped out. The exiting would go on, always reluctantly, until the door would start to close and the elevator begin its halting ascent, banging back and forth against the outer walls as it went. The air was usually foul and stagnant by the time we arrived at our eighth-floor destination.

During the winter, I heard that people would often be trapped in this elevator for long periods of time during one of the frequent power blackouts. There were several evenings when I recall walking home from my classroom annex building, past the main university building when it and the buildings around it were in total darkness. I would wonder if the elevator might be inhabited with a press of folks literally standing through what was usually a two-hour electrical shutdown.

Even though living in greater isolation from English speakers, we were very fortunate to make friends with an American couple who were close to our age and turned out to live just across the little street from us. One fall evening, Judy and I had just exited our metro (subway) station and were on our way through the park toward home when we passed a couple going in the opposite direction. Each had a distinctive look of being American. We both turned back to take a more measured glance at each other before deciding to exchange tentative greetings. Joe and Norma Jenkins were from Provo, Utah. They were in the last seven months of a two-year volunteer assignment directing the work of a large number of Mormon missionaries in eastern Ukraine. Quite ironically, a drunk walked up while we were introducing each other and tried to get us to accompany him in a round of vodka swigs from his bottle.

That evening, I mentioned in an e-mail to our daughters that I hoped that our religious differences would not get in the way of developing a good friendship. Judy and I had been in Salt Lake City for two years while I was doing graduate work, and had found that relationships, across this particular religious line, had been very hard to keep. Fortunately, our new friendship worked out beautifully as we went on to enjoy their company at opera and ballet performances, musical events, and dinners at several restaurants, including home-cooked meals at our dacha.

Judy enjoyed cooking for our guests even though her kitchen was definitely the most primitive of any during our four years in the former Soviet Russian Empire. Her most ambitious effort was an authentic Thanksgiving dinner. Our guests were Newell and Bryce Johnson, a CEP visiting lecturer in sociology posted in Kyiv. Bryce had been a graduate student one year ahead of me at the University of Oregon. What a small world. We had even shared the same favorite professor, Benton Johnson.

Judy had to make quite a scavenger hunt to round up the ingredients for this festive dinner. Even more amazing was that she was able to put this meal together in such a primitive kitchen and in a location where appropriate ingredients were not all easily obtainable. She served turkey with stuffing, homemade cranberry sauce, mashed potatoes, cooked carrots with almonds and basil, brussel sprouts, several relish items, and all finished off with a dessert of apple crisp and vanilla ice cream.

Judy had e-mailed a request back home for a list of the ingredients in seasoned stuffing mix or on a can of poultry seasoning and managed to mix up a good facsimile. However, she could not find celery anywhere until learning that only the hearts were put out for sale. We had seen these in the market, but had not recognized what they were. A quote from her e-mail to our daughters following the successful dinner provides a hint at how an accomplished cook goes about the task in a foreign country:

I made the dressing, which I cut up from two-day-old dry

bread. I got the seasonings at the aptika (pharmacy). I made a sort of by-guess and by-golly combination along with melted butter. It seemed to taste okay, or perhaps I have tasted it so much in the making that it finally seemed right. The proof will be in the eating.

Occasionally it turned out that we were not as isolated as we imagined. It was quite a total surprise to be sitting in the opera theater one evening, waiting for the lights to dim and talking quietly between ourselves when a young man in the seat behind us asked where we were from. "Boise, Idaho," we replied. "I am from McCall [one hundred miles north of Boise] he said. Then revealing not a little pride he said, "Your Bronco football team just lost to the University of Idaho in the big playoff yesterday." *Darn!* I thought. Who would imagine such a coincidence in so isolated a part of the world! We had been hoping that the score could remain a secret from us until, in less than two weeks, we would return to Boise for Christmas and could watch the game on a video replay. Unfortunately, this person was about to return to Idaho in a few days and we lost track of his name and home address. The score would be his last hurrah for a least a while, as his school has not gone on to win a football game against ours in over a decade!

A Typical Day

What was a typical weekday like for us? There was a basic Monday through Friday routine that formed the basis of our time in Kharkiv. Beyond this routine, almost every day could be quite different, so I am taking considerable liberty to describe what might be "typical." However, here is what was marked on our calendar and described in an e-mail for Wednesday, November 11, 1998.

Judy left the dacha at 8:30 and traveled across town by metro to help with English lessons for her Ukrainian friend's grade school students. I left the dacha somewhat later, after a morning spent reading student essays, to walk over to a little store to pick up photocopies of assigned reading for my afternoon class. I returned to the dacha for a quick lunch and then met Judy at a prearranged metro stop for a ten-minute ride and twenty-minute walk to the Academy of Public Administration where we had tea with the foreign language faculty. We then both gave an informal lecture on life in America (with some help from an interpreter) to a class of graduate students who were taking their first semester of English language lessons.

Following the lecture, Judy took the metro back to the dacha. I accompanied her as far as my main university building where I met with the two staff members at the International Office to pick up my employment contract. I got our passports stamped with an indication that I was working in Ukraine and not just visiting. It had taken almost a month and a half to ready my contract for signing. With regretful looks, the two men informed me that I would not be paid for this period of employment. I took this news to be an indication of the way bureaucracy operated in Ukraine, the poor state of the national economy, and the fact that the two staff members were former KGB employees who certainly had no clue as to the importance of customer service. I didn't need the small amount of money but, I thought, what about the locals who were also subject to such crass and arrogant treatment?

Back outside, I made the twenty-minute walk through the park to my classroom building to give a lecture to my Welfare State in Transition class. With help from a short paper delivered by one of my students, the subject of the lecture was the pension system in Ukraine. Finally at about 5:30, I left school for a walk home, with two of my students tagging along for the conversation. We talked about the possibility of obtaining a summer job in America. Some resorts on the East Coast were hiring temporary workers through the J1 visa program. One of my students was a very accomplished accordion player and wondered about employment as an entertainer. It was dark and the sidewalks were icy. We stopped so that I could exchange some money in the back of a small jewelry store. It was a legitimate exchange even though its typical hole-in-the wall location might give the uninitiated pause to wonder. I ended up buying Judy some gold earrings for Christmas. By the time I arrived at our dacha, I was tired and frozen—but married life came through as Judy had hot soup and biscuits ready for dinner and a shot of vodka helped to get me warmed up. That was our day.

The Year of the Student

Our isolation in Kharkiv never became an issue. This was partly due to the rather frequent professional trips which Judy and I made to other parts of the country, including trips out of the country. Our record was three long trips spending six full nights on the train—all in one week. We were also able to break the isolation with a trip back to Boise for a long Christmas vacation. As was so often the case, we were able to count on my students to help us in facilitating our travel.

Our Christmas trip was a good example. At about 9:00 PM on a clear and very cold evening, two students arrived at our dacha in two taxis to accompany us to the train station. The second taxi was necessary to hold all of us and our baggage. The students were along for the ride, using the excuse that they could help us carry all our baggage. After a long delay out front of the train station, and worrying about making our scheduled departure because the taxi driver could not get the trunk lid on his Volga to open, one student showed him how to kick it open.

As the students carried our bags over the snowy platform to the train car, they added an obviously rehearsed reminder. "We are your students, don't forget to come back to us." they said. It was hard for them to believe that we had the wherewithal to make such a long trip for such a short period of time. I think it was even more difficult for them to think that we would come back after getting reacquainted with the comforts and pleasures of American life. I reassured them that we had every intention of returning, and it was students like them who had the most to do with our gladly coming back.

Some of my students had become our best friends. They provided the majority of our English-speaking opportunities, and they went out of their way to assist in our well being while in Ukraine. Another example took place early in our stay in Kharkiv when we needed to make our first overnight train ride to Kyiv. Still not used to even some of the basic requirements, one student helped me find out how much to pay the taxi driver in Kyiv to take us from the train station to our CEP office. He also gave us a translated copy of the address. Another student, knowing how difficult it would be for us, after class, took the money I gave him, went to the train station, and purchased our round-trip tickets. A third student met us at our dacha and offered to call a taxi for us (instead we went by the metro) and even offered to accompany us to the train station.

My students were some of the very best! It was like it became the "year of the student" in my professional career. In response to their attention to our needs, Judy and I spent unusually large amounts of time helping them with classroom assignments and other academic projects. Students were constantly visiting our dacha, getting advice and spending precious time on my laptop computer to write their research papers, having lunch or dinner, or all coming together for a party. Several of the students continue active e-mail correspondence with us even now after several years away from Ukraine. Here are some other examples of my students and the experiences which they helped us to enjoy.

Shortly after our arrival in Kharkiv, Judy and I met a young man that would soon become one of my students. Alex Shupta had seen us enter a small store on Sumskaya Street, near where we lived, to look for bed sheets and a blanket. He followed us in and started a conversation. Alex was a second-year student in engineering at the prestigious National Aerospace University on the outskirts of the city. I invited him to consider attending one of my classes at Kharkiv State University. Not only did he end up taking one of my classes both semesters, he recruited others from his university to do the same.

Alex helped us purchase a kitten shortly after our arrival in Kharkiv. We had left our Estonian cat, Saku, in Boise with our house sitters with the plan to get him a friend while in Ukraine. Alex accompanied us to the big outdoor market on the edge of the city where it seemed just about everything was for sale, including a large selection of cats and dogs. Pets are quite popular with Ukrainians, especially big dogs, if what we saw in the parks was any indication. We approached the edge of the market from the metro station exit to see a long line of babushkas holding wicker baskets, standing in front of cardboard boxes, or just keeping one or more animals near them on a leash.

The scene made me think of an open-air animal shelter arranged like a flea market. Judy went to the beginning of the line and picked up a small kitten from among several in one of the boxes. Alex began to interpret. The woman said she wanted five hryvny (about two dollars), but a few moments later, she was willing to give us the cat for free after we were all treated to a loud critique of her cats by another woman standing nearby. "Those are common alley cats," the woman said. "They are probably sick, and they all have fleas." "You need to take a look at my cats," she went on, holding up a couple for us to see. But, Judy and the little kitten had already bonded, fleas and all. I could see that the search was over. Upset over the impoliteness of the other babushka's remarks, Judy made a point of paying the full asking amount for the kitten. It turned out to be a wonderful bargain for the best cat we have ever owned. We put it down in the bottom of one of our shopping bags where it quietly remained during at least a couple more hours at the market.

On the way home, we decided to call the kitty Pyat, which means "five" in Ukrainian, a reminder of how much we paid for her. Pyat had fleas alright, but anticipating this we had also purchased some imported German flea and tick powder at a nearby "zoo," the Ukrainian name for a pet store. Pyat became the center of attraction, quickly revealing a loving and very amusing personality.

Pyat also would become a world traveler with her own passport, dutifully, and expensively, stamped by the Ukraine Ministry of Agriculture and Foodstuffs upon official evidence that she was healthy and had a rabies shot. For another sum of money and official testimony that she had "no economic value," Pyat received a "Certificate of Permission to Leave" the country from the Ministry of Export. Two years later, Pyat would fill her passport with an additional stamp by the Uzbekistan Ministry of Agriculture and Water Resources. After all the effort and expense to get the proper documentation, no official at the international airports ever seemed interested in looking at Pyat's documentation. Back home now in Boise, reduced to pampered domesticality, Pyat remains an important part of our family and a constant reminder of our last two years in the CEP.

A few weeks later, Alex took us for a visit to Kharkiv's Gorky Park, a large expanse of walkways, trees, and concessionaires on the outskirts of the city within walking distance of our dacha. The three of us spent a late August Saturday in the park. It seemed that practically every large city in the former Soviet Russian Empire had a park named after Gorky, one of Russia's most famous authors. This park featured long tree-lined promenades outlined with rows of park benches, food venders, and an amusement park of sorts. Most rides were no longer operable. We drank beer and ate the Ukrainian version of hot dogs, that is, two dogs on sliced hoagie-type bread with mayonnaise, mustard, and pickled carrot strings, for a grand total of $0.37 each.

On another outing, we all went to the circus together. The circus is an important feature of Russian culture. Like many other cities, Kharkiv had a pavilion specially built for this form of entertainment. And, yes, it contained quite a few dancing bears, but scantly clad young ladies seemed to be the most prominent and appreciated feature, at least for the adult men.

Judy and I invited Alex to our dacha several times for dinner, and he invited us to join him one evening to celebrate his nineteenth birthday. Alex met us at the end of the tram line. From there it was a twenty-minute walk in total darkness to the apartment building where he and a roommate shared a single bedroom/study. His roommate had invited his girl friend to share what turned out to be a full multicourse dinner the three of them had cooked in a small kitchen shared with an elderly couple who were the apartment unit's main tenants.

We enjoyed a typical Russian meal: several kinds of hors d'oeuvres, fried chicken, mashed potatoes, two kinds of cabbage salad, pickled tomatoes, pickled egg plant, and two types of bread. All this was washed down with mineral water and homemade vodka or *samagon*. A few rounds of cognac topped off the festive routine of eating, toasting, drinking, and repeat and repeat. Alex had brought most of the food from his parent's house in the Crimea. It was all homemade. We would later have the chance to enjoy this good food once again. As we prepared to leave, Alex showed us how to skip the dark walk and catch a direct bus back to the city.

A Home Stay in the Crimea

Early in the summer when Alex heard that we were planning a sightseeing trip to the Crimean Peninsula, he arranged a few days home stay for us with his parents who lived in a small village in this part of Ukraine. Alex accompanied us for the overnight train ride to the town of Dzhankoy, where we were met by his parents. It was about a two-hour automobile ride to their village.

Like many others in the village, Alex's parents raised pigs and chickens, had a cow, and grew a large vegetable garden. Peasant farmers riding in wooden horse-drawn carts could be seen traveling through the village carrying hand-cut hay. Geese were running everywhere, while goats seemed content to remain within the confines of their tethers. Out in front of most of the little wooden houses were small green stools, each containing an old-fashioned green-tinted gallon-size glass jar ready to be filled from a milk wagon that would pass by each morning.

For two days, Judy and I dined on the products of this village and our host's backyard plot, including many glasses of homemade vodka—always accompanied with the appropriate toast. The vodka and the toasts would go on until bedtime. It is hard to believe I could drink so much, but, like so many other similar occasions, this much vodka drinking did not seem to leave me inebriated as one might expect. Russians had an explanation for this. They would note that normally the drinking of vodka always occurred in the context of eating quite a bit of food. And our guest's food was delightful.

The garden and farm animals were not just a hobby. They were vitally important, especially since many people in the area were experiencing great economic hardship resulting from the closing of a large collective fruit growing and canning operation located near the center of the village. It had provided work for many villagers.

The next day, Alex was our interpreter for a formal meeting. His father, a head accountant, was anxious to have us meet his employer, a sixty-year-old department chief of the regional public electric utility called the All Ukrainian Energy Supply Company. For the occasion of our meeting, the chief's office desk was set out with small copies of both Ukrainian and American flags along with cookies, bottles of Coke, tea glasses, and the ever-present Nescafe instant coffee.

Judy and I started the meeting with polite conversation. I then discussed the need for energy conservation in Ukraine and the problems connected with recently proposed measures to implement a reduction in wasteful electricity use in the country. Secretaries, who had never seen an American before, found excuses to pop in and out of the office, to ask about more refreshments, to bring a new plate of cookies, or just to stare at us through the open office door.

As a young man, the chief had been attracted to the ideology of

Communism and later, after much training, became a propagandist for the party. The assignment had turned out to be a difficult and unsettling experience as, "increasingly I could not resign myself to the wide disparity between the ideal and what I saw in practice," he said. Now, seven years after the fall of the Soviet Russian Empire, the chief indicated to us that the condition of personal freedom "is what I consider to be the most important change that the fall of Communism brought to my life."

The following day, the chief lent us a company car and his personal driver to take Alex, Judy, and me to the city of Yalta on the southern tip of the Crimean Peninsula. We spent over three hours driving through lightly populated farm land and an occasional small village before reaching the city of Simferopol where we turned south and began driving up through a range of mountains, reaching upwards to five thousand feet in elevation. The mountain pass offered several opportunities to take in the view of the northern Black Sea coastline. Within a short time, we had descended to sea level and entered the famous coastal resort city of Yalta.

The area had a distinctive and delightful Mediterranean look with lots of cypress trees and a scattered number of palm trees. The bougainvillea was in blossom. What a welcome sight after a long difficult Kharkiv winter. Either Alex's father or the chief, we were embarrassed to ask who, had booked us into a beautiful historic old hotel right on the beach! It was far more than I wanted to spend on lodging, but what could we do? After all, from their perspective, I was a rich professor from America! Our top (third) floor room looked right out on the long curving beach and blue sea.

We spent four days wandering the beachfront promenade, naturally called Lenin Street, and investigating the shops and the houses of the Russian rich and famous who, it appeared, had all lived in Yalta at one time or another. Names like Chekhov, Gorky, and Stanislavsky were in evidence: in pictures, books, and a wide variety of tourist mementos. Chekhov also had a street named after him.

There was also a Roosevelt Street, a reminder of the famous Yalta Conference that took place here in February 1945 just before the end of the war. Roosevelt had met with Churchill and Stalin to decide the shape of postwar Europe. Judy and I were anxious to visit the site of the conference. It was located a short way up the hill above Yalta in the summer dacha built in 1911 for Russia's last czar, Nicholas II, and his family.

To reach the dacha, we took a shuttle bus part of the way up into the hills behind Yalta. From the bus stop, we walked through at least a couple hundred acre park that had been the autocrat's private grounds surrounding the dacha. The site presented a fabulous view of Yalta and the Black Sea coastline, probably a thousand feet or more down the hill below us. I was reminded a bit of the Hearst Castle at San Simeon, California. The overgrown and unkempt park contained many inoperable fountains, and what seemed like examples of every flower, bush, and tree that might grow in the region.

The czar and his family had only stayed on four brief occasions in the palatial-sized two-story dacha. The family preferred the climate at another summer home located in Finland. Incidentally, Kharkiv also contained a large estate built as one of several way stations for the czars' travels, which, I was told, he never used. It is now a "wedding palace" and is used constantly. It was hard to believe, when thinking just about all the czars' houses we had seen, how much wealth the czar personally lavished upon himself!

The formalities of the Yalta conference had taken place in the dacha's grand ballroom, which is where we headed first. And there it was, the famous round table sitting in the middle of the big room, the chairs all in place just as they were over fifty years ago, little flags signifying the seating arrangement. One could almost smell Stalin's pipe (he only smoked good capitalist tobacco: an American burley and bright mixture) and sense the intrigue that went on in the adjoining anterooms. Pictures of the three leaders revealed Roosevelt to be tired, and tragically, a terminally ill man.

Some historians have judged Roosevelt critically for the compromises he made at the Yalta conference with Stalin regarding the fate of the Central/Eastern European people, whose freedom was bargained away in the false hope that this would bring peace and security in the world. Of course, neither peace nor security came to pass. Standing there alone in the big conference room, I could not help but wonder how the face of this region and the lives of millions of people could have been so different had the stroke of Roosevelt's pen set a different agenda—

one for liberty. We hired a guide. Alex interpreted, and we toured the remainder of the building.

Later, as we walked the city's long beachfront promenade for the last time, we noticed venders selling T-shirts embossed with the famous picture of the three Yalta conference leaders, all sitting next to each other in a little open-air atrium just next to the conference hall. The T-shirt entrepreneurs had modified the picture to place a scantily clad young lady on each man's lap. I kind of liked this modern view of history. Unfortunately, they didn't have my size, and it was time for us to leave Yalta.

As good public transportation was no longer available, we decided to take a taxi for the long ride back to Alex's parents' home. All three of us needed to catch the overnight train back to Kharkiv. Alex started asking cab drivers out front of our hotel what they would charge for such a long trip. The price started at about eighty dollars and decreased the further we walked toward the bus station. In front of the bus station, we were quoted just twenty-five dollars. The driver informed us that he would first have to drive to his apartment to notify his wife that he would be gone for up to six hours. Then it was off we went. We stopped once for the driver to purchase a coke and we got some beer. The driver showed us how to open the bottle caps by prying them off under the edge of the Volga's metal dashboard. Refreshed, we reached Alex's village in time for dinner followed by a trip to the train station.

It was a warm evening and just starting to get dark as we waited for the train to leave the station platform. There were two other trains on adjacent tracks also filling with passengers: one headed for Moscow and the other for Kyiv. A large number of women were running between the trains and up and down the cars selling plastic buckets full of beautiful dark red cherries. Babushkas were hawking other food and drink items from the station platforms to the waiting arms of train passengers, creating quite a chaotic scene. A whistle quickly cleared the tracks, and we were on our way but not without a big sack of cherries. How delightful.

I remember the shopping trips with Sergey Koltakov. He would take us all over town, happily assisting us in the purchase of at least half of a big duffel bag of pirated computer software and music CDs. He was a computer techie and knew where all the best buys were to be had.

Typically, the best buys were in out-of-the-way places. One example starts with a small sign hanging from the street side of an old building. The sign said CDROM with an arrow pointing to a decrepit-looking archway leading into a small courtyard. An old wooden outside door lead to four flights of very rickety wooden stairs. At the top was an old converted apartment containing a couple of rooms full of young people examining the paper covers of several hundred CDs and CD-ROMs slipped into Ziploc bags closed with a paperclip through which a push pin would stick it to the wall. We made our selection, pulled the bags from their paperclips and handed a young attendant our plastic covered paper covers. He disappeared behind a blanket covered door into what was probably the kitchen, and in just a few moments, handed us our selections. The sale was in cash, $2.93 each at the current exchange rate. One CDROM contained all twenty-three albums of the Beatles!

Sergey had spent a year in America as an undergraduate college student. He had taken the opportunity to become well acquainted with McDonald's restaurants. Back in Kharkiv, he worked for a while as a crew trainer for the city's first McDonald's. Sergey also had a great marinade recipe for pork *shashlik* (kebab). He used this recipe as chief cook at our end-of-the-school year backyard party. These chunks of barbecued meat were served with a tangy sauce and large slices of bread to help soak up the sauce and fat that remained on our plate.

Sergey had a photographic memory and sailed through my classes with "A"s, even though he could never get his assignments in on time. Probably the reason had to do with the impossibly heavy course load he was carrying. In addition to my classes and his full-time coursework at the university, Sergey was enrolled in the university equivalent of a required ROTC program. He was also taking weekly Ukrainian language lessons.

If this schedule was not enough for one person, Sergey's year in America had taught him the personal sense of accomplishment that comes with doing volunteer work. Judy and I remember spending a full Sunday on a field trip with Sergey who played guide and big brother to a bus load of about thirty orphans.

On a sunny but cold March day with still quite a bit of snow on the ground, we got up at 5:30, walked a brisk twenty minutes to our rendezvous location, and boarded a chartered old bus at 7:00 in the morning. From there, we went to an orphanage that was operated by the Orthodox Church. There were quite a large number of children playing outside by the time we arrived. It was a dismal-looking place trying to do its best to keep up with all the children who came to places like this for many reasons, often because their parent or parents could not afford to keep them. Some of the children were disabled. They had likely been placed in the orphanage as the result of the still widely held Soviet practice of separating such children from society, community, and family.

Our field trip took us to the small, but very historic city of Poltava. Upon reaching the city, we picked up a local guide to take us for a bus tour of Poltava and the surrounding area. The city sits on the edge of a large bluff overlooking the site of the most famous war in Ukraine. In 1812—the year the British invaded our country and burned Washington DC—the Swedish King fought Peter the Great here for control of the Ukrainian region. Sweden lost, thus giving Russia undisputed rein over the land reaching all the way to the Black Sea. The local museum had a pin-lighted diorama detailing the battle. The diorama scene reminded me of one like it we had seen in Gettysburg. They are very helpful in gaining an overall sense of the battle maneuvers.

On our way back to Kharkiv, we were each given a fresh baked loaf of garlic bread. We opened tins of canned fish that had also been passed around for our dinner in route. The bus began to smell like a seafood cannery. It was a long but enjoyable day. Judy and I got back to our dacha thirteen hours later absolutely exhausted. Sergey was probably less affected by it all. He often went several days without sleep trying to keep up his studies along with all his other activities.

Another student, Yuriy Abramenkov, helped us locate a veterinarian for Pyat, made all the complicated arrangements for our cat export papers, and accompanied Pyat and me for the necessary examination and rabies shot. Yuriy picked us up at our dacha in a cab. His girlfriend was along to "make sure everything went OK," she said. She had previously obtained the necessary "no economic value" certificate that was required to get Pyat out of the country. "Official" pet clubs provided these certificates for a small fee. It was a long trip across town to the veterinarian's office. Pyat was quite young and frightened by her first car ride and proceeded to urinate all over herself and her carrying cage.

The veterinarian wore a white smock that looked more like a butcher's apron at the end of the day. I set a somewhat wet cat on his examination table. He reached into a large plastic bag and fished out a small bottle and syringe. Without first sterilizing the area, he gave Pyat a poke with the needle. The price was $0.50, including the office visit. After the paperwork had been filled out, I tipped him about $2.00, which visibly seemed to embarrass him. It was hard to believe that Pyat needed rabies, economic, and export certificates in order to get out of the country.

Two of my students, Daria Golovcheniko and Yulia Yakovleva, both took Judy and me one cold snowy evening after class for a walk to an old czarist-era mansion near the university. Here we meet and listened to a small group of men and women dedicated to preserving old folk songs. There were eight singers in attendance for their twice weekly meetings. They sang about twelve songs for us, some having their origins in pre-Christian times, that is, pre-tenth-century Ukraine. The folk singers visit the old people in the outlying villages and record what they can of the ancient music, then try to piece it all together. They have become popular enough to travel to folk festivals around the world. We all had an enjoyable evening, even if we did badly miss the dinner hour. The remedy was my treat at a little nearby pizza place. It was then an icy walk home long after dark.

Another of my students, Maria Dikhtyaryova, tried her best to teach us Russian. She spent two afternoons a week at our dacha's little kitchen table patiently going over the fundamentals. Judy stayed with the tutoring long after I gave up. Thinking this would surely be our last year in the CEP, even Judy finally called it quits. We felt badly about the loss of income this would mean for Maria. In the end, she settled for babysitting our apartment and Pyat whenever we were away from the city, which was quite often, it seemed.

I once asked Maria about getting some catnip for Pyat. She had never heard of catnip, and nobody else seemed to know, either, but Maria was trying to be helpful and understood the effect we were describing it had on cats. She wrote down an over-the-counter ingredient that she said was available at any pharmacy. Fortunately, we happened to show her recommendation to another of my students who explained that the ingredient was digitalis! No doubt this ingredient would have sparked a lot of activity in poor little Pyat. Maria was very apologetic when she discovered the harm that her prescription might have caused. She needn't have been. Like my other students, Maria had only tried, sometimes too hard it might seem, to be of help to us.

And certainly not to be left out of the accounting was Igor Ustyuzhyn, a tall rather lanky high school literature teacher, in his thirties, who always had a big smile. On the first day of my fall semester class, Igor volunteered to be our "right-hand man," giving me his telephone number and urging me to call if I needed anything. During our year in Kharkiv, Igor ran an innumerable number of errands for us, especially ones that required Russian or Ukrainian language proficiency. Igor was very helpful right to the last day. He even located a friend with a car and utility trailer to take us and our baggage on our final trip to the train station. For this trip Igor also had an ulterior motive: he needed to get to Kyiv but did not have the money. We offered him a top bunk in our crowded compartment.

Igor often accompanied me home from my late afternoon class for a snack and a drink. He taught me how to eat black caviar on thick white bread covered with loads of butter. He didn't like vodka straight, but I successfully introduced him to the vodka screwdriver. I don't think that there is a person in Eastern/Central Europe who does not have a fondness for orange juice!

In our discussions, I worked hard to provide Igor reasons to be hopeful about the future. Like so many others of my students, he was pessimistic over the possibility of political improvement in Ukraine, but much more so than the others it seemed. The vodka screwdrivers helped lighten Igor up a bit, but skepticism ran deep in his personality nonetheless. Certainly, Igor and the others had reason to be pessimistic. By most accounts, corruption was rampant throughout the government, and evidence of human rights violations brought constant threats from the international community to cut funding and or apply sanctions to the country.

The enumeration of our Kharkiv student friends could go on. There were so many attractive female first names in my classes that I actually sent a long list of them to our daughter Kimberly and her husband

David, who were considering names for their first child, a girl. Ksenia, Katerina (or yna), Tanya, Elena (or Alena), Irina, Katja, Yana, Natalia, Evelina, and Natasha were some of the names on my list that sounded especially nice to my ear. They chose the equally nice sounding name of Natalie. I also suggested some Lithuanian names, but I doubt most Americans would be able to pronounce them.

Time to Kick Back

Our fall CEP retreat was held in Chernivtsi, a small picturesque city on the western edge of Ukraine near the border with Romania. It took Judy and I two full nights of train riding with a day layover in Kyiv to get there, but it was well worth the effort. Sasha, our young country director, had picked this location, I think partly because he had graduated from Chernivtsi's historic and very beautiful university. Constructed in the mid-1800s, it was initially a Hapsburg-period residence. It remains without doubt the city's centerpiece with its multiple stories of red brick, arched leaded-glass windows, and red tiled roofs topped with intricately crafted cupolas.

I envied our CEP lecturer Albert Ringelstein, who was posted here and was thus able to enjoy the architectural beauty and medieval ambiance of this university every day. Alas, he had to put up with some of the most impolite students imaginable. Part of the problem was the result of his chairman making his classes a last minute additional requirement of students who had already finished their coursework for graduation. They were mentally out the door before Albert ever stepped into the classroom. I was awfully glad that I had been given the option to make my classes completely elective.

We held some work sessions at the university. Our assistant director, Sharon, set up her makeshift bank in a corner of our work room. It consisted of a small suitcase with cardboard dividers for each of the U.S. denominations. She made sure that everybody was paid up to date.

We played the rest of the time. Several of us hired two taxis for a day trip into the nearby Carpathian Mountains that form the western border with Romania. We drove through several little alpine-style villages, stopping to have an early dinner in one of them. The food was scrumptious. Two years later, my colleague, Carter Johnson, would spend New Year's Eve in this same mountain region, having an obviously less scrumptious but more authentic meal with the family of a local CEP faculty fellow. His description of the experience, with his permission, is worth quoting in full.

> The place was beautiful, covered with mountains of snow and every farm animal imaginable. When we arrived, they had just performed the annual pig-slaughtering ritual, which takes four huge men to hold the beast down and one to drive a spike in its throat. Then the women clean it up, and they throw chunks of dead pig into soup at every meal. Apparently delicious, but I found it difficult going as you pick up the chunks in your hands and gnaw away on the bone and chew off the meat, gristle, and occasional coarse hair.

Carter enlivened the evening's celebrations with a bottle of expensive Canadian whiskey he had brought from home (he was from Toronto) for just such an occasion. He was somewhat chagrinned that none of the men present knew how to sip whiskey, instead preferring to throw it back in shots.

The following day, a chartered bus took all of us about fifty miles to visit the little town of Khotyn and its magnificent fortress. It was rather complete, but forlorn and totally unattended, a condition that added to the appeal of this nine-hundred-year-old fort that has seen battles involving Poles, Lithuanians, Russians, and Ukrainians. In 1621, Ukrainian Cossack troops defeated a much larger Turkish army here, thus, as the locals like to point out, "saving Europe from Middle-Eastern domination."

We were put up in a quite flamboyant-looking Soviet "Intourist-"style hotel at the edge of the city. On Saturday evening, we made our way to the large dining/ballroom for dinner. We were considerably less than half of the diners present, which was a good thing because the room was almost filled with a large wedding party intent on spending all evening eating and drinking in the company of family and good friends. The bride wore a lacy white gown, a small orchestra was playing, and the mood had become quite celebratory by the time we arrived. It wasn't long before we were all dancing and getting to know one another over glasses of Russian champagne and endless shots of vodka. Almost every drink, it seemed, was preceded with a toast. As the evening wore on, the toasts grew longer and were more often directed, full of emotion, tactful and flattering, toward the women in the room.

I didn't remember too much else about the evening except coming downstairs in the morning with a faint headache and queasy stomach to face an all too common hotel breakfast: boiled eggs, boiled wieners, and canned peas and carrots left over from last night.

Many of us took the Sunday overnight train back to Kyiv. From there Judy, Newell, and I took a domestic plane flight to Kharkiv, arriving Monday morning in time for my classes. The plane was an old Antonov turboprop that made a hell of a lot of noise but got us home in one piece. We did not fly in any local planes again until our posting in Uzbekistan, where we came to know the Antonov quite well. Judy liked to purposively confuse it with the name of past Soviet Chairman Andropov, calling the plane the type that was good only to "climb up and drop off."

Odesa: The Complement to St. Petersburg

Our spring retreat was held in Odesa, the world-famous city on the northern coast of the Black Sea. Odessa reminded me a bit of St. Petersburg. It was mostly built in the late eighteenth century and featured many wonderful examples of classical Georgian architecture. By the early 1800s, Odessa had become a fabulously rich seaport city largely due to the business of exporting Russian grain to Europe. This economic boom didn't last very long. Following our Civil War, Americans began to sell ever larger amounts of grain to Europe. The price was well below the European market, and Odesa would forever look back on its better days.

We arrived in Odesa from Chisinau, Moldova, after a five-hour ride on a very broken-down bus. The bus was so worn out that even my seat back broke and I ended up, accompanied by much laughter, in the lap of the lady sitting in the seat behind me. A drunk had passed out across the backseats but continued to again roll off the seat cushions into the rear stairwell. Gas fumes remained a constant reminder that the bus had long since seen better days.

Judy and I had gone to Chisinau for me to finish up the remainder of my class evaluations and also to give two days of afternoon lectures at what was referred to as an "invisible college." This just meant that there was no physical plant and that classes were portable, scheduled on demand, and could be held anywhere in the city. This type of nongovernmental organization (NGO)–funded arrangement was becoming popular in many locations in the former Iron Curtain countries as the demand for higher education in the social sciences expanded rapidly.

In talking with the students about prejudice and the concept of social distance, I was reminded of the famous test created on this subject in 1927 by the American sociologist Emory Bogardus. He was interested in understanding how Americans reacted to the prospect of having to socialize with members of nationalities they knew little or nothing about. One of the groups in the test was Moldovan. I remember taking this test in an undergraduate sociology class in 1959. I had never heard of Moldova. Now, here I was forty years later, teaching about this subject in, of all places, Moldova! The college gave me a small honorarium, which Judy promptly spent on a new Italian leather purse. What fun, and this time we made sure to have multiple entry visas so that we could get back into Ukraine.

It was warm and lightly raining as we pulled into the Odesa bus station in the early evening. We were thankful to have arrived and very grateful to get out of the bus for good. There seemed to be more than the usual number of people out in the streets of Odesa. As our taxi entered the downtown section, the driver was unable to reach our hotel on account of the mob of mostly young people filling the sidewalks and much of the streets. We were to find out later it was April Fool's evening. A big celebration was underway. It seemed rather fitting that Odesa host such a festive event as a large number of very prominent humorists were from this city.

We left the cab and managed to carry our bags the remaining distance to the beautiful old turn-of-the-century hotel where we met up with all of the other CEPers from our region. It was noisy outside the hotel almost all night, but our room was quiet, and what a delight to stay in such a charming place. Our ornate accommodations were composed of two high-ceilinged rooms with a bathroom containing the largest shower space I had ever seen.

We had arrived in Odesa far too early in the year to witness the even larger crowds of people who would flock to this party city and its beaches later during the summer. The Black Sea was still very cold; there were even a few pockets of soggy snow remaining in shady sections of the ground. This did not prevent a few hardy CEPers from taking a quick swim anyway, just to be able to say that they had done it.

The weather was nice, so Judy and I spent most of our free time just walking the streets of the city, soaking up its beauty. We lingered around the park at the top of the Potemkin Steps, a famous series of broad steps and landings that climb practically all the way from the water's edge several hundred feet up to a park running along the edge of the city. The park provided an almost uninterrupted view of the Black Sea. There were people selling food and tourist things. I bought several Soviet Army belts complete with their brass buckles emblazoned with the red star and crossed hammer and sickle. Just think, these belts and buckles were now just their former Cold War enemy's tourist souvenirs. It felt a bit like the old days of plunder, except there wasn't much intrinsic value to a brass belt buckle. Nonetheless, the experience made me think about how social reality is shaped, how dangerous it had become in this instance, and how rapidly it can change.

Judy and I accompanied our colleagues on a guided tour of the network of catacombs that ran under Odesa. We learned that the complex is one of the most extensive anywhere in the world, having been made through the removal of stone to build the city. During World War II, a large contingent of Ukrainian resisters lived in this network of tunnels for over two years during the Romanian Nazi occupation of Odesa. Parts of the catacombs, which run almost directly underneath the city, have been turned into a museum. It would have been hard not to feel a great deal of sympathy for what these people endured and for the courage they exhibited. Deep underground were all the basic necessities for maintaining what had to be an obviously miserable life dedicated to making the Nazi's life equally if not even more miserable, nasty, and, hopefully short.

Chernobyl

I was reluctant to write about this subject until I realized how strongly many Americans associate Chernobyl with Ukraine. It was not a subject I thought very much about while living in Ukraine, probably because Chernobyl was quite a distance northwest of Kharkiv and the April 25, 1986, explosion had not spread nuclear contamination in this region. It also seemed that, at least as a historical occurrence, the matter was not often the subject of conversation or was much written about in the popular press as far as we could tell. My students never brought the subject up, nor did the CEP staff talk about it except to warn us not to eat fish taken from the Dnipro River that runs through Kyiv, a location much closer, about seventy-five miles, to the accident scene.

It is quite possible that a lot of people may still be in shock, considering the immensity of the disaster and large number of deaths it produced. No local person ever brought up the subject in conversation with me. It had been twelve years since the tragedy. Was it possible that most people had just gone ahead with their lives, letting the shortness of human memory run its course? There may not have been much to talk about anyway as government officials continued to be very reluctant to release information, and no highly charged lawsuit or large compensation program was going on that might have stirred up old memories.

What was said about Chernobyl in the media involved a continuing debate over the advisability of having restarted the remaining portion of the reactor. Certainly Ukraine needed the electric power it could generate. There was also the pressing concern of what to do about a large number of skilled nuclear plant operatives and managers who had been out of work for a very long time. It was hard for me to believe that anyone would contemplate restarting any portion of the Chernobyl plant. Most European countries felt as I did. The Scandinavian countries had not only adamantly opposed restarting the plant, but were on record as willing to pay for its complete decommissioning. They had received a heavy dose of wind-born radiation from Chernobyl and were anxious that this did not happen again. However, negotiations had failed to prevent the plant from being returned to production.

On the day the reactor was to be restarted, the news carried the story of a threatened strike by the plant workers who were owed as much as four month's back wages. Other nuclear plant workers were saying that their wages were in arrears too, and they would also strike Ukraine's other thirteen reactors, bringing the whole power grid to a halt. Intense negotiation averted these threatened actions, thus allowing the plant to begin production.

Chernobyl will remain a world-class symbol of disaster. Judy and I visited the Chernobyl museum in Kyiv, which was dedicated to preserving the gruesome story and to documenting its radiation effects, especially on the children. The museum was not a very large place nor were the displays particularly elaborate. There were a lot of pictures and a diorama that would slowly reconfigure itself to exhibit each of the stages in the explosion and fire that destroyed one of the main reactors. There was no safety containment dome or shell covering the nuclear reactors, so the fire was able to spew its lethal radioactive smoke directly into the atmosphere.

The museum contained quite enough exhibits to leave me with some particularly strong impressions. The explosion's release of deadly radiation had taken an immediate and death-dealing toll on approximately four thousand Ukrainians. Other innocent and unsuspecting people would die in Belarus, whose southern border was only a few miles from Chernobyl. I had not realized how extensive and serious and long term the painful effects had been. Moreover, it was absolutely dumbfounding to learn how irresponsible the Soviet authorities had been in overseeing the facility, and then when it exploded, they joked about it while sending hundreds of unsuspecting workmen to their death in the most ignorant and primitive effort imaginable to put out the fire and clean up the highly radioactive contamination. Such efforts were like tilting at windmills.

Some of the clean-up crew were obviously considered expendable. These individuals were given shovels and wheelbarrows and sent to the site armed against the massive radiation with nothing more than rubber boots. They were touted with the appellation "Liquidators" as though one could naively liquidate deathly radiation effects that would last a million years. These brave workers all died within two weeks. They were buried in lead coffins.

This naive and shamelessly cynical attitude of the authorities could also be seen in the name of the Soviet Politburo's official Chernobyl

Commission, which actually translates as "Commission for Liquidation of Breakdown." At about the time of our museum visit, I had occasion to read an interview with past Soviet President Mikhail Gorbachev that was published in the March 1998 issue of *The Ukrainian* magazine. He said he was shocked to hear the commission members react to the incident by saying that breakdowns had occurred before and the best and only thing to do was "drink a lot of vodka and have a hearty meal."

Some of the most poignant photographs in the museum told the story of the large number of people, several hundred thousand families, both Ukrainian and Belarusian, who were displaced as the result of radiation contamination of their towns and villages. It seemed such a contrast, as well as a lesson on the incredibly uneven speed of change, to think that highly sophisticated nuclear technology, the epitome of modernity, could exist in the midst of peasant communities, a place where people lived right out of the set of *Fiddler on the Roof,* complete with thatched-roof homes surrounded by farm animals. I thought about the large coal-fired power plants located on Indian reservations in the American Southwest, but this was nowhere near the scale of the Soviet's incautious Faustian bargain with the atom that gained these people absolutely nothing but for which they suffered everything as a consequence.

Displaced from the only place they knew, ignorant of the invisible radiation remaining in the region, many of the displaced peasants continue to attempt to return to their homes, in many cases undeterred by the ineffectual threats of authorities to stay away. The region with its empty homes and farms has also become a magnet to even poorer people from other ex-Soviet republics. How poor does one need to be in order to find such bleak prospects attractive? I left the museum reflecting on the inability of seventy years of Communism to improve, even infinitesimally, the lives of such a large segment of its people. What a shoddy operation it had been.

At Christmas, we had learned that both of our daughters were pregnant. We would be grandparents toward the end of summer. Shortly before we left Kharkiv for the last time, we received a separate e-mail letter from each of our twin daughters. Kimberly and Karen had both been to their doctor for an ultrasound examination. From

Germany Kim wrote; "Congratulations, you are going to have a granddaughter!" From Idaho, Karen wrote three days later that there was "an 80 percent chance it would be a boy!" These e-mails served only to further heighten our anticipation of the first two grandchildren that were about to arrive in our life.

We stayed home the following year, Judy flew to Germany for our granddaughter's birth, and, of course we were both in Boise to celebrate the birth of our first grandson. Yet, as the year reached its end, we began to have an antsy feeling and could not resist the thought of returning once again to the CEP for just one more episode in having the carefree time of our life. It was also just too hard to turn down the chance to finally be able to live in Central Asia.

So off we went to Uzbekistan. However, having grandchildren had marked a major turning point in our life. Although neither of us understood the impact of the change initially, it was no longer quite the same feeling for just the two of us to escape to exotic lands, totally unfettered by the cares of the world. We thoroughly enjoyed our year in Uzbekistan, but we also noticed that living so far away from home increasingly began to feel isolating. This was surely because the attraction of grandparenthood was growing stronger.

5

Tea and Totalitarianism in Uzbekistan

The Land of the Golden Horde

In August 2000, Judy and I had come fairly close to being posted to the Central Asian region. This time we got our wish. We were on our way to Tashkent, the capital of the former Soviet Republic of Uzbekistan.

Uzbekistan is located about in the center of Central Asia. It is the most populated, at twenty-two million, of the several "stans" of this vast region. "Stan" means "country of," and so we were in the country of the Uzbeks. Similar "stans," several of which were once part of the Soviet Russian Empire, indicate the territory of the Kazak, Krgyz, Tajik, and Turkmen people. Adding "stan" to the ethnic identity of the people thus provides the name of the country.

The Central Asian region has remained very remote and little known to the rest of the world. In part, this resulted from the Soviet practice of forcibly isolating its people. They in turn, knew even less about the world outside their confinement.

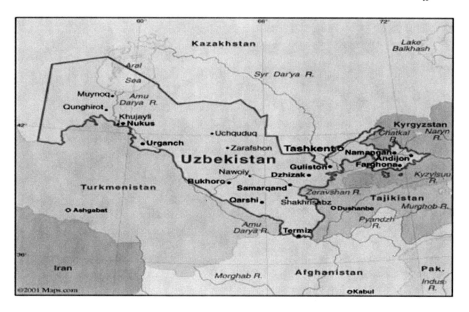

Uzbekistan. Notice the angular lines in the western area and islands of land penetrating Kyrgyzstan. These are the results of the colonial practice of inventing a country's national boundaries.

The vast Central Asian region of deserts and mountains was first conquered by Alexander the Great. It was again subjugated by Genghis Khan, who came out of the region of Mongolia and formed an empire or "khanate," which stretched from China all the way through Russia into parts of Europe. I had been reacquainted with the story of Genghis Khan while in Ukraine. Now, Judy and I would feel his historical influence practically everywhere we turned. It was the largest empire ever formed in the world. His domain came to be known as the land of the Golden Horde.

*Judy and Kimberly stand in front of Tamerlane's (1336-1405)
statue in downtown Tashkent, Uzbekistan.*

Roughly two hundred years after Genghis Khan, in 1336, an individual from a small village near Samarkand, in what is now Uzbekistan, managed to accumulate such power as not only to subdue what remained of the Golden Horde, but to spread his armies through much of their former territory: from the Mediterranean to China and south to India. Known as Tamerlane, he located his capital in Samarkand, where, showing his good side, he set about making it into reportedly the most beautiful city in all Central Asia. He was also gratuitously brutal, maybe even more so than his predecessors. Like Genghis Khan, he sometimes slaughtered every inhabitant of the cities he conquered, piling up a mountain of their skulls at the main gates to the cities as a threat to those, who in the future, might attempt to resist him.

Uzbekistan and the Central Asian region have known nothing other than the power of a *khan* or strong man. More recently in history, the region and its khans was the location for historic Cold War–style maneuvering. Referred to as "the Great Game," the struggle was between Czarist Russia on its north and the British to the south.

The British occupied India and wished to use much of Central Asia as a buffer between themselves and the Russians. Official and unofficial agents, secretive maneuvers, and soldierly forays between these two powers spread across Central Asia during the nineteenth century. In the long run, the Russians prevailed, and the czar became the new "khan of khans" for the region.

The Soviet period of occupation followed, bringing a series of new "khans," especially Stalin, and a great deal of change to Central Asia, much of it forcibly. Agriculture was collectivized, cities were modernized, and women were granted equality and told not to wear the *burka,* their traditional full-length coverings. The Soviet policy of militant atheism resulted in Stalin's closing of over twenty-five thousand mosques in Central Asia, ultimately leaving most Uzbeks, along with most of Soviet Central Asia, somewhat more moderate in their Muslim faith.

Fancying himself an expert on ethnic matters, Stalin had personally drawn up boundaries where none had previously existed, and thus in 1924, at the stroke of a pen, he created the "republics" whose borders now define the present newly independent countries of Central Asia. These boundaries did not so much try to reflect ethnic concentrations as they attempted to pacify through a policy of "divide and conquer." One outcome of these gerrymandered divisions was that Uzbekistan ended up containing a sizable number of Tajiks, and Tajikistan, which shares its eastern border ipso facto came to be made up of about one quarter Uzbeks. Such border turns and twists means that today Uzbekistan also contains several strange little "islands" of sovereign property under its ownership in neighboring Tajikistan. When the Soviet Union fell, each of the "stans" watched, quite helplessly, as their authoritarian Communist Party secretary become their new "khan," aka president.

Each former Soviet Central Asian republic declared its independence as a brand-new country while keeping almost every element of its prior Soviet social structure and political economy. And, naturally, each new country sought mainly to reinvent itself by creating and touting a new nationalism. The most visible result in Uzbekistan was the removal of all its Lenin statues and the replacement of many of them with the personage, normally seated on his horse, of the thirteenth-century conqueror Tamerlane, now with the added title, "The Great."

Cooling Our Heals at the Airport, or Where Is Zarbog Street?

The stories in this chapter begin with our arrival at the Tashkent airport. The arrival was a memorable one, but not for the usual reasons. Judy and I took the opportunity to make a learning experience out of what turned out to be a very long ordeal. We had not been met at the airport as planned. This had left us stranded in the middle of the night, rendered almost immobile by our luggage, generally unable to communicate with the people around us, and facing not only a profoundly new culture, but one which included a rather undecipherable new system of street addresses unknown even to most of the taxi drivers.

Irena An, our Tashkent CEP administrative assistant, in front of our hotel in Almaty, Kazakstan

The story began August 15, 2000, with us sitting on our baggage out in front of the Tashkent International Airport. We had arrived about 1:00 AM. Seven hours had passed and we still were waiting for Irena An, our CEP representative to appear. By 8:00 AM, we started calling the CEP office; however, it appeared there was nobody available to answer our many calls. Finally, we decided to take a taxi to the CEP office, which was located at 31 Zarbog Street. If necessary, we could wait out front of that building just as well as the airport.

There must have been at least eight or ten self-styled Tashkent "taxi" drivers standing next to Judy and me and our new CEP colleague, Carter Johnson. They were each sounding out different pronunciations of the printed address appearing on a small sheet of paper I had handed to one of the drivers. Nobody seemed to recognize the name "Zarbog Street," especially so as the writing was not in Cyrillic letters. We never thought to rewrite it in Russian as all the signs around us were written in English. Almost an hour passed with many variations of the word being offered, but with no consensus. A few drivers dropped out of the circle as new ones arrived, but most persisted, motivated by the prize of an immense taxi fare.

We were joined by an old man with an even older baggage cart, anxious to carry the nearly 500 pounds of baggage, including our cat, Pyat, and her carrier, to the cars of the lucky taxi drivers. We would need at least two cars. Finally, leaving to make a telephone call, one enterprising driver returned with what he claimed to be knowledge of how to get to 31 Zarbog Street. We decided to trust his air of confidence and broad smile. He and one other driver were able to take us to the correct address, but not before they had each made more than three week's worth of wages from our two ten-dollar fares.

We arrived at the CEP office at 31 Zarbog Street, hoping that Irena, our missing local contact might be in her office. She wasn't, but staff members showed us where there was a clean toilet and made us some hot tea. We were able to set up a proper bathroom for Pyat. Our program assistant was supposed to have picked us up at the airport more than nine hours ago! I started thinking back over the whole experience.

Judy and I had sat next to our baggage out in front of the airport most of the night. At least we had been able to share our misery and first impressions of Central Asia with Carter Johnson. We had first met Carter while waiting to transfer planes at the Istanbul airport.

We had flown in from Frankfurt, he from London. We each had the same final leg of our flight to make to Tashkent. Wearing a pair of green leather shoes, Carter had immediately signaled his delightful, independent character. He was a young Canadian with an MA from the London School of Economics who was beginning his first year as a CEP lecturer.

Now we were all cooling our heels out in front of the Tashkent airport. It had been more than twenty-four hours earlier that Judy's and my plane flight left Frankfurt. The adrenalin rush brought on by landing in such an exotic place as Tashkent and all the bureaucratic folderol of going through customs was beginning to wear off. Lack of sleep and adequate nourishment was beginning to catch up with us. The situation was really urgent for our cat that had been in her carrier and not able to make a bathroom call since before we had left for the Frankfurt airport!

We continued to sit on our baggage out front of the airport, in the wee hours of the morning darkness, surrounded with duffel bags, boxes, and assorted containers. We were repeatedly approached by a young man who told us of the high price of hotels. He offered to take us to his grandmother's apartment where we could get a few hours of sleep. Leery of his intentions, we politely, then insistently declined, but did allow him to change money for us even though we knew such a transaction to be illegal. We needed money to buy food and drink, and the single official exchange in the airport would not open for several more hours.

As dawn approached, a student working part-time as a security guard walked over to us to enquire if we wanted something to eat. He took me across the street in front of the airport to a vender who was rapidly selling *piroshki,* a Russian favorite, consisting of small fried pies filled with onions and ground meat. They were being kept hot on a large baking sheet covered with a thick felt blanket. I bought several of these delicious, however greasy, morsels. The three of us washed our meal down with tea sold from a small kiosk, while continuing to watch over our large stack of baggage.

The unplanned wait provided ample time to contemplate the matter of luggage. We were surrounded by six large U.S. Army duffel bags, a big cardboard box, a laptop computer and portable printer, several carry-on items, and a cat carrier. As usual, we were traveling way over the standard weight limit. Also overweight, Carter's luggage was even more interesting and creative. It consisted of a large backpack fully shrink-wrapped in clear plastic: like his green shoes, something I had not seen before. However, the centerpiece of his luggage ensemble was a giant, almost coffin-sized, blue and white plastic multipurpose container. Numerous yards of duct tape had been wrapped around this monstrosity, which was considerably outside the parameters of acceptable luggage dimensions.

My thoughts were interrupted by foul, eye-watering smoke. A metal cigarette butt receptacle anchored into the concrete nearby had filled to overflowing and was beginning to smolder. There was no place to move our baggage as the area was filled with people, more every hour, who were crowding around the airport's front doors and big glass windows hoping to get a glimpse of arriving passengers, maybe friends or relatives, making their way through the last of several customs and baggage checkpoints. A few people held out small signs containing a name or organizational acronym. We checked each carefully, however none were for us. By 9:30 AM, we had decided to leave the airport for better or worse.

Both Carter and I had given advance e-mail notification to Irena of our arrival date and time. Each of us had received confirmation of this information. Unknown to us, Irena had written the date on her planner as one day later. At least our two taxi drivers had been correct in their address. All of our baggage was off-loaded in a carport next to the Open Society Assistance Foundation building where the CEP had its office. Unhurried by any sense of urgency, Irena didn't arrive until 11:30 AM. She was absolutely stunned with embarrassment when she discovered us in her office.

So where was Zarbog Street? It was right where it should have been, of course. Granted, it was a fairly out of the way residential address for an unofficial "taxi" driver to know right off. More to the point, Zarbog Street, like most other streets in Tashkent, had been changed beyond the recognition of most people, including even the most knowledgeable taxi drivers.

The changes occurred in two ways. The main source of consternation for Uzbeks had been passage of the national "Law about Alphabet."

Since declaring its independence in 1992, a new sense of Uzbek national identity had inspired an attempt to rapidly shift to Roman from Cyrillic script. Cyrillic was a Russian imposition no longer seen as appropriate. However, this was the second major language change in a little more than two generations. First, Cyrillic had replaced Arabic, and even now some insistent nationalistic and religious groups were pressing hard to return to Arabic. This was a losing effort, however, the idea having been quickly overruled by the quite dictatorial President Islam Karimov, as contrary to the country's Western-looking development and need to adapt to global communications technology. I suspect that the move also made it easier to control the perceived growth of religious extremism. Either way, the move to the Roman standard meant that most people now found themselves virtually illiterate once again.

To complicate matters even further, Uzbekistan had renamed most of its streets, this also being a part of its effort to quickly shed its Soviet past. Gone as well were the landmark statues of famous Soviet political and military figures—including the many iterations of Lenin that might be used to triangulate a particular location. Some of the pedestals remained bare while others now contained a personage more appropriate to Uzbekistan's new sense of nationalism.

Zarbog means "garden" in Uzbek. The street was formally Roza Luksemburg (Rosa Luxemburg) Street. European history students will remember her name as probably the most famous member of the *Spartakusbund,* the precursor of the German Communist Party. Rosa was murdered in Berlin in 1919 by someone from the officially illegal *Freikorps*, an ultra-nationalist paramilitary organization, many of whose most promising killers would later form the basis of Hitler's storm troupers. Rosa Luxemburg became a martyr in the Soviet Union where many cities named a square or prominent street after her. For example, not much over a year earlier, the two of us had spent several afternoons sitting out front of McDonald's, the icon of capitalism, gazing out on Kharkov's Luksemburg Square. How ironic was that!

Judy and I needed to visit the CEP office on Zarbog Street quite frequently over the year. To get to there, I would walk into the street in front of our apartment, wave, (or "flutter" as the locals referred to such signaling) my hand at a passing car, which would usually jam on the brakes and pull off to the side, thereby instantly becoming a taxi.

A famous landmark near my intended location was given to the driver through an open window, a price was negotiated, and, almost always successful, we were off, all with a minimum of language being spoken.

In transit, I might have given directions by indicating that we should turn off of what was formally Rustaveli Street, now Usman Nosir Street, named for a prominent early-twentieth-century Uzbek poet, and go to…, and so on in this manner. However, this approach along with my extremely limited abilities in either Russian or Uzbek would likely become a recipe for confusion. Instead, to get there, I would usually just reiterate to the driver the name, Red Hotel. Located just a few blocks from my destination, when we got to the hotel, I would then tell the driver, "Continue a little further." "Turn there." "Turn here." As I almost always sat in the front seat, I also found hand motions to be quite useful.

There were no hard feelings over the long wait at the airport. All was well that ended well. Apologies for failing to meet us were made. Our program assistant had our apartment rented and ready. The cat got her proper sandbox, and the school year began successfully. Tashkent quickly turned out to be a fascinating place, more than fulfilling our most important reason for traveling such a long way.

Touristfarting

Our life in Central Asia began with a quick start. In the first two days, we changed apartment flats to one with an elevator and at least minimal air-conditioning, rifled through our duffel bags in order to find enough stuff to pack a couple of small backpacks, and were back at the airport for a flight to Bishkek, the capital of neighboring Kyrgyzstan. From there, we joined approximately thirty other CEP visiting lecturers and local staff from throughout Central Asia to make a four-hour bus ride to Lake Issyk-Kul for three days of orientation, business, and pleasure.

The plane flight was the first of several we would make in small Soviet-period Yak jets. The ride was often quite bumpy, making our tummies a bit queasy. We would soon learn to just say "We are Yaking over" to here or there. In fact, we averaged one flight every ten days during our stay in Tashkent—and lived to tell about it!

The little Yak airplanes looked sleek and fresh from the outside. They were newly painted with the bright blue, white, and green colors of

Uzbekistan, or one of the other newly independent Central Asian countries. They each seemed to have had quite a fleet of them. In contrast, the inside of these planes did not receive a similar freshening up, showing, instead, a typically high state of dinginess and wear. The seat belts never seemed to work, and the seats were low backed and folded forward like the front seat of an automobile coupe. There was no overhead storage, so most people put their carry-ons in empty seats, even up and down the isle. Needless to say, it was always a good feeling to be back on the ground. Praise Allah!

On this first flight, the stewardess gave us a glass of water before disappearing through the arched front cabin door where she remained for the entire trip. The flight went east over a mass of snowcapped mountains. About an hour and a half later, we descended into Bishkek, itself bordered by high snowy mountains on three sides.

Once on the ground, we were transported to the American University of Kyrgyzstan, the single oasis of U.S. culture and higher educational practice throughout entire Central Asia. After lunch at the school cafeteria, including a bout of giddiness over the good food and clean surroundings, we all gathered out front of the school at the entrance to a small park to await the arrival of our bus to Lake Issyk-Kul. Next to the sidewalk, just inside the park, were the life-sized statues of Marx and his friend and financial benefactor Fredrick Engels, seated together engaged in conversation. Marx was probably explaining socialism to Engels, who, the son of a prominent English textile manufacturer, was probably telling Marx about what he had seen of the misery of working-class life.

Our bus was brightly painted on all four sides with the word "Touristfart." This translates roughly as meaning in German "a taker of tourists." I knew that Bishkek had a sizable German community that had resulted from Stalin's forced relocation there of German Russians during World War II. Was this where this bus description originated? Anyway, it was obviously good for a few laughs.

We left the city going east through sprawling outskirts composed of little weathered one-story frame houses and finally crossed an expansive agricultural area. The ride followed a river through dry grass-covered foothills that grew steeper the further eastward we went. Several canyons later, eventually the narrow valley through which we had been traveling opened out on Lake Issyk-Kul, the second largest glacial lake in the world.

It is 2,800 feet deep, four times the size of the glacial Lake Tahoe in California, and, like Lake Tahoe, it was mostly bordered by mountains. The most impressive on the east was the snow-topped peaks of the Tian Shan mountain range, on the other side of which was China!

Modern yurta dwellers (note the boom box hanging beside the lady of the house). Issyk-Kul, Kyrgyzstan.

We had traveled through a number of small villages during the course of our bus drive to the lake. There were more villages scattered along the lake shore. Most structures in these villages were one and two story mud brick, looking a little bit like American Indian dwellings one might see near Taos, New Mexico. Here and there were picturesque felt-constructed yurts (or *yurta* or *ger*), the traditional nomadic home used by people in this part of Central Asia. With the exception of one yurt, which was sitting on a wooden trailer—a sort of Central Asian RV—the rest of the yurts looked permanent in contrast to their original use by nomads. Writing about the yurt for our CEP *Guide to Life and Teaching in Eastern Europe and Eurasia,* CEP alumnus Tom Wood added something of his firsthand knowledge of yurts and yurt activities and etiquette. Here is an interesting quote from his observations:

Step to the left, the male side when entering. When having dinner in a yurt in a rural area: The sheep's head. Oh yes, you do have to eat it. The most honored guest must eat the brains, via prying open the cranial plates of the unfortunate sheep. The eyeballs are for the second most [important] guest. Prayers over meals, ("grace") are normally said at the end of the meal, not at the beginning. The Moslem prayer involves passing your cupped hands downwards over your face at the end. Also, in Kyrgyzstan, horses aren't just for riding. That tenderloin you're about to bite into ain't prime USDA beef.

Apricots were in season. The fruit had been mostly picked and was now drying on the flat roofs of buildings everywhere. The apricot pits are soaked in a salt solution and roasted to a point that the nut can be easily extracted. The technique for opening the pit is to force one half of another pit into the crack created by the roasting process and pry and twist until the two halves come apart. Eating the apricot nut, with its salty taste and flavor of arsenic, is a national pastime everywhere in Central Asia. These nuts are illegal in the United States, but they certainly do not seem to adversely affect the millions of people in this part of the world who have been eating them for hundreds of years! At one time it was popular among some Americans to travel to Mexico to purchase these nuts, thinking that they helped to cure cancer.

Dried fish from the lake were equally plentiful. Besides appearing in the open markets, we first saw them hung in long lines strung between trees and any other upright object along the bumpy highway. A quick "fish stop" could be made by the traveler. We initially sampled the fish and the fruit at a roadside bathroom stop. Hawkers stood around our bus with its bright reddish orange touristfart insignias, selling these items and much more. I bought a Russian beer to wash down my sample of fish while trying not to be smothered by the smoke from a large number of nearby char-braziers cooking up *shashlyk* (kabob) made from chunks of mutton. Other grills were roasting corn on the cob.

We stayed three days at the edge of the lake in the "Castle," the most oddly constructed hippie-style place one could imagine. What appeared to be a single original building had been continuously added to and extended with one-of-a-kind structures that eventually covered more than an acre of land. There were tree-house bedrooms, a sprawling waterfall/swimming pool, and several flower gardens. Judy and I stayed in the castle tower. Our octagonal room had the most sumptuous gilded bathroom we had yet to encounter anywhere in the world.

Our castle quarters were quite a contrast to those of a group of twenty Germans who were camping (touristfarting?) in their specially constructed double-decker bus, complete with kitchen, bath facility, and convertible sleeping bunks. Their bus was parked just past the castle moat near the lake's edge. They had come from China and were on their way back to Germany via Uzbekistan, through the Caspian Sea area, Russia, and Ukraine. They would get a new guide in each country while taking a little more than two months to make the trip. One can travel the reverse direction as well.

Handicraft broker, Issyk-Kul, Kyrgyzstan

Before leaving Lake Issyk-Kul, Judy and I again stopped by the home of a lady, probably in her seventies, who made, or brokered for others, a variety of handicrafts mostly in felt, carpet material, or silk. Acting on a tip from our country director, we had visited this lady and placed our order soon after arrival at the lake and now some of the items were ready. The rest we would pick up on our second visit to the lake in October. With no knowledge of the language, we were able to conclude our purchase orders, including those we would pick up later. It is interesting how the international language of the consumer, involving lots of pointing and other hand signs, is adequate for these occasions. And, of course, money can be counted out regardless of language. This would be our experience throughout our stay in Central Asia.

Following our return to Tashkent, it took both of us several weeks to recover from *giardia*—a fairly serious parasitic infection that frequently strikes foreign visitors soon after their arrival in Central Asia. We had picked up the bug while at the lake, but we called it "Tashkent Tummy" just the same. As the symptoms fit closely the description provided in our travel book, we just purchased the recommended medicine (tinidazole) over the counter at a local pharmacy. It was made in Bulgaria and was so inexpensive that we wondered if it could be any good. It seemed to work. In spite of our tummies, Judy and I spent most of the next three weeks getting used to Tashkent, getting my office and small library quarters at the university ready, meeting my initial classes, and trying to cope and adjust to the consistently hot, well-over-a-hundred-degree weather.

Back to Issyk-Kul

In late October, we again made our way to Lake Issyk-Kul, this time for a four-day CEP semiannual retreat. I had suggested a desert location near Bukhara in central Uzbekistan where we could take camel rides, among other activities. However, we were told by our country director that the travel logistics to get all the CEPers from three Central Asian countries to such an out of the way place would have been too challenging. Instead it was another "Yak over" plane ride and another glass of water, although this time in a turboprop Antonov 10. I had forgotten, from our trip while in Ukraine, how noisy these planes were and how much they looked like they were made out of old tank parts. Our ride to the lake was again by a "touristfart" bus, but before we could get to the bus, we first had to spring Judy out of "detention" at the Bishkek airport.

After retrieving our bags from the airport's single carousal, we were to exit through passport control and customs stations into a second room. I went through first. After waiting for Judy, it became obvious that she had been detained for some reason. It turned out that her visa and passport numbers did not correspond. As she told me the story later, the passport officer indicated that she would need to remain confined to the first area until she could be put on the next flight back to Uzbekistan! Corruption appeared to be rearing its ugly, but predictable head again. This time with the help of local CEP personnel, money passed hands and Judy was allowed to rejoin me to depart the airport.

This incident again brought to mind the continuing Soviet legacy of personal scrutiny, restriction, and corruption, all of which still characterizes so much of life in authoritarian Central Asia. However, I should mention that there was a glimmer of progress I noted as we left the Tashkent airport earlier that afternoon. Below the usual Russian-language PASSPORT CONTROL sign had been added an English translation that read "Passport Service." I was told by Victoria Levinskaya, my Russian Uzbek colleague, that *service* is a word with no Russian equivalency. Somebody had to have deliberately chosen this word for its English meaning. Things are getting better I thought. And to think that McDonald's probably had something to do with it!

One further example shows just how far away the Soviet system was from understanding the meaning of service, but how quickly all of this may be changing. I got an e-mail letter from one of my best students shortly after arriving home from Uzbekistan. Having just graduated from a prestigious university in Uzbekistan, my student had applied for a job with a foreign airline company. "Please tell me what the words 'Customer Service Officer' means," he had inquired. He was about to go for an interview and wanted to know what suggestions I might offer. I mentioned several things, concluding with the admonition to look the interviewer in the eye and make sure to wear some deodorant. Both are considered essential to customer service, I wrote.

This time at the lake we stayed in a giant Soviet-era sanatorium. Incidentally, the slightly different spelling of our resort hotel from the English word *sanitarium* signifies that we were located in something quite different from a convalescent home or a hospital for the mentally ill! The Soviets built their sanatoriums as hotel complexes for the holiday leisure of working people. In addition to having hotel rooms, these places usually could be counted upon to contain a pool, sauna, doctor, hairdresser, a place to get a massage or a manicure, plus a wide range of other indoor and outdoor activities. Today, many sanatoriums tend to be underutilized and not well maintained, a bit threadbare and always drafty, but predictably gaudy and oversized in every dimension.

Fortunately, our sanatorium was a notch above most, the literal flagship of Central Asian sanatoriums. It was called the Aurora, built in the best of "Soviet modern" design to look vaguely like the famous navy cruiser whose cannon shot in the harbor at St. Petersburg in 1917 signaled the start of the Bolshevik Revolution. The real ship *Aurora* still sits at the same place in the harbor in St. Petersburg where Judy and I had a chance to tour it three years earlier.

Our purpose at the lake was fun mixed with business. Among our business activities we were preparing for our annual Regional Student Conference, which would bring CEP students from five Central Asian countries together at this same place later in the year to deliver papers in an academic conference format. Our theme for the conference was: "Creating Democratic Central Asia: Diversity, Interdependence, and Development." Rather optimistic I thought, but then such statements usually were, such being their function. I wished that the actual accomplishment of this state of affairs could happen as easily as it was to put those words on paper!

We also selected a few student paper proposals from outside the region. I was quite proud to see that one of my former students, Yana Tsymbrovska, from Kharkiv had been invited. While in Tashkent, I had helped her via e-mail with her research proposal. Yana had been a sophomore in economics at Kharkiv National Aerospace University when, by accident, she heard of my social policy class from her tram seatmate while traveling to school. She was very poor, had bad, but correctable eyesight, yet still managed to do very well in her studies as well as to sew the few simple but fashionable items of clothing that constituted her school wardrobe. Judy and I remembered her as a very polite person with a broad warm smile. We looked forward to seeing her again and listening to her paper on "Media Economy in Central Asia: Looking Forward, Moving...Back?"

It was a rather scary experience in more ways than the usual stage fright for students from the region to participate in these conferences. We had heard several, but unconfirmed, stories about censorship and intimidation surrounding student's written personal expression on sensitive themes involving government operation or policy. Our organization liked to publish the best of the conference papers, which were then circulated in universities throughout Eurasia. The year before we arrived, a few Central Asian students had declined the opportunity to be published for fear of the problems such publicity might create. One student, on reentering Uzbekistan following attendance at a conference held outside of the country, had been threatened with revocation of his external passport (everybody also had to carry an internal one) after airport militia found a copy of his conference paper to be "threatening to state interests."

Our first personal experience with authoritarian censorship and control was when some of my and Carter's students declined to attend a voluntary weekly informal "Current Events Discussion Club" Judy and I had organized for Wednesday evenings at our apartment flat. The students felt uncomfortable around criticism of the government, especially given that meetings of this kind and size (twenty to thirty individuals) were illegal without prior permission from the government, which, we were told, was usually not given.

I was also reticent to provide criticism of the government, not so much in the classroom or in discussion club meetings, but in my e-mail correspondence. It was generally believed that all five or six of the city's Internet providers were required to send all forwarded communications through a government filter. What that meant, as I understood it, was that all Internet transmissions were subject to a scanner that could identify key words or phrases that might indicate communication potentially critical of the government. Should the communication be found suspect, they were not sent on. Judy and I did not make long-distance phone calls, but Carter did so frequently. He found that the line would usually go dead immediately should he begin to describe some aspect of the government in critical terms. For similar reasons, I had long since quit referring my students to Web sites that might be useful in preparing their research papers. First of all, few students had computers with Internet access and commercial access was expensive. What was most disturbing though was that students who tried viewing some of my Web suggestions received only a picture of the national flag on their screen.

Life in Tashkent

Tashkent is a big capital city of a little more than three million people situated on the northern edge of a giant desert. It was the third largest city in the former Soviet Russian Empire, behind Moscow and Kyiv. It is today a mostly modern city with bragging rights to being one of the oldest continuously inhabited cities on earth. Its history as "the stone city" (completely surrounded by a stone rampart), begins around the second century BC. Later, it became a major intersection on the caravan "Silk Route" made famous by Marco Polo. The city had been thoroughly destroyed and rebuilt many times. Most notably it was torn down in the early thirteenth century by Genghis Kahn, and most recently it was leveled by a huge earthquake in 1966, an earthquake that would come back to haunt us as I will explain later in the chapter. Soviet architects rebuilt much of the city on a grand scale. Everything seemed to be in giant proportion. On a self-guided tour we took of the city center very early in our stay, Judy and I walked across the largest square ever constructed by the Soviets. It looked like a military parade ground, bordered by a narrow waterfall much longer than a football field. We could walk the whole way just below and inside the falls; a wonderfully cooling opportunity on even the hottest of days.

Although in some disrepair, the streets of the city were often as wide and the blocks as long as those we had experienced while living in Salt Lake City, Utah. There were numerous plazas and fountains, man-made lakes and waterfalls, unfortunately, many also in disrepair. Near the edge of the city, the view from our fifth-floor bedroom windows was of a giant granite and concrete plaza containing a big fountain and a pedestal where an oversize statue of Lenin once stood. Behind the plaza were six, twenty-story apartment buildings arranged in a semicircle. When it infrequently was operating, we could hear the sound of the fountain's tumbling water echoing off of the apartments as though the fountain was practically next to our bedroom. In traditional Muslim fashion, water was designed to be running somewhere, all the time, in just about every major city block. Along with irrigating parks and gardens, water is taken from curbside canals by bucket to splash down the sidewalks thereby cooling the customers standing or sitting in the countless number of outdoor eating places.

As was our approach to living abroad, the key was to get out as much as possible and explore new areas and try new things. Because the city was large and spread out, we usually began our forays with an initial trip on the metro. Quite conveniently, there was access to the metro within a block of our apartment. In two stops we could be in the center of downtown. A few hundred feet from the metro exit, past a large reflecting pool that usually was a bit on the green side with algae, was the beginning of Saiyelgokh Street. Colloquially referred to as "Broadway," Saiyelgokh Street ran for several large blocks directly through the city center, ending in a large circular garden where there was a bigger than life statue of Tamerlane seated on his horse holding his sword high in the air in a gesture of triumph. Previously, the middle of the garden had featured a statue of Lenin, reportedly one of the largest in the Soviet Union. That would have been big! I would have loved to have seen it.

Saiyelgokh Street had become a very popular pedestrian mall. We visited "Broadway" quite often. It was always full of people, a jumble of lights and sounds mainly stemming from one side of the street where numerous open-air kiosks were selling recorded music, cheap jewelry, snack food, even the opportunity to try a bit of karaoke. Located mostly along the other side of the street were a dozen or more restaurants. They were sometimes placed one behind the other, thereby extending their presence back into a long strip of grassy park that bordered the street.

Most of these drafty little restaurants were made from tents of various sizes and colors. The open-air portion of their seating out front was usually demarcated by long smoky braziers cooking chunks of marinated mutton, the ever-present *shashlyk,* the national, indeed now international, Russian fast food. In between the tents were large cauldrons filled with *plov,* a pilaf-type of dish containing rice, vegetables, and lamb with plenty of fat to hold everything together. It is the other ubiquitous national delight. The other end of Saiyelgokh Street, aka Broadway, was given over to hundreds of artists featuring paintings, sculptures, wood carvings, and an always-changing variety of other handicrafts. Toward the end of our stay, we purchased a beautiful hand-carved wood backgammon set from one of these artists. This game and chess are both very popular. It was not hard to spot these game players sitting surrounded by a knot of faithful observers. They were a common sight in parks and outdoor restaurants.

Only a couple of blocks from Broadway were the Navoi Opera and

Ballet Theatre, of a rather interesting design in cream colored brick with elements of Islamic architecture. We were told by locals that the building was constructed right after World War II by Japanese prisoners of war. Judy and I attended performances quite often in this theater. For example, a glance at our large appointment calendar for May 2001 shows that we had circled five ballet possibilities and four separate operas, two of which, the evening performances of *Troubadour* and *Figaro,* we managed to attend that month. We considered most of the performances to be quite good. They were certainly a bargain at less than two dollars for the best seats. We both agreed that the absolutely best performance of the year was our favorite seasonal specialty, *The Nutcracker.* It turned out to be a Russian favorite as well. The hall was unusually quite full for this performance.

The theater usually contained many empty seats. We had not experienced this in Lithuania, Estonia, or Ukraine. I concluded that this Tashkent theater was principally subscribed to by Russian and Ukrainian nationals who certainly appeared to have once made up most of the performers and a majority of the audience. Their numbers in Tashkent were now in a steep decline, choosing to leave the city as quickly as they could find new jobs, sometimes in Kazakstan just to the north, but usually in Russia. Their significant presence in Uzbekistan during Soviet times had been principally urban, educated, and professional. But since independence, Russian and Ukrainians quickly began to lose their advantage occupationally and politically to the Uzbeks who now hold power. I know of at least three of my ethnic Russian students who have left for Russia in order to have a fair chance at a good job. Many of the informal taxi drivers we met were Russian or Ukrainian nationals, quite willing to talk about the lack of job prospects and their plans to leave the country. Several had been school teachers. Knowing only the Russian language, they were being displaced by Uzbek-speaking teachers. The displacement of Russian nationals was a common phenomenon, being repeated, more or less, in every one of the newly formed countries.

We went out to eat several times each week. In fact, eating out was so cheap and easy that Judy just about swore off cooking any evening meals. To do much cooking or eating in the apartment flat would have been foolish. In addition to a variety of regional dishes, we easily located absolutely outstanding Indian, Georgian, and Turkish restaurants. At the top end, we might pay four dollars a person. As an example of dining in the middle-price range, there were eight people we took to dinner to celebrate my sixty-third birthday at one of our favorite restaurants. It was close enough to walk to. Some of the tables were located inside a renovated turn-of-the-century home with the remainder of the dining area under a big tent with tables arranged around a large fountain. We enjoyed dinner outside by candlelight accompanied by violin music and good Georgian wine. The bill for all ten of us including a 20 percent tip was under forty dollars!

On the low end of the eatery price scale, there was a traditional Uzbek restaurant nearby with a large open-air patio surrounded by cozy carpeted individual alcoves containing low tables and cushioned benches. Meals here usually cost us twenty-five cents. Yes, a U.S. quarter! For half a dollar together, Judy and I got a large loaf of *nan* (hot, fresh baked, round, unleavened bread). We each received three small skewers of *shashlyk* and a sliced tomato and cucumber salad. All of this came with a pot of tea, and the wonderful ambiance of a small family run restaurant. These prices make more sense if I put them in the perspective of what people like me earned. University professors were paid about ten dollars a month.

Removing samsa (meat and dough pastry) baking in a tandoori oven.
Tashkent, Uzbekistan

This one particular restaurant also served *samsa,* a commonly found meat-filled pastry that is baked while stuck to the inside of an earthen clay oven called a *tandoori.* It resembles a giant three to four foot high and equally wide pot. When done, the cook leans over the top opening to the oven with a long-handled wire basket and a separate metal poker that is used to pry the pastry from the oven wall into the basket. The pastries were very tasty, but you needed to eat them hot before the lamb fat began to jell up; and also make sure you drink lots of hot, preferably green tea.

A heavy dose of lamb fat is hard to escape when eating out in Uzbekistan. The fat comes from a very unique type of lamb commonly raised in Central Asia. It can have a mass of pure fat bulging out as large as a soccer ball just beneath its tail. Hot tea is, according to folk wisdom, supposed to keep the fat from solidifying in your stomach. Not always following this advice, I was repeatedly approached by fellow diners who would come to our table, whatever restaurant we might be visiting, to warn me about the dire effects of my preference for drinking cold beer with these fatty meals. I took their advice and switched to green tea. During our stay in Tashkent, I drank lots of tea, mostly green tea. Judy drank a lot of tea also, but not of the green variety, finding it to upset her stomach.

We continued to get out and explore the city as much as possible. Yet, by the time I was midway through the first semester and almost two months had gone by, our life had become quite busy and our long walks were less frequent. The academic pace seemed to grow as our veteran status became longer and the CEP looked to us for a greater effort. I began preparing material for a series of teacher training seminars. Deadlines for conference proposals and scholarship applications to study in the West were coming due. My students were also expecting a lot more. Each week, in ever larger numbers, they began to fill the cramped little university office following my late afternoon classes, all pushing around me for a chance to express their concerns with conference arrangements, their research papers, or any of the enumerable questions students normally have concerning their progress in the class.

These informal after-class sessions were in addition to the office hours I always held earlier in the afternoon before class. I would make an effort to stay into the evening in order to help each student. However, we could ill afford to dally too long in the office as Judy and I found out the hard way. All the lights (at least those that were working) were turned off at once, leaving the building in total darkness. We might as well have been coal miners deep in the earth without a light on our helmet. The ensuing effort to exit the building proved to be quite an experience. Some of my students shuffled ahead to locate the entrance to the narrow stairwell. Slowly, we were able to find our way down the five floors from our office in total darkness. It was a difficult task.

Our beacon as we headed down the staircase was the odor emanating from the first floor bathrooms. It was the worst facility of its kind in any university I worked in or visited! At the beginning of the second semester, Judy and I, with Carter's assistance, actually bought cleaning supplies and paid the cleaning lady extra to do something about the bathroom situation. Our action made our assistant country director uneasy and clearly embarrassed the dean, but the bathrooms stayed at least a bit more presentable.

Having found our way to the ground floor, there was just enough light to see the main entrance door and make out the shadow of the night building guard who had turned off all the lights. After giving us a scolding for staying too late, he let us out, but not without a flick of his finger under his grizzled chin as an invitation should Judy and I wish to stay and drink vodka with him. We begged off.

A Note about Crime

Uzbekistan did not appear to us to have much of a problem with crime, let alone evidence of a Mafia-style element. There was just no indication that we saw at least, of the conspicuous behavior and material lifestyle that we had observed in Eastern Europe. Fellow CEP lecturer Tim Wood humorously speculated that the apparent absence of Mafia-like activity might be due to the few tourists available to take advantage of. Another of his musings had it that CEP lecturers were safe from the Mafia since most of their children were probably in our classes. I think a realistic answer follows from the fact that Uzbekistan is a police state. I would have to say, in a fit of envious jest, that life in an authoritarian society can be rather simple and relatively crime free if enough of a threat is made and the penalty put up sufficiently high.

My students told me that just prior to our arrival, there had been a spate of car thefts and the burglary of automobile stereo radios. The cars and their radios were most often newly imported from Germany. However, both of these crimes ended quickly when President Karimov went on television one evening to announce that a car thief had been officially shot and that this was the new penalty for car thieves. Theft of auto stereo radios would henceforth be "punished by life in prison," he had gone on to say. The students said that both problems quickly went away.

A Look around Uzbekistan

CEP activities and especially my involvement in a teacher-training project provided Judy and me an opportunity to visit several of Uzbekistan's major provinces and regional cities. Unfortunately, our working visits never seemed to last long enough, being usually four days to a week long. This was at least enough time to take in the main attractions.

Three weeklong trips were made with a teacher-training team to which I belonged. The first was to Nukus, located near Uzbekistan's southwest border with Turkmenistan. Nukus was a surreal and deeply disturbing place to visit if there ever was one. I have devoted a whole chapter to this visit. Another training workshop took us to Samarkand, the jewel of Uzbekistan's ancient Silk Road cities. A final trip with the training team was to Ferghana, located in Uzbekistan's eastern silk-producing province. Judy and I also made a pleasure trip to Bukhara, in central Uzbekistan. It is one of the country's main cities of antiquity and a tourist's delight. I will turn first to Samarkand and then to Ferghana, concluding this segment with a description of our experience in Bukhara and some thoughts about cotton harvesting.

Samarkand

Judy and I visited Samarkand twice, first with the teacher-training team and somewhat later, with our daughter Kimberly, to participate in a CEP-sponsored conference on women. The city is undoubtedly Central Asia's premier, most beautiful, and historically significant location. About five hours drive southwest from Tashkent, the trip took us on one of Uzbekistan's few four-lane highways, across a mostly semiarid landscape. Along the ride, the scene would shift back and forth between mainly desert and sections of irrigated agricultural land. The last few miles of road follow a river through a low pass between barren foothills then drops quickly into the outskirts of Samarkand.

Described in MacLeod and Mayhew's guidebook, *Uzbekistan* as "a city resonant with enigma and romantic legend," Samarkand has a substantial place in history. Its ancient period is ranked by historians as the equal of Babylon (near Baghdad) or even Rome. Samarkand was the home of Tamerlane, the ruthless empire builder, who, beginning in the late fourteenth century, first revived, and then went on to build the wealth, artistic, and cultural life of the city to its greatest height. The city features that were mostly built during his reign were what Judy and I gazed upon as we made our entrance toward the city center.

The view was of one absolutely beautiful gleaming tile-domed structure after another. There were mosques, *madrassahs* (Islamic seminary), and mausoleums scattered throughout the city. Much of the wealth needed to reconstruct and build these gleaming edifices was the result of conquest. Much of the remainder came from transit taxes as Samarkand was a principle crossroad in the silk trade route between the Persian lands to the west, China to the east, and India to the south.

Tamerlane had recently been given the appellation "the Great," and raised to the iconic stature of "founder of Uzbekistan." In some respects this title seemed to be rather ill fitting. For one thing, Tamerlane was an important figure throughout Central Asia and beyond, hardly someone to be appropriated by just one small country, but Uzbekistan got his statues erected first. The claim was apparently uncontested by other countries in the region who may have thought twice about identifying themselves too closely with this famous man.

Also commonly referred to as the "conqueror of the world," Tamerlane actually did subdue more territory than any other single ruler in the history of the planet. He laid waste wherever he led his army, from Moscow to Baghdad and Delhi. His calling card was a pyramid of skulls which would be stacked near the gates of the cities his men had sacked. MacLeod and Mayhew cite estimates that about seventeen million people died in a trail of blood and suffering that even surpassed Mongol barbarity. In one incident they describe, thousands of troublesome inhabitants of a city were piled, alive, one upon another, and cemented into newly constructed clay towers. On another occasion, after the sack of the port city of Smyrna (on the coast of Turkey), Tamerlane was known to have bombarded the escaping Christian fleet using knight's heads as cannon balls. Such an event may never have taken place, at least not quite as reported, but it is definitely within the range of myth which surrounds this towering figure of history.

I mention these observations about Tamerlane, at least in part, because I think that such a show of barbaric strength—ruthless action, seemingly without a care for human suffering—is a quality of power and governance still admired, and to lesser degrees still practiced by strong men in this part of the world.

Shir Dor madrissah (1619), a part of the Registan ensemble. The madrassah departs from Koranic tradition by portraying pictures on the facade rather than geometric designs. This picture is featured on the country's money. Samarkand, Uzbekistan

From the many remaining structures dating from the Tamerlane period in Samarkand, the most impressive is what is called the Registan, an ensemble of three fully restored madrassahs that occupy a parklike area near the center of the city. The main building was reconfigured from an earlier mosque. Of the other two, one takes the place of an original hospice for dervishes (whirling religious dancers) and the other a *carvanserai* (a hotel for travelers and their camels).

For most of their approximately seven hundred years, the madrassahs were schools for Islamic and secular studies. The three huge buildings are arranged around three sides of a large courtyard, two facing each other with the larger third madrassah centered behind and just off the front corners of the other two. As many as one hundred students lived in separate "cells" arranged around the two-story inner courtyard perimeter of each building.

By far the most beautiful and flamboyant part of the madrassahs were their gigantic rectangular-shaped front structures containing huge arched portals. These impressive edifices, which reminded me of giant bookends, were over one hundred feet tall. They were covered in glazed ceramic tile in green, light and dark blue, and yellow colors, all set on a tan background. Each edifice was flanked by twin minaret towers also covered in tile. The rear madrassah was topped with a large turquoise tile-covered dome, one of many similar domes shining brilliantly throughout the city. Everywhere on these edifices the tile were arranged into floral motifs and geometric patterns. In some places the tile contained exquisite examples of calligraphy.

Each of the three madrassahs had been simply and tastefully converted into tourist mini-malls featuring a wide variety of handicrafts, among other things. Each student cell, including the corner lecture halls, were filled with things like rugs and other knitted items, ceramics of all shapes and functions, paintings, an almost endless variety of knives, leather goods, metal stampings, and antiques. We spent part of three days wandering in an out of most of the shops, finally settling on the purchase of two silk robes, half a dozen knit hand bags, some embroidered materials, and an antique ring and necklace set that was around three hundred years old.

I wish I had purchased an old but still functional *burka* that was for sale. It would have made an excellent teaching tool for my sociology students back in Idaho. The burka is a full-length covering for women, made from heavy unbleached cotton with a crosshatched place to peer out at the world that reminded me of the bars of a jail cell. These full enclosures were once mandatory anytime women stepped outside the home. Were they "jails," as we in America would surely conclude? This question might produce an argument from at least a few Uzbek women, who might, for instance, indicate how their use is associated with a much lower instance of sexual harassment, even rape . One thing that can't be disputed is the meaning of the word *mandatory.* That fact sounds jail-like to me. The use of the burka was outlawed by the Soviets in the late 1920s as part of the Movement of the Godless, the mostly successful effort to suppress the power and influence of Islam in Soviet-controlled Central Asia.

Traditionally dressed Uzbek, possibly Tajik women with red hand decoration made from henna dye. Samarkand, Uzbekistan

Judy and I found two other medieval sites to be especially interesting, jaded as we were in a city of so many superlatives. The first was Shah-i-Zinda (the Street of the Dead), the holiest place in the city. It is a steep hillside necropolis of mausoleums near the outskirts of the city. Begun in 676, these elaborately and gorgeously tiled burial structures, marched, on the left and right, wall-to-wall, up the hill until reaching the top. We counted over thirty buildings, in various states of preservation, as we ascended the stone staircase that runs between them.

Some of the mausoleums contained passageways that allowed us to walk from one to the next. Some provided access to underground tunnels that would open into a series of cavelike rooms. While exploring one of these tunnels, Judy and I found ourselves quickly surrounded by a least a couple dozen people who filed rapidly into the room we were examining, making it impossible for us to escape politely until about a ten-minute extemporaneous ritual of chanting and silent praying was brought to a close.

The second site was particularly impressive for what it revealed about the high state of scientific knowledge that had developed in Islamic Central Asia at a time when Europe was still in the Dark Ages. The site was the Ulug Beg Observatory located further out of town on the same road as Shah-i-Zinda.

The beautifully tiled, three-story round structure of the observatory was demolished in a fit of fundamentalist fervor in 1449, only twenty years after it was built. This was, fortunately, a long enough period for Ulug Beg, like Galileo two centuries later, to have severely challenged religious orthodoxy. Galileo was allowed to recant, while Ulug Beg was beheaded through the connivance of one of his sons. His severed head was displayed in the Bibi Khanum mosque in Samarkand. The mosque, commissioned by Tamerlane and named for his Chinese wife, is the largest and most elaborate in the city.

Ulug Berg was Tamerlane's grandson. However, no longer powerful in death, Tamerlane's influence had been unable to prevent this grotesque reuniting, in his mosque, of grandfather and grandson. What a fantastic story!

The observatory building had originally contained a thirty-six-foot astrolabe that hung from its ceiling and swung the length of a gigantic meridian, a sixty-degree arc constructed of marble beneath the observatory's upper structure. This underground portion was not destroyed, remaining intact until it was unearthed by a Russian archaeologist almost a hundred years ago.

Unfortunately, our sightseeing had to give way to the main business of our trip. The teacher-training sessions were held in a beautifully preserved czarist-era home located in the city center. I conducted my classes in the gorgeously decorated ballroom while Judy sat in the back of the room knitting. I suspect she had pretty much tuned me out as she had heard most of my lecture material on several previous occasions.

At the end of the week, our hosts treated us to a delicious late-afternoon meal complete with many vodka toasts. It was early evening and raining hard as the teacher-training team pulled out of Samarkand for the van ride home. In time-worn fashion, going back to the life of Tamerlane, we stopped along the road at the edge of the city to buy several loaves of "Samarkand *Non.*" This was a special recipe, developed during the time of Tamerlane, for Central Asia' traditional unleavened flat bread. He had always taken a supply with him when leaving the city on the way to his next conquest. A bit wet from the rain, but with big smiles, several brightly dressed ladies in traditional silk costume came out from a small roadside bakery to poke the bread through the open van windows, take our money, and wish us a safe journey, thus helping to ensure that the tradition continued. The big round loaves of unleavened wheat bread, crispy on the outside and soft textured inside, were still nice and warm from the clay ovens.

Our van got into Tashkent around midnight. Everybody was tired. It had been a busy week. Carter was the first to be dropped off, about a half block from his apartment. As we left, he was immediately approached by two militiamen who wanted to know what he was doing out so late at night and what was in his large bag. Carter was standing on a main thoroughfare used by the presidential motorcade to move at very high speed between the airport and government headquarters. The militiamen remained curious, and, when they found out he also lived in a building facing this same thoroughfare, they decided to accompany Carter to his apartment whereupon they began to make a security search. When they located chilled vodka in the freezer, Carter decided it was probably time to host an informal round or two of toasts to the president, the brotherhood, and whoever else might be necessary. Several more toasts later, it was early in the morning when the two militiamen finally decided to leave the apartment. Carter had fallen asleep on the sofa. What a strange party that must have been.

Ferghana

We conducted our teacher-training workshop in Ferghana early in the spring. The weather had already turned quite pleasant in this town of about two hundred thousand people. A new season of leaves was in evidence on the cottonwood trees that lined the city streets and filled its parks. Judy and I, and the workshop team, had arrived Sunday afternoon after an approximate five-hour drive from Tashkent in a late-model Japanese van. The trip had been quite scenic. We drove through several small mining villages while climbing past an immense reservoir framed in a blanket of snow. At this point, the road turned to coarse gravel. A short time later, we bumped our way into a roughly hued and very leaky tunnel cut through the Chatkul Mountains at an elevation of 7,450 feet and then began our decent into the very picturesque Ferghana Valley. Located in Uzbekistan's peninsula-shaped eastern border with Tajikistan, the Ferghana Valley is a huge flood plain of the Syr Darya River. Surrounded on three sides by high mountains, the valley's rich land is intensively cultivated and contains about a third of Uzbekistan's population. The Syr Darya is a large river, made even more impressive during our visit, swollen as it was by spring run-off. I had meet this river before, a thousand or more miles northwest, dammed and diverted to just a trickle of water passing through Nukus in a doomed effort to reach and replenish the dying Aral Sea.

Ferghana sits just a few miles from the town of Margilan, the most ancient settlement in the valley and reportedly the location of the easternmost of nine cities founded by and named for Alexander the Great in 329 BC. A popular debate topic has it that silk making may have been practiced at the time of Alexander's arrival in the valley, although the evidence suggests a much later begining—around the sixth century as an import from China. Today the Ferghana Valley is widely known as a center for sericulture, the raising of silk worms and production of raw silk, and Margilan has been granted its historical place as a major Silk Rout city.

Orchards of mulberry trees were a common sight as we drove through the valley toward Ferghana. Individual entrepreneurs purchase silk worms from the state, feeding them fresh-cut mulberry leaves until such time as they have grown quite large and have spun their cocoon of silk. The cocoons appear as white, fabriclike capsules measuring about an inch and a quarter in length and three quarters of an inch around. The cocoons are taken to a processing and weaving factory where they are steamed and then boiled. Silk thread may then be drawn out of the cocoons, dyed, and ultimately turned into the most colorful patterns of cloth. The most popular pattern is referred to as "iridescent rainbow," although Judy and I felt it looked very similar to Christmas candy cane. To make sure that all goes well in the weaving process, a special grass is burned with incenselike smoke to keep the weavers protected from the evil eye.

Judy and I visited the Yodgorlik Silk Factory in Margilan. It is the only factory that continues to use the traditional methods of silk extraction and weaving, all the many other factories being highly mechanized. Of course, all the tourists make their visit here. Adjacent to the factory is a small sales office containing a variety of handmade items. Judy bought a couple of emerald green and dark blue scarves.

The Ferghana Valley is famous for at least two other reasons. It is the birthplace of a highly respected horse breed that history records as being so fast and powerful that it literally sweated blood. In fact, it was the result of a pernicious skin parasite rather than perspiration. The other reason for infamy is that the Soviets had their first experience fighting with *Mujaheddin* here in 1918. They won this battle after killing thousands of civilians in their drive to quell the effort to create a moderate Islamic, socialist government in the region out of the void left by the fall of the Russian czar. Ironically, a little over a half-century later, the Soviets would lose in battle against the Mujaheddin in their proxy battle with the United States over Afghanistan.

The teacher-training workshop was held at Ferghana State University, quite recently christened as a university from its mid-1930s origin as a teaching institute. With a faculty numbering over four hundred, the university offers bachelor's degrees in twenty-three majors, and masters degrees in five specialties. The professors who attended my workshop were outgoing and very appreciative of my efforts. With the help of my two CEP colleagues, Victoria and Carter , we had a very frank exchange of views about the responsibilities of the teachers to speak out for education reform, and to establish their classrooms as a place to introduce and reinforce democratic principles. Carter and I quickly put together a large flip chart during a break period that diagramed civic organizations in relation to private, nonprofit, and governmental spheres of society. Each sphere was represented as a circle, sized in relative proportion to the other spheres. The circles overlapped, suggesting the interrelationship and degree of dependence each sphere has on the others. The diagram was a success in stimulating much discussion. It was hard for me to realize just how small the civic sector is in Uzbekistan, and how reluctant the professors were to take the initiative in developing educationally related organizations, or speak out for reform. I came away from the discussion knowing that we had sparked interest and enthusiasm for change, but wondering how long it might last in the face of the everyday realities of the existing academic structures.

The efforts of the teacher-training team were generously recognized by the university president in a closing ceremony held in his large office. I received a beautiful, multicolored silk robe and a traditional Uzbek skull cap. Judy was given a six-by-eight-foot *suzani,* a beautiful item of Central Asian needlework folk art. Elaborate silk embroidery, featuring four doves of peace, had been sewn on black velveteen. Tradition requires that girls and young women are obliged to sew a certain number of suzanis—we have been told as high as forty—as part of their marriage dowry.

Filled with the joy of Ferghana's hospitality, the time to pack our treasures and "yak over" to Tashkent arrived all too quickly. What an enjoyable week it had been.

Bukhara

I would like to finish this chapter with a trip we made earlier, in November of the previous year, when Judy and I, along with Carter and Zulfiya "Z Girl," who would act as our interpreter, flew to Burkhara, a one-hour trip into the southern Uzbekistan desert on a new French-made airplane—what a pleasant surprise. With about a quarter of a million people, Bukhara was the only one of the three principle dynastic khanate cities along the famous Silk Route that lasted into the nineteenth century. As a consequence, it remains today as the best place to get a reasonably little-changed view of what life might have looked like hundreds of years ago. During the ninth and tenth centuries, Bukhara was the religious and cultural center of Central Asia. Later, in the 1500s, the Uzbeks made it their capital. It was essentially in this historical form that we enjoyed the old portion of the city for three wonderful days.

Our student companion and interpreter was a practicing Uzbek Muslim and a bubbly, self-assured junior majoring in foreign languages. While very respectful and committed to her Uzbek origins, she liked to travel anywhere in the world, but especially to America. Using an advance on her wages, she had traveled there on at least two occasions, both of which turned out to be during very traumatic events. She had been an au pair in Littleton, Colorado, arriving there just in time for the Columbine High School shootings. Two years later, Judy and I visited her while on her second try at this job, this time in a suburb of New York City. Not more than a week earlier, she had been a witness to the 9/11 terrorist attacks on the World Trade Towers. Neither of these tragedies soured her enthusiasm for travel, or for America, one bit. As testimony to her attitude, the night before our flight to Burkhara, she had stayed up until 2:00 AM, taking almost four hours for her mother to put beautiful long dreadlock braids into her hair. "This is popular in America," she said to us.

Sixteenth-century Kalan mosque. "Bukhara rug" merchants are off to the right. The front section of the Ark is in the background. Bukhara, Uzbekistan.

Bukhara in the late fall was a very quiet place, its older central area remarkably devoid of all but a few tourists. Like so many colonially influenced cities, Bukhara was separated into two distinctive sections. One was the Russian, and later Soviet sector, consisting mostly of newer drab-appearing concrete structures. The other section of the city contained the buildings of the old traditional quarter.

The center of the old sector was composed of dozens of large, absolutely beautiful partly tile-covered madrassahs and mosques. The mosques were flanked by their tall slender minarets. There were caravansaries and colorful outdoor restaurants bordering on small artificial lakes and canals. The old buildings in this sector spanned the seventh to the seventeenth century. In the center of the city's traditional quarter stood the high walled fortification called the Ark. It didn't look as mighty as a European fort, being much more plain and simple in its features. Yet, it was definitely commanding in presence as we first encountered it, standing high, absorbing the morning sun on its mud-brick ramparts. Elegant in its simplicity, historically it could hold its own with any fortification in the world. It had also been a very gruesome place. Public executions were held near its main gate. People sold their children to its royal inhabitants to be used as sexual toys. In the middle of the 1800s, two British officers became famous for being beheaded here, accused by the local khan of plotting against him. The Ark had been originally built in the fifth century, being destroyed and rebuilt many times, but continuously used until about one hundred years ago. Even then, the Ark was far from being historically classified as an old structure in this part of the world. Some sections of Bukhara's old center actually have a history which dates back over 2,500 years.

A typical mixture of traditional and contemporary clothing. Bukhara, Uzbekistan

The four of us sat across the street from the Ark, under big shade trees, having tea, trying out the bedlike seating arrangement, admiring the Ark's ochre shades of reddish brown, which are carried throughout all the mostly earthen-walled structures of the old city. Yet, in this mud-shaded environment, color abounds in the blazing blue and green tile of the domes and large flat entrance facades of the religious buildings.

Also adding color to our surroundings were bright patterns of the traditionally dressed women, and the many "Bukhara" woven wool rugs, most in wine-colored red shades, spread out for sale along the sidewalks and hanging in front of the little shops. Actually, the famous "Bukhara" rugs are not usually made in Bukhara. They are made in neighboring Turkmenistan. This was one of the many observations provided to us gratis by a tall, dark-haired, and quite attractive young lady with a reasonably good command of English and a wonderful outgoing personality. Her name was Za Za. She had met Carter, Judy, and our student companion and me on the street our first day out, and had invited herself along as a tour guide. She met us again each of the following two days of our stay in the city. Along with this young lady, we added to our tour retinue a young man, whose self-appointed job was to carry our purchases, including our large and heavy "Bukhara" rug purchase. The most we paid for all this help was these two young people's lunch and dinners. Neither would accept a gratuity.

Before leaving on our trip, our young apartment manager in Tashkent had set us up for a home stay with one of his aunts who lived on the outskirts of Bukhara. Home stays are a good way to get to know the local people, so we had taken up our manager on his offer. Our decision turned out to be informative, even having a few exciting moments.

Our taxi from the airport could not find the address of our home stay (shades of Zarbog Street), but fortunately we remembered that the lady occasionally worked in a medical clinic near the airport. The clinic turned out to be easy to find. At the clinic, we got new directions that led us to her very cramped and basic apartment. It was located on the third floor of a typical four-story "falling to pieces" Soviet apartment complex. There was just room in this cramped little apartment for all of us to gather around a big dining table piled high with local fruit and several kinds of little crumbly things to eat. We consumed pot after pot of tea while sitting around the table sharing stories.

Storytellers included the four of us, the lady of the house, and her three children. Our student interpreter was kept busy interpreting, and in pouring the tea, something which she insisted on always doing. In Central Asia, pouring another's tea is a sign of great respect. That evening, she and Judy slept in the bedroom while the children and their mother slept in the second bedroom, which also doubled as the TV room/den/sewing room. Neither room contained beds other than covered foam pads, which were laid on the floor. Where possible, Uzbeks prefer their beds to be outdoors, but Soviet-built apartments rarely were designed to allow for this custom. In traditional settings, outdoor beds are large king-size structures that often double during the day for places to spend time in the company of friends sitting on them, cross-legged, talking and drinking tea.

Carter and I slept in an apartment one floor below. It was cold and vacant except for two, very stiff, old convertible bed chairs and a couple of blankets. The apartment was a duplicate of the one above, right down to the little bathroom. The toilet ran heavily mineralized water all night. Next to the toilet was a small basket containing torn chunks of paper to use in place of toilet paper. Rather expectedly, there was only cold water for washing in the dark brown stained sink in the morning. The bathtub was so brown with stain that I would have thought twice about using it even if there had been hot water.

The action picked up considerably in the middle of the night when a very drunken man managed to key his way into the completely dark apartment. He was as surprised as we were to find us standing there in our skivvies, all three of us together in the darkness, attempting to communicate in Russian that we had squatter's rights. Using his best Russian—Carter was in his second month of language lessons—he told the man to leave the apartment immediately. The man promptly did! Upstairs next morning over a breakfast of tea and bread with homemade fig jam, we told our story. The intruder, it was explained, was the apartment owner who used the place only when he was too drunk to go home next door without getting a bawling out from his wife.

"At Cotton"

Our host in Bukhara was a typically short, heavyset middle-age Uzbek lady. She and her husband, whose picture was prominently displayed on the front room wall, were both teachers at the regional state technical university. At the time of our home stay, her husband was away fulfilling both his and his wife's obligation to work in the cotton harvest. It was a matter of "volunteering" or face the possibility of job dismissal. The government cotton monopoly was "king" in Uzbekistan, and forced labor was the way it was harvested. In this instance, the role reversal was somewhat uncommon. When adults picked cotton, it was women who usually did most of the work. In the rural communities where women work more often, they are paid, in part, by the right to harvest the cotton stalks for winter heating fuel.

More commonly, the harvesting of cotton falls to the youth. Our hostess's husband would be away for up to five weeks, but never mind his missed lectures, as all his students were "at cotton" as well. While admittedly using the definition somewhat loosely, "slave labor" may have disappeared from most of the world, but such is definitely not the case in Uzbekistan. Following the prior Soviet practice, it continues to be mandatory in most places outside the capital, for thousands of school children, some reportedly as young as eight to ten years old on up through university students, to pick cotton for little payment or often for free, and for their teachers to "volunteer" as supervisors. Everybody gets a pep talk about reaping prosperity for the Motherland.

Cotton, as one might guess, is the number-one industry in this country whose export of this commodity is the second largest in the world after the United States. As a vestigial survival of their colonial and Soviet history, almost all Uzbek cotton is shipped in raw form out of the country, generating just over a third of Uzbekistan's national budget revenue, while the people continue to purchase back their cotton clothing mainly from Russia, India, Korea, or Turkey. However, there are small signs that this practice may be changing. Just before leaving the country, I was able to find a pair of cotton trousers in a department store that said "Made in Uzbekistan" on the inside label. I was unable to determine if the trousers, the material, or both were made there.

Students living in Tashkent are not required to pick cotton, so my students did not have to worry about missing class for this reason. I was told that this was because a national selection process had brought the most talented students to Tashkent and that it was better that their studies not be interrupted. I suspect that social class was also a factor. Several of Tashkent's places of higher education contained large numbers of children from families of high-ranking government bureaucrats and officials. The Soviets referred to these people as *apparatchiks* or *nomenklatura*, terms denoting privilege.

Students from the regional schools and universities therefore got the brunt of the cotton picking requirement (no pun intended!). Not only must the students "volunteer" to pick the cotton under threat of university expulsion, but usually they also had to reimburse the government for their food and housing costs.

My CEP colleagues from Northern California, Brian Farley and Lesley Champany, were obliged to make major changes to their class and teaching schedules when most of their students at Samarkand State Institute left for almost two months "at cotton." Being government funded, as are all the other schools, Samarkand State didn't dare complain about the educational handicap resulting from this practice, even though students lose almost a full year of study out of every four years spent in school. During our visit in Bukhara, we were told that most of the city's 4,200 university students were "at cotton."

The more fortunate young people pick cotton while living in vacated high school buildings on cots or mattresses that they bring from home. Accommodations for others were progressively worse to outright appalling. There was usually never enough to eat, and sanitation could be less than minimum level. Some students managed to buy their way out of cotton. Many of those who do go to cotton get sick, and some students suffer permanent damage to their health. One of my local CEP colleagues told me about picking cotton as a young girl, around fifteen years ago. She was assigned her living space in an inadequately cleaned-out horse barn. She drank contaminated water and ended up with permanent liver damage from type-C hepatitis. Her story could still happen, and it did not include the dangers all the young people continue to face from working in areas where herbicides and pesticides were liberally used and had been for decades.

The Uzbek government seems to be in no hurry to stop forcing young people to harvest the nation's cotton. Some of the most outspoken critics of the governments' cotton policies go beyond the concern for forced and child labor to consider how the economics of cotton further entrenches the poverty and consequent discontent of the majority of small cotton farmers who are paid only what the state decides. Within the past decade political stability in Uzbekistan has been increasingly challenged by a small but apparently growing number of political activists. Their recruitment base is certainly made larger by the very inequitable way in which cotton is grown and the serious human rights abuses connected with its harvest. In several locations in the country I ran into people quite willing to complain, quite openly, about these issues.

A Final Two Months of Travel

It was the Soviet custom for professors to take a somewhat longer holiday break at the end of the calendar year than we were accustomed to back home. Most universities continued to honor the practice. Students had to come back to school briefly for examinations, but there was often as much as two months separating semesters. Over our four years with the CEP, Judy and I always took full advantage of this time, making our first priority to visit family. We had managed to fly home while in Tallinn and again while posted in Kharkiv.

Predictably, the semester break in Tashkent was going to be two full months long. It was too far to fly all the way back home for Christmas, but fortunately, our daughter Kimberly and her family were stationed near Frankfurt, only an overnight flight away. There was actually a bit of Christmas in the air as we prepared to leave Tashkent. We bought some holiday music to "get in the mood," and noticed some shops selling little plastic Christmas trees and various cheap-looking ornaments. It was more than I expected, considering that we were living in a Muslim country. One of my students agreed to cat-sit Pyat for us in our apartment. Actually, this arrangement apparently led the landlord to believe that we were subletting the apartment without her permission. We heard, quite clearly, about the error of this action upon our return.

We began our holiday celebrating Christmas with Kimberly and her family in Germany. We then took a train to northern Germany to stay with friends we had met over ten years earlier when I was teaching in Spain. We had shared Christmas with them the year we were living in Lithuania. This time we were hoping the Christmas tree with its real candles would still be set up–it was. Then it was back to Tashkent for six days of rushed business before leaving on a three-week-long trip to

India. Being as close as we would probably ever get to this exotic part of the world, this seemed to be our best chance to go.

We left Tashkent in the morning and flew via Air India in a Russian-made Ilyushin, which seemed like the largest plane we have ever been in. There were two full floors of seating. The flight took us south over a line of snow-covered mountains separating Pakistan from Afghanistan. These majestic mountains, rising over eight thousand feet, disappeared eastward seemingly without interruption, merging with the Himalayas. The view out the plane window reminded me of flying over the Rocky Mountains except on a much grander level.

I was also aware of how different life was on the ground. This was the Waziristan region below us, Pakistan's most ungovernable autonomous tribal area: the home of ethnic Pashtuns. Rather neglected by Pakistan, and for good reason, as it can be volatile and is almost inaccessible, the area has never been under outside control. Neither Alexander the Great, Genghis Khan, nor the British Empire were successful in gaining dominion over this region, which is now well-known as the hiding place of Osama bin Laden.

Sensational India

From the moment we departed by taxi from the Delhi airport, India became the most intriguing, most colorful, but also the most intense and stressful place we have ever visited. Everybody knows that India has its poor people and crowded places, but it is impossible to be prepared for so many people, cows, elephants, camels, pigs, rickshaws, bicycles, and gaudy-looking trucks piled dangerously high with cargo, all sharing space in the same small street or roadway that was almost always awash in plastic bags.

The urban crush of humanity was dramatic and unnerving. People were everywhere, living in makeshift shacks along the dusty edge of the roads, railroad tracks, or sleeping and living right on the sidewalks. Judy and I were never sure as we stepped over these shroud-covered people whether they were dead or alive. It was a disorienting experience. Adding to the stress of such cultural shock, on July 26, we were violently tossed about on a train traveling quite close to the epicenter of a very damaging 7.9-level earthquake. We expected the train car to tip over. It didn't. After a wait of a couple of hours, we were the first to slowly cross several high-canyon trestles. Wondering if the trestles would hold was the scariest part of the whole experience that killed at least 2,500 people.

We normally prefer to travel on our own, but there are times when travel can be very difficult for even people with as much experience as ourselves. India quickly began to overwhelm us. We had eaten in an area near the Taj Mahal containing small restaurants, an area which was not recommended by our travel guide, and I was beginning to pay the price for such indiscretion.

We visited a small travel agency and arranged to hire a private car and driver, including some upgraded hotels for the next nine days of our stay. It was very inexpensive and improved our comfort level considerably, even though I needed a doctor's visit to our hotel to see if there was anything that might be proscribed to mitigate a very bad case of diarrhea. After that bit of luxury touring, we again struck out on our own, heading along the west coast, visiting Mumbai and spending several delightful days living right on the beach in Goa, a former Portuguese colony. This last stop allowed us a chance to rest, get over my "Indian tummy," and for both of us to get ready for the long flight back to Tashkent.

We had only been back in Tashkent for about a week when Judy and I were again struck by a fairly large earthquake, smaller than the one in India, but enough to give our apartment building a good shaking. It happened during a raging storm at 7:30 in the morning. Judy and I were up but only dressed in our pajamas and robes. Remembering how Tashkent had been practically flattened in 1966, we took off down the five flights of stairs, but the shaking had stopped by the time we reached the front door of our building. There was no apparent damage, but even as much as a day or so later, I still felt as though I could not get my bearings, occasionally feeling like the floor was moving underneath me.

Preparing to Leave

All good things come to an end. Toward the conclusion of our stay in Tashkent, we were fortunately kept so busy that we didn't have time to think much about the possible significance of what was to be our last few weeks with the Civic Education Project. As we had done so successfully two years before in Kharkiv, we arranged an end-of-the-year barbeque for all my students.

Scoping out a good place to hold the party, one student suggested the Tashkent Botanical Gardens. This young Russian Uzbek lady and her boyfriend took us out to this place by bus. We paid the 12-cent entrance fee and went in to find a totally uncared for, massively overgrown jungle of trees and vines, small paths, and what was left of paved sidewalks. Mostly young couples were surreptitiously wandering in and out of the dense almost impenetrateable undergrowth. It was certainly no place for a picnic even though I could see that it once had been a most lovely spot for such an occasion.

We ended up our search by renting a spot in a big park located just a few blocks from our apartment. One of the many park concessionaires agreed to provide the tables as well as the food and drink, all quite within Judy's and my budget, as might be expected. Just about all the students in both of my and Carter's classes came to the party. There were speeches, funny antics, and lots of picture taking to help preserve the memories. Several of these students still manage to get together at least once a year to recall the good times. They refer to themselves as "the CEP gang."

End of year plov party for Carter's (seated front right) and my students. Tashkent, Uzbekistan

We began the long careful process of packing our many duffel bags and cardboard boxes. On her last housecleaning day, we gave our housekeeper, Svetlana, several bags of household items and a large brand-new rug that we had proudly hauled all the way from Bukhara thinking it an original only to find it was a high-quality fake and too heavy to lug home anyway. We gave our boom box to one student and our trusty little shortwave radio to another.

Two days before we left, one of our favorite students came to our flat with her boyfriend, and the two of them spent about three hours cooking a Sunday plov dinner for all four of us. The evening before our departure, we had dinner at our favorite restaurant with our two CEP local colleagues, our assistant director, and program assistant (who first entered our life on Zarbog Street). Then we all went back to our flat to wait out the abysmally poor timing of the Turkish Air flight departure at 3:30 in the morning! Shortly before leaving our apartment flat, we were joined by at least a dozen of my students who had hired a large van to accompany the rest of us to the airport. I will never forget their waving arms and sad faces on the other side of the airport's large plate-glass windows as Judy and I slowly made our way through customs and up to the airline ticket counter. Our next stop was Istanbul, then Frankfurt for a visit with our daughter Kimberly and her family. From there we flew back to Boise. It was a return home filled with many wonderful remembrances and considerable mixed emotions.

6
Getting to Work

Culture Shock

The remaining eight chapters change the focus from the general to the topical, and from centering observations and impressions on our day-to-day urban life and travel, to stories of events or places. Also, I take time in these chapters to describe a few of the central features of my work. As always, the stories are sometimes serious, usually lighthearted, and often humorous. This chapter clearly exhibits each of the above features. It is more than about the rather mechanical nature of the commute to work. We Americans learn to treat commuting maybe with frustration but usually quite nonchalantly. People get habituated to the everyday routine of traveling back and forth to work, whatever it might entail. After a while, we stop thinking about the immediate experience. We focus on the day ahead, take care of our cell phone calling, or maybe just daydream the trip away.

The situation was quite different during our stay in the former Soviet Russian Empire. For one thing, we just didn't stay long enough in any of the four countries to allow getting to work to become habitual. Much more important, though, was the fact that my commuting was made in conditions very different than I was used to, in one instance almost unbelievably different. In every case, the trip to work always took on a quality of being an end in itself, a significant event in the day, a stimulus for many new impressions.

With the possible exception of traveling on our own through India, getting to work on public transportation in Vilnius was undoubtedly the closest I have ever come to a personal understanding of the meaning of intense cultural shock. It was all about adapting to an overdose of a very different way of doing things. In this instance, right in your face! See if you don't agree with me.

In Lithuania, I was assigned to teach at the suburban branch of the University of Vilnius. Constructed in the mid-1980s, the school was a sprawling campus of rather stark-looking red brick buildings spread out between weedy fields. The campus was a stark contrast to the gorgeous four hundred-year-old buildings of the original university that were located in the very cramped Old Town section near the center of Vilnius. Unable to expand, the university quickly became overcrowded and unable to accept the new social science programs that we were helping to develop. As a result, my teaching occurred out at the school's suburban branch. I still had many chances to visit the old university. There were occasions such as business meetings with some of the professors and visits to the basement coffee shop with its marvelous pub-style ambiance. I also picked up my monthly salary at the main campus building. The old university was only a short walking distance from our apartment. Still, I always wished I could have taught a class or two in one of the medieval-looking arched-ceilinged classrooms.

The branch campus was situated up on a hill out on the perimeter of the city. If everything went well, I could make the trip from our apartment to school in a little under an hour by a combination of trolley and bus. Of course, we could have elected to live near the branch university, in which case I probably could have been close enough to walk to work. With this arrangement, there would have been a long trip each time we wanted to be in the city or the adjacent Old Town—which was practically a daily occasion. Judy and I were always glad that the CEP staff had not located us out near the branch campus in one of the multitude of ugly Soviet-built apartments. I much preferred to commute to work.

The Vilnius public transit system was absolutely worn out and hopelessly overtaxed. I doubted that it was ever able to properly serve the upward of six hundred thousand people of this city, but either way, it had certainly seen much better times. I used to think my body would be the last straw whose ride would bring the system down.

The system consisted of red and cream-colored buses and trolleybuses, mostly of 1950s vintage. There were a few more recent bus models, some articulated in the middle for easier turns. For people who didn't mind paying a little more, there were also a large number of licensed, privately operated ten-passenger minivans making regular stops throughout the city. Called *marshrutkas,* these vans had been made in neighboring Latvia, were distributed over much of the Soviet Russian Empire, and looked a lot like the first American passenger vans of forty years ago.

Public transport took place in far less than ideal conditions. Main streets in the city were narrow and sometimes paved in cobblestones. Trolley connections were constantly coming unhooked from their overhead electrical grid. Power outages or broken sections of the grid would stop long lines of trolleys, leaving the streets hopelessly tangled in traffic from a burgeoning number of private automobiles, which were beginning to flood the city.

Riding the buses and trolleys to school looked to be a hellish trip from start to finish. Unless you were really lucky, the wait for a correct bus or trolley number resulted in a large gathering of people who all fully expected to enter with you. Having absolutely no sense of queuing, a small mob scene would usually occur. Everybody would push in an effort to all get in at the same time. About half of the time, the busses would arrive already full, actually over-packed, when they pulled to a stop. The obvious fact that few, if any, prospective riders would find a place inside seemed to deter no one. Space depended upon the number of people getting off.

There would be barely enough time for passengers to exit before those near the front of the waiting crowd of people would surge ahead, being pushed by the people behind them. A few would manage to get in the door, leaving a large knot of would-be riders still outside unable to move, being pushed ever harder from the rear. After a few minutes of this, when no more forward progress was obviously going to be possible, the driver would attempt to shut the doors. The mob would continue fruitlessly to push ahead. The driver would start yelling and begin to slowly move away from the curb. At this point, a collective surge by those yet outside would usually manage to cram in a few more souls.

The bus or trolley was now well in motion. As it pulled away from the curb, the doors were usually still not fully closed, trapping clothing, even body parts between the door's rubber flanges. My canvas briefcase went between stops that way on more than one occasion. Typically short, heavyset *babushkas* (Russian grandmothers) were the most expert at entering buses and trolleys under these impossible conditions. Ken Smith, a CEP visiting lecturer in economics, who had been posted in Vilnius the year before, once mentioned to me that he had learned that babushkas usually had small ice-pick tips surgically implanted in their elbows in order to make them a more effective weapons as they pushed their way through the bus doors!

Once on these aging public conveyances, we literally became vertical sardines, jammed up so tightly that it was difficult to move our arms up or down in front of our body. At times we were packed in so tightly that it was unnecessary to hold on to anything—anything appropriate at least! I once got pushed into a bus so violently that I ended up falling into the lap of an old peasant lady who sat facing me. She had just returned from a mushroom picking trip in the woods: a favorite Lithuanian outing. I crashed, face first, into the large wicker basket of mushrooms she was holding on her lap. The mushrooms faired quite well, but the lady started yelling and continued to glare at me, almost continuously between the next several stops. As we exited the bus together, she was still treating the situation as though it had been all my fault.

Judy thought this incident quite funny. She hated the frequent occurrence of such over packed transport, particularly in warm weather. She is just five foot three, and most Lithuanians are quite tall. This would leave her buried in a crowd of armpits, and practically nobody used deodorant!

This particular smelly problem went away in the winter as bulky jackets pretty much took care of the odor problem, not to say that the damp fur coats worn by many of the women smelled much better. Remember, this is the land of rain. And, by the way, just where was I supposed to place a wet umbrella when all of us are squeezed together like this anyway? I closed it up and hung on to it as best as I could.

Such intense crowding also raised the problem of how to pay for the ride. Tickets could be purchased at specially designated kiosks near the bus stops. They could also be acquired on board the bus or trolley—if the person who sold them just happened to be close by. Then there was the problem of punching my ticket. In less crowded circumstances, it was a simple matter of mechanically (it took two hands) punching the ticket in one of a few little metal contraptions protruding, dangerously, from the inside walls. When this maneuver was prevented by jam-packed conditions, I could get my ticket punched by handing it over to someone in a position to punch, or hand it over a second or more time, and then hoping the validated ticket would get back to me with reasonable dispatch.

Faced with such cramped ridership, some people, including myself at times, chose not to worry about having a ticket, or getting it punched. This meant that at any moment, some plainclothes person, even one crammed up right beside me could decide to flash his or her identification and request that I pay a fine on the spot! This happened to me once. It was doubly embarrassing. Not only was I obviously wealthy enough to afford a ticket, but the incident involved Judy and our two guests, John and Jan McFadden who were on a summer travel vacation with us. It was late in the evening, the trolleybus was not crowded, and I had suggested we all board without first obtaining tickets. The least I could do was pay all four fines—about a dollar each.

Winter brought much bigger problems in my effort to get to work. When the weather fell below freezing, which it did early and often during the long winter, the inside of the bus or trolley windows would cover over with a thick sheet of frosty ice, making it impossible to see outside to confirm my stop. The heating systems in these rattle traps had long ceased functioning to help reduce the ice problem. If one were short, they would then need to count the stops in order to keep track of their location. If you were tall enough, as I was, you could, at every stop, get a quick glance out the open door past the pushing crowd at some familiar landmark. The "lookout" method better not confirm that I was at my desired stop as there would be absolutely no chance to get out the door on such short notice.

Either way, counting stops or looking out, I anticipated my stop well in advance and began taking advantage of any movement, no matter how small, in order to edge ever closer toward, usually, the front door. Even though generally not followed, the custom was to enter the back door and exit the front door. My lack of attention to proper positioning made it necessary several times for me to trudge back numerous blocks through the snow and ice to my intended stop. Positioning was also important on the articulated buses for an additional reason. In these buses, I did not want to get caught standing in the jointed section where the usually torn rubber roof fabric would leak volumes of rain or icy water on me at every turn!

It seemed a strange thing to acknowledge at the time, and Judy thought I was "losing it," but I actually grew rather fond of riding the overcrowded buses and trolleys. There was a skill represented in practicing and then perfecting good riding technique. There was a calculus to be mastered in the loading and unloading process. Once inside, creativity was required in maintaining the fiction of personal space when none existed. All the time, I had to keep a watchful eye on the babushkas. Drunks needed to be helped in and out and a place found for them to sit. Sadly, drunken people were a common occurrence. Despite all these twisted attractions, after a month or so I stopped using the bus and trolley connection to get to work—at least for awhile. As the deep snow and ice of winter set in, I came back to them, more out of fear than out of loneliness. As you will see, I just felt a lot safer in them.

A Minivan Interlude Turns Scary

The time-saving and convenience of the marshrutka minivan could not be ignored. No transfer was necessary. The minivan could take me to work in half the time, and most invitingly, it was never overcrowded. The makeup of their ridership would change along the route, but when the ten spaces were taken the van was full—no pushing and shoving. Period! Riding in minivans was a hoot. Being privately owned, each van ride was a unique experience. Some vans were dilapidated beyond reasonable repair, similar to the one we had used originally to travel to Lithuania. Most were elaborately decorated inside in what might politely be called "cabaret gross:" a dozen or more gaudy pictures of naked women. These were usually small pictures, the size of baseball trading cards. But there was nothing small about the women in the pictures! In some vans the pictures were glued across the dashboard, in others they dangled from a wire strung across the top of the windshield between the sun visor mounts.

Van drivers sped through the city seemingly paying no attention to pedestrians, in crosswalks or anywhere else for that matter. I would later discover that this was standard driving practice throughout most, if not all, of the former Soviet Russian Empire. For their part, people did all they could to contribute to the chaotic scene by darting across the streets, halting like squirrels in the middle of the road, and exhibiting just about every characteristic associated with randomness. The absence of pedestrian right-of-way was something we saw repeated in each country we lived in or visited. The view of this scene from the front seat of a minivan was unnerving if not spectacular! It reminded me of driving at dusk in eastern Idaho trying to negotiate the multitude of jackrabbits that constantly ran back and forth across the highway. The difference was that, while I did not hear or read of any pedestrian fatalities, the jackrabbits weren't so lucky.

By late October, the snow season began in earnest. Soon the snow and ice started to pile up and the city quickly ran out of money to get it removed from the streets. The metal containers of sand that had been strategically located at sidewalk's edge throughout the city did not get refilled. Taking the van ride back from my branch campus now was more like a toboggan run for the initial half mile trip down the hill. We would race down past all the ugly apartments, then around a wide left-hand turn, and finally, miraculously, come to a stop at a main arterial.

I concluded that the majority of van drivers were playing "Russian roulette" as they hurtled down the unsanded street while trying to keep their wheels in the narrow tire tracks that had melted through the ice and snow. I managed to get through a few of these trips by glancing at the girlie pictures and keeping uppermost in mind that within the hour I would be back to a warm apartment where a partially frozen shot of vodka would begin to take effect and settle my nerves. However, these ameliorative actions were not enough. Out of fear for my life, I decided to go back to the ponderously slow but safe bus and trolleybus riding.

Back to Bus and Trollybus Riding

The bus let me off toward the top of the hill at a cluster of large, ugly apartment buildings and the dismal-looking but still functioning remains of a mini-shopping mall. In the Soviet period these two things, mini-malls and apartment complexes, were almost always built adjoining each other.

From the bus stop, I had about a fifteen-minute walk before reaching the campus. I first would cross a busy four-lane arterial, dodging the speeding cars, including people who did not want to wait for the traffic light. Once across the highway, I would climb a long crumbling concrete staircase separated by large, often muddy areas, before reaching my building. I was teaching classes that began in the mid-afternoon, and by late fall, I would have to find my way back down to the bus stop in total darkness. All the campus lighting had long since worn out. The bulbs had blown out or the bulbs, and even the sockets, were missing. Sometimes nothing but electrical wires would hang out from underneath the light shields atop their rusty poles. When the early winter ice and snow arrived, the way would become quite treacherous, even with the help of a flashlight.

There is one final note on the topic of Lithuanian bus and trolleybus riding. A newsworthy event took place in the spring that helped to highlight the problem of excess bus and trolleybus passengers. The problem was not just confined to the capital city. Judy and I had found the same overcrowding in Kaunas, Lithuania's second largest city. To prove this point, and also hopefully set a world record, a group of fun-seeking university students in Kaunas spent part of a November day carefully packing themselves into one of the city buses, a standard seventy-passenger Hungarian-made model. I suspect that they were being coached by a watchful number of babushkas who probably also helped in pushing a record 278 students into the bus!

A Pleasant Walk to Work

In rather stark contrast to our Lithuanian experience, getting back and forth to school was much easier in each of my following three lecture postings. Still, each involved something new; each different from anything we had experienced in America. None involved a freeway, as no such thing existed. In every case, getting to work involved quite a bit of walking, and in Kharkiv and Tashkent, a person also had to be able to climb up and down a lot of stairs. I was often reminded that older people or those with a handicap were at an almost impossible disadvantage under these arrangements, which meant almost every Soviet city of any size.

The trip to work in Estonia was quite simple. Tallinn Pedagogical University was only a twenty-minute walk straight away from our big concrete-block apartment complex. The walk took me along the outside edge of the historic Old Town. The views into Old Town with its turreted walls, cone-topped towers, and Gothic cathedral spires were always a stirring experience, and quite a contrast to some of the newer parts of the city that had grown up around it. The architecture along my walk was varied, including a beautiful old opera and symphony building and several old wooden buildings, tucked in here and there, and dating from the early part of the century. But mostly there were just a lot of plain-Jane three and four story, brown or gray stucco 1950s and 1960s vintage Soviet structures. At this point in my walk, my attention would usually shift to what might be for sale inside the stores and small shops. Even though it was a smaller city, Tallinn seemingly had twice the shopping opportunities as Vilnius.

Toward the end of my walk, I would turn onto Narva Maantee, the main avenue leading east out of town, along the Gulf of Finland, toward the Russian border. At this point, the avenue became a three or more story concrete canyon, crowded, noisy, and obnoxiously fume laden. That is unless a stiff wind was blowing off the gulf, which made the avenue take on the feel of a high-speed wind tunnel.

Down Narva Maantee a few blocks was my university, whose broad three-story front faced this crowded thoroughfare. Little Soviet-built Lada automobiles and much larger Volgas raced up and down this four-lane street, dodging city buses and a procession of clanging trams running along a center set of tracks. I could easily smell all the uncatalyzed exhaust fumes from the traffic. The air was better inside the university, but my second-floor classroom faced the street and could only partially mute the traffic noise. The room gave a faint jiggle and the windows rattled like a small earthquake each time the trams went by.

Winter seemed to come very early during our year in Tallinn, but I was prepared for the walk to school. After slipping, sliding, and constantly fearing broken limbs in Lithuania, Judy and I had found the answer to our dreams in a small shoe shop in a Finnish-owned department store that was located only a block away from my route to work. They were flat black rubber soles with a hole in the front that slipped up over the toe of our shoes. The sole stretched back to a strap that went over the heel. There were several little stainless steel pins protruding from the rubber, enough to bite into the slickest of ice. Never mind the skating rink nature of the sidewalks; oh yes they were here in abundance. With these contraptions the walk to work was as safe as on a summer day. We referred to them as our "cleaty feet." They could be easily slipped off when not in use. I carried mine wrapped up in a plastic sack in my book bag. It was a wonderful invention. I just wish we had known about these earlier during our previous year in Vilnius.

Confronting a Variety of Challenges as We Continued to Walk

We continued to make good use of our cleaty feet during our year in Kharkiv, Ukraine. While the ice did not last as long as it had in Estonia or Lithuania, it seemed twice as slick due to the large amounts of freezing rain that often fell on top of it. During the weeks before and after the winter months, if it was not ice that was the challenge, it was muddy rainwater that would flood the streets where we lived.

Lacking grassy areas to catch some of the water, and storm sewers to take the rest, when the ice melted, or the rain subsided, our neighborhood was just mud, mud, and more mud. We slogged to the market and school in well oiled high-top hiking boots. I must say that my boots presented quite a muddy fashion statement in the classroom. Most of my students had to put up with somewhat similar walking conditions, but usually managed to wear nicer looking street shoes.

In Kharkiv, It took about the same amount of time, thirty minutes, to walk to work or to take the *metro*, the term used by the Soviets for all their subway systems. Signs with a big, lighted, red plastic "M" designated the locations where there was aboveground access to the system. However, Kharkiv enjoyed a fairly long fall season in 1998, one filled with color from the wide variety of trees in the city, especially the many horse chestnut trees. During this gorgeous weather, we hardly ever took the metro to school. Instead, we walked.

Most often we took a walking route that followed along Lenin Prospect. This was a pleasant route with its big trees and large sidewalks full of people. We would pass large numbers of students hanging around between classes on the steps of a medical school. Many of them were smoking cigarettes. Medical students no less! Our pet store was on this street, including some limited opportunities for upscale shopping. There was even a Baskin Robbins on this street, but we only went there once as it was quite expensive.

After several blocks, Lenin Prospect emptied out on a giant cobblestone square. More in the shape of a long rectangle, it was the second largest in the former Soviet Russian Empire. Near one end was a grassy, tree-shaded island. At its leading edge, facing the square stood the powerful, dramatic presence of Lenin. It was an immense dark-metal statue, at least thirty feet high, in the usual style with right arm outstretched. There were always freshly cut flowers at his feet.

Old (ca. 1980s) Soviet postcard of Liberty Square with Lenin in the foreground, the House of State and Industry in the background, and Kharkiv State University on the left.

Looking at the statue, still standing seven years after the end of Communism, prompted me to think of the contrast in the way people dealt with their Lenin statues in the Baltic states. There, Lenin statues were torn down at the first opportunity following independence. Many other places in the former Soviet Russian Empire also removed their Lenin statues, but not eastern Ukraine. Here the ubiquitous Lenin statues remained in place, along with Soviet hammer and sickle insignias protruding from building friezes and hovering over the doorway transoms of every government building. A lot of people in this part of Ukraine, maybe even the majority, were ambivalent at least, if not downright unhappy, over the fall of the Soviet Russian Empire. I told my students about Lenin and the dog poop story I had heard in Vilnius. They said few people in Kharkiv would find this humorous. This conclusion was rather obvious. In addition to all the statues and symbols, the Communist Party still paraded through the main street of the city, and older men continued to wear their faded and tattered suit jackets displaying all their medals from the Great Patriotic War.

Behind Lenin's statue, facing the other side of the square, was the large, eight-story main building of Kharkiv State University. I could see where one part of it had been bombed by the Germans and later rebuilt in a slightly different color brick. The building had a slightly art-deco look to its porte-cochere entrance above which was a tower filled with a triple column of tall slender windows. The architecture fit in with the flamboyant, and definitely art-deco appearance of the Building of State and Industry next door; the one whose front I often thought of as looking like a giant tic-tac-toe game.

I taught in an annex to the main university building, so our walk continued along behind the university through a big tree-filled park containing a zoo, some small restaurants, and, in good weather, several little outdoor beer gardens. These were great places to stop before or after class and people watch; especially the impromptu spring coed fashion show made up of the skimpiest West European inspired miniskirts and two to three inch platform shoes. Ahh, the life! On the way home, Judy and I would often stop in one of these places for a soft drink or a beer. My reverie in the passing fashion show would inevitably be broken by Judy's request for my attention, or a few destitute old people who would visit our table to request that they be permitted to take away the empty beer bottles. On one occasion when both of us were in the midst of enjoying a drink at one of the little tables, a young man sat down, identifying himself as a philosophy student, and asked if I would buy him a bottle of water. Saying he had recently converted to Judaism, he proceeded to launch into a discussion of the pros and cons of having a circumcision.

Toward the end of our walk, the main path wound out of the densely forested park onto a small square with a beautiful statue of Taras Shevchenko. Living only a brief life of forty-seven years, Shevchenko wrote passionately in support of Ukrainian nationalism in opposition to czarist policies of Russification. Shevchenko was imprisoned, and later exiled, but not before he had become Ukraine's most revered literary hero. Early in the spring, women would sit near his statue selling bunches of little white flowers called *podsnezhniki* ("under the snow") and blue flowers that looked like crocus. Pussywillow branches could also be purchased here.

Across the street and up a couple of blocks was the two-story university annex. This was where I held my classes. The building was originally constructed in the 1930s as a place for training officers of the KGB. Their headquarters had been across the street where the far less intrusive Ukrainian version of this police-state menace continued to operate. Out front of their building, in clear view from my second-story classroom, was the larger than life bust of Felix Dzerzhinsky, the founder of the *Cheka*, later to become the KGB. Sometimes, while giving a lecture, searching for a way to make a critical observation about the Soviet system, I would salute his likeness over there. It made a great shorthand way of contrasting good versus evil. The students found quite good fun in this gesture.

There was a second route we could walk to school. It went in the opposite direction from our dacha, past the little store where I had all my course reading assignments photocopied. A block or so further was the big farmer's-style market where Judy and I did most of our shopping. In one more block we would reach Sumskaya Street, a main thoroughfare where we would turn right, passing in front of the czar's dacha, now the wedding palace, and continue walking the remainder of the way to school. Sumskaya Street contained Kharkiv's best collection of pre-Bolshevik architecture. Sculptures abounded on the facades of the buildings. Street venders filled much of the sidewalk on the other side of the street, often slowing down my progress and forcing me to cross the street where the view was less interesting but the sidewalk was, at least, clear of venders by city ordinance. The ordinance made sense. All the venders would certainly have been an eyesore in front of such beautiful buildings.

This was my most often-used route to school, and Judy also took this route, frequently accompanying me—until the rain and the muddy season began, followed by ice and snow. Then it was time to begin taking the metro to work

The choice to take the metro began with about a five or six block walk from our dacha down a gentle slope, through a wooded park that opened out on Lenin Prospect, the same beginning which we had used when walking this way all the way to school. The last metro station on the blue line into the city was located where the park bordered Lenin Prospect. Here I would open one of the glass doors in a small above-ground entrance building and we would head down the stairs that turned into a long hallway. Crowding both sides of the stairs and hallway was a long line of makeshift kiosks selling primarily food and clothing. A second set of glass doors led into the metro station proper. A set of turnstiles, requiring a plastic coin for passage, led to one more flight of stairs down to the spotlessly clean, chandelier-lit, train platform.

As a quick aside, one might wonder, as we certainly did, why there were so many portable kiosks, more often just folding tables, scattered throughout the city, and in the metro areas, selling small quantities of practically everything. We had encountered this multitude of venders in other cities in Russia and Central/ Eastern Europe, but never as densely as in Ukraine. The answer is simply that when the Communist system collapsed, unemployment shot up, sometimes to well over 50 percent of the workforce. Street and metro vending was one of the few legitimate ways for unemployed people to make a little money. Judy and I came across people with all kinds of employment backgrounds working as venders, even former teachers and medical doctors!

Once inside the underground station, we could count on being in a meticulously clean, beautifully decorated oasis. The journey consisted of three stops, including a transfer, plus another three block walk, and there I was, out front of my classroom building, ready to again salute Mr. Dzerzhinsky.

No matter if I took the metro or walked, the only difficult part of the trip, besides the winter encounters with mud and the ice, involved the evening walk back. There was no way to escape having to make part of the walk in almost pitch-dark conditions. Whether after school, after the opera, or dinner out—after just about any trip away from the dacha—returning after nightfall meant that our trip home ended with a walk back through the park. It was, by far, the quickest, most convenient route.

The park had once contained adequate lighting, but these conveniences had long since fallen into total disrepair. Bare wires could be seen sticking out at all angles from uncovered junction boxes in many of the lampposts. It didn't take very long for Judy and me to get used to walking in the dark. It was comforting to almost always have other people walking near us or toward us on the path. Frequently, when it was both dark and really foggy, we would meet these people suddenly, almost right in front of us. This was an experience that took a little bit of getting used to, especially when, in order to prevent a crash, we needed to quickly step left or right on the slick ice and snow. During this part of the walk it was always nice to think about how close to home we were and how it would only be just a few more minutes before we would arrive there.

Metro riding was almost always a pleasure. However, the best place to describe metro rides other than Moscow—the showcase of the mother of all metros—was at our next and final posting, in Tashkent, Uzbekistan. Incidentally, we didn't throw away our rubber traction soles when we left Ukraine. As the cleaty feet were still in good condition, we gave them away. Mine went to my student Igor. Judy's were destined for his mother.

The Metro: Undoubtedly the Soviets' Best Travel Legacy

In Tashkent, our metro entrance was less than a block from our apartment. How much more convenient could a subway stop get! The station was named after "Khamid Olimjon," although nobody I asked could tell me what this person was famous for. He was an early twentieth-century Uzbek poet.

Out on the sidewalk in front of the stairs to the metro entrance, seated in a white plastic chair, was our unofficial greeter. Luda was a seventy-one-year-old ethnic Russian babushka, whiling away her time talking to friends and selling a few items she had spread out in front of her on the broad entrance railing.

Luda

Judy and I would normally pause to signal a greeting, wave at the sky, and smile at the good weather. Once, while entering the metro with one of my students, she realized she could get something she wanted to say interpreted. She motioned us over to tearfully tell the story about her daughter's husband, a soldier, who, the story went, had recently lost his life in a skirmish with Taliban-type militants trying to cross Uzbekistan's short southern border with Afghanistan. He had left his thirty-six-year-old wife, Alisandra, with two small children. Alisandra knit baby things for her mother to sell. Judy had purchased some of these items—mittens, a hat, and booties—early in our stay in Tashkent. We took them to Germany at Christmas for our granddaughter Natalie.

As fall approached and the morning weather began to get a bit chilly, I decided to ask Luda if her daughter would consider knitting me a wool sweater. My pantomimed suggestion was immediately accepted. An appointment was made for 10:00 AM the next day for Alisandra, to take a few street-side measurements and for us to settle on a style and color. I chose a dark green heavy-ribbed pattern. Again, our transaction was pantomime with sketches and prices written on a small piece of paper. Unfortunately, the sweater took far more time to make than promised. Winter came and went, short as it was in our desert location. Finally, one warm May morning there was a knock on our apartment door. My name was being called out over and over from the other side of the door. It was Luda bringing me the sweater. How she knew exactly where we lived, I don't know. Our flat was hot, the air-conditioner was running full bore, but I could see that Luda expected the sweater to be tried on. It was a perfect fit, a real beauty, and only about eight dollars, including the price of the yarn. Judy wished that she had ordered one, too.

Once down in the metro station, the physical layout: elevators, token sales windows, turnstiles, even the olive-colored subway cars, were the same as we had experienced in all the other cities with Soviet metro systems. What was different was the decor, which was always unique to each former Soviet city and to each metro stop. The metro stops in Moscow were the oldest, and while deep enough in the ground to feel as though we might just as well be deep shaft coal miners, they were absolutely gorgeous, containing a wide variety of artwork. Several were like museums showcasing reproductions of classic sculpture. The metro system in Kharkiv, in Kyiv, and the stops we used while in Minsk, continued this same upscale look except in a less elaborate manner

The metro stations in Tashkent were also very striking in design, containing many different materials and featuring themes celebrating famous personalities and historical events. My favorite was "Kosmonavtlar." This metro stop was decorated in bright-colored anodized aluminum. There was a mural running the full length of the loading platform—maybe forty or fifty yards—depicting major space-related events and celebrants: beginning with Galileo, next Sputnik, and ending with the Soviet Cosmonaut Yuri Gagarin, the first man in space. In just about every stop, there were beautifully crafted chandeliers reflecting off of highly polished marble floors.

The decor inside our stop was fashioned around the cotton plant, in keeping with the main economic staple of Uzbekistan. Wrought-iron light posts held lamps shaped like cotton boles with petal insets constructed of dark green hand-blown glass, all bubbly and irregular in their composition. The walls of the main platform contained additional artistic renditions of the cotton plant. No matter how rushed or preoccupied, Judy and I always found time to admire the insides of these metro stations. They were always a spectacular sight, a wonderful way to mask the naked functionality of underground transportation. It was also a superb way in which to make taking mass transit to work and back an acceptable complement, if not an alternative, to the automobile.

Spoiling the great effect inside of each metro stop was always a couple of military police with scary-looking automatic weapons. Judy and I were constantly asked by these *miltisia* for our "documents" Early on; I discovered that I could reduce the incidence of apprehension by not wearing my "parachute" style bloused nylon trousers. These, apparently fit me into a suspect profile. Either way, being stopped was an unnerving experience. Once we were taken to a small room near a metro entrance to have our big bulky grocery bags searched. It was quite terrifying; all this unwanted attention, but we began to expect it and get a bit used to the experience.

Noting that these military uniformed police were generally ethnic nationals from the villages, a CEP colleague suggested a technique for dealing with their harassing behavior. "Begin by shaking hands" he said "and offering a polite greeting." He gave us a greeting, which we promptly memorized. It had to do with asking about his wife and children. "Also make sure to mention that you are a university professor and show them your faculty ID rather than your passport." This advice looked to have a good chance of working, as I knew that shaking hands was the standard way to begin conversations in Central Asia, that teachers were very highly respected, that old people were also highly respected, and we were senior teachers. However, we never got a chance to try out the advice. Soon thereafter, we were issued diplomatic visas by the CEP. This did not prevent being stopped, but the result was now only a quick glance at our documents and a salute.

Being hassled by the authorities was a way of life in Uzbekistan. Local foot police stopped at least half of all our taxi rides. It didn't matter whether they were official or informal. The police were especially aggressive in pulling over the informal type, the private cars we had flagged down when we were late to work or had to get somewhere quickly and no taxi was available. Standing out in the street, the policeman would point his red tipped baton at our car and motion us to the side of the road. The driver would grumble or sigh, as his personality would dictate, while gathering up his documents, from the sun visor or glove box, in preparation to exit the car. There would first be an obligatory handshake. This would be followed by a discussion, more precisely a price negotiation over the size of the bribe that would ensue.

It reminded me of what is called "the bite" in Mexico, only it happened much more often. Money would change hands, and we would again be free to go. I wasn't anxious to jump into this exchange and flash my diplomatic credentials. Would I have received a salute? Probably I would. Would we have had to pay a bribe? Probably we wouldn't. I was not interested in testing these guesses. Instead, I usually just tipped the driver an extra amount for his loss. Getting places by car was definitely faster and certainly reasonably priced, at less than a dollar, to go from one side of this immense city to the other. Just the same, when not short on time, we preferred to take the metro and enjoy the underground life of the city.

Waiting on the loading platform, we would look for an uncrowded train car going in our direction. Approaching the nearest car door, we stood aside for those exiting and then quickly moved in. We had about twenty seconds to get in, find a seat, or pick a place to stand. The cars were lined on each side with brown vinyl covered benches. The great respect given to older people in central Asia could be seen in the young people who would quickly stand up to give us their space. If they were a little slow about moving, it only took a fleeting moment of eye contact to remind them of their obligation. Older people who preferred to stand could expect to have their bags held by someone who was seated.

Not being designed to accommodate the advertising detritus associated with capitalism, the cars had no place for product announcements, but they were showing up anyway, usually stuck to the inside of the windows. Most ads featured imported personal care products, some of it rather intimate. I wondered how the older Uzbek women felt about this effrontery to their sensibilities.

The metro passengers exhibited a reasonably accurate cross section of the Tashkent population. Outside of the matter of age and sex, they could be mostly classified into two categories: ethnic Russians/Ukrainians or one of several indigenous ethnic/racial groups. The latter categories could each be divided by those who were wearing Western dress and those who were wearing traditional dress. Ethnic Russians and Ukrainians were usually taller with fair complexions. Older men might be bald, and both men and women wore Western-style clothing. Passengers representing one of the indigenous ethnic groups, mainly Uzbek, Tajik, Kazakh, and Karakalpak (in descending order of number) were shorter and darker complected with brown eyes and always a full head of black hair.

Most of the young men dressed in Western clothing, while far more than half of all the women, young or old, remained more traditional, wearing head scarves and very brightly colored long dresses made from either synthetic material or silk, which they wore over a type of pantaloon. The older more traditional-minded men might wear an old suit, but on cooler days, this would be covered with a long silk or quilted cotton coat that looked like a Western-style bathrobe. The coat may have been accompanied by a colorful silk sash. Older men almost always wore a black-and-white printed or embroidered skullcap, although the exact nature of headgear could vary by ethnic group. Just about everybody carried one or more plastic store-label sacks or bright plastic woven bags full of their purchases. This was almost always the case if people were entering the car at the Chorsu metro stop located directly underneath the city's giant central outdoor market.

After one change of metro cars and a total ride time of a little more than half an hour from our starting point at the Khamid Olimjon station, Judy and I would walk through the exit tunnel at the end of the line. I would stop for a minute to peer over a knot of willing betters crowded around an obvious scam artist. It was almost always the same person. There he was in the metro tunnel, one hand full of paper money, and his other hand quickly moving playing cards around the top of his portable table. My bet was that he had paid off the police to be allowed to continue his undoubtedly lucrative operation. Then, for us, it was up the final set of stairs and out into the bright sunlight and heat of early afternoon. The immediate area was crowded with people selling vegetables, fruits (including a wide variety of melons), and traditional baked snacks. All of this was accompanied by the pounding sounds of Central Asian popular music booming out from the speakers of at least a half dozen cassette venders.

From the metro exit, it was a fifteen-minute walk to school. The sidewalk led past a large weed-infested turn-around for one of the city's tram lines. Just past this was a state-run service station (the only kind), with cars waiting for gas, usually lined up in several long rows. (Gas was fairly inexpensive, but there were not enough stations to meet demand.) From here a path led to a one-lane road that followed the mud-walled edge of a line of houses in a traditional Uzbek village. The one-story houses, while sharing common walls, each had their own courtyard. Clothes hung from wash lines. Fresh mud plaster was being applied to the outside of some of the houses. Large adobe-looking bricks were drying on the ground in a cleared space nearby. Keeping a sharp eye out for fresh cow pies under foot, we would pass the village garbage dump, often with eye-stinging fumes emanating from smoldering plastic containers. Cows, chickens, and the ubiquitous sheep with the bulbous rear ends would all share the little road with a few cars, some students, and us.

We would soon come to the edge of a large soccer stadium and indoor gym, both in poor condition like everything else on National

University's large campus, which once held upwards of forty thousand students, now shrunk to a population of fewer than two thousand. Finally, after entering an open gate in a high wrought-iron fence, we were only a few hundred yards from my office and classroom building.

The university's student population had dramatically declined after independence, in part because it lost most of its students from other regions of the Soviet Russian Empire, and there were no longer scholarships for foreign students. But, an equally important reason was fear by state officials of the consequences of student protest. Shortly after national independence was declared, there had been a student sit-down strike at the university over a reduction to unrealistically low scholarship stipends. The protest had grown quite large and lasted for several weeks and had resulted in a number of lives being lost: a classic example of authoritarian response. The Ministry of Education quickly decentralized Uzbekistan's higher education system, scattering most of the students throughout the country, in part, so the story told to me by my students has it, to reduce the threat of future large-scale student disturbances.

Now several places of higher learning are physically blocked off behind concrete and spiked fences, requiring passage through a guarded turnstile to gain access. Norma Jo Baker, our country director, once discussed with me the problem of the CEP having to get special documentation to allow students from one school to visit classes or special functions at another. She regarded openness of a university, its willingness to let others come in and be involved, as a "litmus test" of the real nature of the "education" that is occurring inside the walls. As such, Uzbekistan pretty much failed this test.

It didn't usually snow much, if any, during Tashkent winters. But sure enough, it was lightly snowing one evening as we walked from the university back to the metro entrance. We have since thought it quite ironic that, on that brief walk, all it took was a little slick spot for Judy to fall down on a culvert crossing a small ditch and end up with a bad cut over her right eye. We hailed a private car cum taxi for a quick trip across most of Tashkent to a little outpatient clinic that served Western clientele. Judy needed a couple of stitches above her eye. After all we had been through in surviving three previous hard winters getting to work and back, and now our good luck and Judy's pride had evaporated over a small patch of ice.

During my four years of commuting, whether in Vilnius, Tallinn, Kharkiv, or Tashkent, I often thought about the uniqueness of what I was experiencing. There were many pleasant encounters with everyday life. In some cases, the experience would seem onerous, difficult, or tiring. I would think about how much easier it had been to get to work back home in Boise. For example, I didn't have to walk along busy streets choked with uncatalyzed automobile exhaust. I wouldn't find myself cringing while being driven down steep, icy streets at high speed or arriving home in the evening half frozen from standing more than an hour in the bitter cold. Probably most comforting, I would not have to be subject to body searches by an Uzi-toting militiaman. Actually, I hardly needed to give these situations a second thought to conclude that they were really very positive events. The common denominator of these and many other little adversities—and I have said this before—was always a heady sense of being alive, of the unanticipated opportunity to feel or reflect on things differently. Such is the pleasure of purposive travel.

7
Teaching "Over There"

Shock and Awe

"Over there" was a term the CEP staff used when referring to the great expanse of the former Soviet Russian Empire. It was a short-hand expression all of us found useful. "Over there" was a vast territory where life, and the job of an educator, would be a challenging one. In one form or another, all of us would face trials and tribulations, often of major proportion. Yet, while making a life and getting to work were challenging then, and memorable now, being "over there" was fundamentally about a new and very unusual venue in which to experience the many little joys of teaching.

The CEP *Position Announcement* said they were looking for people willing to teach in the former Soviet Union in a "challenging environment." When I signed up, Judy and I both tried to imagine what it would be like to live and work in a country whose way of life neither of us knew anything about. Like others of our generation, we had spent the majority of our lives facing, as we believed, the Soviet's world-ending threat of mass death by nuclear bombs, yet we had remained essentially ignorant of the realities of life behind the Iron Curtain.

I began to think about what it would be like to be a visiting lecturer. What would be the pleasures and frustrations both of us might face? What adjustments would I need to make in order to teach "over there"? What kind of students would I have? Would they be able to understand me? Would I be able to understand them? Would I be able to fit in with the other professors and make friends? What would the university be like? I was full of questions that would soon be answered.

As I thought about the question of what it would be like to teach "over there," I was reminded of a humorous story told by Mae Shores about her initial experience as a CEP lecturer, a year ahead of me, in Moscow in fall 1994. She wrote about it in our little CEP *Guide to Life and Teaching in Eastern Europe and Eurasia*, which was given to all new lecturers. Ms. Shores's story is a great example of the challenges of teaching we all faced, although, I am very thankful in my case, not quite to this extreme. Mae knew she would likely face challenges "over there," but after landing in Moscow a few days ahead of the start of the school year, Mae discovered that her lectureship at Moscow State University had been canceled—unilaterally.

Without any warning, school authorities had changed their minds. Now they were citing the reasons to involve matters of housing and salary, details previously settled in a written contract prior to Mae's arrival. Faced with no job and no place to stay, Mae later wrote that she thought about "teaching inside one metro stop and sleeping on a bench at another." She was helped to find a place to stay, and her local CEP director quickly arranged an audience and an impromptu one-hour lecture before faculty at a different institution: the Academy of Public Administration. Not wishing to be left without a job, Shores also met with officials at a third place of higher education. Everybody seemed suspicious of the motives behind what appeared to be last-minute job hunting—which was exactly what it was! A second presentation was arranged a few days later for a small number of professors at International University, the last school on the list of possibilities. Instead of a presentation to faculty, when Shores arrived at this school, she was asked to give the first class lecture for the semester—in a subject she was not prepared to teach. Afterward, she was hired for the position. Shores concluded the story of her year in Moscow, by considering it to be like Dostoyevsky's description of Russian life in *The Inquisition*. Shores wrote, "When events in this part of the world go well it is, indeed, to quote Dostoyevsky, 'a mystery and a miracle.'"

Now it was my turn to test my luck against the vagaries of the once mighty but enigmatic Soviet educational system. It only took an initial trip to my branch of the university that first year in Vilnius to come face to face with one very significant fact: my teaching that year was going to occur in what I could only describe, without exaggerating the point, as an educational black hole, created by an absolutely minimal amount of financing and characterized by a physical plant that was suffering from severe, even extreme, long-term neglect. It was the typical situation I would later face in almost every university where I taught or visited throughout the former Soviet Russian Empire.

With some exceptions, notably in Estonia, the universities seemed to be barely functioning. Teaching and research appeared to be running mostly on minimal inertia from the past. It seemed questionable whether most students were getting anything approaching a decent education, although I would have to admit that most of my students seemed adequately prepared, some outstandingly so. It was just that the material state of the buildings and classrooms were in such terrible shape. Initially I was shocked by what I experienced. I found it hard to concentrate on what I was trying to teach. All I could think was, "My God, this can't be for real." Then I remembered the words of the position announcement and thought about why I joined the CEP. Within a few short weeks, I was more often thinking, "What do I need to do to make my stay here effective?"

Over the four years with the CEP, I not only adjusted to the adverse conditions, I thrived on them. What really made the difference was that both Judy and I got much more involved in the education and in the informal life of my students. What began as "my job" became very definitely "our job" by the second year. Both our pleasure and my teaching effectiveness went up accordingly. From then on out, the poor students had to contend with two teachers who ganged up on them!

I was reminded of Shore's story of finding a teaching job in Moscow, and especially about the fact that it would be a mystery and a miracle if things were to go right, the day Susan Cooper took me for my initial visit to my university. We made our way across town to a suburban area filled with high-rise apartments, then up a large hill to the university's branch campus.

I had a brief meeting with Birute Pociute. She was the dean at this campus and responsible for setting my teaching time schedule and signing off on my contract. I then got a look at my small office and assigned classroom across the hall. The classroom was furnished in the standard Soviet form. The following day, I decided to bring some books and supplies to my office and examine my classroom more closely. The classroom was devoid of any frills. It had a plank wood floor and eight or ten tables, each covered on top in laminate and long enough to hold two or three persons. There was a variety of single chairs, some usable and some not. Students sat down in them gingerly as it was not always obvious which ones would hold their weight and which might bring them crashing to the floor. There was a practically unusable blackboard located in the front of the room. On the wall just above the blackboard was a long naked florescent light that flickered incessantly when turned on. I washed the blackboard with a dingy old rag and water from a little sink that sat in the corner of the classroom.

I began to replace constantly missing incandescent lightbulbs from the ceiling fixtures out of my personal supply. The story was that students would take the lightbulbs from the classroom fixtures in order to replace those burned out in their dormitories. I wondered if my students would have heard about the "How many … does it take to screw in a lightbulb" joke. I decided not to tell the joke as I knew that several of my students were of Polish background. Quite probably, all of the students would have had difficulty understanding the basis of the humor, and I didn't want to get in trouble. Jokes do not often translate across cultural lines very well. Of more concern was that Polish jokes just did not seem so humorous, considering the extensive stereotyping and persecution Polish people had received in this part of the world over at least the last two hundred years.

Having now made my peace with the classroom and its blackboard, having tidied things up a bit, I was now set to offer two elective classes for the fall semester: one on criminology and the other on social change. Neither of these two subjects had probably ever been taught before in Lithuania.

One essential part of teaching is the same everywhere: "Have lecture notes; will travel." The students, a classroom, a blackboard, and some chalk will always be there, right? Not necessarily. The students were there, enthusiastically so, often far too many of them, but getting the rest of the basic ingredients together always required flexibility and a fair amount of initiative. Several times at Kharkiv State University and at National University I would come to my classroom only to find someone else's class in full swing or the room used for a faculty meeting, or decked out for a party. Parties were a constant feature, usually in honor of a staff or faculty member's birthday. In fact, partying was far more common than anything I had ever witnessed at home, or while teaching in Spain where the university seemed constantly to close its entire operation in order to celebrate one of many saint's days.

Chalk and chalkboards were a luxury. I tried having chalk sent to me from home. It turned out to be too hard to be of much use. In Vilnius, I supplied classroom lightbulbs. In Tashkent, I frequently had to move classrooms to find a lighting system that would work. Sometimes to get the lights to turn on, I would carefully bend together two wires that protruded from the open switchbox on the wall. There were other distractions. In Vilnius, the classroom came close to freezing. In Tashkent, it would bake close to 100 degrees, and if I opened the windows, noxious smoke from leaf and general garbage burning in nearby outdoor oil barrels would usually pour into the classroom. Also in Tashkent, my blackboard was often a large piece of unpainted hardboard leaning against the wall. Throughout the year in Kharkiv, I used a small portable chalkboard that I would park on top of a chair that I sat up on a table in front of the classroom. Occasionally, it was a matter of not having access to any of the basic teaching ingredients at all, except students, where I always had plenty of the very best.

Class Preparation, Scheduling, and the Small Matter of Salary

Being almost fanatical about the need for thorough preparation, I was initially comforted in knowing the serious effort the in-country CEP staff would make prior to my arrival to obtain a signed contract specifying what courses I would teach, how many different courses I would be responsible for, and, although it mattered much less, how much I would be paid. Of course, the university had to then uphold their end of the bargain. These three items of business barely worked the first year in Lithuania, were never a problem during my second year in Estonia, seriously faltered the third year in Ukraine, and received no attention at all during the last year which we spent in Uzbekistan. This was not the fault of my country directors. It was mainly that Western–style contracts, course titles and teaching schedules, office hours, payment amounts, and many other institutionalized practices and routines were little understood, or worse, purposely ignored.

Getting paid in Estonia meant only a short walk across the hallway to the paymaster's office once each month, while in Lithuania I was paid the best of all four teaching locations, about $350 a month over a full twelve months. The payment routine in Lithuania was so out of my ordinary experience that I will briefly describe it.

At the end of each month, I would go to my department office at the branch campus and fill out a form listing my course titles and number of lectures I gave during the month. I always put the same number of lectures each month regardless. Then on the last working day of the first week of the following month, I would walk to the main university campus in the Old Town to visit the paymaster. There was always a long line of people waiting to be paid. The paymaster's little office opened onto a big arched hallway on the main floor of the university. The paymaster sat behind the lower half of an open Dutch door that faced the hallway. There was a small shelf attached to the inside of the lower part of the door in front of which sat an older lady. Next to her was an old wooden cabinet divided into several cubby holes, each filled with stacks of different denominations of *litas,* the Lithuanian money. In front of the paymaster were a couple of plastic egg cartons containing an assortment of coins.

After a long wait, I would make it to the paymaster's door. It was a wait made much longer by the large number of people who would "cut" into the line ahead of me. I asked about this practice a few times, always being told that a friend was holding the "cutter" a place in line as a favor for previously having been invited, by the same person, into this or some other line. This was obviously a vestige of Soviet line-waiting etiquette that I was going to have to get used to. I was told that during Soviet times, food and consumer staples were often in short supply. People would wait in long lines for lengthy periods of time, carrying what came to be known as their "perhaps bag," waiting to see if, perhaps, there might be something to buy, or worth buying at the front of the line. The practice of reciprocal place holding for friends was said to have developed as a result of these frequent long waits.

When I finally arrived at the paymaster's door/window, I would show the lady my passport picture page with my name written below it, and she would quickly find my name on a master list in front of her, check it off, and then begin to count out my monthly salary. This could be quite a wad, as the exchange rate was four Lithuanian *litas* to one dollar, and the paymaster typically paid me in small denominations.

I always felt rather conspicuous trying to stuff all the money into my pockets. I felt even more conspicuous when, on a late summer vacation trip with the McFaddens, we stopped by the paymaster's window to collect my final three months salary. I had to ask for a large bag. Then Judy, Jan, and John, and everybody else in the hallway area got to watch me stuff a fairly large plastic bag nearly full of money. Talk about being conspicuous!

It began to look as though I might not get paid while teaching in Ukraine. The process of finally receiving my salary was quite complicated and ended up rather farcical. Within the first few days of my arrival at Kharkiv State University, Judy and I were taken to the police department for registration. I then had my initial meeting with two university officials who worked in the Office of Foreign Relations. Don't be confused about the office title. This place appeared to be primarily an office to monitor people who came to the university from abroad. I was to present my credentials, a birth certificate, certificate of marriage (an interesting requirement that was also necessary in Uzbekistan), and a copy of my PhD diploma.

The office was sparsely furnished, including three or four desks, side chairs, and a few very out-of-date travel picture advertisements on the walls, for example, Paris, Istanbul, Rome, etc. The place was cold and unfriendly. Everything looked quite worn out. This included the secretary's old typewriter and the dark, threadbare suits of the two older men whom I had come to meet. One appeared to be a silent prop. I concluded that he probably could not speak English. The other man did all the talking. When he smiled, I could see that he was missing a few front teeth. Both men smiled a lot anyway while intermittently waiting for the secretary to slowly type the information being given to her about our conversation.

I examined each man carefully, as it had been reliably mentioned to me that both had been KGB officials during Soviet times. This was my first known encounter with this social type, and my imagination had conjured up several scenarios of possible intrigue in their biography. The teaching contract was finally produced and, in reversal of expected practice, I signed first. I left the office, along with another toothless smile and the promise that the university president would promptly sign the contract with a completed copy ready for me in just a few days. It was ready in exactly two months!

Back at the Office of Foreign Relations two months later, the smiling KGB men happily reported that my salary, the equivalent of eighty dollars a month, would now begin. "What about payment for the past two months?" I asked. They smiled again. "I am sorry," the English-speaking man said, "It is impossible."

I saw the inside of the Office of Foreign Relations several more times during the year, as Judy and I could not travel outside Ukraine without first visiting this dingy little place to obtain a permit. I put this and my ridiculous salary arrangements down as just one more example of incompetence and rigmarole held over from Soviet times.

By the time I began my fourth year of lectureship, I was used to preparation, scheduling, pay, and many other academic snafus. The bottom for higher educational competence was reached at National University in Uzbekistan where I never saw a contract, never discussed possible classes, nor got paid the whole time I was there. Pay, if I had received any, would have only amounted to about ten dollars a month. As it turned out, it didn't matter. I was able to select my own classes. My salary was paid by the CEP, which had a backup policy of guaranteeing a minimum monthly salary of one hundred dollars no matter where the lecturer posting might be. This amount, of course, was a handsome remuneration in Uzbekistan.

Managing a Regional Needs Assessment Survey

Early in my first year as a visiting lecturer in Vilnius I was asked to participate in a multi-country survey of the state of higher education in the social sciences. The CEP had received a large grant for the purpose of conducting a needs assessment within the universities throughout Central/Eastern Europe. I was responsible for conducting the survey at the University of Vilnius and coordinating a similar survey at two other university locations in Lithuania.

The CEP wanted to determine what social science professors knew about their specific disciplines, what they were teaching in their classes, and the manner in which they were conducting their classes. It was felt that this kind of information would help in deciding where CEP needed to focus its activities and resources as well as provide solid information to support further grant applications. The CEP would no longer have to rely on antidotal and impressionistic information to make its case.

The questionnaires, one for professors and one for students, were in English. My initial job was to get them translated into Lithuanian. This involved first having a translation made and then back-translating the questionnaire into English as a check on the accuracy of the Lithuanian translation. I was given money to hire a few of my most capable students to do the translations. This turned out to be very difficult and should have been done by an experienced professional. The translations, while being a financial God-send to the students, were usually not very accurate and sometimes very funny as well. They had to be translated into Lithuanian and back-translated into English more than once. I can only imagine what this process must have produced as professors and students filled out the questionnaires.

The worst part of my involvement in the survey came as a result of being the person in charge of the project. I enjoyed doing the work: arranging questionnaire translations, hiring and supervising students to administer the questionnaires, and making an initial collation of their results. Nobody, it turned out, had been assigned to brief university central administration about the nature and objective of the project. I was not asked to do this, should have thought about the importance of doing it, and ended up doing it anyway, but not before the damage had been done.

About half the way through the project, I was summoned before what American universities would call a university Presidents Council to explain what it was that the CEP was doing. My student interpreter and I found our way through the labyrinth of halls at the University of Vilnius, leading to the ornate chambers of this imposing gathering. The room was quite large and had a beautifully decorated arched ceiling that reminded me of a small version of the Sistine Chapel. Seated around a long carved and highly polished wooden table were the university rector (president), vice rectors, and deans.

Fortunately, some of the administrators spoke English. They wanted to know about the survey project. They were polite, but they were clearly upset by what they felt to be CEPs presumption that conducting the survey, without their prior consent, was in the best interest of the university. The fact that the resulting data would be widely circulated outside their country concerned them deeply. I explained about the project as best as I could and emphasized the anonymity individual participants and their schools would have in published reports. It was a very uncomfortable experience. I had been scolded, rightfully so, for trying to "do good" for people who very much wanted to control their own affairs. The meeting ended with permission given for me to finish the survey.

Making Sure the Students Had Enough to Read

The most important part of class preparation, besides collecting and organizing lecture notes and a few essential reference books, was making sure that the students had enough good quality assignable reading material. I had been lucky to find a few textbooks that I was able to use in several criminology classes during my first two postings. Otherwise, there were small (fifty to two hundred books) English-title libraries located in our teaching offices at the universities in Tallinn, Kharkiv, and, surprisingly, the best one, at National University in Tashkent.

Each library contained a few titles from which I was able to gather some additional useful material. However, most of the reading I assigned to the students came from article reprints, magazine and newspaper clippings, textbook chapters, and selections from anthologies I collected at home, making one photocopy of each document prior to leaving for each of my CEP postings.

Once in country, and following a final determination as to which classes I would be teaching, I would quickly go to work making up the initial portion of a packet of photocopied reading material for each student. During the semester, I would pass out additional reading material so that the student's packet grew in size until shortly before the end of the semester. This much photocopying was time-consuming to set up and operate, and it was expensive, but, it was far less expensive than trying to ship books over from the United States. This was true even if the books had been donated free of charge. CEP had initially tried to ship books such as those I used for the criminology class, but the practice was discontinued, in most cases, due to high freight costs and customs agents who could be very uncooperative unless given significant bribes.

Therefore, the CEP began to make extensive use of the photocopy approach to reading materials. Copyright waivers had to be arranged from the publisher for every bit of my material before copies could be printed. Once I made a decision on what material to hand out to the students, I sent a long e-mail letter containing all references to the CEP headquarters at Yale. Following copyright approval, each piece of my assigned reading had to contain on its front sheet a statement to the effect that photocopy permission had been granted.

Copy machines were almost nonexistent in the universities, so most of what seemed like tons of my copying needs was done by local merchants. Two of these merchants were small, commercial copy centers. One was a tiny owner-operated stationary store with a single copy machine. The other, our favorite, was located in Kharkiv, just a ten minute walk from our dacha near where we shopped at the farmers market. We often lugged home both groceries and a ream or two of photocopies together in our large shopping bags.

Igor and Dima. Car parts are to the left, copy machine in the back, kitchen and bath supplies behind Judy, stationary items behind my camera. Kharkiv, Ukraine.

Igor was the owner of this micro-sized department store. He looked to be in his midforties. When he was in the store, we always received a warm greeting. A big smile would appear on his typically unshaven stubbly face. His glasses were the kind that had a permanent yellow-green tint, darkest at the top and shading off toward the bottom of each lens. Igor kept a Xerox machine near the back wall of the store. It was old and overtaxed, but Dima, his young assistant, seemed to know how to keep it running.

Knowing where we lived, one of my students had mentioned this store as conveniently located and having a very low per-sheet copy price. I later noted that the price was prominently displayed out in front of the store. The main door opened into a hallway. To get to the copy section, I would first pass an adjoining room where Igor rented space to a couple of dentists. I would then pass the automotive product counter. Next was the kitchen and household cleaning items counter containing cheap, rough textured, toilet paper—which we bought and used following the guide "when in Rome...."

All this, plus a few business connections in Cypress that seemed a bit murky to me, kept us wondering if Igor had Mafia connections. He even sported the stereotypical close-cropped crew cut and drove a brand-new Toyota SUV, also de rigueur for someone in this position. Whatever his dealings, business was good enough, beyond our photocopies and toilet paper purchases, to keep his attractive wife and young child in enough money to live high above the average Ukrainian standard. Judy and I had the pleasure on one occasion of accompanying Igor and his family, in the new Toyota, to a graduation dinner function at their son's private grade school.

Igor discovered that I was a car restorer. We would talk about the good and bad qualities of Soviet-made Volgas, Zhigulis, and the Ukrainian-made Zaparosia. None could be called beautiful or sexy; in fact they were all terribly ugly. That wasn't the point, anyway. They were Soviet made. There was one especially cobbled-up-looking early 1960s vintage model called the "Victory." In this sense it was like so much else that had been named after the Great Patriotic War. It looked a bit like a botched-up cross between a Studebaker and a Ford. Igor showed me a sheet of classified car ads and said he would help me purchase a Victory and get it shipped back to Idaho. I was tempted. Newell Cook urged me on and promised he would buy one, too. How unique would this be! That's just it, too unique. I backed out. So did Newell.

Either one or the both of us made the trip to Igor's business at least twice a week. Following our return to our dacha, we would spread our sack full of photocopies on the floor, sort the copies into stacks and begin assembling and stapling together the multiple copies of each assigned reading. It took a lot of time, and, of course, we had to lug all this material to school within the next few days. It was a worthwhile endeavor. The students really appreciated all the preparation work, and the fact that much of the reading material was current, sometimes only a month or more since original publication.

Getting Used to the Students

Over the many years of teaching, I have always found each class to be a little bit unique, to have its own personality, and hopefully not to be distinguished in some adverse way. In my CEP classes, a very positive kind of uniqueness was the expected order of the day, the most sought-after and appreciated part of my lecture appointments. I was never disappointed in this expectation.

My first class at the University of Vilnius branch campus met all these requirements. The room held about thirty individuals. It was full to overflowing on the first meeting for each class. This was followed for the next few weeks by a lot of coming and going of new faces. It seemed like every student at the university wanted to see what I looked and sounded like. Some more serious students came to see what I was going to do. I recorded well over a hundred students who flowed through my two classes that first semester before I was finally able to identify the regulars and a somewhat smaller group whose attendance and class work ultimately earned them a grade. This final group turned out to be a dishearteningly small number, eight in one class and ten in the other. I was hoping for more.

I wished my classes were bigger that first semester. I learned that one reason for the small numbers was the workload I assigned. It was about the same as I assigned at my home university. I was running up against the Soviet practice of keeping students in the classroom as much as forty or more hours a week. This is in contrast to American college students who spend about half or less this amount of time in class. In the Soviet system, students were used to doing most of their work in class, thus having little or no homework. I was assigning too much homework, including a required research-style term paper, weekly take-home essays over assigned reading, and preparation for a midterm and comprehensive final examination. All this turned out to be too much for many of the students, especially considering that they were working in a second or third language. I also failed to consider that my students were used to taking only one test: a single end-of-the-semester oral examination. They had rarely, if ever, been given a written examination, and no one had ever seen true-false or multiple choice questions. I had to slow up and change a few things. The true-false and multiple choice questions were never my favorite way to test. I started by throwing them out.

I tried calling the roll. Vida Beresneviciute, Giedre Rindzeviciute, Liutauras Kraniauskas, Nerijus Mllerius, almost every name contained a variety of pronunciation marks. My tongue would just not work properly. I switched to first names and, with the student's permission, at least initially, even gave a few students nicknames.

The following year in Estonia, I found the student names were much easier to pronounce, for example, Kristi Eichen, Tuuli Tang, or Sven Kaldmaa. In Ukraine, most of my students had Russian names like Olga Nosova, Yuriy Abamedkov, and Tatyana Losinskaya. By then, I was having little difficulty with pronouncing names. There were also many Russian names on my class rosters in Tashkent, but a majority of the names were indicative of regional ethnic backgrounds. These names, like Muftuna Niyazbekova, Alisher Abdusattarov, Nafissa Usmankohodzhaeva, or Mamirdzhan Atuzhanov, took a while for me to learn to pronounce correctly. In every class, no matter in Idaho or whatever country, I never liked calling roll, it ate up valuable time and always produced giggles no matter how hard I tried. So while in the CEP, I usually would give the job to a student and then just watch to see whose hand would go up with each name.

In Lithuania, as in each of the other three countries where I taught classes, my first impressions were always of how almost uniformly young all the students were, most no older than twenty years of age. This presented quite a contrast to the majority of older "nontraditional students" I was used to teaching at Boise State University. It reminded me that this important aspect of higher education policy was at least a generation or more behind the United States. Higher education was still primarily for young people as it was when I went to university.

The students were smartly attired as well. The women usually wore dark dresses while men wore black slacks. In addition to looking nice, an effort was made to wear nothing that would need frequent washing, a task generally done at home by hand in the bathtub. It was a pleasant change to see such nicely dressed students. No baseball caps, sweatshirts, or grubby jeans in class here!

I was also immediately struck by the politeness of the students. In all four countries, students would stand when I came into the classroom. In Estonia, the females would curtsy on various occasions, such as when they came forward in class to receive graded assignments. When has anybody last seen a curtsy in America? It was actually quite widely practiced up until the 1950s. In Uzbekistan and throughout Central Asia, older people were treated with a noticeably high level of respect. As I fit into this age category, in addition to being a professor, which was also a highly regarded status, I received the benefit of a double dose of politeness. Wow, what a life!

Another attribute I quickly noticed about the students was that they were not used to being asked in class what they thought about anything, or to take a position on an issue and defend it. The legacy of the Soviet system of teaching was, as I have previously mentioned, for the professor to "read the class" as the students referred to teaching, that is, to lecture with absolutely no student involvement. Thus, students were great note-takers—and class skippers. They could take notes for each other, and for individuals in the next class, as the lectures rarely changed. The students didn't skip my classes, in part because they enjoyed practicing analysis and critical thinking or the novelty of discussing topics and issues in class.

To their immense pleasure, my classrooms emphasized "active learning," a buzzword for less lecturing and more group work, individual paper presentations, panels, question-and-answer periods, class discussion, and in general, trying to assist students in being more responsible for their own learning. While students were initially a bit timid, I could usually get them to open up if I suggested he or she ask me a question about the United States. Students had heard a plethora of stories about our problems with drugs, poverty, racial prejudice, individual gun ownership, road rage, and other violent behavior, and so on, all negative matters mostly. They wanted to know what was really true and why. I found short answers hard to come by. I am reminded of my first year as a visiting lecturer when a young student asked me a question toward the end of the lecture I had given in front of students, faculty, and administrators in Estonia. "What do you think of Bevis and Butthead?" he asked. I dodged a direct answer and mentioned something about the globalization of American pop culture. To add a story here, the young man's name was Teet Kung. Just a year later, Teet was able to get a better answer to his question—firsthand.

Teet and his girlfriend Teele, two typically reserved, short, blond, and youthful-looking Estonians, visited us in Idaho the summer following our stay in Tallinn. For them, the trip was an impossible dream, save for the fact that as an Air Estonia employee, Teele got free tickets for herself and Teet to fly as far as Seattle.

As their stay with us in Boise and McCall neared its end, I suggested they take in some highlights of the American West on their way back home. They did not have very much money, so I recommended they take a morning flight to Reno so as to experience a bit of Nevada-style gambling. From Reno, I suggested they could take a bus over the gorgeous Sierra Mountains to San Francisco for a few days of touring, and a then hop a bus to Seattle where they could tour that city while staying with my niece who was a graduate student at the University of Washington. They could then easily make their scheduled return flight from Seattle to Estonia.

Once back at home, Teet wrote me an e-mail entitled, "What we learned from our trip." He was happy to report that "now we don't have to believe other people's rumors about America, we know it for ourselves." In Reno, the casinos had overwhelmed these two shy people who were constantly being given "free" tickets to food and shows—some rather ribald to say the least. Everywhere they were asked to show identification proving their age. They were over twenty-one, but definitely did not appear so. They gambled very little, not wanting to lose too much of their small amount of money. Instead they walked the glitzy main street of the city and ended up spending the afternoon in the public library.

Arriving in San Francisco the next day, Teet and Teele saw an ad in the bus station for an inexpensive hostel on Market Street and ended up booking it for their stay. Out on the street, "we learned how to get familiar with people in less than a few minutes," Teet wrote. "The first evening was shocking; people were always asking us for money. There were so many black people. It was the first time we felt ourselves to be a minority everywhere we went. Teele wanted to lock the door at our hostel and stay there for the next two days. The next morning," Teet went on, "it [the panhandler situation] did not look so bad, so we were able to be tourists."

Getting ready to leave San Francisco, their lesson in familiarity with America continued when the driver of their bus to Seattle would not let them board, as their tickets mistakenly listed them as the "Wungs" in place of the Kungs. I have no idea why they were passing themselves off as married, but the name, at least, wasn't working. "The driver said we could not be the Wungs because we did not look a bit Chinese." They ended up making the trip to Seattle on a second bus—still as the Wungs. Teet did not mention the name of the company who owned the second bus other than to write that it was crowded and decorated in psychedelic paint. The Wungs ended up sitting "in the back together with some people who were smoking cannabis and playing Congo drums. You can imagine how much sleep we did get." How ironic. There they were, face to face with a busload of Bevis and Buttheads!

As is typical in sociology classes, we read about and discussed such topics as race, ethnicity, and gender. I was amazed at the way the men would argue for their superiority over women. This belief was especially prominent in Uzbekistan, where male students felt strongly about their rightful exercise of dominant power in the home and in society overall. Where was the legacy of Soviet equality? Local sociology faculty members told me that the Soviet effort to create equality between the sexes basically fizzled out. It was never a high priority in the first place, they said. However, many of my women students, particularly in the Baltic countries, felt quite strongly about equality. During class discussion, I could tell from their eyes and body language that they didn't agree with the vocal males who were unabashedly monopolizing the conversation. I encouraged the women to speak out.

A useful exercise for starting class discussion, which I learned from my Scottish CEP colleague, Colin Spurway, was to randomly pick a group of about twelve to fifteen students and have them line their chairs up in front of the class. In this case, those most in agreement with a policy of gender equality were to move their chairs to one end of the line. Those who were not in agreement were to move their chairs to the other end. Then class discussion got underway among the remaining students. My "barometer" student subjects were encouraged to move their chairs as many times as they wished more toward one end or the other of the line, if so persuaded in their view of the subject by the class discussion. It is a great technique and usually produces quit a bit of chair moving. Toward the end of the exercise, students who had moved their chairs were asked to summarize what it was that persuaded them to move. On this topic, it was a bit hard to tell if many of my male subjects were listening, busy as they were standing their ground. There was the constant claim from the males in the audience that physical strength made the essential difference in role assignment. I thought about bringing in a couple of those pushy babushkas from Lithuania to challenge the men to arm wrestle.

At least the students were honest in expressing their views. It was very refreshing not to have to face the deadening effects of political correctness that was such a handicap to class discussion at my university in Idaho. Would any of my students have lined their chairs up on the antifeminist end of the line? Would they have dared to?

On the topic of ethnicity, I also found another major contrast to America. For example, my Lithuanian students defined their nationality on the basis of ethnicity. They told me that no matter if I learned their language perfectly, or how long I might live in their country and accepted it as my own, I could never be a Lithuanian. To qualify, they said, one needs to have "Lithuanian blood." This was an ethnic categorization with a racial element to it. This produced some lively discussions when I pointed out that, by this definition, there were a number of students in the class who were not "Lithuanian." I asked them to tell me about their ancestry. They were usually Polish and came from families who had lived in the country over a period of hundreds of years. The students were fascinated with the way "Americans" were simply defined by an ideology they practiced—or at least tried to.

In what might be called a more liberal stance, many of my Estonian students opposed the widespread view, officially upheld in Latvia and

Estonia, that a person could not gain citizenship until fluent in the native language. Upwards of a third or more of the population of these two Baltic countries were Russian nationals. Many of them had spent their whole life in the country and may have had parents—even grandparents—who did as well. Of course, this was when the country was a militarily occupied Soviet client state and Russian was the official and only sanctioned language. Now the ethnic table was turned, but the same narrow mean-spirited approach continued. At least most of my students could see through this punitive, overly nationalist, and xenophobic policy. I told the students about the American treatment of Japanese Americans during the Second World War.

My effort to encourage my female students to express their views on women was generally successful. A great example—with just a perfect ending—took place in Uzbekistan, a country that shared its southern border with Afghanistan. All my Uzbekistan students were opposed to the recently established fanatical Islamic rule of Afghanistan by the Taliban. These were an indigenous people, the majority of whom had only a few years earlier flooded into the country from neighboring Pakistan following the defeat of the Soviet's aggressive effort to occupy Afghanistan. The Taliban were extremely oppressive in their treatment of women.

Summing up the attitude of what appeared to be every woman in my class was an unforgettable remark made by Anna Korotkih, a tall dark-haired psychology major whose hobby was knowing everything about American stockcar racing. She had been selected to give her research paper, "Taliban Treatment of Women," at a CEP-sponsored regional student conference held in Samarkand.

Anna had no problem holding her audience's attention while detailing a litany of Taliban abuse toward women. A few examples from her list included: they must wear full body covering in public, were severely restricted in educational opportunity and in access to paid work and health care, must observe special curfews, and only appear in public if accompanied by a man. There was usually severe punishment for violations of these rules. Obviously frustrated by not having hit on a constructive solution to bringing the Taliban around to the Western view of equality, Anna ended her paper by declaring, "The Taliban should be bombed!" As a discussant for the panel, in my following remarks I cautioned her, saying, "Anna, you can't just kill people you don't like." Not more than a month later, I was back in Boise and the Americans were bombing the Taliban. At about this time Anna wrote me an e-mail. She began her message. "Do you remember what you said about my research paper's conclusion?"

My early impressions also included two additional qualities about the students. Always seated together in threesomes or in long packed lines in the big lecture halls, students had learned to work together, and in Lithuania especially, they didn't hesitate to help each other on their examinations! Little or no effort was made to hide this behavior as they spent long periods of time looking on each other's test papers. In-class examinations in Lithuania initially turned into a fiasco of collective effort. CEP lecturers had been warned to expect this behavior throughout the former Soviet Russian Empire, where what we call cheating had been defined differently as a benign if not accepted practice. In partial defense of the students, I had to recognize that they were almost totally without experience with written examination, with my testing format, or with the idea of in-class examinations. It was difficult to convince them that it was not just an in-class exercise.

I began to change my testing methods. As an alternative to their way of looking at things, I lectured on the American definition of proper test taking etiquette and brought Judy in during the second semester of my year in Lithuania to help proctor examinations in my big class. The students had never seen a test proctor before. We had several class discussions on the Western view of cheating. Was this really cheating? If so, why was it done so often and so openly? It was quite frustrating to me either way. The students understood and agreed with my reasons against cheating. Moreover, they realized I was serious about preventing it. Thereafter, and with Judy's presence as a gentle reminder, the problem went almost completely away. In retrospect, I think I may have been too hard on my Lithuanian students. Rightly or wrongly, it is certain that they got a good introduction to Western academic standards and procedures.

Student's research efforts produced a second problem that quickly became apparent. Students, from Lithuania to Uzbekistan, thought absolutely nothing of plagiarizing. Again, I had to consider their behavior in the context of Soviet educational practice. I concluded that the West was far more stringent about this mater, and that another lecture and more discussion were needed to make these differences clear and to indicate exactly what standard I would expect of their work. As with cheating, what we think of as plagiarism was practiced, it seemed, in some ways, even encouraged, in Soviet education. I was able to pretty much eliminate plagiarism from student research papers by talking about it in class, spotting it in early research drafts, and by making it clear that a plagiarized paper would disqualify the student from competing in international research paper competitions, which were very popular with my best students. They also knew that plagiarism could seriously risk not receiving an equally sought after CEP certificate of course completion.

New Challenges Keep Teaching Far From Being a Routine Affair

As fall and then winter came, unusually early during my first year in Lithuania, one other very lasting impression I have of my Vilnius classroom is of looking out over the partially darkened room. It was dark because several lightbulbs were missing and because, at shortly after 4:00 PM in late October, it was already dark outside. We were all bundled up in parkas and mittens. The women wore scarves across their faces with only their eyes showing. Snowy wind was blowing in through the cracks in the windows and through a hole in one of the panes.

There was no heat in the building. What little heat we could count on would not begin until some unrealistic formula of cold days and average temperatures had been reached, and a central heating system somewhere nearby was fired up, and that had yet to occur. The students said that a government bureaucrat would make this decision for every building in the city. Even then the heat at my university would be barely enough to keep us from all turning to ice. The students had been valiantly struggling with my reading material and course requirements. Now we were all struggling with the cold as well, but we were happy. It was amazing.

There was no sense complaining about the heat. I was told that absolutely nothing could be done to get the boilers fired up any earlier. I thought about bringing the matter of the broken classroom window to my department chairwomen, but thought better of it. Mine was not the only classroom that had such problems. My department chair was Vida Kanopiene, a tall, slender (it seemed like almost every Lithuanian woman was tall and slender) lady in her forties with a doctorate in philosophy earned during Soviet times. Earning her degree had made her a survivor: definitely a useful trait in the present conditions. She once told me of the grueling effort and sacrifice she had made to gain her advanced degree. All graduate degree in-progress evaluations and other academic rite-of-passage rituals, right up to the granting of the degree, took place in Moscow. It seemed to Vida that she made at least a hundred of these overnight train trips, sometimes to satisfy the most picayune of requests. My own experience with graduate school rituals, although certainly far less extreme, was sufficient to make me quite sympathetic.

Vida seemed always so nonchalant as to leave me wondering about our relationship. It was definitely unnerving. While very polite and sociable, nothing about my presence or my teaching appeared to be of much concern to her. I once asked her if I could be absent from my two classes for a single day. She said, "That's no problem. Just let me know if you will be gone more than a month."

Vida did at least remember the concern I had expressed to her early in the fall semester about the small number of students in my classes. The following semester with no advance warning, she assigned a large lecture hall for my class titled Comparative Welfare Systems. There were nearly a hundred students in attendance for the first lecture, and each of them was fully expecting to stay through the semester. I quickly discovered that less than half of the students could understand any English whatsoever. That afternoon, I complained about this to Vida who suggested that I get one of my graduate students to interpret my lectures for me.

Professional interpretation as a lecture arrangement was not unheard of. It was being used tolerably well by a few CEP lecturers stationed in some of the more remote locations within the former Soviet Russian Empire. I often used paid expert interpreters when I gave guest lectures and multiday workshops. But even a good interpreter slows the class progress by up to a half, and there is always the uncertainty of obtaining a reasonably accurate translation. Under the present circumstance, I decided not accept Vida's recommendation. Using an inexperienced graduate student was a recipe for disaster.

Later in the week, at the beginning of the second class meeting, I asked all the students who could understand what I was saying, to raise their hand. I then asked these students to please inform those around them, who did not raise their hand, that they were permanently excused from my class. They needed only to come up after class and sign their name on a piece of paper. I gave the paper to Vida. It was a fait accomplit. Most of the students were happy, but not the dean. Learning of my action, Ms. Pociute was faced with the prospect of finding alternative elective classes for the non-English-proficient students. She protested my action, but I held firm. I was not going to use an unpaid novice to interpret the entire class.

During my first two years as a visiting lecturer, I taught only graded classes that were either required or elective in the student's major. This presented its share of difficulties as I have just illustrated. Another interesting example concerned grading of these classes. The grading scale in both Lithuania and Estonia, and I am pretty sure it remained the same in other prior Soviet areas as well, was based on a ten-point rather than our five-point "A" through "F" scheme. I had a devil of a time trying to understand how to get the two scales to correspond. I brought the problem to each of my first two department chairs. Apparently 7.5 was middle "C." Of course, the students were always all too eager to assist me in calibrating my scale to theirs—upwards of course. After the first semester, I stopped worrying about the granting of lower grades when I found out that a dean or department chair could unilaterally adjust them upwards, and sometimes did! I was stunned at first by such a flagrant ethical and professional violation. I dutifully submitted my grades anyway. At the end of the semester or early in the following semester, students who knew they were obtaining a good grade would bring a little passport-sized book to me so that I could enter their grade and my signature. It was the equivalent of a pocket-sized transcript in progress. I remember wondering about the students with the lower grades. They never seemed to bring their grade books to me.

Equally or more important to the students than the university grades, was the "CEP Certificate." (Appendix 1) This was especially the case during the last two years when I taught my classes outside of the formal department curriculum. All of my students who successfully passed or audited my classes would get a fancy looking 8 by 11 certificate printed in two colors on good quality heavy stock. The certificate with the student's name and Western grade carefully hand printed, was stamped with an official seal and signed by the CEP lecturer. I was able to control these grades.

A good grade on these certificates was worth its weight in gold. This was because many of my students dreamed of an opportunity to attend graduate school in America, Western Europe, or England. This was especially true of my students in Ukraine and Uzbekistan as several were very anxious to get out of their country. I could hardly blame them. Another popular graduate school destination was Central European University located in Budapest. This well-organized school was created and financed entirely by George Soros. I heard that he had made a commitment to the school to provide around $15 million each year to the school for at least the first ten years of its operation! Some of this money also meant that students who attended this university could count on a full scholarship for the normal duration of their studies.

I was fortunate to be able to help at least eleven students make the all-important leap to a Western-based graduate education. I am sure that there were others as well who successfully "cashed in" one or more certificates that had been signed by me.

Judy always made sure that there was lots of pomp and circumstance to accompany end-of-the-academic-year certificate awards ceremonies. We hadn't done this in Lithuania, but by the second year, she always took the lead in organizing the festivities and fanfare. As I look at the announcement Simon and I posted for our Estonian classes for both semesters, I see that we had a total of thirty-five students between us who were invited to receive graded CEP-certificate awards. In later years, the number grew by almost half.

In Estonia, the ceremony was held in a classroom with Dean Mati Heidmets as our guest along with Jana, our CEP country director. Simon and I joined the dignitaries in making a short speech. We handed out awards and everybody drank champagne and nibbled on cookies. We followed essentially the same awards routine in Kharkiv. I recall that unseasonably hot and humid weather that day had everybody perspiring in their suits and party dresses. In Tashkent, a special banquet section of the main university building was opened up for our use. We followed an elaborate evening awards ceremony for Carter's and my students with a disco dance. This was Judy's last unofficial job of organizing a CEP function. Attendance was 100 percent, and there was champagne and soft drinks for all.

Drawn into a Power Play

There was always some difficulty in gaining an accepted and useful role in my newly adopted departments. All CEP visiting lecturers faced this problem to one degree or another. Except for Estonia, my experience proved to be no exception. Language barriers were usually the biggest factor. Some faculty members seemed indifferent to my presence. Some might have just been shy and probably a little intimidated. No school seemed to have something like a faculty lounge where we could all meet informally.

It was also the case that professors were often very busy with second or even third jobs, trying to make a living, and thus did not have time to strike up a new acquaintance. In Uzbekistan, Carter and I tried removing, or at least lessoning these barriers by holding a tea party early in each semester. We invited the department chair, Gulmira Khamidovna. Obviously quite delighted to be at such an occasion, she gave a little pep talk to the assembled faculty members. Judy organized the provision of tea and cookies. This seemed to help improve relations. We should have done this in my earlier postings. However, I doubt that something like this would have helped in my Lithuanian posting where making friends with the school's sociology professors turned out to be inappropriate. It took me a while to figure this out although Vida, my department chair, was giving me more than enough hints to know that something was going on.

Vida had offered me a standing invitation to have afternoon tea and cookies in her office. On the few occasions when our schedules coincided, I always tried to take her up on her offer. We were usually joined by her secretary, who never seemed to have any work to do except to lay out the tea and cookies along side the manual typewriter that sat on her desk.

Vida always managed to shift the conversation to nonacademic topics. She carefully avoided discussing how I might contribute to the department, even though outreach activity was strongly encouraged by the CEP and was a natural for someone like me with over thirty years of experience in academia. To my inquiry as to the whereabouts of all the other department sociologists, Vida answered that they worked at an institute for social research located in the city. She promised to take me there and facilitate introductions. She never did, even though I reminded her of her promise more than once. I felt left aside and underutilized. It was disturbing. Subsequently I found out that larger forces were at work.

I never was able to make contact with any of the other sociology professors who worked at the institute. Beyond just being busy trying to make a living, for these institute professors, it was more of a matter of trying to stay employed! And here lay the major reason for Vida's behavior. Although, in all likelihood her job was secure, Vida was caught in the middle of a high-stakes power struggle between the institute and the university. It was a struggle to maintain the jobs of the institute members.

The brief history behind this struggle, and similar efforts like it that were occurring at other universities, was that the Soviets had established a long-standing policy of splitting academic instruction off from basic research, giving the latter responsibility to specially designated institutes. Every major city had at least one of each: a university and an institute. After Communism collapsed, efforts began in many of the newly independent countries to disband the institutes, folding their research function into the universities. However, putting these two functions together often did not include continuing the employment of many of the institute's older, Soviet-trained employees!

Vida was a pawn of the institute. With the blessing of one of the university vice presidents (vice rectors), the institute had recently been able to get its foot in the university and establish the formalities of a sociology department. The institute put Vida in charge, while considering how to move its "sociologists" on to the campus. However, Professor Aleksandras Dobryninas, a mavrick philosopher at the university, had a different idea. With the backing of the other university vice president, Alex, as he was called, was busy planning a second university sociology department that would replace the existing department, its shadow faculty, and maybe even Vida!

Through his excellent connections to the local Soros Open Society Foundation—until recently he had been one of its board members—Alex had managed to get me to Lithuania and placed in Vida's department. Alex discussed his plan for a new department with me shortly after my arrival. It was to be a department of social philosophy, a complement, but I naively concluded, hardly a replacement for the existing sociology department. Alex kept his ultimate intentions hidden from me while gaining my compliance in reviewing and signing off on his curriculum plan, which was part of an application for an Open Society Foundation grant.

The plot and the nature of the struggle finally became clear to me late in the second semester. The board of the local Soros Foundation requested my presence one afternoon in order to hear my comments on two large grant requests before them. Each proposal was to develop a sociology department at the university! I was aware of Alex's proposal, but not the other proposal. To my surprise, it was submitted by Vida! Alex's proposal included no institute personnel while Vida's relied heavily on moving institute members into several proposed new university sociology positions.

The board wanted to know about my role in Alex's grant proposal and to advise them as to which, if either, proposal they should fund. Having not read Vita's proposal, I respectively declined to offer any advice other than to say that Alex's proposal was solid and attractive. They were surprised that Vida had not shared her plan with me. Shortly after leaving Lithuania, I learned, to my amazement, that the foundation had split the rather sizable grant money between both proposals, thus insuring that the power struggle would continue. Alex was anxious for me to stay another year, but I found his ways a bit devious and his friendship too conditional. Instead, and on my recommendation, the CEP pulled its sociology lectureship program from the university. Judy and I left for Estonia.

A Much-Improved Teaching Environment

The standard of living and the quality of university life in Estonia was an obvious improvement in comparison to our initial year in Vilnius, really too much of an improvement to justify keeping the CEP in the country for very long. Estonia was one of the most well off of the Soviet republics and was making rapid economic progress since becoming an independent country five years earlier. Even though its buildings were poorly constructed, Tallinn Pedagogical University was fairly well maintained and staffed with what I considered to be quite a few outstanding faculty members. George Sootla was one of the best examples. He had established a modern Political Science Department and was known to be a favorite teacher to many of my students. I always enjoyed providing guest lectures for his students.

The university was contained within a single three-story building spread out over most of a city block. Quite conveniently, I held all but one of my classes in the computer lab that was only a short walk from my office. There was a computer at each desk. This meant that I had to look around the big computer monitors to see some of the students' faces, but the layout was perfect for weekly take-home essay assignments. The students could write their essays at home or at school and bring them to class on a disk. The essay papers could then be cued up and printed on a machine that sat right in front of my desk. I could also do short in-class quizzes the same way.

I was the happy beneficiary of an early policy Estonia had made to get all students computer literate by the time they entered university level. This policy, and good students, made teaching easy. In addition to the computers, the class had an up-to-date whiteboard, a better classroom feature than any of the best blackboards, and something that even most of my classrooms at Boise State University had not yet installed.

In addition to my CEP visiting lectureship, I had the delightful opportunity to provide a criminology class for students attending a recently established Institute of Law, a nonprofit private school with a student body of about four hundred young men and women. I taught two mornings a week at this institute, while Judy donated one morning each week to help the law students with their English lessons.

Unfortunately, having so many good students at both schools also meant that I had a good many highly employable students, and this presented a problem; I could not keep some of them in class through a full semester. The rapidly booming Estonian economy was enticing them right out of my classroom with good job opportunities even before they could finish the class, let alone graduate. As I have previously explained, the quickly growing economy was partly the result of location and language, but very aggressive government free-market policies were, in my opinion, an even more significant reason. This was an economic point of view I often reinforced in my classes but which, it turned out, didn't thrill my department chairwomen in the least.

Wrangling over "Welfare"

I was invited to team teach a class the first semester with my department chair, Anu Toots (remembered as in "what's up toots?" noted my CEP colleague) to teach a large class on comparative welfare states. Anu was a tall slender stylish woman in her early forties. While she appeared to be busy with the press of department affairs, which I have no doubt she was, it was widely known in the department that, just down the hall, another affair was also seriously competing for her attention. As a consequence, there never seemed to be a good time to work together on our class. Our lectures, planned by topic at the beginning of the fall semester, were always a surprise to each other in their specific content. On the few occasions when I did manage to visit with Anu or her office partner Tu (pronounced tee-you), both liked to add a few stories about the good old days and how easy academic life had been under Communism. I probably should have taken these reminiscences more seriously.

Anu and I would alternate lecture days for the Welfare State class, with her interpreting for my lectures, and one of my students personally interpreting her lectures for me. By now I was used to sitting toward the back of a classroom or lecture hall, listening to the speaker with one ear while having someone speaking English in my other ear. The lecture days were further alternated with discussion classes in which I took students who were capable in English—about half the students—while Anu took the others.

Anu was a strong proponent of the heavily socialist Scandinavian welfare state model. In this model, extensive state assistance is viewed as a birthright, an entitlement for all citizens. The course syllabus specifically stated that we would "examine the arguments both for and against the continuance of the welfare state," so I countered Anu's positive remarks with a libertarian view, beginning with an analysis of welfare in the U.S.

context. I suggested that the way "welfare" operated in my country was ironically somewhat similar in effect, if not in definition or extent, to the Scandinavian model. I pointed out that, while not called welfare, our system included welfarelike subsidies, tax deductions, off-budget spending, and transfer payments of all kinds primarily set up to assist the rich and the middle class. Even more perversely, both Scandinavian and U.S. welfare spending was providing well paying work for an increasing number of welfare-related occupations. Welfare, like a rose, is, by any other name, still welfare, I pointed out. My argument was that, for the sake of fairness, as well as economic efficiency, I supported a scaling back of welfare in all its forms and guises.

While socialist-leaning Anu was a welfare proponent, I was enjoying being her libertarian critic. One of the articles I had the entire class read was called "The Upside Down Welfare State," written by my Boise State University colleague Dan Huff, and published in the winter 1992 issue of the journal *Public Welfare*. Translating this article for her students to read, Anu found herself having to define tax deductions and loopholes, business subsidies, off-budget expenditures, and other forms of assistance as "welfare." Apparently this made her quite uncomfortable.

Additionally, while I didn't realize it at the time, I was also not winning any points with Anu when I invited my English-capable students to write a three thousand word essay on the topic of "Capitalism: A Solution to the Welfare State." The CEP frequently provided all its lecturers with an e-mail list of current supplementary classroom resources, and I had noticed a writing award competition on this topic sponsored by the J. E. Davis Foundation in Florida. I thought a good essay on the benefits of capitalism might get favorable attention for having been written by a student from a former Communist country. It turned out that none of my students won a prize, but two received honorable mention. It was a great learning experience for them and one for me as well. In reading their papers, I was amazed at the persistence of the narrow and inaccurate view of capitalism espoused by some of my students. I decided it was just another legacy of Communist propaganda. Several students really struggled in their papers, and not always successfully, with the novel idea that capitalism could be a big part of the solution to poverty rather than the main, if not the singular cause, of the problem.

What I learned from the paper assignment helped me refocus my lectures on what needed to be learned.

While always polite, Anu finally started to make it clear that she did not like my approach, and began, taking steps to do something about it. Judy and I might have stayed a second year in Estonia, except for the fact that Anu was opposed to the idea and secretively managed to go around the support I had from the dean and block my continuing contract. Oh well, it was not uncommon to find politics taking precedence over academic practice, at home and now apparently abroad as well.

During the year in Estonia, the government proudly announced that it would no longer require nor accept foreign development assistance. This fact, along with Anu's sabotage of both Simon's and my contracts for the following year, was enough to convince the CEP that its presence, at least in the capital city, was not really needed. The CEP pulled its lectureship program from the university. Being the second time this had happened following my appointment as a lecturer, I began to wonder, "Was this coincidence or what?"

Perfect Classes Are a Professor's Dream

It was not until our third year in the CEP, when Judy and I were posted to Kharkiv, that politics did not, at least knowingly, interfere with my teaching. By chance, I also hit upon the ideal way in which to teach my classes, in English, to appreciative students. The credit for this belonged to my new department chair, Vil Bakirov. At Kharkiv State University, I was assigned to the Department of Applied Sociology, a well-run, highly respected forerunner of modern sociology departments that were beginning to spring up at various locations in Central/Eastern Europe. Vil was a soft-spoken, slightly heavyset man in his early forties who had a warm, inviting personality. He was a harried man, with a very busy schedule, unfortunately, as I would have liked to have had time to know him better, but Vil was under pressure as a finalist for the rector (president) position of the university. He was awarded the position in the spring, after which I saw him even less.

In our initial meeting, Vil sat impeccably dressed in his smoky little office with the phone to his ear much of the time. I asked him about my teaching schedule and the classes he would like me to teach. His response sounded nonchalant, "Whatever you like, and on a schedule of your choice, but preferably after 3:00 PM." Actually, Vil had offered both an insightful prescription and the freedom to create the perfect visiting lectureship.

I quickly began to design my classes, using this advice and my knowledge of class standards, hours, and credit. The approach was simple. I had not thought of it before, most likely because it meant teaching outside of the department curriculum. Certainly the CEP regional directors had not mentioned anything like this as a possibility. About the closest I had come to what I was about to do was when one of my CEP colleagues, Tom Velik, had organized a series of guest lecturers to speak, at no charge, to evening audiences drawn from the city of Minsk, Belarus. This successful lecture series was done as part of his obligation to perform outreach activity. I had been one of the guest lecturers. Now, ready to begin my academic year at Kharkiv State University, for all intents and purposes, I would be a freelancer and recreate some of the qualities of a lecture series. The difference it made was considerable!

No longer was I concerned about the language fluency problem or the motivation of students who were obligated to take my classes, even about those who might choose them as an elective. I made up a single-page announcement for two classes (Appendix 2). It looked like a flyer, a kind of "Hark, itinerant professor to give lecture series." I met with the university librarian who said she would make sure that some of the announcements were placed prominently within her domain. Potential students who I had met hanging around the department office prior to the start of the semester helped circulate my announcements in other academic locations around the city.

The announcements indicated who I was and prominently gave credit as host, to my university and to the Applied Sociology Department. The announcement went on to indicate that my department's students, with good English proficiency, would have first priority in seating. Otherwise, my classes were open to any registered student or faculty member from anywhere in the city as long as there was space in the classroom and they could demonstrate a reasonable degree of English proficiency.

I measured proficiency in the first class meeting by having all prospective students read a half page description of a controversial social problem and write a page of response. I examined these on the spot, giving thumbs up or down on admittance to the class. In this way, I filled my classroom to its maximum limit, about thirty-five people, with some of the brightest, most capable, and motivated students I have ever taught. In a few instances, when space permitted, I allowed a few students to audit the classes. The audit status turned out to be a popular option with English teachers who were anxious to listen, for the first time in their life, to an English speaker with an American accent. At Kharkiv State University, I came as close as any professor might dream to having the perfect class: no hassles from administration, no hassles from students, just the pure joy of teaching! Too bad we seem bent on making such a bureaucratic nightmare of it everywhere else.

My new approach also allowed Judy to get more involved in my teaching. She held informal "office hours" for students in one class while I was teaching in another. Students would drop in to the department's large all-purpose office/library to chat and get help on editing their research papers. When there were no students, Judy found time to knit, and to drink tea served by the two young office secretaries who seemed to have little to do in the afternoon except play games on the one computer that served the whole department–both faculty and staff. Amazingly, it would have sat mostly idle if it were not for the game use.

I used this same approach again very successfully in Tashkent at National University of Uzbekistan. I introduced it there to my CEP colleague Carter Johnson. It helped to make his first year of teaching a very positive one. I like to think that it contributed to his choice, following one more year with the CEP in Moldova, to go back to graduate school to become an academic.

During the year, Carter and I shared many of the same students. About half of them were students from our host Department of Social and Political Sciences, others came from the nearby Department of Languages, and quite a few came from the prestigious University of World Diplomacy located quite a ways away on the other side of the city. As in Kharkiv, Judy and I made good friends with many of the students.

In Tashkent, for the first time, Judy and I decided to personally finance two full multi-year scholarships for a couple of very bright students. The two young men were working their hearts out for me, but were so financially strapped they could not stay in the university. It is hard to believe that the full tuition including room and board costs for a year of school averaged between two hundred and three hundred dollars a person. I suppose we should have made more such scholarships available. We discovered that there were actually quite a few struggling young students who could have also used some help.

Summing It Up

Shortly before leaving Tashkent, I was asked to give an address to a large convention composed mainly of university faculty and administrators and a variety of NGO people. I decided to offer some contrasts between Western university education and what I had experienced in four years as a visiting lecturer in the former Soviet Russian Empire. I made the contrast in terms of what I called "East" and "West" approaches. I was interested in showing how the differences related to our work in helping create and strengthen democratic institutions.

I began with a rhetorical question: what kind of educational content and practice is most conducive to, and compatible with, democracy? I described the "East" model as persisting largely as an antimodel of good pedagogy, totally incompatible, hostile even, to the prerequisites for democratization. Its features, which I had experienced, had included overly centralized educational administration, lack of faculty or student involvement in the life of the university outside the classroom, passive, rote teaching methods ("reading the class"), high levels of corruption and, especially in Central Asia, the continuing isolation of faculty from Western scholarship.

In Uzbekistan, I observed an additional "East" feature that local educators usually described to me as the "Central Asian mentality." This concept usually stressed the history of clan and kahn, and the wide gulf that existed between them and between this authoritarian part of the world and democratic Western society. The argument was usually made in the context of justifying people's lack of interest in change, including their preference for traditional ways and rule by men of great and uncontested power. I shouldn't overlook mentioning that I never heard this argument advanced with any enthusiasm by women.

I had learned about the "East" model from a variety of sources. I had directly experienced it in my classrooms. While I was happily to discover my students to be personable, respectful, and very talented, it had been quite disturbing to have to contend initially with high levels of plagiarism. I had also discovered that the majority of all my students had little or no personal experience with or understanding of the research process. Students were also much more passive than I was used to. I found there to be a noticeable reluctance, in some instances a fear, of voicing their opinions or a different point of view in class.

Most alarming was discovering that many of my Uzbekistan students would not openly discuss domestic political issues for fear of government retaliation. Many of these students also lived in constant fear of me doing so in class. Worse yet, to some of my students, was the thought of putting a critical view of the government into writing.

As I began to sum up my remarks to the convention, I added that, in almost every sense, the continuing practice of the "East" model of education, especially in totalitarian Uzbekistan, will depress, if not prevent students from gaining the knowledge and practice, the skills, and especially the freedom needed to assist their countries in moving toward democracy.

I offered one final consideration. In no university in which I taught was there any evidence that students had an opportunity to practice democracy. While I conceded that in America we often took such things as student government for granted, I urged that student government needed to become an important part of young people's education.

Thinking back over the four years as a visiting lecturer "over there," it was the most wonderful teaching experience of my life. The students clearly appreciated my classroom instruction and the lessons about democracy that I worked hard to convey. Just as important, Judy and I made a very favorable impression on our students, not just as individuals, but also, if I can be allowed a rather big generalization, as representatives of the "American way." We taught, and practiced, the values of generosity, tolerance, equality of opportunity, individual initiative, and personal responsibility. We touted the value of volunteerism, showing the way by our example. I knew many other visiting lecturers who were doing essentially the same thing with equal impact and personal satisfaction. The CEP very definitely fulfilled its mission, leaving a very positive legacy of knowledge and goodwill.

8

Life in the Flats

Living Quarters, Soviet Style

Before joining the CEP, the notion of "life in the flats" might have sounded like something a football wide receiver might know about, or someone living in Kansas. "Flat" is the British, and general European, term for apartment. While in the former Soviet Russian Empire, Judy and I lived in three furnished flats and one more-or-less furnished dacha, the latter having once been a Russian private summer home. Our living quarters in each of these places were definitely enough of a departure from the normal housing experience of suburban America to be well worth a tour. Even more interesting are the stories about the events and people who came into our lives by virtue of living in these places. I can't resist telling just a few good stories associated with each of these places. They illustrate some significant aspects of Communist life as we found it early in the post-Communist period.

Most Americans, certainly those in the West where we live, experience residential life in a single-family suburban home connected to the city by their cars. In contrast, a large number of residents of the former Soviet Russian Empire live in urban-style apartments or flats, the newer ones located in high-rise building clusters located out near the edge of the city. If the city is fairly large, then they are connected to downtown by underground metro, tram, or bus, usually all three. Closer into the city, the buildings and their multiple flats are typically older, built prior to elevators, and consequently no more than five stories high. People who lived in these buildings typically walked to many places within the city or took some form of city transit.

In this area of the world, people describe their flat by counting the number of bedrooms. Thus, Judy and I lived in one-and two-room flats. There was no need to describe much further the living arrangements as they were almost uniformly the same, amounting to one bathroom, a kitchen, and a front room that doubled as a dining room and often as an informal bedroom as well.

Most of the furniture was also quite predictable. Every flat contained a sofa that could be folded out long-ways into a smallish standard-size bed. The other common furnishing was a usually quite large, even full room-length, bookcase/credenza/china cabinet combination containing a mix of glass doors, shelves, and cabinet sections. These always dark-colored units were cheaply made from high-gloss photoveneer-covered pressboard.

Russian flats exhibited quite a lot of uniformity in other ways as well. Remember, this had been the Soviet Russian Empire where the official Communist view was that having too many consumer choices was unnecessary and bourgeois.

Living in a Small Museum

Our living quarters during our first year in Lithuania was in an older building of the central-downtown variety. We were there when the building turned one hundred years old, but, of course, nobody paid any attention to this fact. Finished on the outside in typical gray-brown stucco, the building was constructed in a large "L" shape facing the sidewalks of two busy streets. Behind the building were a few large trees and an open play area that was also used to park a few cars. Access to this area and to the entrance staircases to the building's approximately thirty flats was through a large tunnel-shaped opening off one of the streets. The building was conveniently located almost exactly in the center of town, kitty-corner from the former KGB building.

Our initial impressions of our flat will forever remain fresh. We had been away from America less than a week and still in at least a mild state of adjustment to the food and our new routine, when the old beat up minivan that brought us from Riga, Latvia, deposited us and all our duffel bags in front of the courtyard entrance to our flat. In the hot, humid August afternoon we hoisted and dragged our bags up four flights of stairs, perspiring, to be greeted by our landlord who had tea and cookies waiting for us. Nobody had heard of ice tea?

My initial impressions of our flat began with the big, wine-colored, vinyl-padded, door, studded with large brass nails, and containing several locks arranged one above the other. Why so many locks? I noticed that the other two entrance doors on our landing also were festooned with locks. Was this a bad neighborhood? No, I found out later, just bad KGB agents who used to like busting into people's flats in the middle of the night.

Once inside, I immediately noticed the smallness of the rooms, and, most of all, how the rooms were wildly overdecorated and overfurnished. The kitchen contained an older gas stove whose oven operated only at high temperature, a squatty little refrigerator with a small inside ice box whose door would not stay attached, a Soviet-made automatic clothes washer, which quickly overheated and steamed our laundry to death, and a single sink with overhead wire racks for the dishes to dry. There was a small white painted kitchen table with leaves that could be opened to seat four. Through a short hall from the kitchen was a small bathroom containing a sink and bathtub over which were stretched several clotheslines

As a one-room flat, the bedroom was just large enough to accommodate a large free-standing closet, a small vanity, a single chair, and the ubiquitous fold-a-bed-type of sofa. This sofa, though, was only large enough to sleep a very loving couple in a pinch. Judy and I ended up sleeping in the front room under what looked like a gigantic down pillow on a somewhat more comfortable, but still rather narrow, fold-out sofa. When made into a bed, it was necessary to rest the outer front corners of the bed on the seats of two matching upholstered chairs from which I had first removed the cushions. I quickly discovered that without such stabilization, the sofa-bed would tip over, sending me, the outside sleeper, rolling onto the floor.

Overcrowding the front room was a full-size upright piano, a large console record changer, an old color TV set, and a variation of the standard faux-wood credenza. Judy and I used a corner of the credenza as a desk, sitting at one edge, with our knees apart, on a kitchen chair fitted with a big pillow we purchased for such use.

We would begin our mornings by turning on the laptop computer that sat on this makeshift desk and, along with a fresh cup of coffee, read our e-mail. Each week the CEP office at Yale would send us *Newsflash*: several in-house-constructed pages of news summary on events around the world. The existence of the CEP news summary said a lot about the remote locations of a good number of visiting lecturers who worked in regional cities and towns far away from access to news media in English. Unfortunately, this news service was discontinued two years later when we were living in Kharkiv where it would have been very useful. I could sometimes get a reasonably up-to-date copy of the European edition of the *Herald Tribune* newspaper and would usually take a day or two to thoroughly read almost all the contents. We also had a half hour television news program each weekday morning in English.

Our Vilnius flat had a separate little toilet room between the bathroom and kitchen. Such an arrangement turned out to be a rather common feature of Russian and Soviet-period apartments. Judy and I had rarely seen such a room before, or the type of toilet that it contained. The toilet drained from the front, behind which was a large "inspection shelf" that was very difficult to flush properly. The toilet paper was a plum color and looked like stiff crepe paper. It took some getting used to, but then, so did the fact that the little toilet room had no proper source of ventilation.

Additionally, sediment and the potential of heavy metal in the tap water meant we needed to boil and filter all our drinking and cooking water. We had to do this in each of the four countries where we lived.

A collection of sediment and heavy metal after boiling a pan full of water. The water will be poured off into the filter apparatus at the top of the picture. Vilnius, Lithuania

We got used to stoves and refrigerators that were poorly constructed and barely worked, bathtubs with overhead clotheslines, fold-a-bed sofas, and those little toilet rooms complete with their oddly constructed toilets. Our picture albums contain a few shots of these toilets. We found them unusually fascinating. In addition to the inspection shelf, the Soviets had frequently made the water tanks out of opaque plastic. Quite visible was the ugly scum and rust-colored minerals that would collect on the inside of these tanks. The tanks were flushed by lifting a knob located on the top center of the tank lid. It was usual for tanks to leak internally, thus triggering a partial fill of water from time to time. In such cases, it was necessary to make sure to close the toilet room door at night so that its leak and fill noises would not keep me awake at night. Judy usually could sleep through anything.

The larger point to be illustrated in these and other similar examples is the very poor quality of what Americans would call "consumer durables." It was not a case of someone buying the low end of a product line. There just was not, and never had been, anything better to be purchased. Everything, or better, what could be purchased, was low end.

Frequent repair was necessary, but decades of a stagnant or falling economy had left most citizens with little money to properly fix things up. Besides, there were usually no parts to buy anyway, save what might be scavenged at a flea market. Equally significant, it was just not the customary practice to fix things up that were not one's own. However, if a repair was necessary to a personal item or an appliance, the Soviet citizen would call a specialist or *master* or, more commonly, barter a repair by participating in an informal network of tradesmen who would fix each other's stuff after work. There was also what seemed to be the popular option of ignoring the problem all together.

Life in our little Vilnius flat was rarely dull. With only a half-hour of English language programming on the TV each morning, Judy and I discovered, delightfully, that we had much more time to read. We would also stand for long periods of time at the kitchen window and observe the constantly changing scene in the hilly park across the street. In the winter months, as many as a hundred or more children would sled around the trees and down the hill, often accompanied by their barking dogs.

To the Rescue of a Flooded Apartment Flat

In the middle of one pleasant afternoon, we were alerted to the sounds of a young girl running up and down the stairwell ringing doorbells and shouting something above the barking of a dog. It was obvious that there was an emergency. Judy and I were the only ones to follow her upstairs to witness her parents frantically trying to plug a large spouting gusher of hot dirty water exiting from a broken radiator in their front room. The wood-covered floors of several rooms had filled to a depth of about two or three inches of water. With no shut-off valve on the radiator or elsewhere in the flat, it was over an hour before a plumber arrived to close the heating valve for the whole building— safely kept under lock and key in the basement five floors below! We started a pan and bucket brigade from the floors to the bathtub. After at least a couple of hours of working in terribly humid surroundings, we got most of the standing water off the floors.

As we were about to leave, our new friends motioned us in close. The lady pointed to the hands on her watch. Judy and I were being invited to return at nine that evening. We went back to our flat, cleaned up, and went out to get something to eat. We had no idea we had been invited for dinner.

John, Evelina, and Larisa Jocyte (2005). Vilnius, Lithuania

The owners of the flat, John (Ivan) and Larisa Jocyte met us at the door. Larisa was dressed in long black formal eveningwear; we were in our jeans. John was a big tall Russian, a retired opera singer who had traveled widely outside the Soviet Russian Empire. Their two pre-teen children, John, Jr., and Evelina, were also in attendance and nicely dressed. Unbeknownst to us there was a full upper story to their flat, paneled in beautiful wood and containing a grand piano. There were many large pictures of John in full costume in the midst of a number of opera roles.

Off to one side of the room, a large coffee table was set with an expansive array of food consisting of all manner of hors d'oeuvres. Called *zaknski* in Russian, there were the traditional marinated wild mushrooms. There were also pickled herring, a Scandinavian delight, which I had quickly learned to enjoy, and a wide variety of salads. There were cheeses, pork fat, caviar, and heavy black rye bread. We had already eaten, but I was ready to at least sample everything. This was a good idea because there was also lots of vodka. I said I would have just one shot. In reply, John said, "OK, one and one and one."

Judy could not eat much of the food, especially the slimly, sandy mushrooms. I continued to eat. It was only polite to do so, I rationalized to myself; however, I have never had a problem eating more than I should, especially spurred on by a little alcohol. I had only a few of the mushrooms, being well aware of stories of previous wind-born radiation resulting from the Chernobyl disaster. The radiation had settled, among other places, in the local mushrooms. Judy couldn't handle the herring either. I ate both, while drinking "one and one and one" in good Russian fashion. Why not? It was only one floor down to our flat. Evelina interpreted all the evenings' lively conversation.

We stayed in touch with the Jocytes through several trips we made back to Vilnius the following year while living in Estonia. On one of these trips, we mentioned our daughter Karen's wedding that was planned for the summer. Evelina wanted to attend the wedding. She indicated that she could come with her father who could sing at the wedding. I wrote an official invitation letter in order for them to get visas to come to the United States. Then, sometime later, Evelina called us in Tallinn to say that they were ready to make the trip and would we please send the money! What money? We had expected them to cover their own airfare and miscellaneous costs. It was an unfortunate misunderstanding. The plan was called off. Karen got violin music instead.

Judy and I have stayed in touch through e-mail with Evelina. She is now twenty years old, is attending the University of Vilnius majoring in history, and working in an international information company called "Findexa" as a sales representative. Her passion is singing jazz.

The Jocytes were the first of many friendships we made. It was also my first experience with drinking a lot of vodka. I later learned that there are ways to drink a goodly amount of vodka without getting too inebriated. Naturally, the best way is to pour mineral water in your shot glass when no one is looking, making sure to swallow hard and grit your teeth as you toss it down. Mineral water is a common item on any dinner or banquet table. Eating a lot of greasy food while toasting vodka shots is probably the second most helpful thing one can do, at least so we were told by a knowledgable friend. The grease would help soak up the alcohol and slow down the pace at which it was absorbed into the bloodstream, or so the theory has it. I doubt most people thought this way, following instead the timeworn tradition, discovered through trial and error, of eating a lot of food while drinking. Either way, drinking habits were certainly different from what I was used to or observed at home in America. It seemed like practically the only hard liquor people drank was vodka, and just about all hard liquor was taken in straight shots . It was extremely rare to see people just sitting at a bar drinking. There were really very few bars except for those connected with nightclubs or restaurants. In most cases, restaurants with bars were normally designed to emulate the West. The most common example of this type was the Irish pub.

A final caution on the drinking front is to drink good vodka and watch out for local "moonshine." It can be mistaken for the real stuff if purchased at a kiosk in a crudely marked bottle, or by the glass in a hotel, which is what happened to me and a couple of CEP colleagues late one evening in a hotel bar in Bishkek, Kyrgyzstan. Just a few shots quickly upset my stomach, sending off warning bells not to drink any further. Somewhat later I read that, according to official Russian statistics, 42,000 Russians die each year from drinking counterfeit vodka.

Just a Little Deep Cleaning

In a most bizarre incident, Judy and I returned a week early from our Christmas vacation in Sicily to find Vito, our landlord, living in our flat with his girlfriend. Vito had arranged for her to be our house cleaner, and, we suspected correctly, an in-house spy. We had mentioned to her that we would be gone for five weeks and would not need her weekly cleaning. We showed her our calendar carefully marked off with our leave and return dates. Obviously, the two of them felt that this was their golden opportunity.

It was late in the afternoon, cold, snowing hard, and already dark, when the bus from the airport dropped us off near our flat. I was rethinking the advisability of having come back from sunny Italy a week earlier than originally planned. We had been in our shirtsleeves there. As we climbed the four flights of stairs to our flat, Judy mentioned a premonition she was entertaining of Vito living there. When I could not get my key in the main door lock for want of one already in the door on the other side, Judy shouted out, "I knew it!"

Vito opened the door looking very sheepish. He claimed he had stayed only one night in order to do some "deep cleaning" to the flat, which, of course, we had left spotless, no thanks to the housecleaner whose approach to the task was never more than hit or miss. However, it took him and his son, who arrived shortly after a quick telephone call, an hour to pack and lug away his and the house cleaner's several suitcases of food and clothing. Even then, they overlooked all their medicine in the refrigerator.

Vito had been a bit sneaky all along, so I guess his behavior didn't come as too much of a surprise. A few weeks before we left on our holiday, he had showed up one day to announce that the monthly rent was going up immediately one hundred dollars. Fortunately, our country director happened to be in town and was planning on meeting us that afternoon. I called Vito to invite him back over to the flat. Jana arrived and came quickly to the point. Vito needed to leave the rent as specified in the contract or we would move out of the flat immediately. Such brinkmanship made Judy and me quite nervous. The last thing we wanted to do was move in the midst of a snowstorm, but Jana's threat was enough to make Vito change his mind. After all, he was getting an amount in considerable excess of what he could rent his place for to any Lithuanian. We found this considerably higher rent charge to be the case in each place we lived while in the former Soviet Russian Empire.

We closed the door to the Vilnius flat for the last time in early June on an interesting note that proves how, indeed, we live in a small world. Following arrangements made through e-mail, we met Nick Miller and his wife, Lynn Lubamersky, at the front door of our flat. Nick, who was a colleague and friend of mine at Boise State University, was on his way to the Balkans to do historical research. His wife was completing a doctoral dissertation on Polish Lithuanians. They planned to stay in our flat for a month or two. We introduced them to Vito, who was obviously excited with a few more months of high rent, and over the Polish connection to his new renters. At this point, we had just enough time for Nick, Lynn, and the two of us to walk to our favorite restaurant for breakfast and return to the apartment building, load our bags, and leave. Our upstairs neighbor, John Jocyte, had insisted on taking us and all our baggage to the airport. He was waiting for us when we arrived back from breakfast. Somehow, we managed to get us all, including baggage, in his compact Russian Moskvich car.

Life in a Modern Krushchabki

We spent our second year in the CEP in Estonia, in a flat on the fifth floor in a cluster of high-rise buildings. This interesting type of flat was the most frequently encountered arrangement found throughout the former Soviet Russian Empire. Its basic form originated in the late 1950s when postwar industrialization triggered a massive rural out-migration that rapidly filled the cities and created major housing shortages.

In response to the shortage problem, the Soviets designed universal high-rise prefabricated building complexes that came to be called *Krushchabki* in mocking honor of Chairman Khushchev who, shortly after Stalin's death, moved quickly in response to the critical need for urban housing. The effort evolved over time to include apartment complexes that reached up to twenty floors high, consisting of one, two, and three room flats. Constructed of pre-formed, reinforced concrete slabs trucked to the site, these large building pieces were hoisted up with the help of giant cranes and notched together into various rectangular patterns.

The suburbs were filled with these monstrosities. Each flat usually had a small balcony, providing just enough space to store a few household items and to hang out a couple days laundry. Sometimes the flat occupants framed in their balcony space to make an extra room/sleeping porch. The exterior of the buildings might be decorated in swoops, geometric patterns, or bands, all from colored tile, most of which long ago had faded to a dull pastel or had just fallen off. The buildings were set back from the street, usually by several hundred feet of well-trampled bare earth and minimal ground vegetation other than a few weeds. Some of the older complexes contained a few mature trees. We never saw any flowers or flowering bushes around these apartment complexes. We never noticed any lawns to mow.

Each of the numerous buildings of the general type we lived in while in Tallinn contained two or three small entrances. Each entrance led to a staircase and to a single tiny elevator that provided access to between two to four flats on each floor. Each flat had a large personalized entry door similar to the one I described for our Vilnius place. Entry to each flat was usually through two doors, one immediately in front of the other. Some of the outer doors were padded, others were wooden covered with glossy varnish, or just made of steel. No matter in what shape or design, all of the doors were inevitably secured with multiple giant locks.

The entrances, stairwells, elevators, and landings were invariably filthy and missing most or all of their lighting. As neglected public spaces, they had almost always deteriorated into dilapidated and smelly places. It took us a long time to adjust completely to these surroundings. Homeless people often spent the cold winter nights sleeping in our lightly heated stairwell in Vilnius. No matter how familiar we became after constant use of these entrance structures, entering into these often totally dark places at night, I couldn't help thinking about the remote possibility of danger.

Over more than two decades, these Krushckabki-style apartment building complexes ended up growing to a massive scale, lined up in block-long rows or arranged in snakelike or circular clusters of various shapes. The buildings often stretched out over a mile or more, only the color schemes varying now and then. Judy and I were so impressed with the constant presence of their ugly banality that we kick ourselves for not purchasing the definitive remembrance—a large oil painting we saw for sale in an Estonian art gallery. It consisted of nothing but a close up of the bottom floor corner of one of these buildings with most of the painting being taken up by a standard building number sign affixed to an otherwise blank wall! With only a little variation, this was the type of housing we lived in while in Estonia and Uzbekistan, and which surrounded our dacha in Kharkiv.

Our first experience with prefabricated Krushchabki housing was in

Tallinn, Estonia. We located the flat through a realtor, a newly arrived profession to post-Communist times. We lived on the fifth floor of an eight-story building in a fairly large complex located just on the edge of downtown Tallinn. It was a convenient location, being just across the street from a big farmers market. Also across the street was the new Japanese embassy, still under construction.

The flat was large and airy compared to our previous place in Vilnius. The kitchen was large. It had bright red window curtains and, thank goodness, a full-sized refrigerator. There were comfortable twin beds in the bedroom, which opened onto a long hallway lined with storage cabinets, all full of the landlord's stuff. It was typical of each place we lived that the landlord used half or more of the available storage in which to keep what normally looked to us as junk.

The front room contained the usual large wood-looking, press-board china–book case combination, a fold-out sofa, a dining table I converted to my work area, and an oversized and out-of-kilter homemade rocking chair that migrated across the floor when rocked in for any period of time. There was no separate toilet room. The toilet was located in the small bathroom: a departure from the standard for most Soviet-era flats.

Located in the bathroom was a washing machine, of sorts. It was the typical Soviet kind. It was basically a plastic tub that we would lift up to straddle the bathtub. We would fill the tub with water and soap, toss in our clothes, and turn on the agitator. The contraption looked like a large ice-cream maker, and it was important not to run the agitator too long as it could rather quickly beat our clothes to a pulp. There was no spin cycle. Instead we would pull the drain plug, drain the soapy water and then repeat the agitation with clean water. In the last step, we would remove each item, wring it by hand before hanging it on clotheslines above the bathtub to drip dry. Communism was not about making people's life easy, and this "washing machine" was just one more example.

No capitalist frills in a Soviet Krushchabki bathroom.

Most features of our flat were typical of the more modern Krushchabki. Once we had seen the inside, let alone the outside of these flats, we had pretty much seen them all. The joke was about the numerous occasions when folks, having drunk a little too much vodka, easily stumbled into another flat. A standard feature was that all of the plumbing ran exposed along the inside walls of the flat. In the bathroom, this meant that the toilet sat out about two feet from the back wall in order to accommodate the large soil pipe that exited behind it. The bathtub sat up about a foot higher than Americans would consider normal so that all its plumbing could fit underneath.

Also in the bathroom was a set of hot and cold water faucets and a single two-foot long spout. The faucet was mounted on the wall between the bathroom sink and the bathtub. We moved the spout back and forth as needed. The bathroom walls were covered in light green tile. Other bath units might be tiled in baby blue. I concluded that these had been the only two color choices of tile available at the time.

Vinyl floor covering was laid throughout the entire flat. All the vinyl had one of four embossed designs and was usually medium brown in color. Of course, we had ours in medium brown. Just about all apartment walls were covered with heavy, faintly patterned wallpaper in an off-white color. Ours was, naturally, off-white and faintly patterned. Our wallpaper was also home to cockroaches that lived behind its protective veneer, consuming the paste that held the paper to the wall.

Hanging from the ceiling of the front room was a cheap-looking ornate chandelier containing several naked, unfrosted, lightbulbs. All flats contained a variation of this chandelier. In the evening, we could see them in the other flats, starkly glaring away, doing nothing to enhance the ambiance of the room. Floor lamps, table lamps, or any kind of indirect lighting was rarely found in apartment flats, except, as in our case, where we enjoyed a Swedish modern lamp at the end of the sofa.

One thing we did have that was especially appreciated was a color-TV set with a cable connection providing a very limited selection of British programming. We watched the Sky News network each night. We learned all about British politics in the run-up to the election of Prime Minister Tony Blair. We especially enjoyed the commercials, which were very funny and actually appealed to a person's intelligence. Our Tallinn flat was a great place to stay, but the best stories occurred in our next posting in Ukraine, and again in our second Krushchabki-style flat in Uzbekistan.

A Dacha Triplex

The Russian word *dacha* referred to a second home, a place somewhere away from the city. Dachas originally were enjoyed only by wealthy families. During the Soviet period of urbanization, the dacha became the province, it seemed, of just about everybody. Much reduced in size, dachas could be found by the thousands just a short drive or train ride from practically any big city. Judy and I traveled by train through many a countryside filled with these little houses and shacks. They were most numerous just before we would enter the ring of suburban apartment complexes surrounding cities like St Petersburg, Moscow, Kiev, or Minsk. Large open areas cut out of the forests would extend right down almost to the railroad tracks. These areas were filled with dachas lined up in rows and separated by individual vegetable gardens. Many of the units were not much larger than a tool storage shed, just large enough to hold garden tools and a couple of beds. It is certain that the average Soviet citizen maintained their dacha mostly out of the necessity for food consumption rather than the more traditional upper-class need for conspicuous consumption.

Our dacha in Kharkiv, Ukraine. Our quarters were in the left front half, with our "cooks entrance" around the left side. Krushchabi apartmens can be seen in the distance.

Our Kharkov dacha had once been definitely toward the ostentatious end of the scale. Once, about a hundred years ago, it had been a grand statement of wealth, refinement, and leisure. Two years before our arrival, our part of the dacha had been rented by my CEP predecessor, Paul Sloan, who had described the unit to me in an e-mail as "a good place for us to live, a little worn out, but possessing many of the qualities of a single-family home with flowers and fruit trees and its own courtyard entrance." It sounded delightful. Well, by some measure, I guess this might have been true. However, we had to squint our eyes and look very selectively to appreciate this place! I saw our new home as absolutely falling apart, yes, but funky in a way I would never experience again in my life, nor want to, and certainly an interesting relic of history. It definitely looked and felt more like a house than a number on the side of some high-rise apartment. Judy called it "the ugly little place."

In less personal terms, our dacha building was a crumbling single-story red-brick structure of about 2,500 square feet that had originally belonged to an upper-class czarist–period family. It had been built at the beginning of the twentieth century when its location would have involved about a forty-five minute horse-and-buggy ride from Kharkiv's city center. Now it was within easy walking distance from the last stop on the metro in a neighborhood filled with similarly crumbling old dachas interspersed with examples of early Krushchabki apartment buildings. There was a row of these dingy gray-colored buildings right across a single-lane dirt road that passed in front of our house. The road could be a sea of water and mud when we got a good rain. Not withstanding any of this, and more, our stay in this place was memorably humorous and eventful.

Our dacha, and a surrounding weedy acre of abandoned fruit orchard, was both in very poor condition. The building, which had remained in the family since new, was now divided into three flats. In our section, the high, once beautifully ornate ceilings dripped water through large areas of discolored or missing plaster. The floors in the hall and one bedroom sagged to the point of eminent collapse, and the old-fashioned double-shuttered windows leaked a great deal of air. Yet, more in my opinion than in Judy's, this was a good place to stay when compared to the places most other Kharkiv residents we knew called home. We knew a young lady whose father was a Ukrainian Army colonel who taught military science classes at a local military academy. His family's flat made our place look great. We knew another military officer, his wife, and young son. Their flat was newer but exceedingly cramped, as were so many others that we visited during the year.

When comparing places to stay, a large plus for us was that when most city residents were waiting into the mid or late fall, through freezing temperatures, for their heat to be turned on (the typical mumbo-jumbo of so many days below a certain average temperature), we had our own little gas-fired boiler with an adjustable thermostat to keep us reasonably warm. When the authorities would turn off the hot water to large sections of the city, sometimes for as much as a month for "cleaning the pipes," we had our own well and a Polish *klunkla*, a little on-demand gas-fired water heater that would turn on immediately when hot water was needed in the kitchen or bath. All the hot water we needed would then begin arriving within seconds. These two amenities alone justified renting our portion of the dacha for the usual princely sum charged to foreigners.

Russian Air-Conditioning

What we did not have, nor did anybody else, was a back-up electricity supply. Continuing the Soviet-era energy policy, Ukraine was pricing its energy so low as to invite disaster through its wasteful use. Beginning in the late fall, we began to lose our electricity for up to four hours each day. Fortunately, this did not affect our hot water or heat.

Premature darkness came as no surprise. We had been able to see the energy shortage problem coming right from the moment we arrived behind the former Iron Curtain. The supply infrastructure was in shambles. Just as bad, the demand side of the energy picture fostered profligate use with little or no penalty for the consumer. We had also noticed the lack of heat adjustment controls in the typical communally heated flats. The heat was either "on" or "off" according to some remote official's decision to pump hot water into the building's radiator systems. In the fall when it turned cold and no heating water was yet running, the flats remained cold, sometimes really cold. During brief periods of warming weather in the spring, and longer warm periods in early summer, the hot water would remain "on" irregardless. On such occasions, folks would open every window in their flat wide to let the heat pour out. "Russian air-conditioning," they would call it. The whole operation amounted to a giant waste of energy.

Lithuania and Estonia had moved quickly to introduce market signals that would result in energy conservation. Ukraine had not, choosing instead to remain energy poor, backward, and further in debt to the Russians who supplied most of the natural gas used for electricity generation. Twice daily, two-hour-long rolling blackouts were becoming commonplace in our life in the dacha. Everybody else also experienced their hours of darkness. Our blackout periods were usually from 10:00 AM to noon and again from 6:00 to 8:00 PM.

Lack of consistent electricity was also disrupting the hot water heating system at the university. My classroom began to chill down a little more each day. The students started to keep their heavy jackets on in the room. Water pressure dropped to the point that the toilets would not flush. Classrooms on the inside of the building were left in total darkness. Judy and I started wearing thermal underwear. Toward the middle of the winter, there was serious talk that much of Kharkiv would be totally blacked out for up to two weeks or more. An ongoing political squabble over payment of past due gas bills had Russia threatening to further turn down the gas supply. I thought the two week blackout scenario rather implausible considering that this would idle city pumps that circulated hot heating water to most people's flats, leaving them to ice down completely and very likely killing people in the process. Of course, this is exactly what had happened on a smaller scale in Latvia during our first winter in the CEP. What was the recipe behind such a predicament in Ukraine?

Part of the answer for the lack of sufficient electricity was that there appeared to be no political will to begin energy conservation. The heating "on/off" arrangement continued. Ignoring any effort at conservation, the Soviets had routed much of the hot water distribution system above ground along street right of ways, sometimes even up and over intersections. These large pipes had once been wrapped in a thin blanket of aluminum foil–backed fiberglass. Large portions of this wrap had long ago become badly damaged. Some wrap hung in shreds from the pipes while in other sections it was completely missing. Where pipes actually ran underground, they often leaked. During the winter, large plumes of steam would rise up from debris-filled sinkholes in the ground or lidless manholes. With energy prices kept ridiculously low through government subsidy, there was just no incentive to change a tradition of wasteful practice.

One form of subsidy was allowing businesses to pay less than 20 percent of their monthly electric bill while allowing them to try, usually unsuccessfully, to barter the rest of what was owed. Household users were charged less than the full amount of the cost of their electricity and when they fell behind in payment, or did not pay at all, no action was usually taken. Judy and I had experienced this behavior in Estonia where we had a landlord who never seemed to pay our electric bill and another landlord, in Uzbekistan who would let the telephone bill run up for months at a time until our service would be cancelled, before finally making a payment.

A third form of subsidy was the result of a multifaceted system of privilege that meant, among other perks, that almost a half of all Ukrainians were entitled to further reductions in their already small energy bills. Typical examples of these people would be pensioners and military veterans. We knew a man who received both a discount for his age and a second one for his past profession as an entertainer. Well, to keep the story short, the result, for us was inconvenience. For Ukraine, it was the ignominious status of being one of the world's greatest per-capita electricity consumers and overall energy wasters.

In defense of state policy, several efforts had been made, some ongoing during the time we were in Kharkiv, to increase energy rates and reduce subsidies. Every effort had failed to get the necessary support in Parliament from Ukraine's large populist political coalition between socialists and Communists.

We purchased a large battery-operated lantern that could be recharged and, when plugged in, would automatically turn on when the power went off. Lantern light got us through many evening meals and several good books. Walking back from school through the snow and cold, through a partially darkened city and fully darkened neighborhood, it was always nice to have our little lantern shining brightly and to feel the warm air as we keyed open our front door. Of course, the lights were always kept on at the prison, and fortunately, also at our large farmer's-style market.

Our Dacha Neighbors

The other two sections of our building were occupied by relatives, related five generations back to the original dacha owners. Igor Zhukovsky his wife, Raisa, and their twenty-year-old son lived in the back, originally the kitchen portion, of the dacha, sharing a long wall with us. Igor was in his early fifties, tall, stubbly bearded, and usually dressed in well-worn, casual clothes. He had long been out of work, but would busy himself doing small repair jobs on the dacha. When we first moved in, Igor was in the midst of a long-term project having something to do with the plumbing of the family's toilet. The bathroom was in a stoop arrangement attached to the house just beyond the back door of the kitchen.

Raisa seemed to divide her time between cooking and watching Russian soap operas and game shows on TV. The frequent and unwanted greasy cooking odors, along with her throaty laughter, would find their way through an ill-fitting door between her kitchen and our front room. The smell and the noise were only partially reduced by a thick quilt which was hung over our side of the doorway. The quilt and the door were hidden behind a large standard-issue shiny faux-wood bookcase that ran along most of the common wall. Much to our consternation, Raisa also liked to spend a lot of her time on the three-way telephone we shared with her and Igor and with Leonid, the third dacha tenant.

Igor and his son repairing our stove. The oven door would constantly fall open. Kharkiv, Ukraine

Leonid was a physicist who did his best to keep busy with his research. He was middle-aged, divorced, and kept afloat financially through small research grants and a share of our rent money. He was one of many former Soviet scientists whom George Soros was financially assisting in hopes that they would be able to remain in their profession and not be tempted to sell out their scientific expertise to terrorists or other bad guys. Leonid was hardly the type for anyone to be worried about being involved in this kind of event. His financial needs were minimal.

Leonid lived in the smallest two-room section of the dacha. It was dusty and unkempt, stuffed with discarded electronic lab equipment in one room and piles of scientific journals in another. While Leonid had a small kitchen inside, the toilet was a wooden privy located out back in the fruit orchard. Leonid's living quarters seemed surprisingly cramped, spartan in furnishings, and primitive in its sanitary facilities for someone who had spent the better part of a career as a well-respected scientist. His only splurge appeared to be an older but well-maintained automobile. During our stay in Kharkiv, Leonid was working via the Internet on a joint project with scientists at Lawrence Livermore Laboratory in California.

Leonid was always in a good mood. I only saw him agitated and upset once when describing how Igor had been tossing empty vodka bottles down his outdoor privy. "It is time he finished his own toilet repair project, stopped using mine, and also quit drinking so much," he said. Leonid spoke reasonably good English, which aside from allowing us to become friends, also turned out to be helpful in our adjustment to life in the dacha. He was the one who met us on our arrival at the Kharkiv train station, managing, in two trips with his little car, to transport all our baggage to our new quarters. He put in fresh batteries and set the time in a giant five-foot-high replica of a gold wristwatch that hung from our entry wall. He carefully tacked up a long run of telephone wire in order for me to use my laptop computer in one of the bedrooms that we had turned into a study. I cleaned up the fresh wood chips while he cut and nailed a tin patch over a large recently made rat hole that went through the front room baseboard behind the sofa. Leonid warned me not to leave any food sitting out overnight. It was beginning to look like home? Far from it, but it would do for us over the year.

Leonid took us to musical performances. We reciprocated by having him for dinner. He patiently interceded on our behalf when Igor and Raisa tried to raise our rent shortly after we had settled in. The Russian ruble had recently tumbled to less than half its worth, taking the value of Ukrainian money down with it, and Igor was going to make up for it! The telephone rang. He made his usual announcement of intent to meet with me. "Martin, open door," he blurted out. This took a little bit of time. Two back-to-back main doors had to be unlocked in order to step out into a covered, screened stoop containing an old bumpy sofa and miscellaneous worn-out wooden furniture. From here, I was able to turn the lock on homemade French doors that opened to the outside.

With his stubby little pencil, Igor ran through the math on a piece of paper. We struggled over the language differences, but it was obvious that Igor wanted to raise the rent. This sounded familiar. I was sorry that the rental agreement had only been verbal, a slip up, because the CEP normally insisted on a written contract. I suggested that he bring Leonid to interpret for us. A few days later, Leonid informed me that the matter had been dropped; $350 a month was more than enough to pay for this "ugly little place."

Not long after Igor got his toilet reinstalled, our toilet seat broke away from its connections. I got on the phone. "Igor, I open door," I said, in Russian, using the simplest of words. It was an obvious case for a new seat. Igor arrived to our green-tiled bathroom to supervise his son in the removal of the toilet seat, spending enough time in the process of removal to thoroughly leaven every square inch of the small bathroom with his garlic and vodka-laden breath and strong body odor. Soon we could hear some banging around on his side of the front-room wall. Later in the afternoon, following the usual telephone announcement, Igor returned with the toilet seat. The seat was remounted on the toilet, which again necessitated a thorough airing out of the bathroom. The seat managed to stay on for a couple of days, then water started to squirt out the back of the stool with each flush. The porcelain was broken around the lid attachment hole. Again I called on the telephone; "Igor, I open door." Igor looked at the toilet and said some expletives in Russian, then said to me, in the word of Russian I understood, "tomorrow." Back he came the next day with some foul-smelling glue formula that he liberally applied to the back of the toilet. Now the bathroom really needed an airing out. The glue job held, and the seat managed to stay on for the remaining months of our occupancy, although as far as I was concerned, it was no longer capable of being "properly" operated. At least Judy was happy, as the seat could not be lifted and would thus never again be left in its usual up position. The new aluminum bandage would not allow it!

Completing the bathroom accoutrements was actually something that worked quite well: a small portable French-made washing machine that we purchased shortly after our arrival. Sitting in the bathtub, it knew not only how to agitate, it also knew how to spin. This was an improvement over our washing machine in Estonia, but that was all. The rest of the washing was up to us.

In addition to the bathroom, the remaining portion of the dacha consisted of a small, more recently added, kitchen and a fairly large original master bedroom with a row of windows looking out on the covered back porch. This room served as our front room. It contained a cheap folding sofa-bed and two matching upholstered chairs Paul had purchased new and I in turn bought from him. The room also contained the bottom half of a large antique credenza that served as a useful cabinet. There were two original children's rooms. The one we used for our bedroom contained a double bed, free-standing clothes cabinet, and dresser.

The third bedroom I used for a study. It contained a rustic and very worn desk over which was a large wallpaper mural of a woodsy scene in fall color. The room also contained a free-standing electric fireplace, which, although abominable-looking, did put out a bit of heat when needed. In the hallway that connected these rooms were strung several wires that served as our winter clothes-drying area. We were able to hang our clothes outside in good weather. The high ceilings in the study and hall had large green mold areas and places where the plaster had previously become so wet it had fallen down. These two areas stayed wet during the winter but fortunately never dripped on anything important.

Our front bedroom and study windows looked across a small one-lane street to an old apartment building. The windows provided an opportunity to see the people coming and going, including large funerals on two occasions involving residents of the apartment building. People would wait around outside the front entrance as the body was brought down the staircase wrapped in a white sheet. A brief ceremony would ensue before the body was loaded into the back of a closed truck. Several people, probably the immediate family, also climbed into the back of the truck, after which everybody would leave. We had surreptitiously taken photos through our dacha windows of the funeral proceedings only later to be thoroughly chided for this by some of my students who saw the pictures scattered about on my desk. They considered my actions to be in very bad taste.

The view out the kitchen window took in a daycare school playground and the lower portion of our front street where the open garbage dumpsters were located. Mostly old people were constantly sorting through these dumpsters for something to eat, as were a fair number of stray cats. On occasion, I gave these people money as I walked to or from our dacha. I couldn't help making some gesture of assistance. I always left my beer bottles by the dumpster. The bottles could be returned for money to a roadside collector. I frequently noticed the bottle collector on my way to school, sitting by his car and trailer partially filled with glass bottles

The Sounds of Life

Living in our part of the dacha involved getting used to several new features. One involved a number of different sounds. Of course, our houses in America also contain important sounds as well. Think of the microwave, the washing machine, or the smoke alarms. Here, ours were uniquely different. In the kitchen, sitting on top of a very noisy refrigerator was a little red plastic box. When someone came to see us, the visitor, by prior arrangement, had first to know to reach around a metal post in a large gate at the front corner of the dacha and push a hidden button. The red box would then make the loud sound of a bird chirping. This would be my signal to grab the three door keys and the gate key and begin the laborious opening procedure to exit the dacha and open the gate. Why not enter the front door of the dacha, you might say? Only our part of the building was blocked off from this entrance.

A second sound involved the telephone. All three dacha families shared one line. In a way, it reminded me of the multiple-party line my parents had when I was a kid. Each party had its own special ring. In this case, there was only one ring. Not being very conversant in Russian, we rarely picked up the phone when it rang. Instead we would wait for a buzzer located next to our phone to sound a signal that we were being paged. Picking up the standard Soviet rotary dial telephone receiver, it was usually Raisa in her heavy accent and specially affected voice for such a cheerful occasion, "Martin (or Judy)… telephone."

There was also the long hours spent listening to the sound of our laptop computer ringing: first one, then another of a series, usually ten busy telephone numbers, over and over, trying to make a connection to our local Internet provider. After what seemed forever, and with a lot of luck, the sweet-sounding screechy noises and bong sounds would be emitted. I was connected! Now all I had to do was pray not to hear what might be the next sound, that of a rotary phone being dialed and Raisa's voice coming out of the little modem next to my laptop computer; "Ahalo, ahalo," she would shout, wondering why the line was busy but no one was talking on it. She never seemed to understand the reason for the strange screechy sounds when she picked up our communal telephone, even though Leonid had cautioned her about this on several occasions. I soon switched over to sending and receiving our e-mail either very early in the morning or in the middle of the night.

It was vitally important that the e-mail system work as it was our main connection to the CEP and to the outside world. We sent no postal mail as the service in, at least our area of Ukraine, was very unreliable.

A Potpourri of Activity

In early May, Judy and I attended a birthday party for our military family's ten-year-old son. We were getting to know this family fairly well. Judy had been volunteering for his mother, Yuliya, in her grade school classroom, and we had recently attended a school play all done in English. We would soon be invited to watch their son Anton perform at a ballroom dance club competition. Now we were off to the birthday party. We brought Anton a birthday gift of a new soccer ball. Yuliya's mother and father were in attendance at the party along with her sister and a journalist friend and his wife.

Judy and I sat in the flat's tiny front room on a broken-down sofa eating open-face sandwiches topped with cheap caviar or little sardines. We enjoyed a salad made from crab and beets, ate mounds of mashed potatoes, and toasted with several shots of vodka. Our friends peppered us with questions, our answers being slowly, carefully, interpreted by Yuliya. In exchange, they all told us stories. The journalist told of writing an article critical of the government four years earlier and promptly having their daughter kidnapped by the *militia* (police) from the sidewalk on her way home from school. She was held for six hours before they were able to get her back. It seemed a little odd, after stories like that, to hear the many references and testimonials to the "good old days" of Communism. We stayed at the party long enough to have to walk back to our dacha in the customary circumstance of total darkness.

During our stay in our Kharkiv dacha, we continued to follow and expand considerably our practice of inviting students into our flat for academic assistance and all kinds of informal get-togethers, dinners, and class parties. Students who were selected to give papers at international conferences would meet together at our flat to practice delivering their oral presentations.

We introduced the American tradition of Halloween with a pumpkin-carving party. We laid out an old shower curtain on the front room carpet, and after a few simple instructions and a warning not to cut themselves, the students began carving while I read funny tombstone excerpts. They produced some very artful creations. Judy served Ukrainian-style hotdogs and homemade potato salad. We fit candles into the pumpkins and put them on the credenza so that we could take some group pictures. The students warned us against placing them in the windows for fear that they would attract too much attention and the police might arrive. The party was BYOB. Just about everybody brought juice. Fortunately, I had two bottles of champagne to share.

When it came time to leave, the valuable pumpkins and their seeds went home with their owners to be eaten. It was interesting to imagine what it must have looked like as the students traveled back to their flats, sitting on the tram or bus with a Jack-o-lantern on their lap. The students had gone to a lot of work to obtain their pumpkins, as whole examples were almost impossible to find in the markets where it was customary to buy only cut pieces. Fortunately, most of the students had a relative or a friend who knew someone out in the country able to provide a whole pumpkin or two.

Pumpkin carving party. Kharkiv, Ukraine.

At our Christmas party, we introduced the idea of a Chinese gift exchange. Students found this twist on gift giving and getting quite exciting and did not want to stop the exchange. We ended up putting a limit on how many times gifts could circulate.

At the conclusion of the school year, we put on a big *shashlik* party in our weedy backyard. We cleared a space for a fire. Using a pile of bricks and two pieces of angle iron, we made a homemade grille. The backyard contained an old bathtub "used by my father and mother," Igor our landlord had volunteered. It would have been a good place to keep the beer cold, but there was no such thing as packaged ice that could be purchased. The backyard also contained a couple of bed frames and an old park bench, which together provided sufficient though makeshift seating arrangements. Judy and I provided the meat, and the students brought the rest of the food as per a checklist we had circulated in the classroom for them to initial (Appendix 3). Some of the female students came early to help prepare the food. A few of the boys drank a little too much beer. It was a fitting conclusion to the year.

Krushchabki with Real Air-Conditioning

Upon our arrival in Tashkent, Judy and I spent our first two nights in a flat belonging to Dildora, our Uzbekistan program assistant. Carter stayed with us, as a place for him had yet to be located. Dildora was hoping we might live in her rental flat. It was nice enough, had a well-appointed kitchen, but required walking up four flights of stairs and was seriously incomplete in furnishings. Most noticeably, the flat lacked air-conditioning. It was at least 110 outside and close to that temperature on the inside! It was unlivable. So, for the first two days, we stayed outside as much as we could while waiting to select a different flat. The first evening, our first in Uzbekistan, we stayed out longer than we should have. Mindful that we had spent most of our first night at the airport sitting on our baggage and now had gone more than thirty-six hours without sleep, the plan was to go out for a quick meal and then back to our oven of a flat, open all the windows, and try to get some sleep.

The three of us found a little outdoor restaurant about five or six blocks away and stayed around after our meal to socialize over a few beers and a shot or more of vodka. The alcohol went to work on our tired condition, leaving Carter and me in a great mood but decidedly wobbly on the walk several blocks back to the flat—and not having a very good idea where it was anyway! None of us had thought to write down the address. Fortunately, Judy had the good sense not to drink so much and remembered the way back.

Two days later, we moved into a very well-worn but spacious fifth-floor two-room flat that belonged to Dildora's mother-in-law. (Keeping business in the family is a very prominent feature of life in Uzbekistan.) The flat could be reached via an elevator. It had the standard room layout with the addition of a large glassed-in sunroom that opened off of the front room. We hardly needed the sunroom in late August, but fortunately it faced mostly north and, most important, this was where a large window air-conditioner was located. Through the purchase and strategic location of three large portable fans, we could move at least some of the colder air throughout most of the flat.

The entrance to our building was also standard in both design and, predictably, in a filthy broken down condition. Judy and I had long ago stopped thinking about the ordeal and the possible danger of entering such places until our daughter Kimberly visited us in Tashkent in the early spring. She arrived from Germany well after midnight. The airport taxi dropped us off in our dark ramshackle courtyard near the "black hole" front entrance to our flat. Kimberly was absolutely horrified as we left the taxi, got our bearings in the darkness, and carefully approached the unlit entrance to our building and proceeded to go into the dark, warm, musty space.

I knew the routine. It was as follows: from the doorless entrance, being careful not to bump into the rows of ramshackle mailboxes on the right, shuffle forward three paces and grab the end of the handrail on the left, then climb three steps and again shuffle forward and slightly to the left several paces while looking for a dimly glowing button on the opposite wall, press the button and wait for the elevator to show up. Fortunately, the inside of the elevator was lit on this particular occasion. In preparation for Kimberly's arrival, I had been careful to make sure that there was a new lightbulb in the socket on our fifth-floor landing. At least our way was lit from the elevator exit to the door to our flat. Of course, the lightbulb would likely go missing within a few days, but for now, the bright light helped somewhat to allay Kimberly's immediate sense of concern. Other than a few "My God" utterances, I am sure that this first impression of our flat must have confirmed her worst fears over what her parents were doing so far from home. She should have tried walking through the totally darkened park, in the dense fog, on the way to our dacha in Kharkiv.

Our apartment flat was furnished in the usual "Soviet shoddy," including the usual green-tiled bathroom with separate toilet room and wallpaper, which was extensively personalized by the artwork of two small children belonging to our landlady's son-in-law. This young man was professor at National University where I was also assigned. Along with becoming a good friend, he doubled as our contact person for all issues related to the flat. On the plus side of furnishings, we had a great little German-made clothes washer and a good color TV set.

We soon discovered a local contact that would take care of all our money exchanges. We would call our contact when we needed to exchange money. He would usually stop by the flat in the morning to take one or two of my hundred-dollar bills. In the afternoon, he would bring me my Uzbek money, usually enough to completely fill a couple of grocery store type plastic bags. On several occasions, our contact brought the sack of Uzbekistan money to our little CEP office at the university. It would completely fill my briefcase as well as Judy's large purse. I felt a lot better about carrying large bulky amounts of small denomination Uzbekistan money around in the city after obtaining a diplomatic visa. This handy little document prevented the police from examining my personal effects. Just a couple of hundred dollars was the equivalent of a year's wages in Uzbekistan.

Our contact also helped Carter change his money. The same day that he moved into his apartment flat, Carter gave our contact person three hundred dollars at school to change for him. The contact decided to bring the approximately five pound bag of Uzbekistan money to Carter's flat the same evening. Carter was not absolutely sure what floor he lived on, but thought he was on the fifth floor and had informed our contact accordingly. It was a humorous picture to think of this man standing in the total darkness (the lightbulb problem) on the fifth floor of Carter's apartment building with a really big bag full of money. The contact later told us about knocking on one of the apartment doors. The occupants had, naturally, never heard of Carter. The contact resorted to his cell phone, which he had just reactivated having finally paid a much overdue bill, and called me to find out what floor Carter lived on.

Standing in the dark, this time on the sixth floor, the contact had to contend with the matter of two doorbells at the door to Carter's flat. The one doorbell, placed where it should be, did not work. The other one was high up on the door. Feeling around, our money currier finally managed to make it ring. Stepping into the apartment flat, the contact found Carter in the middle of his initial Russian lesson. The young lady providing the lesson wanted to know what was in the big sack. Not wanting to reveal that he was about to have this much money around his flat, Carter quickly answered that it was his colleague's school papers, which were left at the university when he had to rush his wife to the hospital. The story went on to note that our contact, a university employee, had brought the papers back for Carter to deliver the next morning. It was an elaborate ruse, more so than necessary, but it satisfied the language teacher anyway. At work the next day, I told Carter that he should be ready to answer his teacher's questions about Judy's condition for at least the next couple of lessons.

On the first night in our flat, our cat, Pyat, decided it was time to disappear. Our flat was equipped with the standard Russian screenless windows. It was feared that the cat had fallen out over five floors to the ground. I went downstairs with a flashlight. It was after midnight. I walked around near the base of the building calling "Here, kitty, kitty" again and again, wondering just where I might see her flattened on the ground. I also wondered what some of the ground-floor tenants must be been thinking, having almost certainly been awakened by my actions.

Having no success, I returned to the flat. I should have thought that no cat would be stupid enough to fall out of a window located that high of off the ground. We were too distraught to sleep. Then about an hour later, we heard a faint but repeated "meow." Crawling past a wooden barrier, Pyat had jumped approximately four feet to the balcony of the adjacent flat. Like a cat in a tree, she was not about to come back without help. So at about 2:00 AM, standing in the hallway with the door to our flat wide open, the light illuminating our landing, and both of us clearly visible through the glass peep hole in our neighbor's door, I rang the doorbell. An old Russian babushka finally came to the door. I pointed to the entrance to our flat and pronounced the Russian word for cat, then pointed into her flat. She smiled. She knew what we wanted. Leaving her front door open, she left and returned a minute or so later, much to our relief, holding our cat.

The next day we made arrangements for screening the windows. A workman, hired off of the street by our flat manager, did a poor job, using what was more like netting than proper screen. The finished product kept the cat in but succeeded only in reducing the number of mosquitoes most of which now were coming up the stairwell and zipping into the flat with every opening of the front door. They also appeared to be coming out of the air vent in the bathroom. A definite third entrance was through the door to the balcony, which got opened several times each day, in most cases to access the clothesline. The mosquitoes were not the only residents lurking out there. They shared the balcony with several pigeons who claimed squatter's rights, cooing us awake every morning and pooping all over their portion of the balcony.

As for the mosquitoes, it was suggested by a few of my students that we get some coiled incense-looking material that slowly burns, producing a sweet smoky fume. I nixed this idea. Good thing, too. In India, we had used something like this in one of our hotel rooms. The smoke would quickly drop big healthy-looking mosquitoes off the ceiling dead in less than a minute! Rather powerful, but what about the day-in day-out use on our lungs? We decided to use a flyswatter.

As a result of our killing spree, the ceiling and upper portions of the walls of our flat began to exhibit an increasing number of smashed and bloody little bodies. Every evening, it seemed, I could swat more than a dozen of these crafty little menaces as they hung around, waiting for us to go to bed. Still, enough always remained, undetected, until protected by the cover of darkness. We tried sleeping with a sheet over our heads, but it was just too hot for this form of protection. On hindsight, I probably should have tried harder to locate an effective repellant. Instead, I came up with the workable idea of placing one of our large fans about three feet from our heads and turning it on full. We got used to sleeping in this gale force wind unmolested by the mosquitoes who found themselves unable to make a landing!

In the spring, we started going out to eat more often. We met a couple of American businessmen while having dinner at a sports bar located just a few blocks from our apartment flat. Dildora had taken us to this quite unexpected Western-style restaurant, which, naturally, was owned by one of her relatives. She promised that we would like the food. We did. The two Americans invited us to join them the following week for a "hash run." No, it was not the kind that you smoke. Actually I am not sure where the name came from, other than it stands for a club made up of Westerners who like to run, jog, or walk before having dinner at one of the member's houses. Members also liked to drink quite a lot. Hash clubs are apparently quite popular in Western Europe with ex-pats. Judy and I attended two hash runs, marveling at the way the local Uzbeks would stand out in the street to watch us jog by as though it were a parade, a crazy American one in this case, all the running around and going nowhere. We did not stick with the club following two meetings as, back at the host's home, too many of the members acted more like out-of-control fraternity boys.

Getting and Keeping Basic Services

After living three years in apartment flats and a dacha, the hot water problem finally caught up with us. Not having hot water for a couple of weeks or more, especially in the winter while the "cleaning of the pipes" took place was such a common event in Soviet-period flats that the local people rarely gave it a thought. We didn't have to either, but for a different reason; we were lucky never to have had to experience the situation until now. Uncomplainingly, we adjusted by heating water for dishes and to hand wash a few clothes. We also heated water to take a shallow bath using more hot water to pour over each other in order to rinse. The alternative was cold showers, something I had resorted to occasionally in hotels. Judy never could manage the shock of cold water. I asked people why the authorities did not try to clean the pipes in the summer when going without hot water would have been much easier. Nobody could provide an answer. Cleaning the pipes was a mysterious process.

We needed a dish antenna if we were going to watch our TV in English. Early in our stay, a local friend looked into this for us and found out that it would cost $150 for the dish and $40 a month for the service. We were prepared to pay this amount. Then he informed us that it would also take at least six months to get the dish installed. With our friend's assurance, and on his recommendation, we moved to the "post-Soviet default setting" instead. This amounted to taking care of the problem outside of official channels. Actually, this approach to services was nothing more than a carry-over from Soviet times.

The Soviet model was that if one wanted just about anything done, one needed to be able to draw upon the installing and repairing expertise represented in a circle of friends, and be prepared to reciprocate in one form or another. Our friend had the right kind of friends for this occasion. A few days later, two men arrived at the flat and took about two hours to set up our black market dish service. One workman went up on the roof and attached a premade approximately six-foot-long tubular metal extension that projected horizontally out from the top edge of the building. According to the installer, this arrangement would hold the (likely stolen) dish out far enough from the roof edge to foil most thieves.

While installing the extension, the workman's big drill ran off a long extension cord that draped down and into the wide open window of our flat two floors below. It drew so much current that all the lights would flicker and dim. This sent me rushing around the flat in an effort to prevent an electrical failure by turning off unnecessary electrical appliances. I had not noticed an electricity panel in the flat and thus assumed that should a failure occur, we would need to contact an official electrician to go to the basement or some other place to replace the fuse. Then there might be questions about what I was doing to cause the power failure, who the men on the roof were, etc. Fortunately the power managed to stay on. In the meantime, the mosquitoes loved the open window holding the power cord.

While this was going on, the second man moved our TV off of the little stand onto the floor, turned it upside down, and opened the back exposing the circuit board. Using a soldering iron he proceeded to perform a rather extensive rewiring job. Soon the TV was back up on its stand and the dish was installed. At this point, one of the workmen gave us a choice. We could have one year of service with twenty-five Western channels for $100 or one year with six hundred channels for $150. I was amazed: six hundred channels? We took the twenty-five-channel offer, handing over a plastic shopping sack full of our money. At the time, it took about eight hundred Uzbekistan "sum" bills to equal an American dollar. The standard notes were in denominations of twenty, fifty, and one hundred sums. I estimate that the sack probably contained about sixteen hundred paper bills.

The telephone service in the places we stayed while in the CEP was always unreliable. Callers on our rotary phones could be practically inaudible, and the line would sometimes break in the middle of a conversation. In our Tashkent flat, our telephone and, of course, my computer Internet connection didn't break connection due to mechanical problems. Instead it was constantly being summarily canceled. It took us awhile to figure out the problem, which turned out to have two related causes. First, people with our telephone prefix were charged by the minute. Unknown to us, we had begun living in our flat with five hours in our telephone "kitty," but with the Internet humming away and our initial cleaning lady gabbing to all her friends each week, we ate that amount of time up in a hurry. Then the phone and my computer would go dead.

Making matters worse, when initially ordering our service, our flat manager had not told the telephone company that we were Americans. To do so would have resulted in an astronomically high monthly service charge. This arrangement would have worked out except that the young man continued to forget to pay the monthly bill or build up the kitty, so, again we would be cut off. Early on, the telephone company began making a warning call to inform us of a pending shut off of service. The unknown lady's voice would begin over the telephone. I would interrupt saying that I did not speak Russian, offer an apology, and hang up. Our service would then stop within the week. I never put two and two together as we often got calls in Russian, sometimes in Uzbek, at all hours of the day and for who knows what kinds of reasons.

Finally, the telephone bills began to be paid on time. By then it was too late. I had answered the lady's call one too many times in English. The service died again. The phone company had realized we were Americans and now they wanted the much higher phone rate. In a very clever move, our manager was able to talk them out of the surcharge by saying we were his visiting company and not the main residents of the flat. Technically, he was wrong. In any case, the answer was sufficient to get service started and, at the lower rate. The phone and our Internet remained in service after that.

We fired our cleaning lady after the first few weeks of living in our Tashkent flat. She was unreliable about her hours and seemed to be "sick" and unable to work half the time. She would also sit for long periods talking to her friends, including our landlady, on the telephone. For the landlady, I figured she was including a report on our activities and treatment of the flat. It unnerved me. The landlady's daughter helped us to get us a new cleaning lady. Our flat was now kept spotless by Svetlana, a big, tall, middle-aged Bulgarian Uzbek lady. She came each week and cleaned, washed dishes, polished glass, and did the ironing from 10:00 AM until Judy would usually say "Enough!" around

2:00 PM. Our CEP assistant director paid the landlady's daughter $20 dollars each month to pay Svetlana. This was in addition to the rent of $180 for our flat. We felt comfortable with this even though it was a third-party arrangement and could easily be abused. Our cleaning lady was being paid $5 dollars a week for about four hour's work. This was a good wage in Uzbekistan, and she did a very good job, even getting down on her hands and knees to wash the floors.

A little more than a month before we were to leave Tashkent, Svetlana arrived early on cleaning day with her sister, who spoke fairly good English and was anxious to meet us and exchange pleasantries. For once we could talk to Svetlana about our lives and families and about how much we liked the quality of the house cleaning. She was more than earning the five dollars each week she was being paid, we said. The sister made the interpretation. There was silence. Svetlana wrote a figure on some paper and showed it to us. Our cleaning lady was getting paid half what she was owed. Actually, she was getting five dollars a week, but for this, she was also spending up to four hours a week cleaning our landlady's daughter's place as well! I should have suspected that this could happen. And, as in so much of life in this part of the world, extended family relations were also involved.

Judy and I brought this scam to the attention of Dildora. It was her responsibility to make the monthly cleaning payment. We insisted that Svetlana be given full back pay for each month she had worked for us and suggested that the amount owed be taken out of the final rent payment to her sister-in-law. This recommendation was obviously hard for Dildora to accomplish. Nothing happened. To insure that the payment was made, and soon, we took the situation up with our country director, noting that we needed to set an example of what the CEP stood for and make sure the housekeeper got what she rightfully earned. A week later, we were given an extra amount of U.S. money to properly pay back our house cleaner. She tearfully accepted the back wages. Svetlana had happily quit working for the wife of the other family. I like to think we modeled a standard that was typical of the way Americans do business and treat each other.

With all accounts cleared, we said good-bye to the Civic Education Project for the last time and left Uzbekistan for the United States. It would be nice to live in a real house for a change.

9
Riding the Rails

A Definite Nostalgia for Trains

Judy and I have always made it a point to utilize public transportation over the more than three decades we have worked and traveled abroad. Renting a car is expensive and well above our "Frommer's Guide" budget. In addition, we felt that using an automobile would cut us off from an important source of meeting and learning about people. I suppose as much as anything else, we found train riding a very pleasurable experience, one which brought back the excitement and sense of adventure of the railroad that both of us remembered from our youth.

I can clearly recall my first train ride sixty years ago. The train was pulled by a big black locomotive as it left the Portland, Oregon, station with all the impressive chugging and blowing of steam. I was about eight years old, traveling by myself for the first time, on the way to Puyallup for a summer visit with my grandparents. Judy remembers traveling back and forth between Oakland, California, and the University of Oregon by train. Since then, here in the West, there has been a long, almost complete, void in train riding.

So it was a pleasant surprise to begin my work in Lithuania and discover that a large portion of our travel would be by train. Lithuania actually had a fairly modern highway that connected its three major cities, but a good road system turned out to be something of a rarity in most of the countries we lived in or visited. Automobile ownership was never very common in the Soviet Russian Empire. Instead, in a way similar to what I had first experienced many years ago in Western Europe, the Soviets created an extensive network of local commuter and intercity rail lines; sufficient to get just about anywhere we needed to go within a reasonable period of time. The quality of the system was not nearly as good as we had experienced in Western Europe, but then we were not expecting such high standards, either.

As the car is central to American transportation, so the train is central in the newly independent countries of the former Soviet Russian Empire. Used strictly for its utilitarian purpose, the Soviet-era train represents quite a departure from anything Americans have ever experienced. A departure it was, pleasant or sometimes otherwise; an adventure it was—absolutely!

The trains probably never went over fifty miles an hour. In most cases, the tracks were just not in a condition sufficient to allow any more speed. I doubt the trains ever went much faster, even though the rails were wider than the Western standard and lay on concrete ties that seemed so much more sensible than our system of constantly rotting wooden ones. One needed to be patient about getting anywhere very fast. Speed usually never mattered to us as we normally traveled between our home city and our destination overnight. We hardly needed to save time under these circumstances. On a few occasions, the travel time extended beyond an early morning arrival, and train speed might have been important, but I don't recall our complaining about the sometimes pokey nature of travel.

The long-distance rolling stock had become a bit the worse for wear, but having been solidly constructed, typically in West Germany or Czechoslovakia, they had definitely not reached the end of their serviceable life. The cars retained their faded but original colors. Most often they were painted "UPS brown," although sometimes they were dark green. I have been told that there were other colors as well, including blue and dark red, the latter being the color of the Trans-Siberian Express.

Most everything seemed to be in working order. These had been some of the Soviet's best trains. Trains of each class of service were usually exactly alike. This was just one more example of the standardization that had been such a prominent feature of the Communist period. The standardization came in three categories. There were the best-quality train cars, called *spal'nyi vagon,* or sleeping wagons, reserved for traveling long distance between major cities. A second type of sleeping car held at least a third again more passengers and was designed for the low-budget traveler. Finally, there were bare bones commuter trains that were usually, but not always, reserved for short distances. Judy and

I rode on some of these that were outfitted with rows of wooden-slat benches. They rarely seemed to contain an adequate heating system.

Wagon Design Influences Life on Board

We usually tried to obtain our ticket a day or so ahead in order to reduce any problem arising from the possibility of last-minute delay, or finding the train fully booked. We also tried to be at the train station at least a half hour ahead of departure, especially if we were unfamiliar with the station and the procedure for gaining access to the platforms. Such good planning didn't always occur and there were several mad dashes, usually involving high-speed taxi rides, and yet in the four years I worked for the CEP, we never missed our intended train.

Porters were normally available, but we would always carry our own bags through the station to the proper platform. Such was the flexibility that came from backpacking or carrying only a couple of small sports-style duffle bags. Sometimes we would get to the proper platform through tunnels under the station yard. Sometimes we just walked over one or more sets of rails asking people along the way if we had arrived at the right platform. It was better to double-check this way than to wait around on the wrong platform or, as happened a few times, to have the train waiting next to an unlisted platform.

Standing in front of each train car was a uniformed *provodnik*, a wagon steward, almost always a lady, who would examine our ticket and allow us to enter the car. It was a very high couple of steps straight up into the car. For this one needed both hands free and leg strength sufficient to manage the steep climb. About half of the time, the wagon steward would place a small portable step below the entrance, but it usually was of little help. Younger people would usually reach down to help pull older people up into the cars. We would hoist our small carry-on bags into the car first, or just climb aboard if wearing our backpacks, being careful not to bump into things on the way up.

Wagons were boarded through an entrance toward the end of the car. Just inside would be a small vestibule. In Lithuania, we would typically encounter a wood stove and log storage compartment set into the side of this entrance area. In the Ukrainian trains, the stoves burned coal. The stoves served two purposes: one to heat hot water that was fed through pipes to separate heating radiators located in each compartment; the other purpose was to heat the water in a large *samovar* located just inside the hallway leading to the passenger compartments. The samovar was a large usually ornate brass caldron with a spigot on its side. Holding as much as four or five gallons of hot water, the wagon's samovar could be used to make tea, cocoa, or coffee anytime we might request it, or we could do it ourselves once provided with a glass and holder by the wagon provodnik. Judy and I fell in love with the beautiful metal tea glass holders used on these trains. At an antique store in Estonia, we found and purchased four early Soviet-period holders of the same general nature as used on the trains, except these were crafted in a sort of nickel silver, highly filigreed in tiny tightly wound circles. They looked very expensive.

The hallway in each wagon began with a bathroom and ended at the other end of the train car with a second bathroom. Inside each bathroom was a small stainless-steel wash basin with a single water faucet. There was a very rugged-looking stainless steel toilet with no lid. It was topped with a thick black plastic seat that usually contained a set of deeply formed ribbed footprints. It was the custom for many, if not most people to climb up and squat over the seat before using the toilet. The explanation for this practice is that the older generation, especially the rural people, are used to floor-level toilet facilities. In fact, most toilets in public buildings were still of this type, and when the toilets were above the floor, they had both the seat and lid removed with a tile-covered box built up around, and (I will leave the pun in) flush with the top of the facility. The box had one or two steps in order to ascend and descend safely.

It certainly was an interesting custom, one even finding its way to America. We met some Mormon missionaries on a Ukrainian train headed from Donetsk for Kharkiv who told us that the toilet seats in the Salt Lake City international airport are constantly being broken from folks climbing up on them.

Back on the train and following another rather universal but old-fashioned standard, all toilet waste exited directly onto the tracks, except in or near the rail stations when the bathrooms were usually, but not always locked. In the train, as in the typical bathroom in the former Soviet Russian Empire, you brought your own toilet paper.

The narrow hallway ran the length of one side of the wagon. On the other side were about eight to twelve compartments (*coupes*) each with its own door from the hallway. The first compartment past the bathroom from the entrance was for the wagon steward. Inside the steward's compartment was a panel of monitoring instruments and storage for tea glasses and their holders along with space for stacking clean sheets, extra blankets, and miscellaneous items.

Compartments were randomly assigned when purchasing tickets. Judy and I always hoped we would be put in any compartment other than the last one at the far end of the wagon. In addition to being right over the noisy train wheels, the door of the adjacent bathroom could usually be expected to make quite a racket swinging back and forth all night if not closed properly. To make things worse, just as the hallway passed this bathroom, it exited through a door into a vestibule identical, minus the heating apparatus, to the other end of the wagon. This small space was used as the smoking room. I did not go into this area, whether in use or not, unless I needed to quickly pass into the adjacent wagon. It was usually filled by several people, all smoking. In such a situation, just to breathe in this room was as good as puffing multiple cigarettes at once! A good deal of smoke would flow out, late into the evening from this small space into the hallway and under the door of at least the first compartment.

The celebration begins. An overnight train to Kyiv with my Kharkiv State University students. The following morning, we flew to Budapest. There the students delivered their research papers at the International Student Conference.

In the best-quality wagons, each compartment was accessed through a sliding door and was designed to accommodate four people, although they sometimes contained less than this number as one or two people would buy out all four berths. Inside the compartment, there were two padded, vinyl-covered benches facing each other on each side of the little room. Each bench could be lifted up to reveal a large storage bin suitable for luggage and other parcels. These benches were more like platforms, only lightly padded and quite uncomfortable to sit on. They also invited a pronounced slouch. Above each bench was a similar-size upper sleeping berth. Four bulky, usually rather seedy-looking mattresses, each rolled around a pillow, were stored on these upper berths. Slightly above the upper berths, at the front of the compartment, was a large open storage space that ran the full width of the compartment and stretched back over the hallway ceiling.

Rounding out the compartment accouterments were some clothes hooks, a reading light for each passenger, and a small fold-up table below the window between the two lower benches. Families or friends would often pack into a single compartment to share a meal. They could lay out quite a banquet: dark bread and sausages, garlic pickles, dried and canned fish, lots of vodka, and always some chocolate for desert. We had a feast like this in our compartment one evening on the night train from Kharkiv to Kyiv. We were on the first leg of a trip to Budapest with six of my students who would be delivering research papers at the prestigious International Student Conference. The train left at 9:40 pm. with at least one of the students, Sergey, managing to sneak on without buying a ticket. Even though students received a steep discount on tickets, riding for free was the more respected choice, if clever enough to manage to do it successfully. The eight of us occupied two adjacent coupes, but the party took place late into the night in our unit, the little table piled high with food and drink.

The wagon compartments were poorly ventilated. It was a rare treat to be able to open the window, any window in the wagon, for that matter, as most were sealed by design and others by lack of use. Our first few attempts to open a window, successfully or not, quickly taught us that many people did not like fresh air blowing around the compartment, although a few would tolerate a partly open window in the hallway.

During the cold months, the compartments would often become quite overheated, to as much as 90 degrees or higher should the wagon steward overstoke the boiler. Thus it was a wise practice to take a bottom bench for sleeping as it was a bit cooler and closer to the air that might occasionally slip in under the sliding door. Often such precautions were not enough, however. I clearly remember the overnight trip across the western section of Ukraine from Chernivsti to Kyiv. It was close to 100 degrees in the compartment and was giving me quite a headache. I had taken a couple of ibuprofen tablets and was lying on my bunk stripped to my undershorts, thinking this to be the trip from hell, while my young Ukrainian CEP colleague in the top bunk was sound asleep dressed in his heavy sweat clothes! The smile on his face made me wonder if he might be dreaming of being in a sauna. He might as well have been. I concluded that he was probably making up for all the cold, heatless nights spent in his flat in Kharkiv.

The compartment's bottom benches could produce their share of problems as well. With only a couple of feet separating the benches on either side, sleepers had little or no privacy. Each individual slept in full view of the other compartment occupants. Although it didn't seem to bother other people, I sometimes felt uneasy about it, particularly when strangers needed to get in and out of bed during the night, maybe to use the bathroom, partially dress or undress for sleeping, make their bed, or leave or enter the train in the middle of the night. To make matters worse, passengers using the upper bunks needed to step up on one or both lower bunks in order to gain the height needed to climb into bed. There were no ladders.

Sophie Howlett, one of our Baltic States lecturers, told us the story of her experience with privacy on a train in Kaliningrad, a little isolated piece of Russia tucked in between Poland and Lithuania on the Baltic coast. Sophie and her life partner, CEPer Steve Schumacher, were sharing a compartment with a young couple, who late in the evening got up from the lower bench where they had been sitting, managed to hang a sheet from the upper birth to give the lower birth some privacy, and preceded to make love rather noisily only a few feet away. It turned out that this was not an especially uncommon occurrence. Train coupes provided one of the very few such amorous opportunities available to young people, almost all of whom lived at home well past their teens.

There was one main variation to the standard long-distance train car I have been describing. Called a *platscat,* it offered second-class accommodations in what, at times, I would judge to be more like third-class surroundings. The compartments appeared somewhat smaller and had no doors. Along the hallway corridor was a long row of upper-level fold-down beds below which were small fold-down tables and seats that could be converted into beds. This overall configuration cost about half the ticket price, managed to increase occupancy of each wagon by over 30 percent, and resulted in the complete loss of privacy for all passengers in the car. Judy and I frequently booked seats in these second-class wagons for the approximately one-and a-half hour trip from Vilnius to Kaunas. The train originated the night before in Moscow. During the winter months, still dark outside, passengers were just beginning to wake up as we boarded these overheated, humid rabbit warrens that smelled of hot stinky bodies. At least the wagons were warm and one could sometimes find a seat. The alternative was for us to take a much longer ride on a commuter train that began its run out of Vilnius completely frozen from sitting all night.

Appropriate Luggage

Over twenty years of train travel, Judy and I have experimented with several types of luggage, trying to find the ideal way to hold our belongings, realizing that all luggage is a compromise of one sort or another. We began with suitcases: an absolute mistake for those who wish to travel on their own. We then shifted to soft-sided bags, sometimes walking a large duffel between us, always reducing the amount we carried in order to match diminished muscle strength and increased travel experience. Part way through our first year in Lithuania, still not satisfied with having the right luggage and anticipating over a month-long winter holiday most of the way to Sicily by train, we turned to using soft, nonframe backpacks. A new outdoor sports store, the first of its kind, had opened on the main street of Vilnius near our apartment flat. It carried French-made backpacks, fortunately in two moderate sizes that fit us each perfectly. Being a small store, it only had one backpack of each type left in stock, so, by default; mine was bright orange and black. I found it to be a little gaudy, but Judy liked hers. It was a pretty teal color. Being of a size that did not invite an excess of weight, the packs kept our backs from complaining too loudly.

The backpacks were particularly versatile for our frequent train travel where, as I have previously mentioned, two free hands were absolutely necessary to manage getting up and down the long steep distance between the platform and the floor of the train car. The backpacks also left our hands free for the occasional need to compete with a babushka in a pushing match. In the worst case, it left our hands free to help break our fall on icy sidewalks, which happened more than once.

To pack our backpacks we first folded and then tightly rolled all clothing items we wanted to keep free of wrinkles. Each roll was kept tight with two or more rubber bands. This procedure not only made packing and unpacking easy, it was also the most efficient way to use space. The only downside to backpacks was trying to figure out what to put in all the multitude of pockets. Zipper, Velcro, or snap-open pockets seemed to be everywhere. Locating the right pocket to put things in could take a lot of time for someone like me who has trouble making small decisions, even more time later when trying to remember where I put something. Once the packs were on our backs, we had to be cautious not to bump or squeeze other passengers in the narrow isles of the train wagon, or to turn around and inadvertently whack someone. And then, on the way to and from the train, whether by bus or metro, we needed to learn how to sit down at an angle in order to create the necessary space for both ourselves and our still mounted packs.

As two older English-speaking foreigners, probably American, traveling with backpacks, we were definitely an unusual sight in the trains and on the streets of Eastern Europe and Russia. This was especially true in the smaller towns. Locals took obvious notice. People were not used to seeing backpackers on the streets and rarely even in the trains, and certainly not people our age. The hordes of young people with their *Let's Go* and *Lonely Planet* guides, a common sight in Western Europe, had yet to appear on the scene in this part of the world. There were even a few times when Judy and I needed to travel immediately following a formal dinner or to an out-of-town appointment where nice clothes were needed but where no time or place was available to change into our usual train attire: jeans, a pullover, or a sweatshirt. In such cases, we would really push the limit of credulity by "backpacking" in pantsuits, sport jackets, even dress overcoats!

Life on Board

We rode Soviet-era trains frequently during our three-year stay in Eastern/Central Europe. We flew everywhere while in Central Asia as the travel distances were usually much greater and the trains reportedly in very poor condition, filthy, overcrowded, and dangerous.

In the majority of cases, our train rides were overnight, stretching eight or more hours in length. This was usually enough time to travel between two and three hundred miles. Travel was particularly slowed by at least a half a dozen stops through the night to pick up or drop off passengers. Sometimes it was even necessary to noisily reposition the train wheels on their axles. And then, there were often borders to cross with their time-consuming examination of passports. Border stops, with at least a cursory look around each train compartment by the guards, were almost a certainty in the Baltic region. Each country was so tiny that one could easily pass through two countries in one night. Border stops were far less likely when we traveled in Ukraine where one full night of travel might only get us half the distance from one side of the country to the other.

Border crossings were not the only thing making it difficult to get much sleep on the train, assuming one could sleep on the trains in the first place. The trains ran quite noisily, swaying and jerking over the tracks. They often came to a stop with such force as to practically throw us out of bed. At first I found it very hard to get any sleep at all, although the rocking motion would usually put Judy right out. Later, as the novelty of the physical jerks and jolts gave way to experience and therefore predictability, I actually found myself able to sleep fairly well.

Scary Nights

The ceiling lights in the compartment stayed off all night. In a kind of military barracks-style approach, all the lights would be turned off in the wagon at the same time and on again in the morning at the same time. Passengers sometimes left their compartment door open all night both to let in light and air circulation from the hallway. We always kept our door closed and locked. If it was necessary to let new arrivals into our compartment, the wagon steward could unlock it with her key.

We knew that our security could be compromised by thieves who had managed to obtain their own pass keys. Stories always circulated about foreigners getting robbed in their compartments at night. The most frightening of these stories involved a robbery modus operandi that we heard from my Russian colleagues to be a rather frequent occurrence on the night train between Moscow and St. Petersburg. American tourists often took this train. Fortunately, we never needed to do so. Some form of temporarily debilitating gas would be fed into the closed compartment from under the door. The door would then be opened by a duplicate key and valuables and money quickly taken from the passengers. Nobody we knew was robbed in this manner, but the story was repeated enough at least to make us think it to have a basis in fact. One person we knew who did traverse this route several times carried duct tape, which he put over the lock at night. He claimed that the thieves sprayed their gas through the lock rather than under the door.

In addition to the Moscow–St. Petersburg train, we had also heard that the famous Trans-Siberian Express train had become fraught with new dangers. Some accounts laid the blame on the burgeoning number of street venders using the train to transport themselves and their bags of imported goods. Others said that the increased danger was due to the pronounced growth of lawlessness and poverty that accompanied Russia's first years as an independent country. Either way, the stories were enough to dissuade us from following through on our plan to start our second year in the CEP by riding the Trans-Siberian Express from Moscow to either Vladivostok on the Pacific coast just above North Korea or to Beijing. We were then going to fly back in time for the beginning of fall classes in Estonia.

The only case of criminal activity that we knew of directly happened to Charles Kroncke, a good friend and CEP lecturer posted to central Estonia. On a Christmas holiday train trip overnight to Budapest, a compartment occupant tried to take his wallet in the middle of the night. The thief cut the back pocket of Charles' jeans open with what was likely to have been a razor in an effort to free his wallet, but apparently lost his nerve and did not complete the job! Hearing of this and thinking of the warnings CEP staff had given us, Judy and I always took the usual precautions. We left most of our jewelry at home in Boise in a bank safe deposit box. When we traveled, we put our money in a special zippered belt compartment or in a pouch tucked inside our clothes. We never left our train compartment unattended. We never took money from our belt or body pouch in places where we might be observed. These precautions were necessary as it was normal to have as much as five hundred dollars split between the two of us when traveling, and on a few occasions, even quite a bit more. Large amounts of money took the place of credit cards and traveler's checks, both of which were practically useless. Personal checks whether written by foreigners or locals were absolutely unheard of.

Even though the amount of cash we often carried was worth much more in local buying power, neither of us worried much about our security on the trains. Maybe we should have, but we couldn't have done much more about it. Maybe our previous good luck had left us a little too trusting. Although I have had pickpockets try to lift my wallet in a crowded market in Tangier, only once had I ever had anybody successfully pick my pocket. This occurred while I was being thrown forward with other standing passengers on a Kyiv metro car, as it braked while pulling into a station. I felt a little more than the usual pressure against my hip, and sure enough, when I felt for my wallet it was gone. Judy had warned me earlier to put my wallet in my front pocket. I had just exchanged a one-hundred-dollar bill into Ukrainian currency less than an hour before!

Even with the usual precautions, carrying large sums of money, which we had to do on a few occasions, could be a bit frightening. The most money we ever carried was during our year in Ukraine when I was asked by the Yale CEP office to act as a courier. Judy and I were in Boise for Christmas when I got a call to bring fifteen thousand dollars back to the Kyiv CEP office on my return to Ukraine.

Regional CEP offices paid stipends to their visiting lecturers and salary to staff members and otherwise operated on a cash basis just like practically everybody else "over there." The Soviets had never bothered to make it easy to conduct business or consumer transactions. This manner of running the economy continued to persist, in most part, following the breakup of the Soviet Empire. Thus, CEP operations in each region needed to obtain a rather large infusion of hundred-dollar bills from time to time. The money was normally brought unofficially into country by air and then over long distances by train. In this manner, Judy and I curried a giant wad of one hundreds all the way from Boise through a four-night stay in London and on to Kyiv! Except to shower—one at a time—we never took the money off of our bodies, even to stay out late one night going pub crawling with Simon, our ex-CEP Estonia colleague, and Jana, our past country director.

The only time I was really nervous about carrying all this money was, rather surprisingly, when I had to stand, very self-consciously, in front of a crowded teller counter in Boise while the lady slowly counted out all 150 of my $100 bills. Several people began to take notice as I cautioned the teller to slow down her count and allow me to check each bill to see that it was of the new "Big Ben" variety and contained no marks or tears. Ukrainian moneychangers, as was our previous experience in the Baltic countries and Russia, were usually very particular about such things. There must be no wear or tear and no hand-made markings of any kind.

I continued to feel self-conscious as well as pretty uneasy about leaving the bank, given that several people knew pretty well how much money I had in the large bank envelope I was carrying. I was even more concerned, and my heart raced a little bit when passing through the customs check in Kyiv. The officer wanted to know how much money I had. I responded exactly with what I had reported on the customs form, about three hundred dollars, if I recall correctly. "Keep it small" I remember saying to myself. Ukrainian customs agents were known to be too corrupt to prompt much honesty on my part, and who knows how word might spread outside the airport terminal. Fortunately, we were able to divest ourselves of all the money soon after arriving in the CEP's Kyiv office. We were hoping we did not have to take any of the money with us on the train to Kharkiv. We had carried all that money long enough. Some of it would get there anyway, but not by me.

Purchasing Tickets

Deciphering train schedules and purchasing tickets presented its share of difficulties. It didn't take us too long to learn the fundamentals our first year in Lithuania, and the adjustment to the procedures in

Estonia were fairly easy. Ukraine turned out to be just the opposite. The system was more complex, the language barrier much more of a challenge, and official indifference was most often the order of the day. Fortunately, two years of train riding had given us enough confidence to face these obstacles—until we discovered how helpful my students could be!

It was fairly easy to figure out the Lithuanian train schedules, which usually appeared on large mechanical reader boards located inside the bigger train stations. Local commuter schedules and the schedules in smaller stations were typed and placed in a plastic jacket on the wall. These schedules were often much more difficult to figure out. Judy was much more proficient at this task than I, but when we both failed, help was usually not far away. I remember standing with Judy in the train station in Vilnius trying to get information about the several different train departures to Moscow. A school-age boy of about ten or eleven years of age walked me to a ticket window, asked the agent for clarification, and then told me, in quite good English, exactly what I needed to know as well as what the ticket would cost.

In Ukraine, train designations and ticket information were written in the Cyrillic alphabet. Judy quickly developed the proficiency to figure out town and city names, but beyond that, the deciphering got much harder. In Kharkiv, purchasing tickets was even more complicated and could be very unpredictable due to a complicated rigmarole and the uncooperative attitude exhibited by most of the ticket clerks. To purchase tickets, we needed to leave the train station where most tickets were sold, and go to a separate building across a parking plaza and busy street where, we were told, there was a ticket window just for foreign passengers. Following our purchase-early guideline, we located this window several days ahead of making our first train ride out of town. In a line of mostly unoccupied ticket windows, we found a window reserved for military veterans, and I believe there was also one for pensioners. What turned out to be the window for foreigners was occupied by a ticket agent who could speak only Russian, or maybe Ukrainian: the two sounded alike to our untrained ears, and was not interested in our going back over her efforts to communicate.

In spite of the language barrier, we managed to get tickets to Kyiv on an overnight train, but that was about all. The rest of the ticket and travel details would be pot luck, as the chance of finding someone nearby who spoke enough English to help us out was between slim to nil. Provincial Ukrainian train stations like this one were a far cry from the much more user-friendly places we had grown accustomed to. We were probably quite lucky to get our tickets at all, when I stop to consider some of the mind-boggling stories of bureaucracy and service run amok that we heard from some of our CEP friends. Here is an example taken from CEPer Janet Helin's humorous remarks printed in our CEP *Guide to Life and Teaching in Eastern Europe and Eurasa*:

> Proceed to the railroad ticket agency. Ask the administrator which window to go to. Wait in line one hour, until the clerk sends you to a different window. Wait in line one hour, until that clerk sends you back to the original window. This is not done on a whim. The rules simply change by the hour. Wait in line one hour and arrive at the front of the line just as the window is closing for "obyed" (lunch break). Wait for "obyed" to end. Get sent to a different window which has just closed for "teknicheskii pereryv" (technical break).When you finally make contact with a clerk who agrees to hear (in a passive sense) your request for tickets, the exchange will end with the clerk doing one or more of the following: telling you these tickets cannot be purchased today, for reasons known neither to you nor the clerk; insisting that your visa is not properly stamped, registered, and/or extended and that you are here illegally; bringing your attention to the poor quality of the photocopied documents and perhaps refusing one or more of them; saying you can't purchase tickets with photocopied documents (but you can); ....(or) claiming that you don't look like your passport photo, to which you respond that this is what dealing with the railroad bureaucracy has done to your appearance: or (it happens sometimes) processing your tickets.

We would usually try to get our tickets a day or two ahead, but not any more than that as three or more days ahead was too far into the future for the ticket clerks to handle. We also tried to be at the station early. I would have to admit that there were last-minute ticket purchases and train connections when all advance planning and precautions were cast aside as unattainable. These cliff-hanger occasions usually began with a wild drive in some stranger's private car. In one example, Judy and I had participated in a late-evening business meeting at our CEP office in Kyiv. The meeting had delayed our preferred early arrival at the train station. Our only option now was to grab our backpacks, quickly descend three flights of stairs in the darkness, and walk as fast as we could over more than a block to a frequently traveled intersection. We were lucky to promptly flag down a car. For what seemed to me to be a surprisingly small sum, the driver happily agreed to take us to the train station, a distance that took at least fifteen minutes to complete. Last-minute situations, no matter how often I went through them, typically left me in a bit of a sweat, even in the dead of winter.

Faced with the potential for so many things going wrong with scheduling and ticket purchase, Judy and I quickly took up our student offers to help us in any way we might request. Having come up to the lectern following the first class to announce his willingness to assist us in any way, Igor was the first to be called upon. For this he earned the nickname from Judy of "Eager Igor." If some of the students were accompanying us on the trip, I would just give them the money to purchase their tickets and ours a day or two early. If Judy and I were traveling by ourselves, there were several students who thought nothing of heading to the train station at practically any hour to purchase our tickets for us! Of course, Igor saw his share of duty on these many occasions.

I should have realized earlier in my CEP postings how helpful my students could be when knowledge of the language was really important in meeting our needs at the train station. For instance, it didn't occur to me that a student who could speak either Russian or Estonian might greatly increase my prospect of recovering the first and only "officially approved" nude painting that Judy was willing to have in our house! I had purchased it in St. Petersburg while we were visiting the Hermitage gift shop. It was carefully rolled in a large protective cardboard tube, which I hand-carried onto the train for our overnight ride back to Tallinn.

The next morning following our arrival back at our flat, I began to empty my backpack when I realized I had left my nude in our compartment on the train! I returned to the train station and tried to find someone who might assist me. After several efforts to communicate my problem, I learned that my wagon, along with the others, was sitting near the station on a spur track waiting to be cleaned in preparation for the evening departure back to St. Petersburg. I was told to come back in the evening just as the train was ready for passengers, and ask the wagon steward of my car if my nude had been found. I referred to it as "a painting," but my problem would have been solved much easier with the help of a student! Lucky for me, however, my efforts to communicate were sufficient. That evening, using the number from our ticket, I was able to locate our wagon. I recognized one of the two wagon stewards and began to tell my story only to be interrupted with laughter resulting from my fragmented Russian, pantomime, and overall effort to politely inquire about my lost "artwork." They had found the tube, had examined its contents, and knew exactly what I was trying to describe!

So with ticket in hand, we would pass through the station to board our train. In the Baltic countries, we would walk through an underground tunnel and up a flight of stairs to the appropriate track, or in many cases we would exit the train station at track level and, beginning at the end of the train, walk along one of the platforms to the wagon number identified on our ticket. In Kharkiv, we could exit from the underground metro stop right under the station, walk up the stairs, and enter the large ornately decorated main hall. Standing on either side of the staircase as it opened out into the hall were the larger than life welcoming statues of Lenin on one side and Marx on the other

All Aboard

Before leaving the Kharkiv station to board our train, we would usually grab a last minute bottle of water, add the purchase of a sausage, some cheese, a bottle of wine, and maybe even a small bottle of cognac for a nip before bedtime. From Kharkiv, it was ten hours overnight to Kyiv, Moscow twelve hours overnight, and Odessa seventeen hours, also overnight. It took twenty-seven hours to get to Ukraine's western border city of Lviv. In contrast, the eastern border with Russia was only an hour's train ride away.

It was always late in the evening as we walked out the main hall toward our waiting train. We would always be serenaded by a lone trumpet player giving a sometimes stirring, often haunting rendition of one or more classical numbers. During the winter, this obviously took some dedication and enough tip money tossed in his horn case to make standing long periods of time on the frozen, snow-covered platform worth while! Being treated to impromptu music in the underground metro passages, at the train station, or in various places around the city was one of the little pleasures of our year spent in Ukraine. In a few instances, we would hear brass or reed instruments, but in most cases, the music was from an accordion, a sound that seemed very appropriate in this part of the world. I usually emptied all my small bills in the musicians open music case, normally less than a dollar, but well worth the wonderful ambiance and sense of place they provided.

I can still vividly recall the summer evening we left Kharkiv for the last time on our way to Kyiv and a Lufthansa flight to Germany to visit our daughter and her family before flying home to Boise. Igor had arranged for a car and small trailer to take us and all of our army duffel bags to the station. It was 9:30 PM, and we were standing by our train car with several students who had arrived to bid us good-bye, waiting for the boarding whistle, making our final good-byes, and listening to the clear, now rather poignant, sounds of the trumpeter.

Already stowed in our compartment were our six duffel bags, two bulging backpacks, a small animal carrier with Pyat the cat, and the bag belonging to Igor, who knew he could get a free ride in our compartment to Kyiv. After all, Igor was the one who had first announced his willingness to be of assistance to us during the year. It was fitting that Igor had also arranged the car and trailer. He had also taken our money to the station to purchase our tickets and buy out our compartment earlier that day.

The Best Train Ride

Thinking back over the experience of riding the rails, the best train rides we took occurred during our stay in Lithuania and Estonia. We needed to travel frequently to our regional CEP office in Riga, an overnight train ride located approximately equidistant between our first posting in Vilnius and our second posting in Tallinn. There was bus service available, actually a pretty decent bus that went between Tallinn and Riga, but we preferred taking the train, especially in winter when the roads could be perilously icy. There were a couple of choices of trains, but the best was the "Baltic Express."

The Baltic Express was easy to spot because of its bright magenta and cream paint. It was privately owned, an example of the nascent beginnings of venture capitalism. Unfortunately, the business folded the year after we left Estonia. The Baltic Express used Soviet rolling stock, so the layout was standard right down to the big samovor. What was different, along with the fancy paint job, was the better service and high level of cleanliness. There were also some two-person compartments available, although we never used one.

During our first year, we would catch the Baltic Express in Kaunus for the trip to Riga. This required taking a very basic late evening local commuter from Vilnius for the approximately one-and a-half-hour trip to Kaunus. Here we would wait at the old, sparsely furnished, and drafty station for a little over an hour for the Baltic Express to arrive from Warsaw, Poland, its southernmost terminus. This would put us on the train about midnight. There would be two stops, one at each side of the border with Latvia for customs agents to wake us, examine our passport, and enter the appropriate stamp. Our arrival in Riga would be a little before 6:00 AM. This would give Judy and me enough time to head out of the station, stop for coffee at the nearby McDonald's—the place where we had our first cup of coffee behind the former Iron Curtain—then walk through the big park, and be in our CEP office at the University of Latvia in time for whatever the occasion might have required.

Even though the Baltic Express trains were the best to ride, getting to our destination was only part of the trip. Arriving in the outdoor portion of the train station in Riga on terribly frigid snowy winter mornings, long before the sun would rise, could be terribly uncomfortable no matter what train was used. However, Judy and I just took it all in stride and walked a little bit faster through the cold and snow. We experienced these hardships as quite a contrast to our comfortable life back in Boise. As such it imparted a wondrous feeling of being thoroughly alive! This, and other hardship experiences I have described, made me realize how much Americans look for convenience first, overlooking so many other realities in life.

The following year, when school was over in Tallinn, before going home for the summer and what we thought would be my last employment with the CEP, Judy and I decided to take the Baltic Express from Estonia all the way to Poland. The border crossing into Poland was quite unique. We not only had to have our passport papers examined, but we also had to change trains, and for a rather interesting reason. It was literally the end of the line on both sides of the Polish-Lithuanian border! The rail tracks did not line up, each coming to a stop at least fifty feet apart and to the side of each other. It wouldn't have made any difference if the tracks did join because the track widths were not compatible. The incompatibly and the separation had been purposefully created by the Russians, and continued by the Soviets, as a way to increase the security of their borders, thus making unwanted rail movement in or out of Russia very difficult if not impossible. All we needed to do was walk across a gravel area to a waiting empty Baltic Express train for the rest of the trip to Warsaw.

Following an afternoon spent touring Warsaw; now using a different train, we continued our train trip further south. On the train that evening, our travel companion was a most interesting and charming lady. Her name was Keti Dolidze a Georgian film director and actress. Judy began the conversation by commenting on the large, attractive, white scarf with lace edging that she was wearing. Keti said she had received it from a Bosnian refugee in honor of her leadership of the White Scarf Movement. In 1993 Keti had led, not without unimaginable difficulty, over two thousand Russian, Ukrainian, Jewish, German, Lithuanian, Azeri, and Armenian women to the front lines of the Balkans conflict in an effort to revive an old peacemaking tradition and help stop the senseless bloodletting. Keti's peace movement had reached back to an ancient tradition in Georgia where fighting men would stop battling when women threw their traditional headdress, a white scarf, in their midst. In the intervening four years, the White Scarf Movement has spread through the Western hemisphere with membership groups first initiated in the Georgian capital of Tbilisi and branching out to Warsaw, Moscow, London, Paris, and even Salt Lake City. Women in white scarves meet in the main squares of these cities on the last Sunday of September each year to think about what war is doing to mankind and to call for a day of peace.

Our train took us to Krakow where we spent a week walking the city, visiting the university where Copernicious taught, and the factory where its owner, Oskar Schindler, became famous for his effort to hide Jews from certain death at the nearby concentration camp at Auschwitz. We spent a second week in the Czech Republic. The medieval ambiance of Prague was breathtaking. Two of the sights of the surrounding region will also stay indelibly fixed in our minds. The first was the fortress town of Terezin, where the Nazis had established a Jewish death camp, killed or starved at least 35,000 people, but were able on at least two occasions to make the camp appear so physically attractive and life there so normal as to fool visiting delegations of Red Cross observers.

The other equally ghoulish site was located in the old mining town of Kutna Hora. Our travel book described a "bone church" located there whose interior was furnished in human bones. We had to see this place for ourselves. A fairly normal-appearing structure from the outside, the church was built in the fifteenth century by the Catholic Cistercian Order and furnished inside using bones from every part of the human body, presumably from deceased members of the order. There were bone crosses, bone chandeliers, bones on the walls and columns, bones everywhere a visitor might glance—by far the most fantastical and morbid display of its kind, far surpassing anything we had previously seen on display in Mexico or Italy.

The border crossing was quite a bit different on our trip back through Poland into Lithuania. The waiting empty train on the Lithuanian side filled quickly with more than just passengers and their personal luggage. Women were frantically running back and forth between train cars carrying gigantic woven plastic sacks one at a time, zippered at the top and wound about with cord as insurance against splitting open from being so tightly packed. Inside was the "Polish crap" which Jana, our country director had deridedly pointed out to us upon visiting our first of many Lithuanian "mugues," the little shops so prominent in Vilnius. By the time we were able to transfer trains, our assigned compartment was packed all the way to the ceiling with these big bundles. Several ended up being moved from our beds out into the hall once it became obvious that we fully intended to occupy the space we had paid for. We saw this same phenomenon again on our way out of India. The airport check-in was crammed with the same gigantic sacks. Was there no weight limitation? Where were the rules about stowage for takeoff and landing? We stepped over these bags all the way back to Tashkent. "Indian crap," I am sure Jana would say.

An alternative route from Lithuania through Belarus into Poland employed a different system of changing from Russian width to European width rails: moving the bogies or wheels in or out on their axles. A CEP colleague and his wife had experienced this method of border crossing several times. Tom and Cindy were posted to Minsk, Belarus. They told us about how the separate train cars would be hoisted up, one at a time, to allow for the wheel moving. They added that the noise and jostling was sufficient to wake even the soundest of sleepers!

Borders and Bribes

So many little countries meant that there were always border crossings. They could be a real annoyance, or worse. Once the Soviet Russian Empire collapsed, every one of the newly independent countries, which had formally been part of the empire, quickly sought to firm up their borders. Disputes were frequent over just where the borders should be set. Some disputes involving Russia have yet to be resolved. It seemed like a thousand check stations were constructed to sit at the outer edge of every highway and train crossing as it went from one country to another. Borders were a major cash cow. Everybody's documents needed to be checked. Most foreigners from outside the region needed expensive visas. Naturally this required a whole cadre of solders who would examine visas and other documents at the many borders. It was a large employment industry for ex-military men, who, it seemed reasonable to conclude, would be otherwise generally without work.

While the border checks for train travel usually went fairly quickly, this was usually not true for the long lines of transport trucks and passenger cars that often waited two hours or more at the borders. The concern was mostly with contraband. This could include people. There were impoverished foreigners looking for work, even young women being trafficked for prostitution.

Without doubt, the most unique approach to moving goods illegally across borders occurred between Estonia and Latvia during our stay in the Baltic region. A few clever entrepreneurial types figured out how to beat the border hassle by burying about a mile of plastic pipe in a shallow trench between the two countries so they could pump vodka across the border without paying any duty!

Vodka seemed to be the smugglers' choice. While preparing this chapter, I read a piece in *The Wall Street Journal* that described the arrest of some Lithuanians at the border, trying to "export" a truckload of manure to Kaliningrad. Buried in the manure were thousands of bottles of vodka!

Borders, borders, and so it went with these officious and sometimes picayune folks who seemed to wait around just for the opportunity to pick off an unsuspecting foreigner, especially an American! You could be turned back from your trip if it was determined that there was even the slightest inaccuracy in your documents. We had heard accounts of this happening to several CEPers, sometimes more than once. It had even happened to us.

Although the following story took place while we were riding a bus, it is the same border crossing hassle. The incident occurred as Judy and I crossed the border between Moldova and the separatist province of Transdniester on our way back from Moldova to Ukraine. There was the expected small bribe to be allowed to pass through the little Russian-controlled area located along the Dniester River that marks Moldova's eastern border. At the border guarded by camouflage covered tanks, I was asked to get off our intercity bus on the pretense of a visa inaccuracy. I was taken into a small office where a second rifle-toting officer carefully wrote the symbol "$," and the number "5" on a little piece of paper. As I produced the requisite U.S. bill, the other man was carefully tearing the little scrap of paper into small pieces and depositing the pieces in an old waste basket. I was then handed back our passports and returned to the waiting bus to hear the collective groan of the passengers who were well aware of what had transpired. They rubbed their index fingers and thumbs together. "How much?" they wanted to know. The small amount certainly speaks to the dismal level of the Transdniester economy, based as it is, mostly on black market activity.

Our bus stopped at an outdoor market area used as a bus stop just across the border. Judy and I got off just long enough to exchange some money and purchase soft dinks and some packaged cookies. I noticed that the denominations on the paper money had been printed over with considerably larger sums. It was an obvious indication of rampant inflation.

Emerging from a bloody civil war with Moldova when the Soviet system collapsed, today Transdniester, amounts to a small narrow strip of land, probably not more than several square miles in total and ten miles wide, sitting between Moldova and Ukraine. The little country is filled with just over half a million mostly poverty-stricken Russian nationals and other Slav secessionists, mostly just people who dream of rejoining Mother Russia. Seized by the Soviets from Czechoslovakia after World War II, Transdniester claims the status of a republic, but it is not recognized as such by anybody, including Russia, over four hundred miles away which prefers to claim it as a protectorate, using the justification that a high proportion of its citizens remain in the area and continue to feel threatened by their neighbors.

Having quickly passed through this little strip of left-over Soviet occupation, Judy and I then paid a second bribe at the Ukrainian border. It was called "medical insurance." It was just a few dollars and was required of only the two of us, but the time taken to fill out a form, and use of the worst outdoor privy imaginable, meant a frustrating delay to all the other bus passengers.

At least this time we had the correct multientry visa to return to Ukraine. On our trip to Moldova the previous December, we had been detained in-country for three days for unknowingly having only a single (Ukrainian) entry visa, which, of course had been used up on our initial arrival from the United States. We had paid for a multientry, but had never checked the stamp carefully. Now we were out of the country and could not return. To make matters worse, I had only a one-day leeway before I was expected back in my classes. With a mixture of urgency and a premonition that things might not go well, Judy and I took a cab to the Ukrainian visa office.

The cramped little office in Chisinau was open only three days a week. We had to stand outside in the snow, in line with the other "supplicants" for well over an hour waiting to conduct business with a solitary clerk who really knew how to take her time! Then it was another two-day wait and more standing in the snow to get—yes—two more single entry visas.

We were required to turn in a monthly expense account to our CEP country director. Judy threatened to put down these border crossing rip-offs and visa snafus under a new heading for "bribes." She was laughingly told that the CEP did not compensate for bribe payments. The visas were paid for by the CEP and the bribes were admittedly small on these two occasions. However, they were not always small.

A Very Expensive Visa Snafu

The most maddening border crossing by train that we experienced, including a hefty bribe, occurred on a trip to Moscow in the summer of 1996. We were in the middle of our late summer backpacking vacation with John and Jan McFadden, about to cross the border between Lithuania and Belarus on our way through Belarus to Moscow, Russia. Prior to leaving the United States, John had obtained the necessary seventy-five-dollar visas for each of us from the Russian consulate in San Francisco. I had not carefully examined the visas before our late afternoon departure from Vilnius. If I had, I might have noticed that the visas were dated for our arrival the next morning in Moscow.

It was about 8:00 PM when the train stopped at the Belarus border. In short time, we were visited in our compartment by two very young Belarusian men in military uniforms who examined our documents. One quickly caught the error. I knew that Belarus would honor Russian visas, but the problem was that we had arrived at the border about four hours too early. Our visas did not officially begin until 12:01 AM the next morning. There we were, in the middle of a picnic dinner in our compartment, and we were without proper visas to enter Belarus!

Pointing to our luggage, then to all four of us, one of the soldiers stated with a heavy, but quite understandable and very authoritative accent; "Bags out, you out!" and pointed, first to the bags, then to us, and finally through the window to an empty strip of concrete platform along side of our wagon. Outside, in what looked like the middle of nowhere, the sun had just set in the open fields. I could see us standing out there, on the isolated little platform, being eaten up by the mosquitoes, until the next day when we would become "official" and be allowed back on the next Moscow bound train, almost certainly at the cost of new train tickets.

My noisy protest of the solder's orders was unintelligible to the two solders, but obviously conveyed our anger and frustration. Soon an older passenger appeared at our open compartment door. He was a Lithuanian businessman who traveled this route quite often and had seen this exact confrontation before. "Just offer to purchase a new set of visas," the man said in reasonably good English. Having no other reasonable alternative, we dished out three hundred-dollar bills. One of the guards soon returned to hand back our passports and visas. Each now included a flimsy little piece of initialed paper! We probably should have tried just a single hundred-dollar bill first. Oh well, we said. Somehow it seemed a fitting and memorable start for a trip into Russia! We got to experience one form of corruption in a land that made such practices into a way of life for most! Anyway, Belarus, like many of the other Soviet satellite countries, was practically bankrupt as it continued, unsuccessfully, to cope with a long-running case of economic implosion. We had just done our part to keep the economy alive and pay those two soldiers. Making no more than twenty or thirty dollars a month—if they even had been paid in the last few months—those three big Ben Franklins probably amounted to a year's worth of rubles!

There is really no end to Soviet-era long-distance train stories; they occur as predictably as the clickity-clack of the rails. None of the stories could be considered life-threatening, even though maybe just a bit dangerous. Judy and I were never tossed off of a train as some of my CEP colleagues were, or had to sit most of the day outside the train-car while it was being repaired, which also happened to a visiting lecturer. Our saunalike compartments sometimes contained people with annoying body odor, most often really stinky feet, and there were plenty of occasions where we endured examples of this! Other incidents involved friendly passengers who shared our compartment along with their food and drink, sometimes far too much of their drink. And there were always the passengers who spent most of the time just staring at us. The trains never broke down as also happened to some of our friends, but in every other way the Soviet-era trains were always an adventure.

Just think of what we Americans are missing when we travel so much of our time by private car with individually adjustable heat and cooling. Where is the life? What stories can take place in such familiar confinement? It is high time to bring back the train, or better yet, head to the lands of the former Soviet Russian Empire and ride these rails before they, too, fall to the onslaught of the automobile.

10

A Trip to the Market

New Forms of Shopping

Consider the typical American way of shopping for groceries. You know the routine: back the car out of the garage, drive to the supermarket, park as close as possible (walking is un-American and to be avoided), make your selection of food and sundries in a warm, odorless environment filled with thousands of choices, hand the clerk your credit card, and perhaps have the bag boy or girl take the purchases to the car. Just in case these grocery shopping habits at the supermarket have become a bit boring, consider the contrast in the stories and descriptions of shopping we routinely experienced "over there."

To do any kind of shopping in the former Soviet Russian Empire, one first had to have cash in hand. Except in very rare instances, markets operated strictly on cash transactions. If Judy's and my cash hoard was low, we would first need to exchange our dollars for local currency. In Vilnius, we would use our credit card to obtain cash at a bank. In Tallinn and Kharkiv, we would bring a hundred dollar "Big Ben" to one of the many little official money exchanges scattered around both cities. In Tashkent, the official exchange rate was so outrageously confiscatory that we would always use an intermediary to exchange our money at a much better rate on the black market. The latter exchange required planning ahead one day in order to complete the transaction and have the money ready to go shopping. Using an intermediary also meant that, for the sake of safety, we converted smaller amounts of money on each occasion, usually one hundred dollars and never more than two hundred dollars.

In addition to what I received in university salary, Judy and I kept a stash of hundred-dollar bills scattered in several hidden locations in our flat. Then, because we would worry that we might forget where we had hidden some of the money, we kept an easily available master location list in cryptic shorthand. On hindsight, I suppose that if thieves had come into our flat and had found the hidden location for some of our money, this would have just spurred them on to tear the place apart looking for other locations. We only knew of one CEP person who was robbed in this manner. He lived in Chisineau, the capital of Moldova.

Most of our shopping was conducted in what we would call a farmer's market. There were only a few places to shop for grocery items that resembled anything like what we would call a supermarket, and this only in Tallinn. Even there, it was a marketing concept that was just beginning to appear.

One end of the scale of indoor food-shopping opportunities was represented by a glitzy market located on the ground floor of a newer high-rise apartment building we stayed in on a couple of visits to Minsk, Belarus. Tom Velek and his wife Cindy Boub, two of our good CEP friends, lived on the eighth floor. The two top floors above them housed several big shot ex-KGB officials and their families. We couldn't go up to their floors for a look around because the stairwells were gated and the elevator buttons for these higher floors had been burned away with what looked like a cigarette lighter in what was likely a drunken expression of ingratitude. Instead, we got to watch those people shop downstairs in the market. Inside the market, the walls were covered in continuous mirrors. Sparkling chandeliers hung down over the caviar and champagne. All the male store personnel wore tuxedos. Judy and I bought a few small things, finding the prices quite high by American standards. It was an impressive store, oddly existing in probably the poorest of the former Soviet republics.

At the other end of the indoor food-shopping scale were the standard stores of the Soviet period. It would be erroneous even to think to use the adjective "super" to describe these stores. Examples of this common type of store could be found in any former Soviet town or city. They were also definitely not self-service stores. It didn't matter if it was a food store, a bookstore, jewelers, pharmacy, or any kind of store: what you wanted was below the counter or behind the clerk on a shelf on the wall. Judy and I would point out our choices to examine or purchase. It was a tough way for us to shop, as, at least initially, we did not know the Russian names for most things, but we learned fast. In the meantime, in food stores of this type, we would stare at the shelves in the distance, squinting, trying to make out the pictures on the product labels. We would then point and direct—no, not that, more to the left, no, up, no, over. The clerk would set whatever it was on the counter. It often wasn't what we wanted. We would point again. The clerks invariably put up with us, I think because they were curious about us and amused by our efforts. Besides, they were indifferent and bored, and we gave them something to do.

I remember buying some imported (it was all imported) deodorant spray for the little toilet room in our Vilnius apartment. The store clerk took several cans down from the shelf. One at a time, she would shake the contents and spray a small amount in the lid for us to sample and approve the scent. When we finally had what we wanted, the clerk would write down the total price on a piece of paper, hand the paper to us and leave the items on the counter. Then we would take the paper to a booth, usually located within the room or somewhere nearby, and hand it to the lady cashier along with the money. She would hand us a printed receipt that we would then take back to the clerk to redeem for our previous selection. If the store had several sections, then we would have to go through the whole procedure more than once. I couldn't help thinking what obviously control-oriented Soviet mind must have dreamed up this procedure. Granted, it did help to keep everybody employed: an important goal of Communism.

In Vilnius, there were two fairly small supermarket-type stores with a name that easily managed to keep Judy and me chuckling. The nearest IKI (pronounced "icky," meaning "come again") market was a long walk from our flat, so we shopped for IKI food only occasionally. Instead, we did most of our shopping at Koops, a little mini-style market not much larger than a 7-11 store.

Koops was located only three blocks from our flat. It contained a little meat market, a dairy counter, a short series of shallow wooden bins that held vegetables—green ones until about October, and then all winter long only a few root vegetables like carrots and beets could be found. Cabbage was always available, which pleased me even though Judy hated the stuff. A special bin held some rather small potatoes. There were about five short double rows of shelves for canned food, packaged goods, and various other grocery supplies. It was easy to tell what was in the imported canned goods from their label, which always contained a picture of the product. On the remaining shelf space were fruits, vegetables, and meats canned in old-fashioned blue-green jars with simple little paper labels, sometimes containing a small faded picture that allowed us to double-check what was inside. Most of the food canned in this manner came from Russia, was usually of reasonable quality, and was very cheaply priced. Just inside the entrance to the store, Judy would get a small cart and begin shopping, while, occasionally, in the late afternoon during the bitter cold winter months, I would hang back for a quick shot of vodka at a busy little bar just opposite the cart storage area.

During the year in Vilnius, we tried shopping at a big outdoor market just once. We had to take a trolley to get there, it was terribly cold and snowy, and I fell down and sprained my thumb. The pork we purchased spoiled the next day. We never went back, and the idea of shopping for most of our food at an outdoor market continued to remain foreign to us. However, our approach to grocery shopping in an outdoor market changed the next year when we moved to Tallinn and really hit its stride during our third posting in Kharkiv. While in Kharkiv, I wrote a story for a few friends and my students about shopping at our local outdoor market. Because it is a comprehensive description of this kind of market, I will turn to this story first.

A Trip to the Market

It was November 1998. Judy and I had made one final check of the thermometer just outside our dacha window to confirm that we would need to wear our insulated underwear and heavy mittens for the trip to the Sumskoy market. It was 17 degrees Fahrenheit outside, sunny with a coat of fresh snow. Along with several large woven plastic bags, we tucked in our Estonian "cleaty feet" straps in case we encountered ice on the way.

With the exception of a very high-end meat market and a wonderful little French bakery, both about fifteen minutes walk from our house, to our knowledge, there were no supermarkets, even smaller markets like Koops in Kharkiv, at least not anywhere nearby. Therefore Judy and I learned to shop and enjoy the traditional, partly outdoor market that served our neighborhood. The trip from our dacha to the market took about fifteen minutes to walk. After leaving our housing area, we would head up a single-lane road next to a run-down but still operating indoor sports facility, past an older apartment housing complex, then up a few stairs next to the outdoor restrooms, and there we were at the market.

On the walk, I noticed the men with their big fur hats going by and wondered where I might be able to wear one like these back in Boise. They could be quite handsome. The little children were dressed so warmly that they were as wide as they were tall. Judy pointed out the many clumps of mistletoe hanging from the leafless oak trees. We made a note to get some to hang prominently in the doorway to our front room. We would have some convincing to do with our local guests who viewed our display of mistletoe with considerable amusement. Ukrainians consider mistletoe to be strictly a nuisance. It was the same kind of snickering sense of incredulity that we got from my students for hanging a pair of otherwise mundane and strictly utilitarian twig brooms on our living room wall. We saw them as folk art.

On the way to the market, the bitter cold began to take its most predictable effect upon us. Judy's eyes had begun to water and my nose was beginning to run. We made a quick stop to get out our constant traveling ingredient, a roll of toilet paper that doubled for facial tissue on such winter occasions. The next stop was Sumskoy market.

Street scene with chicken purchase. Outside a market in Chisinau, Moldova.

Saturday morning was a big day at the market as the selection of things to buy was at its best for the week. We walked past the outdoor restrooms as quickly as possible and entered a large covered area containing long lines of concrete outdoor tables on which were hundreds of small piles of vegetables, each pile attended by a vender. The area was surrounded on three sides with old military trucks. From the back of some of these trucks, we could buy dairy products, while others were filled with piles of cabbages, potatoes, or beets.

Judy had brought along two large clear plastic bags that she handed up to two men seated on the back of one of the trucks. One man scooped out flour, or sugar, as requested, from giant sacks while the other held our bags to be filled. Beside the truck there was a small bright blue utility trailer still hooked to its little Russian-made car. The trailer was filled with walnuts. Judy got in line to buy a kilo (a little over two pounds) of these nuts while I watched a multitude of little birds that had figured out a way to individually carry off a whole walnut when the merchant was not watching. I wondered how they cracked them open.

I made a mental note to put wool socks in my boots next time, as standing on the snowy ground, my feet had begun to get cold. People were staring at Judy's foreign looking earmuffs and giggling. An old lady with wrinkled hands wanted me to give her a few coins. I wondered about the hard-working life that these hands had experienced. Finally, we stopped at our favorite egg lady. There were maybe a dozen women sitting on small stools in front of piles of eggs stacked between layers of molded cardboard. Judy gave the lady her plastic egg carrier to be filled with ten eggs. (A dozen of anything is an odd request to people in this part of the world).

After a few other purchases, we climbed several snowy steps and went in the back entrance to the main indoor part of the market. It was a little bigger than a basketball gym and had a big curved roof. The effect was a bit like being in an aircraft hanger. As we entered, we were glad to have the sunlight streaming through the high windows as electric illumination was barely adequate.

Once inside, a distinct blend of smells from the many different foods, combined with marginal sanitation and a lot of people's smelly clothing and poor personal hygiene, initially created a mildly unpleasant odor. The odor was also a bit unappetizing, thus helping to quell the usual adage about shopping on an empty stomach. The smell would change somewhat as we moved from one part of the market to another.

Directly ahead were tables covered with two-foot-long carp. Several varieties of dried fish stared at me. At the end of one table, a complete pig's head was propped up, signifying that pork was sold at this spot. Another table contained foot-high mounds of butter. Along one side of the market were probably twenty butchers all lined up in front of a long, wide sturdy table, some chopping meat with big axes, others sorting out the small chunks and bigger pieces. Several of the butchers were smoking over their work. Rather generic, medium-size, light brown, short-haired, "Ukrainian-type" dogs darted among the shoppers hoping for a scrap of meat to fall on the floor, which happened quite often.

I noticed the lady in front of me handling several cuts of meat while contemplating her selection. She was hefting them up, turning them over, and then going to the next cut. Finally, after she made her choice, the butcher took her money, made change, and then continued to sort and cut the meat in front of him, all this being quite unsanitary, but at least now I knew one reason why older money looked and felt so grimy. Another woman was busy eating sunflower seeds and spitting the husks all over the floor. Judy was successful in indicating to a butcher that she wanted a big chunk of pork cut into chops. I got bumped hard by a lady working her way through the crowd of shoppers hawking hot sausages, each wrapped within a slice of bread. Such local fast food was especially appealing to the merchants who had not yet had time to eat that morning.

Pork for sale. A much nicer market than we were used to, but the pig heads show off well. Lviv, Ukraine

Next, we visited one of the several middle-age female venders with whom we had become acquainted through frequent visits. They had driven in from their farms and dacha truck gardens that morning. They were all wearing cheap and usually ragged and dirty winter jackets. When we bought eggs inside the market, we always patronized a lady with an outgoing personality and very peroxide-blonde hair. There was also the chicken man and the vegetable babushka. We would examine the stack of chicken pieces to make sure that our selection was still at least partially frozen. Judy preferred the pieces to the whole chickens, which generally contained the neck, gizzard, and liver, individually stuffed inside, not in a little bag as we are used to finding them. Also inside the chicken would be the feet and the head with, as one of our CEPers put it, "it's eyes looking right at you, lids opening slightly as the skin defrosted the last little bit."

One of our favorite merchants was a lady who sold homemade garlic pickles from a big bucket. They were incredibly tasty, but never lasted more than a few days before turning bad. The same lady could usually be counted upon to have a few carrots, onions, and lettuce when in season. Later in the spring, her fresh garlic was the treat of a lifetime—crunchy and sweet. The vegetable babushka always acknowledged us with a warm greeting and a big smile full of gold teeth. On this shopping trip she had taken out her glasses for the first time in order to read a word from our little pocket Russian dictionary. We were trying to find celery, which we later found out is not sold as stocks but only as a root. The lady struggled over the dictionary and was not able to help us. I noticed that one lens of her glasses was badly shattered. We bought some onions and all her carrots. The carrots looked a bit scrawny, wilted, and like most of the other root vegetables, crusted with dirt. "No bother," Judy said to me, "It is more than I need, but this will help her out." All the while shoppers continued to walk by the venders asking prices for the food. It was unusual in this market to see marked prices on food.

By now our sacks had become quite heavy; still, there was more food to find. But wait, an old lady panhandler had recognized us and was on her way over to bless me for a little money. She usually stationed herself near the liquor window where the pickings were good, but she could normally spot me a mile away wherever I happened to be. I got blessed almost every time we went to this market.

We requested a slab of fresh butter be cut from one of the massive chunks sitting on a long table. Then as we passed the honey lady, I remembered that I had forgotten to bring a jar for the honey. I had to pay a little more this time. The honey was ladled out of several large old-fashioned milk cans each containing a different variety. It was customary to first sample the variety from a lineup of small honey jars using a common spoon for each jar. I decided to take pot luck instead. Sampling things was a common practice with a cut, dip, slice, or other form of tidbit always freely offered if we looked as though we were trying to make up our mind to buy.

At this point, we were basically through shopping. We each had two large bags completely full of our purchases, heavy things in the bottom and light stuff on top. We headed out of the front end of the building and made our last stop at a bread kiosk just outside. There was always a line going up the ramp to the waist-high platform from where we would place our order through a small window. The air moving out of the window carried the wonderful scent of fresh bread. There was every size and shape sitting on shelves behind the counter. The French bread was especially good, and the dark heavy rye with its superb taste could cure the uninitiated of constipation in a very short time.

Next to the bread kiosk was a second, smaller building where Judy and I would sometimes treat ourselves to a snacker's delight. It was deep-fried *pirozhki,* about the size and shape of a corndog minus the stick. The outside was made of pastry while the inside was filled with highly peppered mashed potato. They were always freshly cooked, and nice and warm. If one was willing to suspend calorie counting for the moment, they were yummy. We managed to pass up this delicacy for this trip. Our rationale was that our hands were just too full to both eat and walk, as was the custom with this food.

We were finally ready to go back home. It had taken us almost two hours, and our arms were beginning to ache from the load. As we jostled along the path and back road home with several other shoppers in the bright crisp morning air, I remember reflecting on how much we had enjoyed another trip to the lively and always exciting market scene.

I have converted some of the food prices from Ukrainian *hrevnas* into U.S. dollars: a quart of milk, 48 cents; a large loaf of bread,14 cents; ten eggs, 56 cents; two pounds of sugar, 22 cents; two pounds of potatoes, 28 cents; and two pounds of chicken (leg/thighs) $1.27. To us, these were good prices. To the locals, these were very high prices, in part occasioned by a recent devaluation of the Russian ruble.

We usually went to market as frequently as every other day, sometimes taking a slightly altered route home in order to pick up photocopy work at Igor's copy/auto parts/kitchen supplies and dentist shop. Shopping at our neighborhood market was one of the most pleasurable experiences of our year in Kharkiv.

As a result of our shopping experience, we looked forward to shopping in a new variety of outdoor markets during our next posting in Uzbekistan. We also looked back to our first regular use of an outdoor market while living in Tallinn, Estonia. The neighborhood market in Tallinn had also been a matter of thorough enjoyment from the very first trip. It was conveniently located right across the street from our apartment complex. However, our commitment to this new form of shopping never became as exclusive as it would in Kharkiv.

Instead, in Tallinn, we would often travel several blocks out of our way to purchase at least some of our groceries at Stockman, one of the new full-service markets set up by a Finnish company. The building was quite large and on two levels. Above the ground floor grocery was a second level containing upscale clothing and home furnishing departments with prices equal to or above what we would pay at home in Boise. We shopped at Stockman, as much as anything, I think, to reacquaint ourselves with that certain giddy feeling that comes from being in the presence of so many food and other shopping choices. It brought about a sense of well-being that had long been conditioned into us as supermarket shoppers. Judy was less philosophical. She needed some specialized food items and especially liked buying the carefully cut and wrapped meat found in this store.

Yet, even with the advent of the supermarket in the quickly changing Estonian shopping scene, the vast majority of people continued to shop the traditional way in an outdoor market. Here the food was "organic" and had always been so, long before the practice became fashionable in our Western supermarkets. No irradiation, no pesticides, no growth hormones. Just fresh seasonable food, carrots and potatoes usually covered in dirt, and chicken poop still stuck to the fertile eggs. We quickly learned to do most of our shopping in our local Estonian open market.

Homemade products, including spicy sauerkraut right out of the pail. Tallinn, Estonia.

The layout of the market was almost the same as it would be in Kharkiv, except that the inside portion was larger and two stories, with the main floor opening directly up to a balconied second floor that featured many small merchants selling clothing along with typical five-and-dime store stuff. Living so far north, you would think that daily outside grocery shopping in Estonia would just about cease to exist during the short, bitterly cold winter days. On the contrary, there continued to be crowds of people all throughout the year and most every time we were there.

The relatively unprotected little outdoor stands of the venders would be surrounded in the winter by a growing sheet of ice, sometimes reaching as much as six or eight inches thick, making it very difficult for the shopper to maneuver from place to place. Yet somehow, commerce managed to continue. Our metal-cleated boot soles kept us upright, and each time we went shopping, there seemed to be something new to buy.

Judy found a merchant who had just set up his stall and was selling skeins of natural, unprocessed sheep's wool. Going overboard with enthusiasm, she bought, as she now admits, "more than I will use in a lifetime." A little store on the perimeter of the outdoor portion of the market sold absolutely the tastiest bear claw pastries. Of course, this often produced an irresistible urge for a quick "morning breakfast run" to purchase a hunk of cured ham and a sack full of these pastries before they were all sold out.

The ham was especially tasty. Saku, our kitten, liked the ham as well. Starting with eating small pieces from a bowl on the floor, he quickly advanced to sitting in his chair and taking his little ham chunks from a bowl off his plate at the table. We thought this was cute and amusing until we discovered that Saku was becoming territorial about his place at the table. He stopped being fed at the table after jumping on the head of one of our male guests who, rather impolitely, sat in his chair.

Down the way from the bakery, in a shop that looked like a portable fireworks stand, was a merchant who sold gorgeous Belarusian crystal. Judy plotted to buy the store out, but did manage to acquire some pieces for us and for everybody on our Christmas list back in Boise. Vodka shot glasses were a popular purchase. They made a wonderful tinkling sound when tapped together while empty.

Central Asian Bazaars

By far the biggest outdoor markets we had ever experienced were the bazaars in Uzbekistan. They made up a shopping venue like nothing we had ever seen, a gigantic cacophony of sights, smells, and sounds. We got almost all of our groceries in these bazaars during our year in Tashkent. With the exception of a few big sandy windstorms there was no fear of really cold or otherwise bad weather in Tashkent. As the geography and climate was similar to Phoenix, Arizona, almost all of the bazaars operated completely in the outdoors under large shade-providing roofs. Let me take you along on one of our weekly visits to our local Alay bazaar. It was about a twenty-minute walk from our apartment.

Before leaving, we got out our four, by now well-worn, large woven plastic bags. We then filled these with lots of little plastic bags collected from our previous shopping. While we initially thought these little bags to be free, we soon learned that in Tashkent markets, they were added to the cost of our purchases, so we saved them up and reused them as much as possible.

The trip to the market began with a walk up the one-lane tree-lined dead-end street next to our apartment. It was about two blocks to its intersection with a larger neighborhood arterial. At this intersection, in the fall, there would always be a young man selling melons. Like the similar scene at so many other major intersections, the young man would be there with his large stack of melons, his metal frame bed, and his obligation to stick it out, night and day, until all his melons were sold. Walking along the arterial, we would pass a grade school and a couple of small restaurants before arriving at a very busy four-lane highway. With no marked crossing near where we wanted to cross, we had to wait for a break in the speeding traffic, then like everybody else we would dart across to the meridian and wait again to cross the final two lanes. Once on the other side, a small road would angle off toward the bazaar.

Old people would be sitting on the sidewalk along the last portion of the small road begging for money. Prior to leaving for the market, I had sorted out my money and determined how much I would give to these ragged, usually quite deserving-looking people. I was adhering to a custom in this part of the world where it is a person's duty to give small amounts of money directly to the poor. Closer to the bazaar, the sidewalk filled on both sides with an active flea market. An individual blanket or tarp would be laid down to display books, kitchenware, clothing, musical instruments, hardware, toys—many of the kinds of things one might expect at a yard sale back in the United States. The most noticeable difference between the two is the evidence of excess commercialism in our yard sales. Here the things for sale were limited in amount and usually functional in nature. Judy and I had browsed these sidewalk sales in every place we lived in the former Soviet Russian Empire. On this day, we stopped now and then to look closely at the kitchen stuff, hoping to supplement our growing collection of Sputnik commemorative silverware. The handles contained an etched picture of the world's first satellite sailing through starry space.

*Tradesmen sit behind pictures of their work while waiting for employment.
Near the entrance to Alay Bazaar. Tashkent, Uzbekistan*

About a block from the bazaar entrance, the concrete sidewalk gave over on one side to people selling cassette tapes stacked across folding tables placed end to end. On the other side of the sidewalk were maybe twenty or so craftsmen squatting next to each other. Each had a small cardboard display of photographs propped up in front of him showing some of his work, hoping to gain a new commission from a passerby. This line ended at several large stacks of gleaming white porcelain toilets and wash basins.

Now the action and the noise really picked up. Within a radius of a few yards, there were a couple of men working over a large wooden board, re-blackening leather jackets. Next to them was a sidewalk shoe repairman followed by a fellow standing in front of a large case of swords and daggers of all sizes and shapes. At the end of this little queue was a booth selling lottery tickets. At this point, Judy and I turned left from the sidewalk and made our way the last hundred feet to a side entrance to the covered portion of the bazaar.

Near the entrance were kiosks selling most every kind of imported nonfood item: toiletries, perfumes, clothing, and small electronic appliances. The largest percentage of this stuff had arrived by boat in the Arabian Sea port of Karachi, Pakistan, and was then trucked into Uzbekistan through Afghanistan. It was a long and perilous journey as Afghanistan was in the midst of a raging, mainly intertribal, war.

As we approached the bazaar entrance, old ladies were selling traditional round flat bread, smoky charcoal braziers were cooking sizzling chunks of meat, and men were stirring large caldrons full of plov, the delicious national dish made from rice, vegetables, and chunks of lamb, all cooked together with plenty of fat. Having finally reached the side entrance to the bazaar, Judy and I stopped one last time to pick up a couple of pirated music CDs. They were $2.50 each. Then we maneuvered through the bustling crowd into the covered part of the market.

As expected, the temperature was noticeably cooler under the big roof of this gigantic arena as big as a football field and set out with rows and rows of concrete tables on a concrete floor. Hundreds of people were standing or working behind their assigned table space on which were piled or laid out the widest variety of fruits and vegetables, nuts, squash, potatoes, meats, and much more.

Judy and I were unfamiliar with many of the food items for sale. Vegetables, while usually recognizable, were in varieties we had never seen before. Since our arrival in Tashkent, we had already taken home and enjoyed three different kinds of melons, finding each to be delicious. Even at that, there were many more varieties of melons still to be sampled. The merchants held out melon slices for us to try. Following the customary price negotiation, we chose one of the bigger melons that came nestled in a rope sling with a little wooden carrying handle. I gave the melon to a porter, a young man I had hired to pull our big sacks around in his Radio Flyer–style red wagon. Some of the porters were very young boys, some old men. They always looked like they badly needed to earn a little of my money.

Near where the melons were sold was a long line of Korean women selling what seemed like an endless variety of *kimchi*, hot-spicy, finely sliced, vegetable salads. They reminded me of very colorful examples of coleslaw. We had been served several kinds of kimchi in the resturants and quickly discovered how tasty it could be. A trip to the market now almost always involved buying at least a couple of varieties to eat at home.

Tomatoes and cucumbers are a staple of the typical Uzbek salad. Sweet red peppers are in the sack awaiting display. Alay Bazaar. Tashkent, Uzbekistan

After finding out what they were, I had grown to enjoy the taste of green radishes. They were the size of turnips and came in many shapes. Sliced and salted, they made good nibble food. We purchased a few, placing them in one of our little plastic sacks that we then placed into one of our big shopping sacks. This was the routine for each item we bought. Again, as in Kharkiv, Judy and I developed friends among several of the venders. We would wave or stop to make simple conversation and give them each one of our little souvenir pins while arranging a purchase.

Most items in the bazaar seemed reasonably priced, amounting to only a few cents. The price of the more expensive foods, particularly the meat, was almost always subject to bargaining. I got reasonably good at this, while Judy still felt embarrassed to offer a "low ball" price, or any price, other than the merchant's beginning or asking price. Even then the price was a steal by standards we were used to at home in Boise. Occasionally, in the middle of a purchase, we were forced to step aside as a group of men would push a cart stacked high with sides of beef through the crowded walkways. In a tradition that I suspect dated back centuries, men always seemed to handle the distribution and sale of meat.

The market was incredibly colorful. Many of the women vegetable and fruit venders wore the traditional long dresses over pantaloons, both of which were either made from synthetic material in brightly colored flower prints or from peppermint striped colors in silk. And then there were the colorful foods carefully laid out or stacked in patterns repeated again and again throughout the market. Everywhere we turned was color. There were pyramid-shaped layers of an odd-looking fruit about the size of a pear. It was bright orange and very bumpy. A vender showed us how to open it up and eat the bright red fleshy material surrounding the large pumpkin-sized seeds. It tasted very blah. There were dozens of carefully stacked mounds of reddish-colored pomegranates and equally large piles of both white and purple mulberries. Mulberries look and taste quite a lot like large blackberries except that they grow on trees. We walked over their squished remains practically everywhere we went in the Tashkent neighborhoods.

Big sections of the market were devoted to every conceivable kind of dried fruit, although apricots were always the most plentiful. Another section featured a seemingly endless variety of nuts. Salty, roasted, apricot nuts were in abundance. Partially cracked open, their delicious seeds were ready to be extracted. Finally, there was the most colorful section of the market, an area containing a number of carefully arranged displays of spices. Standing high behind their artfully arranged tiers of mounded colors, the proud merchants waved their upturned hands over their displays beckoning to us to stop for a closer inspection and to take in the wonderful aromas. Judy had prepared a translated short list of needed spices written out in Russian. A lucky merchant began to fill her order, placing each selection in a separate little piece of paper and wrapping it up tightly. "America?" he exclaimed, while working on the order. Like so many other Uzbeks who greeted us this way, we knew what the next line would probably be; "Bill Clinton!" Then there was a pause and a big smile. "Monica Lewinski," he blurted out. We resignedly nodded in agreement.

We were finished with our shopping. I motioned to our porter to drag his wagon back to the market entrance and out to the street. I paid our porter about 50 cents for his work. He waited to load our bags into a car I had just flagged down. I opened the front door of the car. Pointing ahead and waving to the left, across the busy four-lane arterial, I stated the destination (we lived right next to a well-known disco bar) and offered my price. It was high enough rarely to be challenged. Then it was a quick trip and another fifty cents for the three-or four minute ride back to our flat.

Shopping Encounters: Have Wedding Ring on and Picture of the Kids Handy

Going shopping, even for a few items, always gave us an opportunity to interact with local people. Usually the people we met through our shopping trips were Uzbeks. This meant that we would get to know such details as age, marital status, and number of children and grandchildren. While an initial conversation may include a comment on the weather, it almost always quickly moved to a sharing of some personal family demographics. Most important was marital status, and if married, how many kids we had. Age usually came third on the list.

The topics of marriage and family are not idle talk for Central Asians. Being very family oriented, even a complete stranger is likely to be treated to raised eyebrows, mildly cajoled, or visited with some other similar sanction for being too old to remain single. At age twenty-eight, my Canadian colleague, Carter, was always getting this treatment. It reminded me of growing up in America in the1950s, but was much more pronounced and potentially more intimidating. Several of my female Uzbek students told me of the pressure they either were under or would soon face to marry, typically in an arranged marriage. Another young Uzbek lady who I knew quite well decided to quit a promising career position and move out of country, in large part to escape from having to marry a traditionally minded Uzbek man.

Worse than not being married by the time you were supposed to, was being married without children. I recall a chilly fall morning while visiting an ancient Persian and Zoroastrian cemetery high on one of the hills near the city of Nukus in southern Uzbekistan. Several young women were there who had been sitting in the graveyard all night. My student companion informed me that their marriages had so far been childless, and they had spent the night among the grave markers, which hold the promise: *barakat*, the blessings of fertility for women unable to bear a child.

Even more unthinkable in the sharing of demographics was the idea of living together–in sin! Our country director, Norma Jo Baker, told us that while teaching with the CEP the previous year in Tashkent, she and her CEP lecturer and life partner, Chad Thompson, felt it absolutely necessary to wear wedding rings. Both individuals, being in their early forties, used these rings to prevent themselves from being lectured by taxi drivers, food venders, and others about the need to get married. The rings were insufficient evidence for the university where I was now teaching, which, upon discovering Norma's living arrangement, had threatened to revoke her invitation letter and therefore invalidate her visa, which depended upon this document. It was at this point that not only were rings purchased, but an official engagement was announced immediately. I should have asked why Chad was not also given this ultimatum. In any case, these two Canadians were officially married the following summer before their return to Central Asia.

The Most Exciting Kind of Shopping

There remains one final kind of market visit. This was the gigantic clothing, furniture, housewares, small appliances, the "you-name-it-and-it-is-there" type of market. Like the open-air food market, this type of market was found with only small variations everywhere we lived or visited, from Estonia to Uzbekistan, but never were they as big as the one we visited in Tashkent. Hang on to your wallet for fear of pickpockets and prepare to be jostled, pushed, and propositioned as I take you into this immense market located on the grounds of what once was a hippodrome, an ancient horse and camel racetrack, on the outskirts of Tashkent.

We left for the market on an early fall day. There was a bit of a chill in the morning air, and the trees were beginning to turn color. We decided to see what local people wore for winter. The answer was leather, black leather—loud and clear. It was time to take our first trip to the hippodrome. Like almost everybody else, we took local transport. There were several buses leaving from the city center specifically designated for taking passengers to this market. Few people drove personal cars. The small parking lot didn't appear to be more than half full, but judging from the size of the market and the immense number of people we encountered, had this been in America, the parking lot would have looked more like a major university homecoming football game.

We were accompanied by Irena An, our young, petite, Korean Uzbek CEP assistant. Irena had an aunt who ran a leather stall in the market. It was one of what seemed like a thousand small alcoves that opened onto a large rat maze of narrow, wood and canvas covered passageways, each alcove, it would seem, containing enough clothing to outfit several hundred people.

Irena led us through the main gate to the market, past an outer ring of prepared food venders raising the usual smoky cloud from their charcoal meat braziers. Then we entered the covered part of the market. She introduced us to her aunt and then promptly returned to the main entrance in order to bet on a card game being run by what I quickly had surmised to be a very capable huckster. We had seen the large, raucous crowd this game had attracted as we first entered the market.

The aunt's stall, like most of the others in the immediate vicinity, was stacked high with leather clothing and accessory items. The smell of tanned leather was powerful, definitely helping to get us in a buying mood. A long pole with a hook on the end was used to reach numerous items hung on hangers high up the walls and across the entrance to the stall. Leather was everywhere. We had never seen so much in one place before. Standing in front of the stall, we began to try on a couple of jackets. As soon as we did, it was as if we had telegraphed our choice of style and color throughout the market. Soon we were besieged by over a dozen men holding out similar jackets while bidding for our attention.

"Auntie" shooed most of them away. Jostling was a constant feature in the narrow passages, as we attempted to try on some of the jackets and coats being proffered. Every merchant seemed to be helping us at once, each holding out mirrors of various shapes and sizes for us to take a look at their selections. It was a madhouse of choice. In spite of it all, we each managed to get what we wanted. Judy purchased a nice three-quarter-length black coat, and mine was a bomber-style, also in black. Unfortunately, my coat sale didn't go to Auntie, who, it seemed had everything but bomber jackets. Thinking about the overwhelming presence of black leather reminded me of Henry Ford's famous line about his cars; "You can have any color you want as long as it's black!"

As we were about to leave Auntie's stall, Irena showed up wanting a loan, a sizable one by local standards. I could see that the scam had been working. I thought about trying to talk her out of spending any more money on the card game, but decided against it as it was obvious that she was determined to continue playing. Irena insisted that she knew what she was doing. She escorted us out of the maze of stalls. I reluctantly gave her the money as Judy and I left the market. We got paid back a couple of days later. Irena claimed that she had not lost any money in the game, but I was not so sure this was true.

Shopping in the open markets and bazaars—so much a part of life in the former Soviet Russian Empire, was always an exhilarating experience for Judy and me. The hardships involved in this form of shopping were small in comparison to the pleasure we gained. Now that we are back home in the United States, we have visited our local farmer's market several times. It is open Saturday mornings during the summer. Fresh produce and home-baked goods are for sale at competitive prices. But the market remains a small operation. The organizers have added live music and a few craft booths to help bring out more customers. We have found it to be a fun way to spend an hour or so. Afterwards we are usually anxious to get our "real" shopping done. On the way home, we drive into our local Wal-Mart Super Center, trying, of course to look for a parking place as close to the front door as possible.

11
Nukus: Coping with Disaster

The Effects of Trying to Do Just One Thing in Nature

By the mid-1970s, a majority of Americans had begun thinking seriously about the environment. The lesson from ecology was that life on earth is a matter of a balance; the actions we take in the environment are almost certain to have consequences beyond those we intend. Again and again, industrial civilizations have overlooked, or ignored, this important piece of wisdom when contemplating interventions in the delicate balance of nature.

The Soviets were, without question, the industrial world's greatest environmental offender. While in Uzbekistan, I visited one of the worst examples—the Soviet's reckless, if not actually criminal, agricultural and hydraulic plan to divert massive amounts of river water to create a gigantic cotton monoculture in the middle of Central Asia. The objective was to create self-sufficiency in this staple for the entire Soviet Russian Empire. However, implementing this plan has resulted in a tremendous ecological imbalance: the almost complete drying up of the Aral Sea, once the fourth largest inland body of water in the world. Such a drastic alteration, along with poor agricultural practice, has combined to produce disastrous long-term health effects on thousands of people living in the immediate area of the lake, and serious air contamination extending far beyond the region.

Americans have done their share of ecological damage as well. Undoubtedly the most notorious example involved the damage from severe wind erosion that resulted from plowing up the Great Plains. The result was a hundred million acre "Dust Bowl" that stretched across parts of six states, ruining the livelihood and health of millions of people. A less well-known example also occurred early in the last century. It took place in California's Owens Valley. A quick review of what happened there will make it easier to appreciate the magnitude of the Aral Sea disaster in Central Asia.

Located approximately two hundred miles northeast of Los Angeles, Owens Lake had been a shallow 110-square mile body of water. In an effort to alleviate a pending water shortage in Los Angeles, land around Owens Lake was quietly bought up and engineers constructed a system of pipelines, pumping stations, canals, even aqueducts, over two hundred miles, to connect the "city of angels" to its newest source of water. In less than twenty-five years, Owens Lake was drained, leaving a dry lake bed contaminated with particles of nickel, cadmium, and arsenic. Ruined was a prosperous and long-standing farming and ranching economy that had been dependent on the lake and its tributary streams. In exchange for the taking of their water by the less than angelic Angelinos, every time the wind blows hard, as it often does, the people of the Owens Valley are treated to blinding "salt outs." On these occasions, the dry lake bed is stirred into life as the single largest source of particulate-matter pollution in the United States!

Environmental degradation stories sometimes contain a report of recent efforts to rectify damage done. An effort has been underway in the Owens Valley to enforce the federal Clean Air Act. This has at least helped to reduce the air pollution and salt outs. It is now required that stream water be reintroduced to the dry lake bed and that a minimum level of about three inches—just three inches—be maintained at all times.

In comparison to the original Owens Lake, the Aral Sea was much deeper and twenty-five times larger in size! And, if arrogance was not enough, the Soviet planners and their Kremlin overseers clearly knew in advance precisely what risks they were going to incur when they sought to do just one thing: divert massive amounts of river water in order to grow more cotton. They chose to ignore the explicit warnings of their scientific advisors.

The result was a death sentence for thousands of people who lived near the Aral Sea. The health problem continues with an almost equally serious effect for people living there now. Similar to Owens Valley, when the wind blows through the Aral Sea region, particulate-matter pollution continues to spread damaging health and environmental effects that are lethal to the local residents and detectable thousands of miles distant. It has been an international catastrophe. The area adjacent to what is left of the Aral Sea should be vacated as unsafe for human habitation. This would include the nearby city of Nukus, a perversely befitting name for a very God-forsaken place.

Early in our stay in Tashkent, Judy and I learned about Nukus, a city in the western part of Uzbekistan on the border with Turkmenistan. I had agreed to be a trainer in a series of four teaching workshops, the initial three of which were to be given in regional university cities. The first was scheduled for late November in Nukus. Judy and I knew something about the famed Silk Route city of Samarkand, and we looked forward to making this our second workshop trip early in December. Less well-known was our third workshop location, a city named Ferghana located on the eastern edge of the country. All we knew about Ferghana was that the center of the ancient silk industry of Central Asia was located nearby. Judy was anxious to stock up on this exotic and beautiful fabric. As for the location of the first workshop on the itinerary, it was time to read up on the city of Nukus.

Nuked in Nukus

I could not have begun to feel more uncomfortable! My two guidebooks were nearly identical in their frank, almost incredulous description of Nukus and the surrounding area. My *Lonely Planet* guidebook spoke of "desolation" and described the city as an "unhealthy and forlorn" place. There was the warning that anyone who planned to stay in the area for any length of time should first seek medical advice. The second guidebook, *Uzbekistan*, by MacLeod and Mayhew, began its account with phrases like "grim and spiritless." Nukus was described as a planned socialist city of at least two hundred thousand people, without a center, surrounded by "a wasteland of cotton fields punctuated by the random, surreal exotica of wild camels loitering in neglected apartment blocks."

What was I about to step into? In a decision she would later regret, Judy decided not to accompany me. It would be the first and only time in our years with the CEP that I went anywhere overnight without her. We began to talk about my getting "nuked" in Nukus. Actually, the guidebooks turned out to be quite accurate. There were even the camels, but there was also much more, some deeply disturbing. Fortunately, in addition to the pleasure of the workshop, a further portion of my experience was quite heart lifting.

Who or what was responsible for this dismal and frightening place? I made it a point to find out. Accepting my fate to be a guest in Nukus for a week, I began preparing my workshop lectures and getting all my handouts translated into Russian. I also started to learn more about the area, undoubtedly one of the greatest, if not the world's premier, environmental and human disaster. At the risk of getting ahead of myself, the story began in this area about forty years ago and continues to unfold its worsening effects. Many observers consider the Aral Sea disaster to be a catastrophe far more devastating than the Chernobyl nuclear "accident." How lucky could I get, I thought, while contemplating the years Judy and I had recently spent in Eastern Europe near to if not within the moderate danger zone created by Chernobyl. We had gone from one danger zone to the next. Now, in Tashkent, we were spending a year in the Aral Sea's toxic chemical fallout zone!

It wasn't long before I was in Nukus. It was late in November on a cold and windy Sunday evening when the big Soviet-era Tupolev-154 jet landed for its stopover on the flight from Tashkent to Moscow. That a big jet would fly out of its way like this, between two large capital cities to land in Nukus, offers an interesting insight into such a relatively small, out-of-the-way place. Nukus had become a mecca of sorts for a flood of nongovernmental organization (NGO) personnel all trying, in one way or another, to make Nukus and/or the adjacent Aral Sea better again. Our plane could have quite likely contained a journalist or two, maybe a writer, even an artist. Sure to be aboard would be international representatives of health and social services organizations, medical specialists, Peace Corps workers, agricultural and hydrology scientists, even social scientists like ourselves.

Our training team descended the movable staircase, entered the dingy little airport waiting room, and rounded up our luggage and several large boxes of teaching materials. There were seven people in our teacher-training team, including Sayora, our former program coordinator. She was from Nukus and had graduated from the regional university there. Her parents continued to live in Nukus. I thought about how proud of their daughter they must be. Sayora had begun a well-respected career in the country's capital city. Having recently gained a promotion, Sayora would be assisting Zulia, our new coordinator.

Not long after we left the terminal, our minivan pulled up in front of a nondescript apartment building. Sayora planned to stay at her parent's flat and had left from the airport in a separate taxi. The remaining six of us were being escorted into a vacant but furnished two-room flat. Once inside, we quickly began to give the place the once over inspection. One bedroom was fixed up with a canopy double bed all decked out in bright pink and red accoutrements. Who would get this room, and just where would all the rest of us distribute ourselves? One of the fellows staked out the front room sofa. Pulling rank as the oldest, I plopped my bag on the one single bed in the second bedroom. Someone else could take the mattress on the floor, I thought. The whole arrangement seemed far from satisfactory.

We asked the university staff member who had driven us to the apartment why we had not been put up in one of the two hotels in town. The answer was that neither was in good condition or safe. It was explained that our university hosts thought the apartment a better location. Just as we were about to reconcile ourselves to the apartment flat, Sayora arrived to say that we would, in fact, stay at the Nukus Hotel. She had just come from the hotel and pronounced it fit.

While waiting for our bags to be loaded back into the minivan, I checked the Nukus Hotel description in my *Uzbekistan* guidebook: "cockroach-ridden rooms with disgusting bathrooms," it said. Sayora responded that the guidebook was out of date, and one of the three floors had been cleaned up to a suitable standard. This was true. The cockroaches were nowhere in sight, but, in my room the bathroom was certainly sub-par and the toilet ran constantly. My bed had a very noticeable swayback look and feel to it and the blanket was at least an inch thick and very heavy. Were the winters that cold here?

To help cheer up the week-long stay, the university hosts quickly and thoughtfully stocked each of our rooms with two watermelons, several bottles of water, a bar of good soap and, just in case, most likely because we were foreigners, a jar of imported instant coffee. This was especially considerate because just about everybody in Uzbekistan drinks only tea. Most appreciated by me at that late moment were two bottles of the best locally made vodka.

Closer inspection showed the liquid to be a very unappealing light green in color. I thought, would this stuff "nuke" me? My university host showed up in the room at about this time and assured me that the green color was the result of a rare and special plant indigenous to the region, a small piece of which could be seen floating in the bottom of each bottle. I tried a double shot out of the rather dodgy looking hotel glass. It wasn't too bad, although it would have gone down much better if it had been chilled. Nevertheless, it wasn't enough to keep me sleeping through the night. At about midnight, it appeared that some of the locals had been in the hotel's basement bar downing far more of this green stuff than I, and were now rampaging about near the back of the hotel yelling and shouting. So much for the first night in Nukus.

By the next evening, our teacher-training group quickly settled into a routine that was repeated, with the exception of one dinner party out, throughout the rest of the week. Following the day's teacher-training sessions, the university van would drop us off at the hotel or a tourist site of our choosing. In the early evening, the van would pick us up at the hotel for the short drive to the Billiard Club for dinner. Fairly new in its plain concrete construction, the two-story club building sat behind a parking area of asphalt surrounded by salty mud that looked exactly like it had just received a light dusting of snow.

The interior of the club was a smoky dive, full of pool tables, overheated, humid, and buzzing with mosquitoes. Off of a hallway behind and adjacent to the kitchen was a small banquet room where we ate our evening meals. The dining table and high-back chairs were crowded into the room along with several large pieces of overstuffed furniture. The food was good, and the tea flowed like water. My student interpreter, Z Girl, again took up her self-appointed role as tea-serving hostess. I had requested that she come with the teaching team to help me and the others with translation and interpretation.

The evening routine began soon after dinner. On the way back to the Hotel Nukus, our van driver would first stop at the same small kiosk, the only place in the city that he knew sold imported Russian beer. A couple of us would buy a few beers; others would by soft drinks, and any snacks that caught our eye. Then it was back to the hotel. We would lay a big blanket on the floor of one of our rooms and sit around talking and eating and drinking until late in the evening. Later, the alcohol would take just enough of the edge off of the physical condition of my room and bed that I could usually get a reasonably good sleep.

A Visit to the Aral Sea

Toward the middle of the week, arrangements were made to allow both Zulia, me, and one other teacher-trainer to take a morning off in order to visit the once-thriving fishing town of Muynak and the adjacent expanse of dry Aral Sea bed. The president of the university lent us his personal car, and his son volunteered to be our driver for the three-hour trip from Nukus. We left the hotel about 3:00 AM. in order to complete the six-hour round-trip, leave a couple of hours for sightseeing, and be able to return for the afternoon training sessions.

The death of the Aral Sea is certainly one of the most compelling case studies of the disastrous consequences of a single action on the web of nature. Some people say that the rapid death of the sea was unforeseen. It definitely was not known to the locals. Like the situation in the Owens Valley, the local fisherman and farmers, in fact none of the citizens living in the region, were told of the consequences that would almost certainly follow the massive diversion of river water away from entering the sea. The majority of the locals I talked to were even now not very informed about the causes, a matter I found hard to believe until I stopped to remember that Uzbekistan has continued the Soviet policy of a tightly controlled media. As such, the state goes to great lengths to control information critical or unflattering of the government. Instead, the locals were left to conjure up outlandish theories such as the one I frequently heard expressed to the effect that most of the Aral Sea water had drained out underground to the Caspian Sea over two hundred miles to the west.

In fact, the rapid loss of river water to the Aral Sea, at the time dropping the sea level by three feet a year, and over fifty feet to date, was an intentional and purposive act of the Soviet central planners in Moscow. They were well informed of the likely consequences by their scientific advisors. Yet, over the decade between 1960 and 1970 the planners chose to overrule the certainty of horrific consequences in favor of their plan to enthusiastically exploit, for cotton irrigation, every bit of the water of the two largest rivers in Central Asia. The two rivers, the Amu Darya and the Syr Darya, have their origins far to the east in the high mountain ranges of Kyrgyzstan and Tajikistan. From there, they flow the many miles through Kazakstan, Turkmenistan, and Uzbekistan to their final destination as the exclusive water sources of the Aral Sea, one river entering the lake from the north, the other from the south.

Obsessed with the rearrangement of nature and, "the devil can take the hindmost," the planners began in the 1960s to construct a number of dams on these two rivers. The number of dams increased rapidly in order to divert the necessary water through miles of unlined canals to irrigate massively expanding cotton acreage. The Soviet's intention was to be self-sufficient in cotton. Its Central Asian republics, especially the agricultural lands of what is now the independent country of Uzbekistan, rapidly became synonymous with cotton growing. Caught up in this great plan, the approximately 1.5 million people of the Nukus region, many of them ethnic Karakalpakstani, became an integral part of what is still referred to as "fulfilling the plan."

After the last big dam, the Tahaitash on the Amu Darya near Nukus, was put in place, the southerly flow of water to the Aral Sea became, for all intents and purposes, only a memory. Stopping at the foot of a relatively new bridge just south of Nukus, I could look out across a great expanse of dry sandy river bed, at least two hundred yards wide, now all but empty save for no more than a width of twenty feet of shallow muddy water slowly flowing next to the opposite river bank. Of course, it was mid-November, the low part of the water year in what had been previously a very dry season, but no matter, a little more water or less, the water was, and continues to be, almost all spoken for upstream. The small amount of water I was looking at would be gone long before it reached the lake.

With expanding acreage and using liberal amounts of pesticides, herbicides, and fertilizer, cotton harvests grew spectacularly through the 1960s and 1970s. The harvest produced great wealth for the Soviet Russian Empire, and, equally great amounts of corruption in the region. In Tashkent, there was a two billion dollar scandal in falsified cotton harvest statistics, and at least one man who lived like a feudal lord with a private estate and his own harem! This was hardly in keeping with the egalitarian ideology of Communism. No matter, the region, with Nukus at its center, was at its zenith of development and good fortune.

Yet, in the midst of the economic good times, all boats, to coin a pun, were definitely not rising. In fact, in Muynak, all boats were coming to rest on the dry sea bottom along with the economic livelihood of over ten thousand fishermen and a prosperous fishing industry that employed as many as sixty thousand people. Still, the planners considered this of small consequence to the overall plan.

The economic value of cotton became and remains an important feature of the present economy. At the time of Uzbekistan's independence in 1991, cotton made up 80 percent of its export earnings and 40 percent of its domestic economy. Yet, the cotton growing monoculture has had a completely different effect on the ecology and people of Nukus and the Aral Sea region. The Aral Sea fishing town of Muynak, once able to boast of catching as much as twenty thousand tons of fish in a day or two, spent the period of rapid cotton growth watching its sea and its livelihood shrink rapidly. Bewildered, never told the truth, and believing the situation was temporary, the people of Muynak even dug an eighteen-mile channel to access the rapidly disappearing water's edge and keep their large fleet of fishing boats afloat. It was a waste of time and energy. The sea level would continue to drop rapidly, its volume quickly shrinking.

Today Muynak is over fifty miles from the water's edge. The Aral Sea has lost 75 percent of its volume, and is now less than two-fifths its original size. The sea can no longer support aquatic life, it now being sludge of highly salty brine, surrounded by two million acres of dried whitish-color seabed.

I stood on an embankment on the outskirts of Muynak, at the original water's edge in a chilly wind, waiting for the morning sun to raise high enough to provide light sufficient to operate my camera. Ahead of me, sitting atop sands that were once sea bottom, were the darkened and eerie silhouettes of a fleet of rusty abandoned boats, all perched at precarious angles, some half buried with silt and sand. Some were small trawlers and some, like great leviathans appearing out of the dark, were the hulks of large freighters. There was even a passenger ferry.

Boats everywhere and no water as far as the eye can see. The author stands beside one of the many eerie reminders of the Aral Sea fleet. Muynak, Uzbekistan.

As the sun rose to expose the scene more clearly, I was able to see boats scattered here and there for as much as a half a mile. The temperature was below freezing, and the wind continued its steady pressure against me, making my inspection of the fleet more difficult and somewhat more cursory. Nearby, a few people began to appear outside of their tightly battened cottages, and the only two streets through town started to show some pedestrian life.

Looking out over the expanse of sagebrush-covered seabed, now so far from the waters edge, I could not put out of mind my visit the day before to the Karakalpak State Museum in Nukus. One section depicted the natural history of the Aral Sea and the surrounding region. Nature had once been bountiful. There were several excellent dioramas exhibiting preserved remains of some of the over five hundred species of wildlife that were, until recently, part of the ecosystem of the area. The majority of these species, as much as 80 percent, have now disappeared. Especially compelling were the dioramas containing specimens of the previous aquatic inhabitants of the Aral Sea. Now as I stared into a brushy sandy desert seabed made temporarily colorful by the sunrise, I pictured an immense variety of fish, among them large sturgeon, and an even larger species of catfish—now gone forever!

The local university professors and others in Nukus with whom I spoke were just beginning to gain a full awareness of the consequences of this tragic case of human arrogance and folly. This recognition was brought, in large part, by the steady stream of foreign experts visiting the area. However, it was difficult for me personally to agree with the professor's typically cautious sense of optimism, however stoic its expression might have been. The human toll on the area's people was and continues to be immense and growing worse.

All the drinking water in the Aral Sea region is chemically contaminated to unfit levels. Drinking water must now be trucked into the region. Recent health studies conducted in the region reveal an epidemic of anemia reaching a level of 99 percent of pregnant women. There are abnormally high rates of kidney and liver disorders, DDT poisoning (most notable in breast milk), and predictably dramatic increases in respiratory diseases. At the time of my visit, studies conducted by a gynecologist and director of The Women's Health Center in Nukus, were exploring the suspected connection between mineral deficiencies caused by heavy metals, including toxic substances in the food and drinking water and a bizarre although commonly known local phenomenon of children eating all the chalk from their school rooms.

What are the connections between intensive cotton monoculture, the death of the Aral Sea, and the badly worsening health of the people of this region? In prehistoric times, this part of Central Asia was, like Owens Lake, once a gigantic slightly salty lake. Now, winds off of the receding lake, and especially the massive irrigation projects, have left large amounts of salt on and just below the surface of the ground, creating an alkaline soil that is so salty that it looks like a heavy morning frost covering large sections of fields. This situation extends into the city of Nukus, right into the spaces between apartment buildings.

Salinization of the agricultural land of the Aral Sea basin is increasing while cotton yields decrease in spite of the continued heavy application of chemical fertilizers. In what remains of the fishing village of Muynak, the exposed Aral Sea bed is releasing a deadly combination of previously accumulated pesticides, including DDT, and salt to ever more frequent periods of high winds that are generally attributed to the ecological changes in the area. It is estimated that seventy-five million tons of Aral Sea toxin and salt-laden dust now blow across central Asia each year. Harmful amounts of this dust have been found as far away as Norway.

The latest environmental affront to the region and its people has resulted from the lowering water level that has exposed a land bridge in the Aral Sea between Vozrozhdeine Island and the mainland. The Soviets had constructed a bio-weapons facility on the island. When it closed, the hazardous material, some of which quite possibly contained anthrax spores, was buried in canisters on the island. The canisters are rusting open and animals, which can now access the island, are thought to be ingesting some these dangerous microbes. This is creating a distinct possibility of spreading this lethal danger into the human food chain. There is also the issue of the large number of weapons stored on the island falling into the hands of terrorists. This latter concern has been sufficient to bring U.S. troops and money to Vozrozhdeine Island to assist in a multimillion-dollar clean-up effort, including the closing of a related chemical weapons plant in Nukus.

The Aral Sea disaster is generally considered to be too far developed to warrant any efforts beyond those that might mitigate some of the most deadly effects of the present situation. There are jokes about the endless procession of high-priced "experts" who come to Uzbekistan to study the problem and make suggestions. "If each of these professionals would bring a bucket of water with them," one Australian consulting engineer working for the World Bank Aral Sea Project told me, "we could easily refill the sea." My alternative suggestion, about as practical, was for the government to mandate that people fix their ubiquitous leaky toilets. Failure to do so could result in a long prison sentence similar to that for stealing car stereo radios. After all, according to one statistic, Uzbekistan consumes up to 90 percent of all the water used in Central Asia. I am sure that fixing leaky toilets would, alone, save enough water to again fill the sea!

Whatever the solution to the problems ultimately may be, it almost certainly will not be sufficient and will require government assistance from outside Central Asia. Several other countries share water rights with Uzbekistan over the two rivers. The two biggest water users, Turkmenistan and Uzbekistan, are poor countries that are economically locked onto the cotton treadmill and undoubtedly reluctant to change their pattern of water use. Lining all the main irrigation ditches could save up to half of all diverted water, but this would cost a lot of money. Of course, this solution would be easy for America. Think of some of the minor environmental issues that we can afford to spend a very large amount of our money on! As a panelist one Saturday at a Tashkent NGO conference, I sat next to a visiting university dean from Monterey, California, who told me a fantastic story. He said that the United States government spent a billion dollars to sift all the lead bullets out of the Pacific Ocean sand dunes, which had been used as a firing range backdrop at the now decommissioned Fort Ord, California, Army base. A long time ago, I had put a few of those bullets into the sand dunes myself. Who might provide—who could provide the "superfund" effort necessary to detoxify the large expanse of Aral Sea bed and surrounding area? What country, or even group of countries, have that kind of money to spend in such an out-of-the way place in the world?

The Aral Sea sits astride the border of Uzbekistan and its northern neighbor Kazakhstan. Each country controls the last portion of one of two rivers that historically kept the sea filled. Kazakhstan would like to put a dam across its northern portion of what remains of the sea and refill it to a lower level with the Syr Darya River water it controls. Uzbekistan might wish at least to partially replenish the lake as well, but at least not now, not while it continues to fight a losing battle on "the cotton treadmill." Beyond its use in growing food, every bit of irrigation water must go to cotton. The shaky economy depends on it!

Then there is Turkmenistan who shares the Amu Darya River border with Uzbekistan, until the river turns north toward the sea. Eighty percent desert, beyond its own cotton and other agricultural uses of the river water, Turkmenistan's authoritarian president announced a cockeyed plan to create both a lake of truly giant proportions out in the desert, and a man-made river to run through his capital city of Ashgabat. It has been officially stated that these projects would not use any more river water. In theory this maybe true, but there are numerous critics who are saying that practice will be quite different.

So for now, Nukus is left to cope with a disaster of increasing proportion. There is certainly overwhelming reason to describe the area as an unhealthy and forlorn place, as my guidebook had warned. It was hard not to feel terribly saddened by the whole experience. I thought about the people who lived here as I headed out of the hotel for the last time. Across the street was a half-constructed multistory building, a web of rusted reinforcing metal rods, concrete pillars, and steel beams. A couple of large rusty cranes hung over the project, everything long ago abandoned. In the next block were the remnants of a large parklike promenade two or more blocks long, lined with benches and ending in a tall statue dedicated to the friendship between Soviet and Karakalpak peoples. Now, along with the friendship, the concrete walks were disintegrating, the trees stunted or dying from salt concentrations, and most of the park benches gone or in poor repair. Across the way was a kiosk that probably once dispensed soft drinks and ice cream to the passersby. Now it stood abandoned, most of its windows broken. Nukus was a living ghost town still filled with people. Without doubt there has been great suffering.

An Upbeat Note

Yet in the midst of the suffering were signs that the human spirit was still very much alive. As one example, Nukus can boast of a very unique and impressive art gallery. Along with its large collection of ethnographic art of the region, the gallery contains some pieces dating back at least five thousand years to the time of Alexander the Great. Also in the collection is the handiwork of centuries of nomadic life and the finest collection of 1920s and early 1930s pre-Stalinist avant-garde art anywhere in the world.

The collection and the gallery were put together by Igor Savitsky (born 1915) for whom the gallery is now named. Savitsky was a Moscow artist who came to Nukus in 1950 to participate in an archeological project, became enamored with the regional ethnic Karakalpak people, and stayed to begin his collection. It is undoubtedly the many examples of avant-garde art that have recently begun to bring notoriety to the Savitsky Gallery. Savitsky collected Russian, Uzbek, and Karakalpak art from the first part of the twentieth century. The pieces reflected a period in which artists working in the Soviet Russian Empire were experimenting with new styles in European modern art. Their avant-garde approach did not conform to Stalinist social realism, which not only cut short this style of artwork, but resulted in the destruction of many existing pieces.

Astonishingly, Savitsky was not only able to put together such a large collection of this art, but was able to retain his collection in spite of ideological suppression and destruction that severely hobbled better-known museums. Savitsky had luckily picked the right location for his gallery. Few of Stalin's censors knew where Nukus was, let alone paid it any attention. Savitsky died in 1984, but not before amassing a collection of over 81,500 items.

Nukus and the Savitsky Gallery continue to remain very remote to all but the most purposive traveler. Understandably, the collection still suffers from years of severe social hostility directed at modern art. Only a small amount of the collection is on view; however, it is a sufficient feast for the eyes to see this exhibit as it is, literally frozen in space and time.

Our university hosts arranged a special evening viewing for me and the other teacher trainers. We met the English-speaking director, Marinika Babnazarova, who presides over a small staff dedicated to securing and preserving the priceless treasures. She personally showed us the original works as well as parts of the thousands of other art exhibits that now make up the complete collection. It was very hard to believe that such a wonderful and precious cultural heritage could exist in such a remote, inhospitable place in the world.

Nearby, in a large remodeled gymnasium, was another very positive example of the human spirit in action. It reminded me of the line from the movie *Field of Dreams*, "If you build it, they will come." "Nukus may not be the best place," said Lily Lagazidze, director of the Progress Center, "but we are doing our life, and it is a pleasure to see the results." About a month after returning from Nukus, I had the pleasure to meet Lily and join her on a panel at a conference in Tashkent. Over a private lunch with Lily, she told me her story of starting her English language school in 1992 in an old abandoned gymnasium. The school was envisioned to operate primarily as a center for young people, particularly those most at risk due to impoverished circumstances. It was an effort to fill a badly needed void left when youth groups lost funding in the collapse of the Soviet Russian Empire.

The Progress Center's Language Learning Center has grown to well over one thousand fifth to eleventh grade students who spend four afternoons a week involved in English lessons, sports programs, music and dance instruction, and more. Speaking softly and with an infectious enthusiasm, Lily described the latest additions to her center. These include a pre-school program with seventy children, a successful effort to bring orphans and disabled children to the center for mentoring by high school students, and a business school with 162 students and 29 professors, 6 of whom are from the United States and Canada. Printed in a little brochure, which Lily gave me, was the anthem of the Progress Center. To quote a few lines: "Progress is a state of mind ... of winning for all time. We are a community of hope ... a family of friends. The most precious thing is the human spirit. Today we are the leaders in Nukus. The future belongs to us!" Lily is a rare and very inspirational lady. I wish her and her charges the very best as she continues to work her miracle.

Addendum: A Cautiously Optimistic Note about the Aral Sea

I have described the Aral Sea as a salt-encrusted wasteland, a planned causality of mass-scale cotton farming. The ecology of the desiccated region and the health of its human population had looked very dismal from the vantage point of my visit in 2000. Then, in 2006, in a pleasant turn of events, the Aral Sea seemed to be enjoying a new lease on life, in large part due to a joint effort by Kzakstan (now flush with oil money), and the World Bank project I had disparaged earlier in this chapter. I was reminded of the improvement that had taken place to Owens Lake through the modest effort to replenish a small portion of its water.

Through repair to the banks of the Syr Darya River, coupled with a strategically placed eight-mile-long dike, there has been a doubling of the river flow into the northern end of the lake. Six years after my visit, the water level in this, the "Small Aral" portion of the lake, has risen by nine feet. This has markedly reduced the salinity of the water, raising the prospect that, through concerted effort (and much more extensive international loans), it may actually be possible to at least partially reverse one of the biggest environmental catastrophes in history. New, salt-tolerant flora is being planted, and an imported type of fish has been found to survive the saline water. Even a new strain of cotton has been created whose deep roots can survive the dry conditions of the area. Unfortunately, the plant produces less, and quite rough-textured, cotton.

There are certainly grounds for cautious optimism, but many issues remain. The lake may be filling from the north, but not from the south. The other mighty river, the Amu Darya, remains as I observed it—just a tiny stream flowing through Nukus, essentially dry by the time it reaches the lake. Any new effort to increase its flow awaits economic improvement in Uzbekistan, who now must also contend with the rapidly increasing diversion of upstream Amu Darya water by Afghanistan, another border neighbor who has become a much more vocal claimant to a portion of this river's water.

12
Doing Civic Education

Exporting the "American Way"

The organization I worked for as a visiting lecturer, The Civic Education Project, was, in the broadest sense, exporting the "American Way." Exactly what is meant by the American Way surely would fill a good number of pages and produce much debate. However, most Americans would likely agree that it includes a belief that the entire world's people should be able to live in a condition of individual freedom with rights similar to those we enjoy. Some people even say that America wouldn't be America if we weren't constantly out there in the world helping people to achieve these ideals. It is assumed that we need not proselytize this belief, but instead, all people naturally have a desire to be free. President George W. Bush's often quoted statement that "Human freedom is a God-given gift to all humanity" might be seen by some as putting it rather bluntly, but what he said follows directly from the belief in the universal, immutable, self-evident truths ("Natural Rights") on which our country was founded. It is important to emphasize the word "universal" in the above statement. It is the key to understanding America's sense of mission in the world. Even though what the president said might not be too fashionable in some quarters, and is without question culturally ethnocentric, the president is on firm, even hallowed, ground in making such a pronouncement.

Whatever might be the current thinking about what the U.S. role in the world should be or how to justify it, going "over there" as CEPers to assist nation building in word and deed, to help spread the ideas of democracy and liberal economy, was clearly our business at hand. I doubt most of us thought about it this way very much, if at all, but, nevertheless, we worked at it, doing civic education every day. My work can be usefully divided between doing civic education through outreach activities, which is the focus of this chapter, and my classroom efforts to encourage civic-minded scholarship in our students, which the next chapter describes.

Building Democracy

We were "over there" to be helpful, yes, but more fundamentally, we were in the land that totalitarianism had ruled, to make a convincing case for the kind of economic and political attitudes that are fundamental to the development of democratic institutions.

We were hardly alone in our endeavors. We were part of a large wave of democratic government entities, international nongovernmental organizations (NGO), even several religious groups, all recently arrived in the newly independent countries of the former Soviet Empire. In one way or another, all of us were there to assist in and further some portion of the prospects for individual freedom, economic competition, and democracy. In the broadest sense of the word, we were all doing our part to develop the cultural and associational foundation for individual freedom and political democracy.

A new millennium was about to begin with an explosion of countries, previously totalitarian, now claming to be pursuing a democratic path. The big question, assuming their sincerity, concerned the prospects for their success. Certainly the history of democracy-development in the world did not leave many grounds for optimism. Even now, it appeared that some of these newly independent countries, especially in Central Asia, were wrapping themselves in democratic rhetoric while their old Communist elite remained quite firmly entrenched in autocratic power. However, other countries, particularly in Central/Eastern Europe, were genuinely making progress.

I had read some of the transition literature and knew some of the issues, but it was quite a different thing to experience events on the ground firsthand. For instance, during my first year as a visiting lecturer, it was obvious that Lithuania was having a very hard time keeping its economy from further deterioration. Such impoverishment appeared to be strengthening the case for a return to socialism/Communism. In stark contrast, Estonia gave every appearance of success in transitioning its economy towards capitalism and its polity into a viable democracy.

Yet it wasn't until our third year, when Judy and I arrived in Ukraine, that we were to witness a really hard-fought struggle to institute democracy. After several years of independence, Ukraine had not managed to make much progress in becoming a democratic society. It continued to be governed by a well-ensconced and very corrupt president and his ministerial cronies. It was at this point that I began to see—on the street and through the eyes of my students—what an uphill and very unpredictable battle the whole democratization process could be. I was also following the situation in neighboring Russia, a country that began its experiment with democracy to much fanfare only to experience severe economic setback and social dislocation. And now it had a leader in President Vladimir Putin who seemed to act ever more like a czar.

Two years later, during our posting in Uzbekistan, I learned what it was really like to live in a totalitarian, thoroughly undemocratic society. It was only then that I seriously began to consider the prospects for democracy and the chance for people to live freely. The importance of civic society and how I might be able to help implement it moved to the forefront of my attention.

Open Society

The mission of the CEP, and the question of the prospects for making a successful transition to democracy, can be examined through two concepts: open society and civic society. The rudiments of open society have a somewhat familiar ring to them. They sound a bit like democracy, only they are much more comprehensive. Its basic elements are listed in George Soros recent book, *Open Society* (p.133) There are seven:

- Regular, free, and fair elections;
- Free and pluralistic media;
- The rule of law upheld by an independent judiciary;
- Constitutional protection for minority rights;
- A market economy that respects property rights and provides opportunities and a safety net for the disadvantaged;

- A commitment to the peaceful resolution of conflicts; and
- Laws that are enforced to curb corruption.

Mr. Soros didn't invent the concept of open society, rather, he attributed that to his academic mentor, the British philosopher Carl Popper. However, Mr. Soros definitely did the most to popularize the concept, in good part because the words he used in his books commanded attention due to his position as one of the world's financially most successful individuals. The concept is also well-known because Mr. Soros selected it as the title for his Open Society Foundation, the international framework for much of his multimillion-dollar philanthropic activities. Through this foundation with its many branches throughout the former Soviet Russian Empire, George Soros has become almost a household word "over there," although relatively few people know of him here in America.

The concept of open society rests on the fundamental assumption that people create their collective reality as a part of developing, maintaining, and changing their culture. Our understanding of social conditions or of what is "real and true" is thus always imperfect and never final. There is no absolute truth other than the self-fulfilling type. We are fallible.

Faced with these limitations or opportunities (depending on one's point of view), it is imperative that we create the conditions for the open exchange of differing ideas: regular, free and fair elections; the rule of law upheld by an independent judiciary; and a commitment to the peaceful resolution of conflicts. These and other conditions define open society. They are the minimum conditions that have proven to be a safeguard against absolutism and the arrogance that accompanies the idea of infallibility, whatever its guise, or however strong its appeal. These are the main conditions that create the basis for democracy. The Civic Education Project was about helping to lay the foundation for open society.

Civic Society

Civic society functions to establish and support an open society. Fortunately, I was familiar with the concept of civic society, having begun to teach about it after Ronald Reagan became president and invited Americans to reconsider the importance of civic society and expand the old idea of volunteerism. President Reagan viewed voluntary social assistance organizations as a modern remedy for our expensive, and he felt, morally corrosive dependence on the government for a vast array of social services. In this sense, civic society meant encouraging more people to work together to solve their own problems.

I like the definition of civic society offered by David Boaz in his book *Libertarianism* (p.127): "all the natural and voluntary associations that grow up around individual and group interests, and through which we express our interests and values outside of and distinct from the state." There can be an amazing variety of such associations: families, churches, schools, clubs, fraternal societies, neighborhood groups, professional associations, benevolent societies, labor organizations, and many, many more!

As the leading example of civic society, America is often referred to as a nation of voluntary associations, "a nation of joiners." It is through all this organized civic activity that our democracy works. After the Communists seized power in Russia, they deliberately suppressed the existence of all voluntary associations. Without any intermediary groups to come to their defense, to stand up for their individual interests, the Soviet people became clients of the state, dependent, controlled, and waiting for government functionaries to act on their behalf. This is a mentality that was easily recognizable from the former Soviet period. I observed it many times over in many of my students. Polls in Hungary, Ukraine, and most other Eastern and Central European states, continually showed that a very large number, sometimes a majority of post-Soviet people, lacking an appreciation for voluntary associations, still thought that the government should take care of them cradle to grave.

I remember a Czech lady who rented Judy and me a room during our week-long stay in Prague. She had been a Communist Party member, working as a tourist guide during Soviet times. Sitting in our second-story room, she looked out the window and began complaining to us of the graffiti on the apartment houses in the area. I suggested that the apartment house owners form a Neighborhood Watch and explained how this type of group might be organized. I mentioned that a paint crew could be created to remove the offending "art work." She responded rather indignantly with, "These things are the government's responsibility."

In another example, when our Ukrainian university grounds became littered with trash, I suggested to some students, during a guest lecture, that a clean-up project be organized, complete with media coverage. Their initial response: "Not our responsibility." I had to work fast, having only one class period to plant the idea of volunteerism in their mind. They were also concerned that such volunteerism might take away people's jobs. The jobs concern was a lingering result of the Soviet effort to artificially create a full employment economy. This often resulted in dividing up little menial tasks so everybody would have some work to do.

In contrast to the above example, my students would have recognized the importance of not relying so heavily on government services. They had heard my lectures, read the photocopied material I had assigned, and written essays about it. For example, I helped my student Olga Nosova gather and organize material to write a research paper on privatizing health care delivery in her country. She was intrigued with the idea as it was such a contrast to anything she had known growing up. Olga's mother was a doctor struggling with the limitations of Ukraine's increasingly deteriorating national health care system, which had been inherited from the Soviets.

Another of my students, Olga Ivanova, came right to the point about passivity and dependence upon government in her research paper, "New Social Identities: How to Get from Totalitarianism to Civic Society." She and Anna Smirnova, a Russian student at Yaroslavl State University, both presented their papers in a session I chaired at the International Student Conference in Budapest. Anna's paper, "Russia in Search of New Identity," saw the problem as how to effect a transition from an ethnically based conception of identity, *russkij*, to a national identity, *rossiyanin*, which would include the absolutely critical ingredient of active involvement in the life of the state. Both students were concerned that the legacy of totalitarianism would make it all too easy for post-Soviet people to support the type of ultra-nationalist antidemocratic organizations that were springing up. Anna concluded her paper by noting the need for a shift to an identity more supportive of active involvement in the civic life of the country. "Admittedly, there exists a certain generation gap in Russia: the younger and the older generations build identities on different bases; for the young, it is new opportunities in self-realization while for the older generation, the concern is for restoration of the former feeling of all-embracing security."

These were the reminders of how the Soviets had created a thoroughly dependent form of mentality. In contrast, civic education was about helping to foster the climate of natural and voluntary associations that make up civic society, all of which creates citizens rather than clients. Citizens understand their own problems and believe in their capacity to work together to solve them; they are "self-actualizing," as Anna stated. In sum, civic society and open society are almost two sides of the same coin. Each of these two concepts describes arrangements and conditions that are mutually interdependent in building democracy.

Doing Civic Education

We CEPers were busy implementing these concepts, not only in our teaching, but also in a wide variety of "outreach projects." One example involved a speaking engagement offered to me as a result of a relationship I developed with a faculty member at a graduate school in Kharkiv. The subject of my remarks would truly have been considered as unimaginable were they to have taken place just a few years earlier. On this occasion, other than a touch of pride, what stood out most prominently in my mind was that I was really where I was and doing what I was doing. It was as though I had to keep pinching myself to make sure I was not dreaming.

This unique speaking and lecturing experience began shortly after Judy and I arrived in Kharkiv, through a chance meeting with Valeri Shur, the head of the foreign language department of the Academy of Public Administration. The Academy had recently become well-known as one of Ukraine's two leading schools offering graduate training for current and prospective government officials. Dr. Shur happened to be standing next to me while we were both having a brandy during the intermission of a ballet performance. He invited me to visit the school. Less than an hour into my visit, as I finished sitting through a long greeting by the school's director, Dr. Grigory Mostoviy, I was offered a teaching position on the spot. We settled for the promise of several guest lectures.

During my year in Ukraine, I visited the academy on many occasions to speak to classes and work individually with many of the students. I frequently lectured on the topic of civic society and volunteerism. One lecture topic was built around the subject of adding entrepreneurialism into government. My main reference for the lecture was the recently published *Reinventing Government* by Osborne and Gaebler. It had become a best-selling book on this subject in America. It was a profoundly ironic experience to have Dr. Mostoviy in attendance at my lectures. He had also been the director during Soviet times when the school was then called the Academy for Truth and Right Thinking, a Communist Party training center. I could not help but wonder what he thought as he listened to the reasons for reducing government, putting the customer first, outsourcing services, assisting civic development, and making government compete in a capitalist market.

What Dr. Mostoviy may have thought of my remarks was surely put to the test later in April when I was invited to give a major address on the topic of civic society to a conference being held at the academy. The conference was attended by government officials from Ukraine as well as Poland and Russia. The theme of the conference, a bit rough in its English translation on the brochure was; "Problems of Forming a Welfare State in Conditions of Transformation of Ukrainian Society." The title, emphasizing the need to expand government, provided an absolutely perfect opportunity for me to make the contrarian case for the absolutely central relationship between limited government, liberal economic policy, and the resultant vibrant, productive array of civic institutions. There I was, sharing the platform with Dr. Mostoviy, formally the champion of Communism. What was his thinking now? I couldn't tell. He smiled at me several times, but he kept his thoughts to himself.

In previous chapters, I have mentioned or described other examples of the civic education outreach activities of my organization: activities such as curriculum design and implementation, preparation of teaching materials, library development, special projects, conferences, and much more. These activities, in addition to my teaching, pressed me to rethink the purposes of social science disciplines such as mine.

As an undergraduate and graduate student, I had primarily learned to think of sociology as revolving around its own internal, "ivory tower" concerns. Such concerns were "pure," rather than "applied," and in my field, this meant that we should be more attentive to sociological problems (matters related to scientific thinking about society), rather than solving social problems. Then, as a CEP visiting lecturer, I began to ask myself why the CEP was built around the social science disciplines and not any of the dozens of others. Why not literature, chemistry, art, biology, or business courses? It was only then that I began to realize just how important some of the Western social science disciplines were in supporting civic society and preparing young people to understand and appreciate democratic institutions, especially citizenship and its all-important ingredient, civic activism. What I discovered was an example of the sociological concept of "latent function:" an unrecognized contribution. The underlying reason for teaching social science classes became much clearer. Not long afterwards, I was involved in a large faculty training project that consequently took on a much more important meaning. I wasn't doing just sociology; I was actually doing civic education!

Teaching Teachers

During our last year in the CEP, while posted in Tashkent, Uzbekistan, I got a chance to put the democracy-building function of social science to extensive use. As an outreach activity, I got involved in a four-week university teacher-training project sponsored by Tashkent-based Open Society Assistance Foundation (OSAF), the only Soros foundation in Central Asia. Zulfya Tursunova, a tall dark-haired Uzbek woman in her mid twenties, had recently become the foundation's Higher Education Program coordinator and the training project director. Zulfya had a master's degree she had earned from Kent State University in Ohio. Through the efforts of Zulfya and her predecessor, OSAF was in its third year of assisting the initial development of university-level social science disciplines in Uzbekistan. The teacher-training project was a brand-new initiative, a start-from-scratch effort.

Like the other newly independent countries of the former empire, the Republic of Uzbekistan had been bequeathed a system of higher education purposely devoid of curriculum in the social sciences, including an understanding of how to do scholarly level social research. Additionally, it was an educational system built around instruction rather than active learning. Increasingly frustrated with the lack of improvement, many faculty members at the several universities were in agreement with OSAF that major changes would need to be made to the old Soviet educational paradigm. However, any changes would have to occur in the context of increased funding. Yet it was extremely unlikely that the state would provide the funding as its overall support for higher education had been declining. Higher education enrollment had also fallen from 14 percent of Uzbekistan's university-age group at the time of independence, to half this amount the year I was there.

What additional funding there might have been, it would quite likely have been held up by a fear on the part of the ruling elite that any educational steps toward an open society leading to individual freedom and the legalization of political parties might result in chaos or worse, civil war and the possible takeover of the state by Islamic fundamentalists. A civil war had occurred in neighboring Tajikistan less than ten years earlier over the rise to power of a radical Islamist political party, and over one hundred thousand people had died as a result. It seemed as though the Uzbekistan government elite were scared to death of democracy, planned to hold on to power as best they could, and did not seriously intend to do much about helping develop the social sciences in the universities, at least not in the short run.

It had been, and would continue to be, an uphill effort for OSAF to make a difference for higher education faced, as it was, with this level of official hypocrisy and intransigence. In the end, they would lose the battle. But for now, undeterred, OSAF continued to fund projects aimed at assisting the development of the social sciences. One of the first foundation initiatives used the assistance of several CEP lecturers. Throughout Uzbekistan and the other newly independent Central Asian countries, a large number of regional college and university professors were struggling to teach the new social sciences. They had none of the right books and only a little knowledge of their discipline or how to teach it.

To help address this deficiency, OSAF began to set up a number of regional libraries containing social science books and curriculum resources. While most of the more than eighty thousand titles placed in the new libraries were written in English, expensive arrangements were ongoing to translate some of this material into Russian and Uzbek. At the same time, the foundation underwrote several special summer school programs, organized and staffed mainly by CEP lecturers with the purpose of creating a pool of academics with a good command of their new social science discipline. All the participants' costs, including transportation and attendance, were paid for by OSAF.

Unfortunately, the foundation had overestimated the qualifications of its target audience. The first summer schools were severely handicapped in what they could accomplish by the fact that they had been unable to recruit academics with at least a midlevel knowledge of their social science discipline. There were none. To help redress this pressing deficiency, OSAF came up with a new, and this time very successful, initiative: the Teacher Training Workshops. Again, they turned to CEP lecturers for help, and this is where I got involved.

The four separate week-long workshops were offered in the smaller regional universities for the few existing social science professors as well as the majority of professors who were about to teach a course in one of the social sciences for the first time. The purpose of the program was to develop fundamental disciplinary knowledge, increase exposure to a variety of active teaching and learning techniques, and offer assistance in curriculum design and implementation.

A team of six trainers was assembled. Hooman Peimani and Carter Johnson were political scientists, one Swiss and the other Canadian. There were two philosophers with specialization in teaching methods; Chad Thompson was our other Canadian, and Victoria Levinskaya, a Russian Uzbek, was a Fulbright scholar and CEP local faculty fellow. Yuliana, a Korean Uzbek citizen, was a local high school English teacher who would offer sessions on critical thinking. I was the lone sociologist. At various times, the team included up to four part-time translators and interpreters as most workshop sessions were conducted in English with full translation into Russian, Uzbek, or Karakalpak as circumstances required. In addition to her workshop presentations, Victoria translated my reading material and interpreted most of my workshop sessions as well. By the third workshop, sitting next to me, in front of the class, she would lean over and quietly say, "Yes, yes, I know what you are going to say, so OK, I will do it." She even knew my jokes! I never realized how quickly we teachers could fall into such predictable routines!

Nukus State University

The teacher training team apprehensively began their first full week-long workshop in early November 2000 in Nukus, the agricultural city and administrative center for the semiautonomous region of Karakalpakstan with its ethnically distinctive population.

We were to conduct our workshop at the regional university in Nukus, a pleasant oasis of trees and grass on the edge of the city, surrounded on three sides by open fields that were covered with ugly salt deposits and abandoned partially constructed concrete structures. Upon our chilly morning arrival at the university in two small minivans, we were met by at least a hundred or more students out cleaning up the school grounds. Was this an example of my long sought-after club project, a lesson in civic education? No, it was Soviet-style "volunteerism" by university presidential edict. The Russian word for this kind of turnout is *subotnik*. It originally meant "Saturday volunteer." It was touted in Soviet propaganda as a glorious example of citizenship under Communism. Of course, there was never anything voluntary or glorious about it. It was forced labor.

Approximately forty teachers from the area's two universities met with us early Monday morning in a banquet hall to listen to opening remarks and be divided into two groups based on pedagogical interest and disciplinary specialization. For the week, we had scheduled two separate morning and afternoon workshop sessions each day. (See Appendix 4.)

My sessions took place in a second-floor classroom. Arrayed around the four walls were large framed pictures of bearded men who represented the most learned of the historical elite of the region. Hanging in the front of the room attired in suit and tie, with no beard, was a big picture of Uzbekistan's President Islam Karimov. I began my first session by putting the desks in a U-shape, constructing large name cards, and watching the class fill to about twenty-five teachers, including the vice rector who was a teacher and regional representative to the national (rubber stamp) parliament. The class was about evenly divided by gender, and ranged in age at least into the sixties. Without exception, all the teachers were ethnic Karakalpaki: short, heavy-set, with dark complexion and black hair. I was the only one without any hair, and Victoria, who did most of my interpretation, had long blond hair. We certainly made quite a contrast.

Using a large easel full of notepaper, my morning sessions covered sociological concepts and principles, basic vocabulary, major disciplinary issues, and the scientific as well as humanistic nature of the discipline. My afternoon sessions were on teaching techniques, internship programs, and the theory of civic society. As part of the civic society presentation, I circulated a notebook full of brochures gathered at my university in Boise during a volunteer fair. They were from dozens of nonprofit social service and volunteer-based agencies and organizations. This made it easy to illustrate a very essential type of civic organization as well as an important way in which these organizations recruited their help.

Capping off the week of workshops was a hotly debated unit on the state of civic society in Uzbekistan and the prospects for the country to transition into an open, democratic society. I found a mix of opinion concerning these topics. There was the expected "it is not my responsibility" response. Some teachers invoked what a philosophy professor in Tashkent had described to me as the "Central Asian mentality." This view expresses doubt over the prospects for a democratic future. It assumes the need for a strongman leader. It sounded to me like a new form of Genghis Khan, although hopefully less brutal, must continue to run the country while severely limiting individual freedoms. It is a view based not only on history, but also a realistic understanding of the continued prominence of ethnic and tribal division and conflict. This kind of potential for conflict appears to be a prominent feature common to all the seven "stans" (countries) of Central Asia. Only a strong, even ruthless national leader, so the argument goes, could manage to keep the peace among the many local factions.

As to the prospects for democracy, other workshop teachers were cynical, for good reason, about the reform intentions of Uzbekistan's president, an obvious "strongman" who had managed to stay at the top of the country's power elite since before the fall of the Soviet Union, and may actually remain as president-for-life, if he so chooses.

Everybody was notably frustrated with the slow pace, if not actually the lack, of significant economic and political change. However, most of the teachers wanted to be optimistic about their future. I tried to build my remarks on this desire. I have always felt strongly that a positive attitude best equips people to work for change. Too much criticism can foster a negative attitude that can paralyze the human spirit. I have seen it more than once in my profession.

The author with CEP local scholar Victoria Levinskaya (to my right) along with "Z Girl" my student interpreter (to my left), finish their teacher-training workshop at Nukus, Uzbekistan.

The first run of the Teacher Training Project in Nukus was not all work and no play. At the end of the week, all of the training team, including our interpreters and program coordinator were invited to one of the teacher's homes to have dinner. A few other teachers pitched in to help prepare the meal, and I suspect they also helped to purchase the food. It was classic Uzbekistan hospitality. Arranged on a very long table was food and drink in overabundance with more food constantly being served from the kitchen. Every so often during the dinner, the customary vodka toast would be made until everyone had his or her chance to complement the women hosting the dinner, at least once if not more times. When we were all completely stuffed, a bit light-headed, and thinking the dinner was over, out came a large fish, taken that morning from the nearby river. I thought about the river's terribly polluted water, but in politeness to our hosts, I tried the fish anyway. It was delicious. Then came one final entree, a complete, well-preserved, smoked turkey! We absolutely had no more room to eat anything more. Saying that we would eat this later, the turkey went back to our hotel in the trunk of the private car that we had borrowed from the university rector. There, in the trunk, remaining quite frozen, it bounced around for six hours all the way to the Aral Sea and back the next morning. A day later, we finally remembered it was still in the trunk, still frozen. We had just enough time to give it to the hotel cleaning lady before leaving for our return flight to Tashkent.

Needing only a little fine-tuning arising from our initial experience, we essentially duplicated our teacher-training workshop in the western regional city of Ferghana in February and once more in the historically famous Silk Route city of Samarkand in March.

The Final Workshop

The defining objectives of the three regional workshops were reiterated and extended in a lively, week-long capstone workshop session held in Tashkent in May. Instruction was in English and Russian, interpreted into Uzbek and Karakalpaki. As selected by the workshop staff and teachers, this session brought together the most active and capable half of all the previous three workshop participants. We held the workshop in a newly constructed hotel built with Turkish money and shortly thereafter sold to a Japanese hotel group. The hotel was one of the few signs of change that had started to affect the landscape of Tashkent before new government policies pretty much shut down foreign investment. Only two metro stops from our apartment, the hotel was also the one location in the city, which I knew of, that sold at least a limited number of Western newspapers and news magazines.

There were four main purposes for this last session. We wanted to follow up with additional exposure to the content of the social science disciplines. Also, we were particularly anxious to review the progress that the teachers had made in designing their new course curriculums. A third purpose of the session was to role-play new teaching approaches we had introduced in the regional workshops. Finally, it was very important that the participants learn how to use the new OSAF-sponsored Curriculum Resource Centers that had been established at their schools. The resource centers would assist the teachers to train additional teachers. And again, not to emphasize all work without some play, the workshop participants came together for a big dinner and last-night session of disco dancing. It had become predictable, wherever we were in the former Soviet Russian Empire, to recognize student's affinity for disco dancing. But, neither Judy nor I had ever seen adults who loved to dance more than we witnessed in Uzbekistan!

Author joins in on the dancing during a workshop lunch break. Ferghana, Uzbekistan

It is not difficult to imagine the positive effects the workshops had on the teachers. Just to think of the opportunity all the teachers had to come together, first in their own cities where they represented different departments and different schools, and then as a single group in the final workshop. We had created a unique, and for most of the teachers, a first opportunity to be able to meet together as professionals representing a common new disciplinary interest.

Almost all of the curricular material and pedagogical method which

I introduced in my workshop sessions were new to the participants. It was as though these teachers were in the global community, but only beginning to be part of it. They had spent most of their lives confined behind Soviet boundaries, isolated from the outside world. Even now, all but a very few of the teachers in the workshops had ever been outside their country, let alone outside their local region. Most of the teachers only lived a few hundred miles from their capital, Tashkent, but the miles might as well have been counted in the thousands. The teachers read one-sided state-controlled newspapers and watched equally slanted state-controlled TV. For most of these people, the OSAF efforts have truly allowed them to become a part of the outside world of scholarly activity!

The Teacher Training Project continued for the better part of three more years after Judy and I left Uzbekistan. Additional workshops were offered and more teachers were included in an ever-expanding pool of social science knowledge and training. New library titles continued to be purchased and new translations made for the regional libraries. Teachers began training more teachers in the new curriculum, and new, much more effective summer schools have been conducted, drawing upon the pool of recently trained academics.

It may appear a bit of a stretch to try to make the connection between civic education, teacher training workshops in social science subjects, and the development of market economies and open, democratic societies. The connection is there, however, even if a little indirect. Our work in Central Asia was a very small part of the whole, a grass-roots effort with none of the glamour of the big projects such as those sponsored by U.S. Aid for International Development, or conducted by the World Bank. The financial credit must go to George Soros who had the foresight to establish his network of foundations and to sponsor the CEP and underwrite its many outreach projects. One dramatic but very unfortunate proof of our effectiveness in assisting social science higher education growth and change was that the president of Uzbekistan forced the Open Society Assistance Foundation to cease operation in 2004, calling it a "subversive organization." Left without its main source of funding, this meant that the CEP had to shut down its Uzbekistan activities as well.

13
Encouraging Civic-Minded Scholarship

Student Conferences are a Priority

The second major way in which the CEP helped to build the foundation for democracy was through its extensive support of a student conference program. Financial and academic support for undergraduate research, conference presentation, and publication was a priority second only to the instructional work of the CEP's visiting lecturers. The year before I joined the CEP, more than two hundred and thirty students from fifteen countries had given papers at regional conferences, while an additional one hundred and fifteen had presented their work at an international conference held in Vienna, Austria. During my tenure with the CEP, regional conference numbers would increase by over a third, while the single international conference would move to Budapest, Hungary and become much larger and more competitive.

A brief listing of some of the conference themes and the research paper titles of a few of my students reveal the connection between their research, conference activities, and the overall objective of furthering civic education in the countries transitioning out of the communism. Here is a sampling of conference themes and the locations: "Looking Ahead at the New Millennium: Choices for Regional Development" (Chisinau, Moldova, 1998); "Between Fear of the Future and Nostalgia for the Past: Social Exhaustion and Reform in Post-Communist Societies at the Dawn of the 21st Century" (Nizhny Novgorod, Russia, 1999); and "Ten Years After: Moving Forward, Looking Back?" (Budapest, Hungary, 1999).

Student papers were usually focused on one aspect or another of the themes of civic society and transition. While the accepted model for transformation had yet to be formulated by Western academic and policy professionals, its expression in the student papers could be summed up as an open society: politically democratic and economically market-based. It was up to each student to fill in the details. Here is a sample of paper titles taken from several different conferences; "The Potential Role of NGOs in Changing the Human Rights Climate in Bulgaria," "Institutionalization of Political Parties in Kyrgyzstan," "The Middle Class in Russia: Society Says Good-bye to a Class that Never Existed," "The Development of the Securities Market in Lithuania during 1990–1996," and "Private Ownership of Land: Problems of Legal Regulation in Estonia." Other subjects examined included privatization, gender issues, educational reform, nationalism, the advent of consumerism, ecological sustainability, NATO enlargement, and several different social welfare issues. It was an impressive level of professionalism exhibited by undergraduate students, some in their first year of university and all but a few having to write and give their papers in English.

The CEP Conference System

The conferences were organized on two levels. The regional conferences were organized by CEP lecturers and staff, and brought together students from one or more adjacent countries. They would take place in university facilities lasting over a three-day weekend. There was typically a welcoming and plenary session for all participants on the first day, followed by a day and a half of paper presentation sessions, roundtables, and discussion forums, all running concurrently. Regional conferences wrapped up on Sunday morning with a few speeches and featured several categories of awards for papers. The best papers were published as conference proceedings with multiple copies sent to all CEP lecturers for distribution to university libraries and other interested parties.

A half dozen or more of these regional conferences held during the fall and early winter throughout the former Soviet Russian Empire, culminated in a week-long international conference held in mid-April in Budapest, Hungary. The venue for the international conference was the dormitory/conference center of Central European University, a recently created graduate school specializing in the social sciences and humanities. The university was the jewel of George Soros's international Higher Education Support Program (HESP), which was funded and administered from within his overall network of Open Society foundations. A number of the best CEP students, including three of my students, won all-expense scholarships to attend this university.

At the international conference, as was usual for all CEP conferences, the paper presentations included a moderator and discussants selected from faculty and VIP guests. These people were asked to stay up usually quite late the first evening carefully reading and judging each paper in their session(s). In addition to the papers, there were several afternoon workshops. Each year the conference week culminated in a dinner and dance cruise on the Danube River. The boat would gently pass through the heart of the city with all of its historic old buildings set off in their flood-lit magnificence. The Danube actually separates what is often mistakenly considered the two halves of the city: Buda from Pest. Actually each half was a city in its own right at an earlier time.

Judy and I attended this exciting international conference in 1999 during the time we were living in Kharkiv. We were accompanied by four of my students. Oksana Bratchikova gave her paper on victim's rights. Sergey Koltakov spoke about the increasing problem of ethnic discrimination in several of the transitioning countries. Olga Ivanova's presentation was about the need for people to acquire a new social identity as part of the transition from totalitarianism to civil society. I had the pleasure of chairing her session. I was glad to see her do so well, as she had stayed up much of the night worrying about the details of her presentation. Irina Yaroschuk's paper was a critical analysis of Ukraine's approach to the small but growing problem of drug abuse.

Boat rides and chairing paper sessions with my students represented the culmination of a long process of preparation and organization. This chapter highlights some of the details and events associated with this process. As one of our CEP lecturers, Janet Helin, experienced, the successful conference was nothing less than a miracle. Janet was thinking of the things that can increase the danger to life and limb associated with attending conferences during the icy cold winter months in most of Eastern/Central Europe and Russia. She ought to know. While involved in conference activities, Janet was attacked by dogs, fell out of a train, fell through a snow-covered steam grate, and was sent tumbling down a flight of icy stairs by another CEP lecturer who stumbled and fell ahead of her. Janet was carried from one conference to her departing train with two broken toes. Accidents like these were surely the most dramatic part of the conference portion of our work. Less recognized were all the details involved in making sure that qualified students were bringing high quality research reports to these conferences.

Assuring a Plentiful Number of Good Conference Papers

Getting students ready to participate in a conference was a mixture of what I had learned at Boise State University coupled with a lot I was soon to learn about how this particular conference system operated. There was much unchartered territory. This was especially the case when I typically had to prepare several students to give their papers at different conferences on different dates and in different countries. And this was only the first part of the effort. There were still all the unfamiliar logistical tasks of getting students, and sometimes Judy and me, to the conferences on time and back home safely.

Needless to say, the student conferences were a university educator's dream. In all four countries where I was a visiting lecturer, I would begin my two fall classes by requesting that each of the students begin immediately to research a social problem topic and develop a policy solution. After a few introductory class meetings, the classroom topic turned to basic instruction on how to properly conduct research. Everyone got one of my guidelines for writing a research proposal (Appendix 5). I set a firm time line with dates for each step of the student's work: topic selection, research proposal, outline and bibliography, first draft, and so on, all the way to completion and presentation of the paper in class and at our flat.

Because students were competing in more than one conference venue, there was always more than one time line to juggle. One "Schedule for Completion of Research Papers" I posted in my Uzbekistan classroom contained separate schedules for four conferences and ten students. Assuming they met my schedule criteria and dates, these students would travel to Samarkand, Nizhny Novgrored, Bishkek, or Budapest, and some would go to more than one location. It is hard not to brag about my students; I typically sent between twelve to sixteen students to a conference each year, well above the CEP norm. They were talented, and they worked hard for a chance to be accepted.

Eugeniya Skkiba gives her research paper at a CEP student conference held at Samarkand State Institute of Foreign Languages, Uzbekistan

Each year, about the forth week of the semester, "call for papers" announcements would be e-mailed to all lecturers throughout the CEP network. I would post a copy of each of these prominently in front of the classroom. I needn't have made them as obvious as the announcements were highly anticipated by the students. The solicitations included suggested fields and topics for research focus (Appendix 6).

Students didn't normally think of the research and paper writing as exposing them to the facts and issues of civic society. Besides offering a rare opportunity for international travel, working hard and having their paper selected for conference presentation could be one of the most important considerations in a successful scholarship application to study abroad. It was also a very important key to gaining a job with one of the increasing number of foreign business and nongovernmental organizations flooding into Russia and much of Eastern and Central Europe.

My students had to conduct their research under the constraint of extremely limited library resources. Journals containing up-to-date research reports were also almost nonexistent. To help matters a little, I loaned out my extensive clipping and article files and brought current newsmagazines and international newspapers to class as quickly as I finished reading them.

Except in Estonia, very few of my students had access to the Internet other than through very expensive Internet cafes. In Uzbekistan, the government blocked many Internet sites deemed to possibly contain material that was critical of their activities or policies.

Writing about Corruption

While teaching at National University of Uzbekistan, I received a call for papers on a large and timely theme: corruption. It was an announcement of the tenth international, NGO sponsored, Anticorruption Conference, which promised to bring together in Prague, Czech Republic, more than 1,500 anticorruption professionals from all over the world. This was the first time the conference was to be held within the territory of the former Soviet Russian Empire, and, most important, the first time the program would include student papers.

Suggested topics for student paper proposals included "attacking corruption in education." I posted the call for papers announcement on the door to the CEP office. Two of my students immediately approached me concerning this opportunity. They were very enthusiastic, but noticeably frightened about the possible repercussions, personally and to their families, that researching and delivering a paper on this topic might incur. Corruption had been, according to my students, a part of higher education for a long time, but it had ratcheted up considerably since independence. I first heard my students complain about it when

I was posted to Kharkiv State University. The causes were the same in Uzbekistan. The government had begun reducing educational funding and cutting the salaries of faculty and staff. Teachers needed to supplement their meager salaries, and many caved into the temptation to take money.

Good grades were available at a price. Even the best students found it necessary to pay bribes in order to obtain earned high grades. The typical procedure was to pay a student intermediary to make the arrangement, for one class grade, or for grades in all the semester's classes. University officials were aware of these practices, but my students told me that they seldom turned their attention to the matter. My students were upset and defeated over the issue, but found themselves with little recourse other than to put up with it. Lucky for them, bribery appeared to be more prevalent in the elite universities where students had more money.

I encouraged both of my students to write research papers about corruption in the university and suggested a methodology that started with interviewing one trusted school confident and branching out through a personal network to confidential interviews with other university students, teachers, and staff members. I showed them the research paper one of Carter's students had written the year before that earned this student a trip to the International Student Conference in Budapest. I felt that this might increase their resolve, and suggested that they should consider following up on this student's research by adding additional empirical verification to some of her assertions.

Carter's student had correctly pointed out that corruption, which included bribery and using connections to get things done illegally, was a cultural legacy of the Soviet regime. Her paper asserted that students were able to pay for answers to university entrance examinations, or that students who had the wherewithal need rarely if ever attend classes but instead pay the teacher for a grade. I told my two students about an essay I received in Ukraine that offered a very perceptive statement on the latent consequences of corruption. One might wonder, as the student did, that if as a result of university corruption, students graduate badly educated and critically illiterate, then where is the hoped-for prosperity of their state to come from?

Sitting in our little CEP office at the university, discussing my students fears about their safety as well as that of their families was, for me, another incredible example of totalitarianism, probably the most disturbing of many I had encountered. One student quit part way through her research following a threat from one of the teachers she was interviewing. The threat was serious. The teacher would see to it that the student was dismissed from the university! The second student cautiously and discreetly completed his research and was accepted to the conference. The conference organizers ended up paying all his expenses, but not before he had to come up with an international airline ticket. Judy and I lent him half the cost, and I was able to get the CEP to match the other half. His brave effort to research this dangerous topic and deliver his paper at the conference paid off for him. He was able to land the rare, well-paying NGO job upon graduation.

Organizing Our Own Conference

Toward the beginning of our second year in the CEP, Judy decided that it would be fun to organize a regional conference in Tallinn. She would take on the job of organizer, including prime mover and shaker. My colleague, Simon, and I would be her "gofers." The three of us agreed to this arrangement, noting also that it would be a good way to fulfill a portion of our responsibility to become involved in useful outreach activity. We approached our university with the idea. The administration was excited about hosting such a prestigious conference. We then brought our idea up at the fall retreat, gaining unanimous approval from our country director and the other visiting lecturers located throughout the Baltic States. It was an easy sell as each vote came with a bus ticket to Tallinn, which was just about every lecturer's favorite city. Students would be selected from throughout our administrative region, which included Kaliningrad, Lithuania, Latvia, Estonia, and Belarus. St. Petersburg, Russia, was added for this particular occasion.

The conference title selected was "Economic and Social Change: A Question of Balance." The title reflected the fact that economic improvement throughout the Baltic region, while significant and growing quickly, was popularly (and quite correctly) thought to be very uneven. A few people were getting very rich while initial economic growth was contributing little, if any, to the welfare of most people, especially the unemployed and those on pensions.

The transition to market-based economy was being widely misperceived. A large majority of citizens thought that the disappearance of Communism and its replacement with capitalism would not only bring immediate economic improvement but also a rapidly rising standard of living for everybody. Such a condition takes some time, but few people seemed willing to wait much longer for life to get better for them. The distinct possibility existed that the spectacle of a few with much new wealth, much of it gained through connivance, corruption, and other forms of illegal behavior, coupled with little improvement for just about everybody else, would drive many people to use their newly granted vote to return Communists back to power! In Russia the Communist Party had retained its name as an official party and had a large following. Communists elsewhere in Eastern/Central Europe had generally changed only their label to something using the words "democrat," "people's," or "socialist," while continuing to woo the disaffected with egalitarian rhetoric. In several countries, such as Ukraine, Communists were being elected to positions of power. Nobody knew how far this might go. An insightful analogy offered by one of my CEP colleagues described the situation as like a horse race between a sometime popular Communist nag who knew how to quickly get out in front of the pack, and the dark horse of market capitalism, expected by the economic handicappers to pull ahead in the stretch and thereby win the race. Capitalist transitions definitely take patience.

Armed with a conference title that tried to reflect the political scene, Judy, Simon, and I started our planning in late October. We consulted the little booklet on outreach activities that was given to each CEP lecturer at the time of initial orientation into the organization. The booklet contained a single sheet on "How to Organize a Student Conference in 26 Easy Steps." Another place in the booklet noted that "Large projects take a great deal of time and energy to organize and might not be worth the effort." There were cautions concerning the difficulty of fund-raising, commitment of local participants, and in several places, speaking of outreach activities in general, the booklet warned about the battle with poor logistical and communications infrastructure. Our enthusiasm remained undampened as we plunged ahead.

The conference was planned for mid-March. As the three of us would fly home for a Christmas break that would extend into early February, we therefore had a little more than two month's planning time remaining. Obtaining the necessary funding turned out to be relatively easy. The Open Society Foundation in Lithuania and its sister organization, the Renaissance Foundation in Latvia, both part of the Soros foundation network, each offered a five-thousand-dollar grant to assist students who would come to the conference from these two countries. Victoria Middleton, public affairs officer at the American embassy in Estonia, helped us arrange a Democracy Grant for ten thousand dollars. Our budget total now came to a generous level that would ensure a good quality conference.

Judy began to kick into high gear. She was operating like a professional. One would never guess that she had no background in event planning, only the experience of attending one previous regional conference with me the year before. Simon had attended a regional conference the year before as a CEP lecturer stationed in Poland. I thought it might be a latent talent that Judy had for this kind of thing, until I remembered her long and successful experience as the chief family planner and manager.

Schedules were mocked up for the conference, and opening addresses by dignitaries were penciled in. Eighteen ninety-minute paper presentation sessions were blocked out. Each session would include a chair and a discussant and four student presenters. VIPs from the university, the NGO community, the American embassy, even the U.S. ambassador to Estonia were recruited to fill some of the functionary positions. Fat Margaret's (*Paks Margareeta* in Estonian) Restaurant, a little pizza place in Old Town popular with the ex-pat community, was hired to cater the reception. The food would be U.S.-style pizza slices, hoagies, wraps, vegetables and dips, beer, wine, and champagne. A closing award ceremony was set to conclude the four-day conference. All the planning was completed before Christmas. We had made good progress.

After the Christmas break, we made final arrangements. Cooks in the student cafeteria anxiously prepared sample dishes for Judy's approval. The students would eat all of their meals at the university. Fortunately, our budget allowed for a significant upgrade to the university's normally limited cafeteria fare, which Simon and I had tried a few times early in the fall and had pronounced quite unappealing. The cooks were delighted to make use of their latent culinary skills in preparing higher quality menus. Even more than the quality of the lodging, we knew that food was a principle factor in making the conference a success. Actually, the lodging was quite nice as well: a modest two-story hotel located just a snow-covered block from the university. Rooms were neat and clean. Bathrooms were at both ends of each floor. Most importantly for this part of the world, there was hot water and the hotel was heated. We booked the entire hotel for students and out of town CEP lecturers and guests.

Participants began arriving Thursday afternoon, March 13, 1997. A big welcoming banner hung in the main university lobby. Students from the small Russian Baltic enclave of Kaliningrad traveled the furthest, having started their bus ride the previous afternoon. Students and CEP lecturers from two locations in Lithuania met up with the Latvian and Kaliningrad contingents in Riga where everybody joined together to board a newer, much larger bus for the trip north to Tallinn. Finally, a group of students and one CEP lecturer arrived by overnight train from St. Petersburg. All together, we had assembled more than seventy of the best economics, law, political science, history, and sociology students from six countries.

It was an on and off again sunny weekend with temperatures consistently below freezing. The ground was partly covered from an earlier snow. It was completely dark each day by 3:00 PM. Undaunted by the weather, the opening festivities went well. The reception food was a perfect hit with everybody, and U.S. Ambassador Lawrence Taylor's opening remarks gave the conference just the right note of seriousness and importance. The local media were there to gather material for the evening TV news broadcasts (the picture of Judy and me on the back of this book was taken at this reception).

The paper sessions began the next morning with three 9:15 presentations: one evaluating World Bank projects in Latvia, and a second on national stereotypes associated with some of the new emerging democracies. The third presentation reported on attitudes toward involvement in political party activities.

The conference was a complete success. The organization, thanks to Judy, was flawless. The CEP mandate was fulfilled, the university officials were pleased, and VIPs and those who had contributed funds were very satisfied with exit survey results. As for the students, most of their work had been successfully accomplished beforehand. It had remained for them to nervously present their paper, attend the presentations of classmates and newly made friends, and to socialize and just have fun. Many students hung around the school lounges or in their hotel rooms in the evening, talking into the early hours. Knowing that most students had little or no money to bring to the conference, each was given a small amount of local currency at registration. Some of this money was spent on necessities; some went for souvenirs. Almost all students used some of their money for trolley fare to Tallinn's historic Old Town, a must-see for anybody visiting the city.

Judy, Simon, and I had decided early in the conference planning to put on a Saturday night disco dance party at the university. Judy and I had seen this successfully done the year before at the CEP regional conference in Jelgava, Latvia. We hired a van to pick up several cases of soft drinks. An overwhelming favorite throughout the Baltic region was orange soda. We also stopped at the Saku brewery warehouse to purchase an equal amount of beer. In the weeks preceding the conference, cases of beer and pop, peanuts, pretzels and chips, and all the necessary party supplies would accumulate in Simon's and my little office on the third floor of the university.

University officials were a bit skittish about hosting a disco dance party. Such an event had never happened before. Still, they were sufficiently excited about the conference to relent on our request. They suggested the cafeteria. It was a dreary sow's ear and would never measure up to the silk purse we envisioned. We preferred the rather ornately designed auditorium. This venue took some convincing, but in the end it was worth the effort as it had a flat wooden floor that turned out to be a perfect dance location. We converted the auditorium into a French cabaret with little tables seating four, complete with colorful checkered tablecloths and little paper cups full of pretzels. We rented strobe lights and a giant faceted mirror ball for the center of the ceiling. One of my students at the law school had a boyfriend who was a well-known local disc jockey. We hired him for the evening along with his sound system and great selection of music. There were several good rock and roll songs that easily moved Judy and me to the floor on several occasions. Most everybody stayed to the end of the evening. Our student clean-up crew went to work at midnight and within about a half-hour, we were all saying good-byes to the night-watch lady.

This chapter, however, is about scholarship, not dancing and drinking the night away. On the other hand, these two things really do go together, certainly at a youthful age. We just thought it better to host and chaperone the party than have all the students wandering off downtown in search of similar entertainment. The final test of our judgment was that a head count revealed that every student and visiting lecturer was in attendance along with our guests the next morning for our Sunday session involving closing remarks and awards presentations—everybody except puckish young Simon, who as the conference master of ceremony, almost slept through his final assignment. We all sat waiting when, all decked out in his suit, Simon finally rushed in, out of breath, only five or so minutes late, but, thank goodness, with his previously prepared remarks in hand.

More Examples of Civic-Minded Scholarship

The Tallinn regional student conference, like the one the year before held in Jelgava, was only the beginning of a large number of scholarly student-oriented activities in which Judy and I participated during our four years with the CEP. As in the student conferences, each activity was designed to further the civic-minded efforts of our students. Additional events included moot court deliberations, formal debate competitions, and other special activities initiated as outreach projects by visiting lecturers or local fellows.

As an example of an additional scholarly activity, Uzbekistan visiting lecturers Leslie Champeny and Brian Farley organized a special topic conference entitled "Women in Education: Working Toward a Better Future." The conference was held in their host city, Samarkand, appropriately on March 4, 2000, which was International Women's Day. The stated purpose behind organizing the conference was very much in keeping with the CEP mission. Quoting from the *Program Announcement*:

Education is the key to effective change. Our goals for this conference are to begin to provide the women of Central Asia with the knowledge and the will to improve their present status and control their future welfare.

Such a program statement as this would likely not sound at all ambitious in America, but in Central Asia, it was not only ambitious, it was very controversial, likely heretical. The idea of women being educated to such a high level of self-actualization went totally against a still viable tradition of male educational privilege. This was part of a way of life that continued to be solidly entrenched in this mostly rural region of the world. Even in Tashkent, at the National University where I was teaching, I was aware of a female student who had to drop her studies due to financial hardship in the family and the fact that her brothers had first priority in tuition expenditures. As her mother had put it; "My daughter's husband will require that she stay home and take care of the children anyway. So it is foolish to spend money on her education."

Admittedly, most patriarchal customs had been weakened by the egalitarian ideology brought into the region by Soviet occupation, but the practice had not been weakened that much. Now, with this conference lead by CEPers Champeny and Farley, Western-style modernity was again, slowly but surely, challenging Central Asian traditions regarding women.

Judy and I were part of a chartered busload of visiting lecturers, local faculty fellows, and students who traveled to Samarkand with research papers to present to the conference. Many of the bus riders had flown into Tashkent's international airport from neighboring Central Asian republics. Also flying in, from Germany, was Kimberly Johanek, one of our twin daughters. At the time a U.S. Army captain, Kimberly was chief of military personnel at Landstuhl regional Medical Center. As a special guest of the conference, Kimberly gave a presentation on gender-sensitivity training in the U.S. Army. This was a completely new topic to almost every student at the conference.

Of equal novelty and high interest to the audience was that Kimberly was a female giving her presentation while in uniform. The armed services, as far as I was able to determine, are not a career open to women in Central Asia, certainly not in Uzbekistan. The lecture hall was packed to standing room only by the addition of a number of very curious Uzbekistan local students, including quite a few military men who somehow had been tipped off about the presentation. It was entirely possible that Kimberly may have been the first U.S. Army representative to step foot in Uzbekistan, and a bit surreptitiously at that, because government authorities almost certainly knew nothing about her presence or activity in the country.

Research for the purpose of writing a conference paper was only the main way that the CEP encouraged civic-minded scholarship. Moot courts provided a chance for law students to get involved in a wide range of court simulations. Simon Bevin led a successful moot court group all the way to the finals in Prague, Czech Republic. Their focus was on a subject in European Community Law. It was quite impressive to see that the judges of the moot court included representatives of the European Court of Justice.

Another approach used to encourage engagement with civic issues involved debating competitions. Judy and I helped to judge Soros-sponsored high school debates while we lived in Kharkiv. Some of the earlier debaters were now my university students. During our stay in Uzbekistan, my CEP colleague, Colin Spurway, applied his formidable acting skills gained as an undergraduate drama major, in assisting two teams of his Samarkand State Institute students through three ascending levels of competition all the way to the World Debating Championship held in his home town of Glasgow, Scotland. One team lost in the first of nine rounds while the other team stayed in the competition through the early rounds, long enough to beat teams from Europe and North America.

Learning about the United Nations: A Very Prescient Experience

Yet another forum for encouraging student civic-mindedness was a three-day model United Nations Security Council simulation. The program was the first of its kind to be run in Central Asia. Looking back at the experience, it turned out that our simulation came eerily close to foretelling a couple of world-changing events that were soon to take place in Central Asia and the Persian Gulf. For three days, over forty carefully prepared students and half again as many CEP fellows and staff members modeled Security Council deliberations in an old Soviet sanatorium located in Chatkal, a small village in the foothills of a very impressive snow-covered mountain range, about two hours drive north of Tashkent.

This was my colleague Carter Johnson's idea, and, having experience with this particular simulation, he took the lead on the project. As his second in command, Judy, predictably, became project manager, working up a new version of her now tried and tested "operations notebook." No detail would be overlooked and everybody knew what his or her assignment would be! Carter and I selected about ten of our students to participate. Each was provided reading assignments including background briefs and instructed to meet at our flat in the evening once a week for a group discussion of the material.

Carter and I were able to obtain financial and in-kind support for the project from the U.S. embassies in Uzbekistan and Kazakhstan, and from the U.N. Development Program, and High Commission for Refugees. Our local CEP assistant, Irena An, was an invaluable help with the many details that required working with sanatorium staff and local food and transportation officials.

Carter Johnson at our flat preparing student delegates for an upcoming U.N. Security Council simulation. Tashkent, Uzbekistan

Early in the planning, Judy and Carter accompanied Irena to the sanatorium to set up the food menus. As might be expected, the place was—no other way to describe it, just dingy. The two-story main building looked like the inside of a low-end convalescent home. Thankfully, our budget was able to at least upgrade the culinary selection. The facility contained a gymnasium, and numerous little cabins were scattered throughout the unkempt grounds. They actually looked rather inviting. There was a rather broken-down and empty swimming pool, which the groundskeeper promised to be full of fresh heated water and running by the time we would arrive in mid-May.

It was Irena's job to make sure that all the out-of-town students and CEP lecturers were picked up at the Tashkent airport. From the airport, everybody was bussed to Chatkal and the sanatorium, stopping briefly in downtown Tashkent to pick up local faculty and students. We had arrivals in Tashkent from Kyrgystan, Tajikistan, Kazakhstan, and, from Uzbekistan, a hired car (unofficial taxi) arrival from Samarkand, a four-hour drive away.

There are two interesting stories connected to these travel itineraries. On their way home from the model UN program, and following a common procedure, CEP lecturer Colin Spurway and his brother who had been a visitor and guest at the conference, flagged down a car in Tashkent for the trip back to Samarkand. Colin and his brother were an hour or so out of Tashkent, driving along, when a police car pulled out onto the highway from his hiding spot, with his flashing lights and siren on, apparently with the intention of signaling their hapless driver to the side of the road. Instead, the policeman succeeded in running his police car into the right front fender of the driver's car. Immediately the policeman took off at high speed down the road. Spurway's driver accelerated, giving him chase. What a humorous picture this must have presented. The policeman turned across the meridian and began to drive back in the opposite direction. Colin described the high-speed chase and bumpy ride as his driver cut across the brush-covered dividing strip, managing to get his car turned sideways to that of the oncoming police car. Both cars came to an abrupt stop.

The drivers approached each other for the obligatory handshake. The policeman was drunk and offered to pay for the damage if the matter could be left at that. Money would soon change hands, but not before both cars followed each other several miles on a side road to the officer's village where he was able to get the money from one of his brothers. The officer had originally planned to coerce a bribe and it backfired on him.

The second story, related, not surprisingly to the first, occurred on our way from Tashkent to the sanatorium. Our busload of students was stopped by two militia men on a rather remote strip of the highway. It was going to require a payment to proceed. We had been tipped off in route by cell phone from our Tashkent office that this was likely to happen and where it would take place. We were told that the militia would say that the road ahead was unsafe and that a fee was necessary for successful passage. Vladimir Paramonov was ready to handle this contingency. Prior to becoming one of our CEP local faculty fellows, he had once held the rank of major in the Soviet army. As we pulled to a stop, Vladimir, a big, tall man who could present a very imposing image, quickly stepped from the bus. His authoritative posture was obvious, except for the customary initial handshake. There was a rather long discussion, including, we found out later, a threat to file a report, followed by another handshake, and we were on our way without the payment of bribe. Our people took care of their people this time.

At the sanatorium we busied ourselves with last-minute details in the setup for the Security Council deliberations. We arranged tables in a large circle within the gymnasium, providing a seat for each of the fifteen students representing the permanent council members. Additional chairs were arrayed behind this inner circle to accommodate student advisors, faculty, and VIP trainers who were volunteer personnel from several embassies located in Tashkent. There were flags and banners and large table markers identifying each country. Each student wore a light blue knit shirt with the United Nations logo on the front.

Following an opening address the next morning by U.N. Resident Coordinator Pavel Kral and a thematic presentation on American foreign policy toward Afghanistan by U.S. Uzbekistan Ambassador Herbst, the Security Council meeting was gaveled to order.

The student council representatives had to determine what to do in two crisis situations Carter had very cleverly constructed. The first was a very realistic scenario, reported in the morning's fictional four page *Afghaner Monthly*, which was handed out to each participant. It reported on the fall of Afghanistan to the Taliban and the flood of refugees that had begun to move into neighboring Tajikistan. As it turned out, this scenario was very close to what actually happened less than a year later.

Then there began a series of brief country position statements about the present situation in Afghanistan followed by separate meetings by coalitions that had formed around the statements. This was followed by a return of all participants to the roundtable for resolutions, more meetings, and finally a majority vote to provide humanitarian aid to the refugees, and assistance to the growing number of displaced persons within Afghanistan. Then it was time for an interesting lunch fare consisting of a bowl of chard soup, a plate of buckwheat with small meat chunks, potato *pirozies* (deep-fried-dough-covered mashed potato), homemade peach juice, and fresh strawberries.

As the second situation was about Palestine, the explosive conflict obviously did not need to be described in any extensive way. It was already happening on the ground. On the final day of deliberations, the student delegates considered the issue of expanding the number of council members who would have permanent veto power. There was a surprise entrance by a Colin Spurway, dressed in traditional costume, playing the role of a renegade Saudi prince. The prince threatened disaster to Western powers by a terrorist organization if they did not leave the Gulf region immediately. This turned out to be an even more powerful statement of what would come to pass on September 11, 2001—just seventeen months later.

During a luncheon the following day, the U.S. and Russian ambassadors treated us to an extemporaneous, polite, but very serious and spirited exchange of views on Afghanistan. Russian Ambassador Ryurikov spoke first, not without some emotion, to the effect that, with Soviet assistance, Afghanistan had been in the process of becoming a peaceful, stable country until the Americans began their successful behind the scenes effort to remove them. He contended that the United States bore much of the responsibility for the utter wartime devastation and consequent rise of the Taliban. U.S. Ambassador Herbst told a different side of the story.

The exchange reminded me of the fact that every event has two sides; it is like the story of Little Red Riding Hood, which also can be told from the wolf's point of view. But, who was Little Red Riding Hood and who was the wolf in these two widely conflicting stories?

Following the ambassadors exchange of views, the student delegates were invited to ask questions. It was very pleasing for me to listen to their well-informed questions, knowing the effort we had made in their previous preparation.

The students who played the part of invited Afghanistan guests asked some very difficult and pointed questions of Ambassador Herbst. They wanted to know why the United States left the region so precipitously following their successful proxy effort to remove the Soviets from Afghanistan. The power vacuum that this created had not only allowed the Taliban to seize control of the country, but also to invite their Al Qaeda friends to establish bases in order to train terrorists. The world was not paying much attention to these developments then. In contrast to such lack of attention, our students were well informed concerning the severe reactionary Islamic fundamentalist policies of the Taliban and blamed the United States for walking away from what they considered a postwar obligation to assist in the Afghan political and infrastructure reconstruction. The students turned out to be quite prophetic on this issue as well!

The final speaker was U.N. Resident Coordinator Pavel Kral. Mr. Kral was directing a humanitarian aid mission in Afghanistan. He described what it was like trying to work in the face of mounting Taliban hostility toward the presence of the international aid community in their country.

The model U.N. Security Council deliberations were a great success not only in meeting objectives, but also as a public relations coup for the CEP. As I mentioned, nothing like this had been done before in Uzbekistan. In fact, it had not taken place in any of the surrounding Central Asian countries other than in Kyrgyzstan, where a much smaller U.N. simulation had been done by a CEPer the year before. Incidentally, on the issue of Afghanistan and the Taliban, the students on the Security Council ended up voting on three resolutions but were not able to pass any of them. Inadvertently, the students had again modeled actions that the real council would soon take over the issue of Iraq.

As in past conferences, the students celebrated their hard work with a Saturday night disco party held on the sanatorium premises. The party went very well for most participants, but we made the mistake of providing access to too much alcohol for young people, many of whom were not used to drinking alcohol. Most of the students behaved themselves, enjoying both the disco and the fact that the swimming pool actually was up and running and warm! But, again, we had underestimated the fact that young people in Central Asia are rarely given so much individual freedom. The alcohol combined with the difficulty in maintaining after-hours supervision became an invitation, which a few could not resist, to carry the party into the cabins and in a few cases throughout the night. One could tell this small number from their tired faces at the Sunday morning session and closing ceremony. We even had to go get a few students out of their beds. I doubt that the sanatorium staff had seen such a display of youthful exuberance in a long time. I also suspect that while several of these individuals were a bit shocked, more were likely amused. Luckily, no harm came from the action of these few.

Back home in Idaho, I was writing the first draft of this chapter while watching the television broadcast of the actual U.N. Security Council debate over a possible war against Iraq. I was reminded of our Security Council simulation and the experience and insight these very fortunate Central Asian students were able to gain. I wondered what they were thinking and saying. They were certain to really understand and appreciate the difficulties facing this important deliberative body in its time of trial. I can be sure that a few of them will teach about it to their future students, maybe one will one day be a U.N. delegate.

There was never any doubt in my mind that all these programs aimed at encouraging civic-minded thinking and habits were worth every bit of effort and pain that went into their planning and accomplishment. We knew we were making a big impact on our student's lives. We hoped they would be making a difference in the future of their newly independent countries.

Epilogue

Bringing the Stories to a Close

It has taken almost seven years to complete this book. I can't say that this comes as a surprise to me, as the self-discipline necessary to speed up the writing process was, at times, hard to muster; so many other projects and activities seemed to make retired life busy beyond what I ever expected. It has been even longer since Judy and I first entered the former Soviet Russian Empire, and six years since I gave my last class as a CEP visiting lecturer. It seems appropriate, therefore, that an ending chapter provide an opportunity to reflect back over the many years while also catching up on some of the changes that have transpired in the region.

I want to indulge in some reminiscences and comment proudly on the early careers of some of my students. The CEP was about helping to develop civic-mindedness in our students. Many of my students clearly have taken this message to heart. Others have yet to make their mark in this way. Perhaps, for them I like to think that the CEP message remains latent, waiting for the right occasion to blossom.

Finally, I have one more objective for this chapter. With so much time having elapsed since Judy and I wrote e-mails home describing our impressions of post-Communism, one would expect a lot to have changed in this part of the world. It is true that much has changed, but, the change has been very uneven, almost dramatically so, and not all of it has been positive. In an effort to update the situation a bit, I have added a few summary observations about the impact of recent changes on the prospects for open society.

Reminiscences

Judy gets the credit for our four-year involvement in the Civic Education Project. While we both have always had a passion for new cultural experiences and to be "on the road again," it was Judy who insisted that we retire early from our teaching jobs and become intentional travelers, able to go beyond tourism to a deeper understanding and appreciation of peoples and places. Credit goes also to the CEP. It had every one of the qualities necessary to help make our time "over there" the most delightful and exciting period of our lives.

An important credit goes to our posting locations: Lithuania, Estonia, Ukraine, and Uzbekistan. Each was a new adventure in so very many ways. The chapters of this book have only touched on a few of the memories of our life in these countries, of working with new colleagues, befriending so many wonderful people, and, most importantly, of being a teacher to a disproportionately large number of the finest students I have ever had the pleasure to know.

There was another, more unanticipated reason for the delight and excitement of these four years, why we kept returning to the CEP, and why a big part of us wishes we were over there now. It was the opportunity to be really alone together. We inadvertently had embarked on a long second honeymoon.

Much of the meaning of life is to be found in what we experience. Our life in the former Soviet Empire, with all of its attendant hardships, rather unexpectedly brought each of us the pleasure of a much-heightened degree of personal awareness. Even more serendipitously, and definitely more importantly, we discovered the delight and satisfaction in a level of companionship that had been difficult to achieve throughout the working and childrearing period of our life. There we were, just Judy and me, taking a night out from our cramped and drafty little apartment in Vilnius to sit in an unheated movie theatre in the dead of winter, eating a homemade sandwich in place of dinner, or walking arm in arm over the ubiquitous ice on the way to grocery shop in Tallinn. There were the innumerable evening meals eaten by candlelight during winter power outages in Kharkiv, or the afternoon walks we would take to explore the fascinating bazaars of Tashkent. These and other events enabled us to experience a degree of closeness, sometimes brought on by necessity, but always nice in its consequences.

And the teaching experience was the greatest! I have always thought of my role as a sociology teacher as being a bit like the secular equivalent of missionary activity. I think it is why I most enjoy teaching the introductory 101 course where I get to make a first case for the importance of thinking sociologically. I never thought that proselytizing a sociological imagination would save the world, but I was sure it could help solve social problems. However, four years with the CEP as a visiting lecturer has allowed me to more fully understand and to teach a most important application of sociological thinking, one to which I had never previously paid much attention: the central feature of citizenship, of taking an active part in the civic life of society. This book is full of examples and stories of how Judy and I worked to establish citizenship as a habit of the heart as well as the mind. I think the two of us, along with our fellow CEPers, did a good job of helping to bring about a fundamental change in the subjective outlook of our students and many of our teacher colleagues. That change was one of moving from passive subjects of the state, who are given directives, to being responsible people who are committed to the exercise of their rights and duties as citizens.

A New Generation of Leaders

What have been the early careers of some of my students? Over a decade has passed since I said good-bye to some of them on the last day of class or at an end of the school year party. Back home, Judy and I have tried to keep track of as many of my students as possible. At first, our e-mail correspondence was a bit overwhelming, taking several hours each week to accomplish. More recently, the volume of letters has slowed to include mainly our favorite students and those who just like to keep us as kind of a pen pal. We are awfully proud of these students and especially the success many of them have had in gaining significant leadership roles in their country's civic sector. Here are some examples by way of illustration. I will begin with the students we have known the longest.

Evelina

Unfortunately we did not develop an e-mail correspondence with any of my students from my first posting in Lithuania. There were only a few students that I got to know very well, and none were active e-mailers. However, we have kept in touch with the little girl who ran up and down the stairs of our apartment one afternoon yelling for help to stop the water gushing into her parents' flat. Evelina Jocyte is now in her midtwenties. She completed a graduate history degree and now works for an international advertising agency.

Following on her outgoing personality and musical talent, Evelina has become a regionally recognized jazz singer, helped along, I am sure, by a nation that is crazy for this music form and even has the only statue in the world of Frank Zappa. The life-size statue is located just a few blocks from where we lived. Judy and I like to think that we had at least a small part in Evelina's successes, given the many afternoons she spent in our apartment practicing her English and getting answers to a never ending series of questions about us, about what we thought and believed, and about our country.

Teet

I described Teet Kung's visit to Boise in an earlier chapter. Teet was one of my Estonian students in 1996–97. By 2004, Teet was working as an advisor to the German-Baltic Chamber of Commerce. He wrote us a special e-mail letter in that year, just a few hours after Estonia officially joined NATO. "I just wanted to let you know how important a moment this was for this little country (and our little neighbors) here on the border with Russia," he said. "This is the biggest security certificate we have ever had in our history … I feel BIG tonight!" Teet wrote his e-mail from Dresden, Germany, on one of his many trips where he specialized in assisting in research and technology transfer between universities and businesses. More recently, Teet has worked as an international trade consultant.

Igor

Judy and I have remained in touch with several of our very talented Ukrainian students. Through e-mails, we have delighted in following Igor Ustyuzhyn's path to his present occupation. It certainly had its entertaining moments. With his permission, I have taken a few quotations from his letters. Igor graduated in Russian literature the year I left Kharkiv. With my very hesitant blessing, he left Ukraine for the first time to enroll in a Bible school in the UK to, as he wrote "study the Bible in the so-called 'Christian environment.'" Igor ran into trouble early on, noting in his letters that "I have a pretty short fuse (I do work on making it longer, though), and it only lasted for about eight months, after which I blew up and upset two of the teachers with my sarcasm and 'liberal' hermeneutics."

With my complete support and glowing recommendation, Igor transferred the next year into a graduate history program at Central European University in Budapest. He wrote that trying to complete his master's degree in only one year was "the most difficult year in my life and the main pain in the neck turned out to be not historiography or art history (which I quite enjoyed), but literary theory." Again, Igor clashed with one of his professors who were "feeding" him "postmodernist/feminist rubbish that I either ignored or vomited back in my papers." To "cut the long story short" as he put it, "all this and my inadequate humor nearly cost me four credits and my MA." Igor finally settled back in Kharkiv where he is affiliated with Kharkiv State University and is an advisor to a championship-winning high school debate team. Knowing Igor, I can easily imagine why his team is so successful.

Sergey

Sergey Koltakov was a brilliant young Ukrainian man with a photographic memory. He wanted to go to America to study subjects such as, to quote from his resume, "multiresolution analysis in geometrical modeling, realistic image synthesis, and ray tracing vs. radiosity." I couldn't speak to his academic interests, but I sent character recommendations to places like MIT, Dartmouth, and Yale. Sergey ended up with a full scholarship to Stanford University. After more than six years in a PhD program in computer science, Sergey wrote me recently that he is ready to give up on his studies because of a not-uncommon academic tactic. Sergey's dissertation chairman has requested a complete change in his research on multiple occasions, thereby prolonging his status as a graduate student indefinitely. Extremely good jobs await him in the Silicon Valley area. Sergey seems ready to leave Stanford and begin his career.

Olga

Olga Nosova was also one of my Ukrainian students. She writes a Christmas letter each year to "some of the most wonderful people that have been in my life." We are fortunate to be on her list. Olga followed her graduation from Kharkiv State with completion of a master's program at UK's Cambridge University where she studied public policy making. Since her graduation, Olga has been working on a variety of civic society NGO projects primarily in the fields of economics and politics. She has helped the Ukrainian Society of Financial Analysts to revitalize the country's stock market. Her assignment with the Council on Competitiveness of Ukraine was to write a strategy on competitiveness, and a procedure to measure its implementation and successes.

More recently Olga has led an NGO project to increase accountability in Ukraine's five political parties. Her group has analyzed pre-election promises and compared them to post-election lawmaking activity, giving each party a cumulative and average grade. Olga's leadership on this project has allowed her to enjoy the limelight of a few press conferences. The project has helped to provide information for others to write two books and several newspaper and magazine articles about the subject. How much happier could a professor be with one of his students! It is actually a success story repeated many times over with my CEP students. In Olga's last Christmas letter she noted, with pride, ministerial level acceptance of her suggested amendments to the new government policy on public participation in state policy making.

Olga

There was also another Olga in my classes, Olga Ivanova, a graduate major in sociology and one of my most accomplished students. She stayed on at Kharkiv State to complete a PhD program. Olga subsequently gained a postgraduate scholarship to the University of Missouri–Saint Louis where she met Shawn, a graduate student in marine biology. She and Shawn are now married and living in Newport, Oregon, where Olga teaches sociology classes for the Oregon State University Extension Division. Judy and I visited them on a recent trip to the Oregon coast. Shawn works as a research marine biologist for OSU's Marine Science Center. Olga spends a lot of her time at the center, often doing her school work in Shawn's frequently vacated office while he is in the lab or as a guide with special visitors in the museum.

Artyom

Artyom Kazantsev graduated with a BS in rocket science from the Aviation Institute, but managed to find his way into a couple of my sociology classes just the same. This sounds a bit comical, but rocket science is not an uncommon degree, considering that Kharkiv had been the production location for the Soviet Union's ICBM arsenal. When Artyom found the going in my sociology class a bit difficult, I used to kid him about the subject being far less complicated than rocket science. However, employment opportunities for his specialization had declined along with missile building, so Artyom went on to add an MS degree in International Marketing. My most recent word from Artyom is that he has decided to follow his hobby and become a professional Web developer. He has buyers from the United States, Canada, and several countries in Western Europe.

Irina

Yet another Ukrainian student, Irina Yaroshchuk is married and recently had a baby named Andrushka. Upon her graduation from Kharkiv State University, Irina joined the faculty to teach English language and literature. After four years of facing unpredictable payment of salary, she quit the university for a job as assistant manager at a publishing house. She likes her job, especially the fact that it pays three times what she made as a teacher. Irina's move inadvertently confirms the continuing financial problems and consequent faculty losses and corruption difficulties facing many of the universities throughout most of the former Soviet Empire.

Oksana

A final example from Ukraine demonstrates, as with some of the students I have mentioned, the extent of the "brain drain" that is occurring in Ukraine as a result of the country's frustratingly slow and halting progress toward political freedom and economic health. Oksana Bratchikova was a very personable, outgoing law student who attended two of my classes, earning an "A" grade in both, along with getting two of her papers accepted to international conferences. Following graduation, Oksana moved to San Diego to be near her twin sister. She is currently working for a small technology company and attending law school with the goal of passing the state bar and becoming an attorney in California.

Albert

My Uzbekistan students are my most recent graduates. Consequently most have just entered the work force, while a few are still completing their graduate education. Albert is a good example of this as well as an interesting success story in the making. Albert was raised by his mother in a little village outside Tashkent. His mother worked in a cement factory and made fifteen dollars a month. Albert was a freshman, living on a very meager state scholarship, the year I taught at National University.

During the year, Albert enrolled in all four of my classes even though he was carrying a full load of regular classes in his political science major. Along with earning "B's"and "A's" in my classes, Albert also found time to volunteer in our small CEP library of English titles and to contribute a research paper that earned him a trip to a regional conference. If this was not enough, Albert participated in our debate team and was a Security Council delegate in our model UN conference.

The following year, working from home, I helped him obtain a partial scholarship to a small, high quality, USAID-financed university in neighboring Kyrgyzstan. Judy and I sent him money to help pay his room and board. Then the World Trade Center terrorist attack occurred, followed by the U.S.-led war in Afghanistan. These events and a serious incident of anti-U.S. vandalism at the school were enough to prompt the CEP to pull its several visiting lecturers out of the school and out of country. This left Albert no other option but to petition for readmittance back home to National University. Here he spent his sophomore and junior year, again with our financial assistance, until gaining a Fulbright scholarship to spend his senior year studying in America.

I remember Albert's writing me from Tashkent, pointing out that he was acclimated to a desert environment and hoping he would not end up in a cold location like Alaska. In fact, he was placed at Concordia College in Moorhead, Minnesota, an even colder place! We sent Albert a "care package" containing long winter underwear and heavy flannel shirts. He quickly grew to love the extreme cold and everything about the school and the city. He discovered Wal-Mart on his first foray into the city, writing that he considered it "the eighth marvel of the world, a superior example of a well-living civilization."

Albert did well in his classes, rooming with some athletes whose lack of academic interest never ceased to astound him. And, as was usual, Albert quickly became involved in a myriad of volunteer activities. Nearing the end of his stay at Concordia, the post 9/11 climate made it impossible for Albert to get his U.S. visa extended or renewed for the purpose of beginning graduate education. Fortunately, Canada came to his rescue, so Albert moved even further north, to even colder surroundings, to complete his masters at the university in Winnipeg. Albert is now finishing a second master's degree, this time in public administration at McGill University in Montréal. Albert is on track to be a Canadian citizen soon.

Judy and I kept a Thanksgiving letter Albert sent to us a couple of years after we left Uzbekistan. His English still needed a little work. In the letter he says that there are "three beings whom I can tell thanks in my life: my mother, you, and God. I was born by my mother. You gave me direction and support, and God give me good luck." "A poor guy from a village now has a great chance to be worthy man and to give something in the future." Judy can definitely take half of the credit for such kind remarks. As for me, I would have to say that I taught for many years before getting a recommendation this good!

Ruslan

Our other Scheffer scholarship recipient was Ruslan. He was also raised in very poor surroundings by a single mother. Ruslan was a freshman political science major at National University who, like Albert, also took all my classes and worked in our library. Ruslan wrote a research paper on the issue of the International Monetary Fund in Uzbekistan that won him a trip to Budapest to give his paper at this prestigious International Student Conference. With my prompting, he arranged to interview some high-placed ministry officials about the topic. They were cooperative but totally unused to giving interviews to students. The subject turned out to be touchy. We found out a couple of months later that the IMF was in the process of withdrawing from Uzbekistan.

Unable to obtain a scholarship to study out of country, Ruslan finished his degree with honors recognition. During his last two years as a student, Ruslan would send us his school budget and grades as a condition of our financial assistance. In his junior year, his full tuition was $310 while meals came to $33 a month. A couple of used books, last year's clothes, and miscellaneous costs came to a grand total of a little over $700. Ruslan had spent the summer working in construction, saving over half his earnings, almost $100. During the school year, he was paid to work in the CEP office library and was giving English lessons at $2 a week. Judy and I sent him about half of his total budget. What a contrast to what higher education costs in America!

From time to time, I would send Ruslan some little missive via e-mail to help him with his English. Here is a sample I got from the Internet titled "Twenty Reasons Why English Is So Hard to Learn." "The bandage was wound around the wound," "Since there is no time like the present, he thought it was time to present the present," and "There is no ham in hamburger." When Ruslan graduated, he was very fortunate to gain a local staff position with Freedom House, an international NGO. Ruslan helped in several important human rights projects and assisted in their resource center. Freedom House paid Ruslan almost two hundred dollars a month, well above prevailing wages for Uzbekistan. He wrote me ecstatically: "Imagine, a shy boy from a poor province far from Tashkent, with a good job in the most important human rights organization in the world. Now I never again [will] be hungry as I was so often, and my mom never will have problems with her health. All my achievements I connect with you and Judy's help."

Ruslan's achievements continue. Recently, Ruslan was selected as one of two individuals from Uzbekistan to gain a two-year Edmund Muskie Fellowship for graduate study in the United States. He was ecstatic about his good luck. He had earned it. Ruslan was glad to be in "real America," as he expressed it, not what he referred to as an "international city," giving as examples New York City, Washington DC, and Los Angeles. He wanted to experience "charming friendly smiles, polite attitudes, and honored values of real Americans and religious persons." Ruslan is now in his second year of study in political science at the University of Missouri. He talks to his fellow students about the difficult economic condition of his home country and his hope for its eventual move to democracy. In the meantime he is very appreciative of the freedoms which Americans enjoy, mentioning especially our right to free speech. It is a great pleasure keeping up with Russlan's life. Ruslan always modestly signs his e-mails, "Your best student."

Alisher

Ruslan had help in obtaining his job at Freedom House from Alisher. Alisher enrolled in two of my classes while finishing his law degree at a neighboring university in Tashkent. Ruslan moved into Alisher's job when the opportunity came available for Alisher to be a project coordinator for the NGO-sponsored Center for Continuing Legal Education. Sponsorship came from the Soros-funded Open Society Assistance Foundation, the same foundation through which the CEP drew the majority of its funding. When the president of Uzbekistan closed down this foundation, the CEP and several NGO programs consequently had to close their operations as well. Alisher found himself out of work and unable to return to his previous job with Freedom House. Sidelined and unable to locate new employment, at last word Alisher continues watching his job prospects stagnate if not decline along with the economy of Uzbekistan. This situation coupled with increasing government interference of one sort or another has prompted several other foreign NGOs, some funded with American money, to also leave the country.

Uzbekistan's economy has not been helped by a continuance of political turmoil. Since Judy and I left Uzbekistan in summer 2001, there have been at least three widely reported outbreaks of protest against government economic controls and political repression. Each has produced violent official reaction. The latest and largest incident occurred in the Fergana Valley in the spring of 2005. It gained considerable world attention. A widely disputed number of people, with estimates ranging from a little over a hundred to more than seven hundred, were killed as a result of harsh and apparently indiscriminant police reaction.. Judy and I had visited the city of Andijan where this took place. I remember the exact location where the people were shot down in the street. I e-mailed some of my students for information about this latest incident. One wrote back that "lots of people living here are concerned over what happened, but we have what we have and I can't comment about these kinds of security issues. I am sorry... but I have to live here." This student had been the young man who was brave enough to write his research paper for me on corruption in the universities. Now he was silenced. Echoing the speech restrictions in this authoritarian country, another student was careful to pick code words that would communicate his inability to write the truth. Speaking of Andijan, my student said "do not worry, it is quiet here and things go well;" "It was just a gangster attack."

Evegenia, Farhod, Anna, and Adelena

The list of names and highlights in the lives of my Uzbekistan students could go on much longer. Four years of teaching with the Civic Education Project had honed our ability to really get close to my students, get involved in their lives, and bring them into ours. Here are just a few more Uzbekistan students to add to the above: Evegenia Skiba moved to Russia, where work prospects were much better, married a Russian man, and has a little son, Ivan. She lives with her husband in Moscow. I recall the Sunday that she and her boyfriend came to our apartment flat and spent all afternoon cooking us a wonderful big dinner of *plov,* the Central Asian pilaf-style staple. It was delicious.

Evegenia's move to Russia was typical of a fairly large exodus of Russian and Ukrainian nationals moving out of Central Asia as the result of occupational discrimination by the various ethnic populations that now hold political power.

Farhod was interested in journalism, which, of course, was tightly controlled in Uzbekistan, thus hardly much of a career, but Farhod dreamed of better times. I last heard that he was working for Radio Free Europe/Radio Liberty, but my contact failed to take note of where he was located.

Anna was a strikingly attractive, impish and funny psychology major who loved Formula race cars and knew most of the major world drivers by name. Anna was the student who, as I mentioned in an earlier chapter, suggested that we solve the problem of Taliban discrimination against women by bombing them. She graduated from National University and moved to Kazakhstan to escape the terrible economic climate in Tashkent. She has since become a part-time actress while working for various foreign companies in administrative and promotional positions.

Adelena was a student and part-time administrative assistant for CEP in Samarkand. Judy and I got to know her as the young lady with the absolutely bubbly personality who became our unofficial guide on each of our visits to this beautiful city. We would have long talks while touring the city. Shortly after Judy and I left Uzbekistan, Adelena received a scholarship to study in Oklahoma. Toward the end of her studies, she became engaged to a classmate from Nebraska. Gosh, a "cornhusker" engaged, of all things, to a "Sooner!" The following summer they traveled back to Samarkand long enough to get married, then it was off to San Francisco where Adelena had a job waiting with the Global Fund for Women. At last account, her income was helping to support her unemployed husband. My colleague Carter Johnson wrote me the news about her, concluding, "How's that for role-reversal: raised to be a traditional mother and not work outside the house and then find yourself in America working to support your American husband! I wonder how her parents comprehend it all." I am sure that her husband has found a good job by now.

Zulia

And finally, I have saved one of our favorite Uzbekistan students for last; Zulia or Z Girl has turned out to be a parapetic world traveler. "Z Girl," was an au pair (mother's helper) in Colorado the year before Judy and I first met her as a student in my classes at National University. Less than a year after we left Tashkent, "Z Girl" was working, again as an au pair, in a New York City suburb. We arranged a day together during our visit to the city. It was just a week after 9/11. The following year, Zulia sent us an e-mail from London where she was taking ESL instruction and working in a sandwich shop. By then, it was obvious to us that "Z Girl" had a very serious case of travel fever. Thus, it came as little surprise somewhat later, to have her on-line conversation box pop up on my real-time computer screen. She was in China teaching English classes.

This much travel might seem even a bit out of the ordinary for a young American girl recently graduated from college, but such a life is almost totally unheard of in Uzbekistan. However, Zulia had started early to signal her intentions by working as a babysitter for American embassy employees and inviting them to her home. We met a few of these employees, having been graciously invited to have dinner on two occasions at her parents' flat. Her mother, a doctor, and her father, a retired railroad engineer, were wonderful hosts, very much in the Uzbek tradition. Both understood Z Girl's love of travel. Her embassy friends, I suspect, were also her best contacts, able to provide overseas job leads. I wonder where Z Girl will show up next! Wait a minute! I just opened my e-mail and there is a message from Zulia. She is working as an au-pair in California and has a scholarship to begin graduate classes at the nearby state university! Her goal is to return to her country and run an ESL program.

The State of the Transition: A Mixed Record of Success

And now to conclude with what might be called the big question about the most general reason why Judy and I were in the CEP. The dissolution of the Soviet Empire produced a newly configured Russian state and opened the door to independence for each of the fifteen former republics that had been part of the empire. This eventful moment also freed the several former client or satellite states in Eastern Europe to again pursue their affairs as independent countries. What progress has all the new countries managed to achieve in their transition out of Communism toward the condition of open society?

My comments on this question are made with considerable modesty. I certainly make no pretense at having even barely figured out the complexities involved in the democratization process, or of being able to provide authoritative answers to questions concerning the prospects for democracy in each, or any, of these countries. What Judy and I witnessed firsthand in thirteen of the countries and have followed closely in the rest has been the aftermath of collapse and the beginnings of recomposition. This is a neutral term that, unlike the word "transition," might better signify that while each state is pursuing its own sovereign path, the outcomes will all be different, possibly very different. Some countries are hewing to the broad parameters outlined by the concept of open society, but, for at least a few other states, the transformation has not been in the hoped-for direction, an initial period of citizen optimism has disappeared in state reaction, resistance, and retrenchment.

As the Soviet Union collapsed, the original challenge for each country was stated quite well in the preamble to a two-page CEP International Student Conference call for papers e-mailed to all lecturer sites in 1999, almost a decade into the transition:

> The fall of the Iron Curtain and subsequent events have necessarily led to a whole set of new challenges and realities: a new geopolitical context for security arrangements and regional relations; economic uncertainty and social instability connected with the movement towards open markets and capitalism; the direct and indirect effects of European integration on the region; new notions of human rights and civil liberties; changing patterns of minority and ethnic relations; cultural change and diversification; and an evolving political culture with new opportunities for political participation.

The preamble went on to list several centrally important questions about whether a decade of reform had met the expectations of the people, questions that will be asked and re-asked about each of the transitioning countries, and about all of them collectively:

How are these developments perceived? To what extent is "nostalgia" for earlier times or for more stable conditions emerging as a force? Have things of value been lost in the process and is there opportunity to regain them? Are these developments responsive to recent global change or do they rely too much on outdated models? What have proven to be the biggest obstacles to the transformation process and how can they be overcome? How far along have reforms come … and will they be able to sustain the momentum to stay on course?

The challenges were extensive and dramatic. The possibilities that the fall of Communism opened up for major societal change were truly revolutionary and nation changing.

First to seize on these possibilities were several of the countries of Central/Eastern Europe. Hungry, Poland, and the Czech Republic immediately come to mind as good examples, along with Lithuania, Latvia, and particularly Estonia. All were quick to make the most of their new opportunities to build democracy and a liberal economy. The road to change was bumpy, but the transition was never uncertain. As the objects of Soviet partition and subjugation, these countries had managed to retain a national identity. There was an historical memory of earlier periods of national sovereignty, and even, in some instances, the institutions of democratic governance. Working within shattered economies, but with a strong sense of optimism, these former Iron Curtain countries have managed to develop fully independent political parties and more than once to change government leadership through fair elections, and even in Lithuania, impeach a corrupt president.

While most Eastern and Central European countries have achieved much in the way of tossing off the Communist past and moving toward open society, Belarus has been one notable exception. Judy and I visited Belarus in 1995 and 1996 and found it to be a poor country in comparison to its border neighbors: Poland, Lithuania, and Latvia. Belarus had not been a lucky country by any means. It had lost a third of its population in some of the most devastating battles of the Second

World War. Stalin's purges sent many more people to their death or to Siberia.

The Chernobyl disaster had blown its deadly poison north to permanently contaminate a fifth of the country's land. During the Soviet period, Belarus had enthusiastically embraced Communism and consequently was finding independence to be particularly disorienting. The year before our visit, in their first postindependence election, Belarussians had chosen Alexander Lukashenka as their president. In the eyes of his county's critics and almost certainly to most outside observers, Lukashenka was bent on bringing more bad luck to his people as he set about consciously turning the country backwards: back to a command economy and back to a dictatorship. Judy and I found life in the capital city of Minsk to be absolutely Soviet in every respect, replete in all its Communist symbolism, even continuing to retain the old name of the KGB. We took pictures, standing next to the giant Lenin statue out front of its headquarters building. Staked prominently in the grass of the parklike surroundings of the presidential building were signs, only in Russian, indicating that trespassers may be shot!

Lukashenka's policies have remained popular with the rural poor, state workers, and the elderly whose pensions have always been paid on time and in full. However, Lukashenka put severe restrictions on the independent media and opposition politicians. Ten years into his autocratic rule, he was able to pass a sham referendum allowing him to run for a third term. He is certain to win this election as well should he choose to use the same campaign tactics and voting procedures employed in his referendum win, an outcome independent pollsters judged to be "implausible in the extreme." Belarus remains a most dismal backwater among otherwise more successful and progressive western Baltic neighbors.

Bordering Belarus on the south is Ukraine, a country similar in many ways to Belarus, with strong ties, at least in its eastern region, to Russia. It is also a poor country although not to the same extent as Belarus. Since its independence, Ukraine has struggled to implement the fundamentals of open society. It has managed to keep from slipping back into a dictatorship, but the ruling party has been notably heavy-handed and lacking in transparency while the economy has tended to remain quite stagnant and insular, reflecting the strong influence of the country's corrupt oligarchs. Typical of its critics was CEP's principle sponsor, philanthropist George Soros, who visited Kyiv during our year in Ukraine. Meeting with President Kuchma and later with representatives of his Open Society (Renaissance) Foundation, Soros announced he was scaling back his charitable giving in Ukraine saying in the *Kiev Post* that "Ukraine lacks political will and any kind of leadership." Soros was just one of many prominent international voices who were drawing essentially the same conclusion.

The political economy of Ukraine continued its uninspiring path for approximately the first five years since Judy and I left the country. However, this sorry state of affairs may be finally coming to an end amidst considerable fanfare. The national elections in 2004 were marked by a high amount of fraud as President Kuchma and his allies in Moscow tried to rig the votes in favor of his hand- picked successor, Viktor Yanukovych.

Protesters quickly gathered in the freezing snow of late November in Kyiv's Independence Plaza. During a week or more of living in a makeshift tent city and growing at one point to an estimated seven hundred thousand, the protesters supported the opposition candidate, Viktor Yushchenko, who they believed had legitimately won the election. Their encampment in the plaza went on long enough, created sufficient international attention, and helped to produce a strong enough backlash to the election, to pressure the Ukrainian parliament to reject the election results. This inadvertently ushered in what came to be called the "Orange Revolution" with the promise of major improvement in governance and economic policy.

Such promises, including a vow by the new president to end corruption and break the political influence of the oligarchs, are yet to be fulfilled. A worsening economy has meanwhile disillusioned many nominal supporters of the Orange Revolution. In the parliamentary elections, the president's liberal reform party came in a distinct third behind the pro-Russian party of Yanukovych, the previously discredited and voided presidential contender. Orange Revolutionary candidate Yushchenko then had to govern through a coalition headed by the party of a very popular prime minister who he had previously fired from his administration. While obviously a setback to his supporters who continue to wait for major improvement in Ukraine's political and economic climate, I believe, from my distant vantage point, that the country has definitely turned the corner in its democratic transition. I am optimistic about the near future.

Ukraine, as well as Belarus, and to a lesser extent all of the newly independent countries, have been effected by Russia's struggle to institute countervailing institutions, democratic practice, and liberal economy. During Soviet times, each of the new countries had been shaped by the practice of centralizing power in Moscow. After the fall of Communism, most of the new countries remained, to varying degrees, economically and politically connected to Moscow through a loose alliance called the Commonwealth of Independent States. While this alliance has continued to remain undersubscribed in its membership, Russia continues to remain the major trading partner for several of the new countries.

Then in 1998, just before Judy and I left for Ukraine, Russia defaulted on its currency, sending its economy into a major recession, which had very serious economic effects on its trading partners. Crippled economically, Russia sought to keep alive its botched effort to turn the corner on its Communist past. Through the first few years of independence a condition of near economic anarchy had allowed a few individuals to get fabulously wealthy and thus to constitute an informal oligarchy against whose interests it became increasingly hard to govern. Efforts aimed at broadening privatization to include agricultural land, to introduce a market-based pension plan, or to initiate a number of bureaucratic and administrative reforms mostly came to naught. In the meantime, taking advantage of the chaos, organized crime became a well-established feature of Russian society. True, this was also a period when reforms created the first of several personal freedoms and the beginning of civic society. But, from a standard of living point of view, most Russians gained little from the early years of the transition other than, more often than not, to fall further into poverty.

Fortunately, rising oil and natural gas prices came to Russia's aid. As a major oil and gas exporter, the second largest in the world, by the turn of the century and certainly since 9/11, the international rise in oil prices has lifted Russia's economy well beyond its earlier doldrums, well beyond its wildest imagination. All citizens have felt the benefits: a solid urban middle class has formed and the number of people in poverty has been roughly cut in half. For how long the Russian economy will be able to ride the dramatic run up in the price of oil remains a very important question. A serious long term decline in world oil price could very well move Russia back towards an economic status quo anti, creating real hardship for many.

However, most world attention has focused on Russia's politics instead. The last several years of the Putin presidency have witnessed what seems an unmistakable turning away from democracy. President Putin accomplished this change by increasingly clamping down on the independent media. He eliminated all independent seats in the Duma (congress), canceled the practice of direct election of regional governors, and imposed new laws to control charities and other private NGO-type organizations. New legislation, supported by President Medvedv and Prime Minister Putin further broadens the definition of state treason by giving the state the power to prosecute anyone, as reported by an *Associated* Press release 12/18/2008, deemed to have "harmed the security of the Russian Federation." By reining in such typical bulwarks of civil society and countervailing powers to centralized authority, The Russian leadership has succeeded in tilting his country back towards authoritarianism. It may not be stretching the point to say that Russia is beginning to look more like Stalin's Soviet Russia where people were separated by those who appeared to support the regime, or whispered their decent, and those who were deemed to be "enemies of the state."

Of course, there are other interpretations for these events. One must remember that the worst-case scenario is usually the one that gets the most attention. It is common for people to point to Russia's long tradition as an authoritarian, antidemocratic country and see only a continuance of this tradition. Nobody doubts that a lot of Russians, probably a majority, are apolitical and unconcerned with the prospects for democracy. I have met people like this, and my impression is that there are many with a likeminded attitude. However, even if only a minority of Russians understand democracy and support the political and social conditions on which it depends, it might be worth remembering that less than 10 percent of Russians ushered in Communism. I like to think that a different 10 percent can lead the way out, and some of those 10 percent are going to be our CEP students!

Certainly the most difficult places for open society to become established will be the newly independent republics of Central Asia. In addition to a long history of life under Moscow's authoritarian rule, first under the czars and then under the Soviets, the new Central Asian republics have little tradition of statehood and definitely no experience with political democracy. The highest level of identity and allegiance tends to remain tribal and sectarian. The longest-standing political tradition is that of the strong man, the warlord, the khan, the one who gains power by might and keeps it the same way.

In Uzbekistan, as in the other four new central Asian countries, the legacy of authoritarianism has produced a strongly centralized state with a strong man at the top. The state continues to be the almost exclusive source of prestige and advantage, and for this reason, those in power are reluctant to go along with the development of democracy and rules of the game that establish free and fair elections. They know they would likely lose power and all that goes with it! If this is not enough to impede the development of open democratic society, there is more.

There are two variables that are closely associated with the rise of democracy. Neither variable exists in a manner that bodes well for democracy in the region. One is a continuously growing and diversified economy. Until recently, all four of the Central Asian economies were stagnant, if not experiencing several decades of decline. This condition is likely to persist in Uzbekistan, while oil revenue may soon boost the fortunes of Kazakstan and Turkmenistan: the two republics that border the oil-rich Caspian Sea area. A caveat here is that economies based on oil revenue traditionally have a dismal record of fostering democratic freedom and civil society.

The second and most important variable is cultural traditions. In addition to strong-man rule, there are very influential religious traditions to be taken into consideration. Almost all Islamic countries remain, to a more or less degree, under authoritarian control. This is no accident, but is viewed by scholars and most observers alike as the result of the Islamic tradition of treating the state as a type of theocracy. This closed-society tradition remains very influential in the Muslim world, in spite of the fact that its influence in Central Asia was considerably reduced and constricted during the period of Soviet rule.

Uzbekistan still continues to severely regulate the expression of religious belief, including censoring the content of sermons and imprisoning any person whose religious behavior, real or imagined, appears to be "fundamentalist" in any way. Ironically, the consequence of this hard-line approach may not only be making Uzbekistan more authoritarian, but more vulnerable to greater levels of theocratic-based extremism.

Due to this policy, several thousand "extremists" are quite likely to be sitting in Uzbekistan's prisons. Some are actually extremists, such as those who are members of the Islamic Movement of Uzbekistan, a group that has routinely attempted to overthrow the government by violence in order to replace it with a Taliban-style autocracy. But, according to Uzbek professors I spoke with in my department, the IMU is thought to be fairly small in number, leaving most of the other prisoners to be not really extremists. Most are more likely to have just been in the wrong place at the wrong time and are guilty of nothing other than bad timing. Without an independent judiciary and the rules specifying transparency and a speedy trial, most of these people continue to languish in prison, making it impossible to determine who really constitutes a threat and who does not.

The conclusion that Judy and I heard most often from the critics while in Uzbekistan was that government heavy-handedness combined with difficult economic conditions will undermine any chance for democracy in the foreseeable future. And so goes democracy! Well, maybe not quite true. I said earlier that optimism is the best approach in fostering constructive change, so I will close with a few reasons to see a brighter path for Central Asia and especially Uzbekistan. Remember that the country is only a little more than a decade in the making as an independent republic. It is being noticed by the world's most economically powerful countries with the consequence of being rapidly connected, pushed and pulled into a condition of globalization. This process was boosted considerably by the recent involvement of the U.S.-led coalition in neighboring Afghanistan, the creation of a U.S. military base in the southern part of Uzbekistan and a second base in neighboring Kyrgyzstan. Only the latter base remains active, the other, now that our Afghan presence has been considerably reduced, have been decommissioned at Uzbekistan's request. Nevertheless, Central Asia is now open to the world for the first time and world influences are bound to open it further. If nothing other, the Internet will lead the way.

Uzbekistan, as in almost all parts of the former Soviet Russian Empire, enjoys a remarkably high level of literacy among both men and women. Being able to read and write is an important basis for citizenship, volunteerism, and the development of civic organizations. Encouraged through the activities of a resilient, if not increasing number of NGOs, women, maybe even more so than men, are leading the way toward social change and civic development. An example of this is the Women's League of Initiatives with headquarters in Tashkent. I have met with representatives of this organization. The league publicizes information about women's issues and rights, conducts training, and helps to find additional training and employment for many disadvantaged women. Another interesting civic-minded NGO is the For the Health of the Generation foundation. Founded in 1993, its members distribute humanitarian assistance and conduct health-promotion programs. The foundation also runs a network of drugstores that distribute donated medicines. During the time Judy and I were in Tashkent, the foundation initiated a program to provide nutrition for mothers with children. It was fully subscribed very quickly.

Another reason for optimism is that throughout Central Asia, there is an old tradition of self-government at the neighborhood level. These entities are referred to as *mahallas*. The Soviets co-opted them and, in Uzbekistan, the Karimov government continues to maintain financial control and thus political influence over their operations. Yet, they have recently been allowed more independence. The mahallas constitute an excellent politically moderating foundation for civic society.

Finally, it should be noted that all Islam does not lead to fundamentalism. In Uzbekistan, as in the other three central Asian countries, most expressions of Islam are modest and tolerant. America, after all, has begun to experiment with encouraging religious organizations to reassume their historic role as unquestionably the most significant element in civic society. Witness the passage of the Charitable Choice provision of the Welfare Reform Act of 1996 and our government's support for faith-based initiatives. Uzbekistan also has a tradition of independent Muslim foundations supporting schools and a variety of welfare services. As in our own country, these religious organizations could be revived as a basis for increased civic activity.

In the final analysis, civic education and civic society will almost certainly be a feature of the newly transitioning countries. I have sought to link civic society to an open democratic society, but there is another bottom-line reality to the growth of civic society. Citizen wellbeing and the economy of modern government depend on it!

Civic society is a necessary feature of social life; a necessity the Soviets considered, rightfully, as a threat to their rule. Gorbachev discovered the importance of civic society too late in his effort to try and save Communism. The warning signs were there. In the *Novosibirsk Report*, prepared for a closed conference in the Soviet city of Novosibirsk in April, 1983, the author, Tatyana Zaslavskaya, a Russian sociologist, had argued that Communism's guarantee of full employment and cradle-to-grave social services not only had produced a prodigious level of laziness, incompetence, and apathy in people, but was also bankrupting the Soviet economy. Gorbachev tried in vain to quickly introduce the basic elements of civic society, even borrowing the concept of *perestroika* (a broad agenda of change), from the report's author. It was a case of too little, too late. The fall of Communism offered a painful lesson that civic society and civic education are both needed features of modern life, and both are fundamentally incompatible with authoritarian government, as well as with heavy doses of socialism and command economy. It is a lesson that offers hope for democracy and liberal economy.

In Conclusion

No one has set specific criteria for judging what constitutes a reasonable time span for any particular democratic transition to be completed, let alone what exactly it might look like when accomplished. Who could judge such things anyway? Democracy is a process, not an end product.

My CEP years began enthusiastically in support of the universalistic view of Western liberal democracy as the final and highest form of government. A year spent in Ukraine made me realize that a democracy movement can be usurped by elite who have no intentions of assisting its development. Fortunately, the condition appears to have been reasonably short lived. This didn't dampen my idealism, other than to reinforce the idea that the democratic process is not linear: setbacks, even reversals are a reasonably common event. It was the last year I spent in Central Asia that significantly moderated my view. I remain an enthusiastic supporter of democracy, but realistically I now must concede that democracy is a much more complex and culturally specific process. It takes root and grows better in some societies than in others. In Central Asia, it looks to be a very long time coming.

Now it is time to put political theory aside even though it remains such a defining feature of our CEP years. It is still hard to believe that Judy and I had such a marvelous opportunity to play our small part in the early stage of such significant political transformation. Our adventures in the former Soviet Russian Empire completed, we came home with considerable reluctance. Along with additional memorabilia with which to almost certainly overdecorate our house, we returned with a great appreciation for all the places we had been, a fond remembrance of the wonderful people we had the opportunity to befriend, and, all in all, the most wonderful adventure imaginable.

Appendix

Appendix 1 – CEP Certificate

CEP
Civic Education Project

Certificate

AWARDED TO

For the Successful
Completion of the Course

At

With the Grade

The Civic Education Project, which is affiliated with the Central European University, offers courses in the social sciences, law and humanities taught by CEP Visiting Lecturers and Eastern Scholars at universities in Central and Eastern Europe and the former Soviet Union.

Lecturer

Lecturer Signature

Date

397

ANNOUNCEMENT

THE DEPARTMENT OF SOCIOLOGY OF THE NATIONAL UNIVERSITY OF UZBEKISTAN IS PLEASED TO OFFER TWO SOCIOLOGY COURSES WHICH WILL BE TAUGHT IN ENGLISH

❋❋❋❋❋❋❋❋❋❋❋❋❋

Professor Martin Scheffer is a Civic Education Project (CEP) Visiting Lecturer from the United States. Professor Scheffer will be teaching the following courses:

- **INTRODUCTION TO SOCIOLOGY**
  Including basic methods of investigation - main analytical concepts - major theories and empirical knowledge of human social behavior

- **CRIMINOLOGY**
  A sociological approach to the study of crime; including theories of causation, types of crime and the relationship between crime and legal and political processes

Both classes are open on a "first priority" basis to English proficient students from the Faculty of Social and Political Science at the National University. Remaining seats will be open to any English proficient student from other universities. A CEP certificate with a western grade will be awarded to students who successfully complete the requirements of the class. Students who wish to regularly attend class without completing requirements for a grade may do so on a space available basis.

- A meeting about the **CRIMINOLOGY** class will be held Monday, September 11 from 2:30 to 5:00 at the National University of Uzbekistan, Faculty of Social and Political Sciences, 5th floor, Foreign Language Reading Room.

- A meeting about the **INTRODUCTION TO SOCIOLOGY** class will be held on Wednesday, September 13, at the same time and place as noted above.

Appendix 3 – Shashlik Party Sign-Up Sheet

SHASHLIK PARTY
FOR SPRING SEMESTER CERTIFICATE STUDENTS
(Dr. Scheffer's Students)
SUNDAY JUNE 13 -- 4:30 PM

DIRECTIONS: Draw a circle around your
name to indicate that you will come (please
no girl or boy friends) and write your name next to the
name of ONE thing on the list that you will
bring

CIRTIFICATE STUDENTS
Sociological Theory
Social Policy

Cucumbers

Oksana Bratchikova
Anton Demydenko
Ksenia Fedack
Avtyom Kazantsev
Olga Ivanova
Kateryna Lapina
Alex Shupta
Alexei Subbotin
Yana Tsimbrovskaya

Cucumbers Irina Yaroschuk
Daria Golovechenko
Alexander Khmel
Sergey Kondrashov
Alexey Matykhin
Anna Sorokina
Yuriy Abramenkov
Maria Dikhtyaryova
Natalia Maksimova
Sergey Daragan
Igor Ustyuzhyn
Martin and Judy

Proidenko
Tanya

LIST OF THINGS TO BRING
Select ONE item or group

1. Pork *Martin & Judy*
2. One katchup and 10 large plates *Maria*
3. One katchup, pack of napkins, 2 Tomatoes
4. Three beers and two tomatoes
5. Three beers and two tomatoes
6. Three beers and two tomatoes
7. Three beers and two tomatoes
8. Three beers and two tomatoes *S. Anna*
9. Ten Tomatoes *Alexey Margulka*
10. One large Coca Cola and one bunch radishes *Daria*
11. One juce and three tomatoes *Igor U. Zevaxoheva*
13. Large bundle of wood and two loaves of bread *AnnA*
12. Large bundle of wood and two loaves of bread
15. Large bundle of wood and one juce *Alex S*
14. Large bundle of wood and two loaves of bread
17. One large Fanta and one bunch radishes *Olga Grace*
16. Large bundle of wood and 20 large plates
18.. One large Fanta and one bunch radishes *Bachynsk Yuliya*

399

Nukus Workshop Schedule

MONDAY

> 9:30-10:30 Get Acquanted - Explain Our Plan for the Week (Martin & Victoria)
> 10:45-12:15 Teaching Problems: Group Discussion and Class Report (Martin & Victoria)
>
> -----------------
>
> 1:30 - 4:30 Sociology: Perspective, Theory and Method (Martin)
> 1:30 - 4:30 (Victoria)

TUESDAY

> 9:30-10:30 Teaching and Learning Paradigms (Martin)
> 10:45-12:15 Discussion (Martin)
>
> -----------------
>
> 1:30-4:30 Major Sociological Concepts: Culture and Socialization (Martin)
> 1:30-4:30 (Victoria)

WEDNESDAY

> 9:30-10:30 Building a Supportive Classroom Environment (Victoria)
> 10:45-12:15 Discussion (Victoria)
>
> --------------
>
> Afternoon free for visits to the Karakalpak Museum and Igor Svitsky Art Gallery

THURSDAY

> 9:30-10:30 Various Classroom Techniques Explained (Martin & Victoria)
> 10:445-12:15 Syllabuses, Proposals, Essays and Research Papers (Martin & Victoria)
>
> -----------------
>
> 1:30-4:30 Major Sociological Concepts: Social Structure, Groups and Organizations (Martin)
> 1:30-4:30 (Victoria)

FRIDAY

> 9:30-10:30 Open
> 10:45-12:15 Wrap-up on Teaching Methodology (Martin and Victoria)
>
> -----------------
>
> 1:30-4:30 The Concept of Civil Society and its Social Policy Implications (Martin)
> 1:30-4:30 (Victoria)

SATURDAY

> 9:30-11:00 Sociological Perspective and Practice (Martin)
> 9:30-11:00 (Victoria)
> 11:15-12:15 Evaluation and Goodby
>
> Afternoon free with late afternoon return to Tashkent

Appendix 5 – Suggestions for Writing Proposals

SUGGESTED PROPOSAL FORMAT

PROPOSED PAPER TITLE

(in the 1st part)

Describe your subject in terms that will make it interesting to the reader. Maybe a couple lines revealing its history would be useful. Come quickly to the specific topic which you intend to study and state it clearly and in as few words as possible. Indicate why you think the topic or problem is important and be convincing about it. If it is an issue that is being debated or contains a policy proposal that is controversial about how to solve the problem , then make sure that you briefly describe the issue or proposal, and indicate how your research will contribute to resolving the problem or clarifying the issue. Finally, it is very important that you keep your topic limited and focused on something you can actually write about in 8 to 10 pages (and deliver orally in 10 minutes before your audience

(in a 2nd part)

Describe the information sources you plan to use in your research (library books, documents, newspapers, memoirs, interviews, surveys, a case study, participant observation, etc.). Will you collect original data and information (primary sources), or will you be using someone else's data or information (secondary sources - a more common source of information)? It is very important that you do not propose to do more research than you will have time to accomplish. Paper judges want to think that you will actually be able to finish your research within the time between the proposal and the delivery of your paper.

(in the final part)

Provide a few brief closing statements that remind the reader of the topic, including the problem or issue, you are going to research and write about. In this last part, you want to be sure to make your statements interesting. You might take this opportunity to again clearly say why you picked this topic (why it is important to you) and in what way your research will help advance useful knowledge or contribute to the solution of a problem, or clarify an issue.

Your proposal must be made on only one page, and you must type it in single space. However, you need not use all of the sheet to explain your proposal (remember that the judges will have a hundred or more proposals to read and a clear, concise and brief proposal will be appreciated and remembered more easily when the sorting and eliminating process begins) You should type the draft of your proposal in double space. This will leave space for editing. Above all, enjoy your work and good luck!

CIVIC EDUCATION PROJECT

is pleased to announce

CALL FOR PAPERS

to be presented at the
THIRD REGIONAL STUDENT CONFERENCE

" LOOKING AHEAD AT THE NEW MILLENNIUM: CHOICES FOR REGIONAL DEVELOPMENT"

to be held on 3-6 December 1998
in Chisinau, Moldova

This annual student conference, organized by the Civic Education Project Ukraine-Moldova-Belarus
with organizational assistance from the Higher Education Support Program, Soros Foundation Moldova
and the Academy of Economic Studies of Moldova
will address the following historical, geopolitical, economic, legal, social and other aspects
of co-existence of the states of the Eurasian region:

- ☐ **historical similarities and differences between the nations of the region**
- ☐ **ethnic issues and nationalism, territorial conflict settlement**
- ☐ **CIS and other alternatives of integration**
- ☐ **participation in international treaties and alliances**
- ☐ **constitutional reform and civil rights**
- ☐ **development of market relations, economic cooperation and integration**
- ☐ **environmental issues**
- ☐ **mass media and social conscience building**
- ☐ **new social structures and social security issues**

The conference is open for participation to undergraduate students,
nationals of Belarus, Moldova, Romania, Russia and Ukraine,
a limited number of participants will be invited from the Baltic States and the Caucasus.
The working languages of the conference are English and Russian.

The applicants should submit a one-page single-spaced typed or printed paper proposal
in English or Russian language and the applicant information sheet before **20 October 1998**
to the CEP Kyiv office by **fax: (044) 229-7319** or **email: cep@gluk.apc.org.**
Following the notification of acceptance for participation, the selected students
will write up-to-ten-page papers and prepare oral conference presentations.

For further information, please contact the Civic Education Project Fellow
at your university:

Works Cited

Boaz, David. *Libertarianism*. New York: Free Press, 1997.

Brochure. Single informational sheet from 1995. The Civic Education Project.

Guide to Life and Teaching in Eastern Europe and Eurasia. Clipbound collection of information and essays. 2000. Printed and assembled for in-house distribution by the Civic Education Project.

Hoffer, Eric. *The True Believer*. New York: Harper and Row, 1951.

Huff, Dan "The Upside Down Welfare State," *Public Welfare*. Winter, 1992.

King, John, John Noble, and Andrew Humphreys. *Central Asia*. Oakland: Lonely Planet, 1996.

"Liquidators." *The Ukrainian*. March, 1998: 47–51

MacLeod, Calum, and Bradley Mayhew. *Uzbekistan*. Hong Kong: Odyssey, 1999.

Noble, John. *Baltic States & Kaliningrad*. Oakland: Lonely Planet, 1994.

Nowak, David. *Associated Press*: "Russian treason bill could target Kremlin critics." *Idaho Press-Tribune* December 18, 2008, Main:12

Osborn, David, and Ted Gaebler. *Reinventing Government*. Reading, MA: Addison-Wesley, 1992.

Soros, George. *Open Society*. New York: Public Affairs, 2000.

"Soros Announces Cuts at Foundation," *Kiev Post*. November, 16, 1998, *Nation*.

s After: Moving Forward ... Looking Back. "Schedule of Events," ternational Student Conference, Budapest, Hungary, April 13–18, 1999.

Vilnius in Your Pocket. #52, June/July, 2002.

Women in Education: Working Toward a Better Future. Program Announcement, Samarkand, Uzbekistan, March 4, 2000.

Zaslavskaya, Tatyana. "Novosibrsk Report." *Survey.* 28 (1984):88–108.

LaVergne, TN USA
02 December 2009
165545LV00003B/4/P